Antonino Falduto

The Faculties of the Human Mind and the Case of Moral Feeling in Kant's Philosophy

Kantstudien-Ergänzungshefte

———

Im Auftrag der Kant-Gesellschaft
herausgegeben von
Manfred Baum, Bernd Dörflinger
und Heiner F. Klemme

Band 177

Antonino Falduto

The Faculties of the Human Mind and the Case of Moral Feeling in Kant's Philosophy

—

DE GRUYTER

Die Drucklegung wurde durch einen finanziellen Zuschuss der Kant-Forschungsstelle am Philosophischen Seminar der Johannes Gutenberg-Universität Mainz unterstützt.

ISBN 978-3-11-048156-3
e-ISBN 978-3-11-035114-9
ISSN 0340-6059

Library of Congress Cataloging-in-Publication Data
A CIP catalog record for this book has been applied for at the Library of Congress.

Bibliografische Information der Deutschen Nationalbibliothek
Die Deutsche Nationalbibliothek verzeichnet diese Publikation in der Deutschen Nationalbibliografie; detaillierte bibliografische Daten sind im Internet über http://dnb.dnb.de abrufbar.

© 2014 Walter de Gruyter GmbH, Berlin/Boston
Druck: Hubert & Co. GmbH & Co. KG, Göttingen
♾ Gedruckt auf säurefreiem Papier
Printed in Germany

www.degruyter.com

To Sandra

Acknowledgments

The present study is a revised version of my dissertation, which I defended in March 2012 at the Università degli Studi di Torino (Turin, Italy) and at the Johannes Gutenberg-Universität Mainz (Mainz, Germany) after a joint supervision ("co-tutelle de thèse") of my doctorate.

I want to begin by thanking Heiner F. Klemme, on the basis of whose commentaries I emended and hopefully improved many passages of the present study and whose forthright and acrimonious comments constantly demanded the improvement of my work, and Luca Fonnesu, whose stimulating critique was my initial inspiration in philosophy and who still affectionately advises me in philosophical challenges. I owe Massimo Mori a debt of gratitude, particularly for encouraging me while writing this work.

While researching this work, which lasted over three years, I collected many further debts of gratitude and, at this time, I thank all the people who helped me in my research, and I conclude by naming Michael Walschots, who very quickly provided me with an accurate linguistic revision of my study.

Special thanks are due to Gabriel Rivero, with whom I discussed, and still discuss my (philosophical) ideas.

And, above all, I am grateful to Sandra Vlasta, who read and commented on drafts of this project, and without whom I could have not written this. To her this work is also dedicated.

Contents

Introduction —— XIII

Chapter 1 **The Concept of Human Mental Faculties** —— 1
1.1   Some Occurrences of the Term *Vermögen* from Kant's *Critique of Pure Reason* —— 3
1.2   The German Term *Vermögen* during Kant's time —— 8
1.3   The 1773/1775 Berlin Academy Prize Competition: *Examen des deux facultés primitives de l'ame, celle de connoître et celle de sentir* —— 12
1.4   Kant's Concept of *Gemüt* and the Epigenetical Reading —— 24
1.5   The Concept of Human Mental Faculties: Some Concluding Remarks —— 33

Chapter 2 **The Mind and Its Faculties in Contemporary Kant Scholarship** —— 34
2.1   Brook's Kantian Mind-Functionalism and the Transcendental Argument —— 35
2.2   Hatfield's Innatist Reading of Kant's Faculties —— 38
2.3   Some Brief Observations on the Distinction between Rational and Empirical Psychology and the Supposed Place of Psychology within Transcendental Philosophy —— 40
2.4   Kitcher's Kantian Transcendental Psychology —— 45
2.5   The Mind and Its Faculties in Contemporary Kant Scholarship: Some Concluding Remarks —— 52

Chapter 3 **Anthropology and Kant's Study of the Faculties of the Human Mind** —— 53
3.1   A Brief Historical Overview of the Relation between Pragmatic Anthropology and Empirical Psychology —— 54
3.2   Anthropology as a Pragmatic Discipline —— 62
3.3   Anthropology and the Worldly Concept of Philosophy —— 69
3.4   The Cyclops Metaphor and Kant's *anthropologia transscendentalis* —— 76
3.5   The Boundaries between Kant's Pure Philosophy and His Pragmatic Anthropology —— 85
3.6   The Boundaries between Pure and Empirical Philosophy —— 93
3.7   The Mind's Activity: *Anthropology*, § 7 —— 98
3.8   A Significant Passage from the Rostock Manuscript —— 101
3.9   The Published Remark to § 7 of the 1798 *Anthropology* —— 108
3.10   The Concept of Sensibility: *Anthropology*, §§ 8 – 11 —— 111

3.11   Sensibility as Strength —— 115
3.12   Kant's Classification of the Faculties in the 1798 *Anthropology* and in the Rostock Manuscript —— 117
3.13   Anthropology and Kant's Study of the Faculties of the Human Mind: Some Concluding Remarks —— 125

Chapter 4 **Kant's System of the Faculties of the Human Mind** —— 127
4.1   The Classification of the Mental Faculties in Kant Scholarship —— 128
4.2   Some Brief Considerations Concerning Kant's Division of the Faculties in the First *Critique* —— 130
4.3   Towards Kant's Tripartite Division of the Faculties in the third *Critique* —— 137
4.4   The Correspondence between (Pure) Reason and the (Higher) Faculty of Desire, as well as (Pure) Reason and (Autonomous) Will —— 139
4.5   The Concept of Pleasure and the Role of Feeling in the *Critique of Practical Reason* —— 149
4.6   Kant's Classification of the Faculties in the *Critique of Practical Reason*: Some General Remarks —— 155
4.7   The System of the Higher Cognitive Faculties and Its Relation to the Distinction between "Philosophy as a System" and "Critique" in the So-Called 'First Introduction' to the *Critique of the Power of Judgement* —— 162
4.8   Kant's Classification of All the Faculties of the Human Mind in the 'First Introduction' to the *Critique of the Power of Judgement* —— 171
4.9   Kant's "Encyclopaedic Introduction" of the Mental Faculties in the 'First Introduction' to the *Critique of the Power of Judgement* —— 178
4.10   Kant's Classification of the Faculties in the Preface and in the Published Introduction to the *Critique of the Power of Judgement* —— 182
4.11   A Last Clear and Comprehensive Classification of the Faculties of the Human Mind: The General Introduction to the *Metaphysics of Morals* —— 190
4.12   Kant's System of the Faculties of the Human Mind: Some Concluding Remarks —— 202

Chapter 5 **Interpreting Kant's Concept of Moral Feeling on the Basis of His Theory of the Faculties** —— 204
5.1   Kant's Account of the Aesthetic: Some Brief Remarks —— 207
5.2   Kant's Ethics: A Rationalistic Account and the Role of Feeling —— 215
5.3   Moral Sense and Moral Feeling —— 217
5.4   Moral Motivation, Moral Incentives, and Respect —— 221

5.5   Respect, Incentive, Feeling —— 225
5.6   Feeling as Susceptibility in the *Doctrine of Virtue* —— 232
5.7   Kant's Moral Aesthetic —— 238
5.8   Concluding Remarks and Outlook —— 240

Bibliography and Abbreviations —— 242
Kant's works – English translations —— 243
Kant's texts (not in AA) —— 244
Other Primary Sources —— 244
Secondary Sources —— 246

Author Index —— 263

Subject Index —— 266

Introduction

In the last few decades a remarkable change occurred in Kant scholarship: in recent research the "other" Kant has been discovered, i.e. the one of the *Doctrine of Virtue* and the one of the *Anthropology*. Through the rediscovery of Kant's investigations into the empirical and sensuous aspects of knowledge, our understanding of Kant's philosophy has not only been enriched by an important element, which allows researchers to correct supposed deficiencies in Kant's work. In addition, this enrichment has contributed to the formulation of further questions concerning the very same nature of Kant's philosophy itself. In fact, the more the "other" Kant comes to the fore of interpretative efforts, the stronger the question concerning the connection between Kant's pure philosophy and his empirical investigation becomes. However, as a look into the secondary literature also reveals, the relation between transcendental and pure philosophy, on the one hand, and anthropology, on the other hand, never becomes completely distinct.

In the present study, my aim is, on the one hand, that of showing that the attempts of reading Kant's pure philosophy on the basis of a psychological or anthropological interpretation is not convincing and, on the other hand, that of nonetheless illustrating some interrelations and connections between Kant's critical investigation and his anthropological one, by means of an analysis of the theory of the faculties. In my work, I focus mainly on Kant's published works, in particular the three *Critiques*, the *Groundwork of the Metaphysics of Morals*, the *Doctrine of Virtue* from the *Metaphysics of Morals*, and the *Anthropology from a Pragmatic Point of View*, and I sometimes accompany these analyses with an examination of some unpublished texts from Kant's Reflections and from the lecture notes taken by students in Kant's university courses.

While I dedicate the first three chapters and partly also the fourth to the study of Kant's theory of the faculties, in the last two chapters and, above all, in the last one, I focus on the concepts of feeling and moral feeling.

In my analysis I first argue against both the "transcendental psychological" and the "anthropological" reading of Kant's theory of the faculties, which try to "psychologize" or "anthropologize" Kant's transcendental philosophy. Instead, I emphasize that Kant's study of the faculties is a constitutive part of his pure, critical philosophy. Finally, I show that there is a close connection between Kant's pure philosophy and his moral aesthetic.

In particular, in the first chapter, which is introductory in its nature, I give an account of the concept of the faculties by referring to some terminological and lexicographical clarification of the meaning of the German term *Vermögen* [faculty], and by furnishing some well-known examples of the term from the first *Cri-*

tique. In addition, I show that not only the concept of *Kritik*, but also the consideration of the concept of *Gemüt* turns out to be central in order to understand Kant's philosophy.

In the second chapter of my study, I turn to some contemporary attempts to interpret Kant's theory of the faculties and, in general, Kant's account of the mind. I expose strengths and weaknesses of the interpretations of some contemporary philosophical studies (A. Brook, G. Hatfield, and P. Kitcher) of Kant's model of the mind, criticizing the fact that these readings too strongly emphasize empirical or psychological aspects within Kant's pure philosophical investigation.

In the third chapter I deal with another interpretive reading of Kant's theory of the faculties, namely the one discussing the possibility of founding the analysis of the faculties in Kant's critical, pure philosophical investigation on anthropological presuppositions. In this chapter I focus on Kant's system of the faculties and the faculties' division as Kant analyses it in his anthropological work and I take into consideration the interpretive proposal of a transcendental anthropology (which must not be confused with pragmatic anthropology). I show that, even though it is possible to find many intersections between the critical philosophical investigations and the anthropological ones, the at times nuanced boundaries between these two disciplines do not imply the identity of anthropology and pure philosophy. I first note the inconsistencies of the reading according to which Kant's pure philosophy is based on anthropology. Afterwards I emphasize that Kant's analysis of the fundamental faculties in his critical investigation corresponds to the analysis of the cognizing, willing, and feeling human being. Finally I conclude that from this it does not follow that Kant's theory of the faculties in his critical work should be identified with psychological or anthropological investigations.

On the basis of these considerations against two contemporary readings of Kant's theory of the faculties, in the fourth chapter I describe Kant's classification of the faculties and its development in some of his published works. In contrast to an underestimation of the study of Kant's treatment of the faculties – which has mostly been considered in the context of a psychological or anthropological reading of Kant's philosophy – I give a precise description of this division in the context of critical philosophy by focusing in particular on the three *Critiques*, on the *Groundwork* and on the *Metaphysics of Morals*. I deal with the history of the development of Kant's tripartite theory of the mental field in his published works and, in this way, I aim to show how the faculty of feeling pleasure and displeasure becomes more and more important in the context of pure philosophy.

After these observations, and in consideration of the increasing importance of the faculty of feeling pleasure and displeasure in Kant's critical philosophy, the last chapter of my work is well introduced. In fact, in the fifth chapter I apply the gained knowledge about Kant's pure philosophical analysis of the faculties to the specific field of moral philosophy. On the basis of the results gained in the previous chapters concerning the systematic nature of human faculties, in the fifth chapter I show how moral feeling reveals itself to be a central component for correctly characterizing Kant's description of the moral life of a finite and sensuous agent. In order to do this, I first distinguish between two possible characterizations of the concept of moral feeling in Kant's philosophy and afterwards, on the basis of these two different accounts of the concept of feeling, I elucidate the role played by the faculty of feeling pleasure and displeasure in Kant's ethics and eventually explain the significance of Kant's "moral aesthetic". I analyse more closely how it happens that, according to Kant, a human being is able to feel respect for the moral law and I frame the analysis of the concept of moral feeling in the context of Kant's theory of the human mental faculties. This clarification requires the proposal of an alternative to many contemporary readings of Kant's concept of moral feeling: in contrast to many other readings, my interpretive proposal is based on the analysis of the faculty of feeling pleasure and displeasure in the context of pure philosophical studies of the human faculties, so that I aim to frame moral feeling within the context of Kant's transcendental aesthetic in general and an "aesthetic of morals" in particular.

In sum, with my work I intend to shed some light, on the one hand, on the inconsistencies of the psychological and anthropological ways of interpreting Kant's pure philosophy and, on the other hand, of its aestheticization (in particular in ethics) which risks to underestimate the role played by (practical) reason. In this study, I hope to have shown that both Kant's philosophy in general and the relation between pure philosophy and anthropology in particular cannot be understood without reference to Kant's theory of the faculties, but also that the role and function of moral feelings in Kant's critical works can be rightly appreciated only in the context of a moral theory which remains, at its core, cognitivist.

Chapter 1
The Concept of Human Mental Faculties

Immanuel Kant is the first philosopher who defends a clear and distinctive tripartite structure of the faculties of the human mind (*Gemütsvermögen*) from a pure philosophical standpoint on the basis of an exact distinction between reason and sensibility. Kant unfolded what other thinkers aimed at doing before or contemporaneous with him in the psychological field by newly interpreting the functioning of the soul. Among others, authors like Christian Wolff, Alexander Gottlieb Baumgarten, Johann Georg Sulzer, Johannes Nikolaus Tetens, Georg Friedrich Meier, and Johann August Eberhard have taken notice of the important role played by the faculty of feeling (*Gefühl*) or by sensibility (*Sinnlichkeit*) and started reserving a central analysis in their studies for the sensitive part of the soul, together with the observations they dedicated to the faculty of cognition and the faculty of desire (*Erkenntnisvermögen* and *Begehrungsvermögen*). However, those authors mostly engaged in this sort of investigation by means of an empirical analysis, which supported the rational psychological part of their studies (as I will discuss over the course of my work). What is central for my study and should be emphasized is the fact that the study of the faculties, which had been characterized by the aforementioned authors as a mere empirical psychological project, gains a philosophical significance in Kant's investigations.

In order to understand the importance of Kant's tripartite division of the faculties in the history of philosophy, I first consider the meaning of the term faculty at Kant's time. In order to accomplish this, in this first chapter I confine myself to take into consideration some occurrences of the German term *Vermögen* (*faculty*) in Kant's *Critique of Pure Reason* and I then come back to a mere terminological analysis of the word *Vermögen* and the related word *Gemüt* at Kant's time.[1] Subsequently, I will shed some light on the discussion concerning the debate on the faculties during the Eighteenth Century in Europe in general and particularly in Germany by focusing on an exemplary event, namely the *Preisaufgabe* of the Royal Academy of Sciences in Berlin, which has been first announced in 1773 and then published one more time in 1775. As I will note, the 1773/1775 call is central for my discussion, in that in this case the Academy expressly asks for the clarification of the nature and characteristics of the basic faculties of knowing and feeling (*Examen des deux facultés primitives de l'ame, celle de connoître et celle de sentir*) and the text by Johann August Eberhard (*Allgemeine Theorie*

---

1 I propose to translate the German term *Gemüt* with the English term *mind* for reasons that I hope I will render clear in the proceeding of this work.

des Denkens und Empfindens), to whom the academy awarded the prize, together with the two other works mentioned, that is the ones by Johann Gottfried Herder (*Vom Erkennen und Empfinden der menschlichen Seele*) and Joachim Heinrich Campe (*Die Empfindungs- und Erkenntnißkraft der menschlichen Seele: die erstere nach ihren Gesetzen, beyde nach ihren ursprünglichen Bestimmungen, nach ihrem gegenseitigen Einflusse aufeinander und nach ihren Beziehungen auf Character und Genie betrachtet*), are good representatives of the philosophical debate that took place during this peculiar chapter in the history of ideas and give us an insight into the lively discussion on the faculties at Kant's time.[2]

As a counterpart to the animated discussion concerning the faculties during the Eighteenth Century in Germany, in chapter two I turn to the discussions surrounding the mind and its faculties in contemporary Kant scholarship, in order to show how these debates and examinations show differences and similarities over the centuries. This will become clear if we consider how the faculties are still analysed from the various perspectives in contemporary scientific discussions, based on their psychological, philosophical and anthropological meaning.

I will then complete my analysis of the term *Vermögen* in Kant's philosophy by approaching the more precise description of the tripartite division of the faculties as a specific, pure philosophical project in Kant's work in chapter four, which ideally concludes the discussion on the faculties which I begin here in these first two chapters of my study. The urge to discuss these themes is occasioned by the astonishing circumstance that, in spite of the fact that the term *Vermögen* is central and often appears in Kant's critical works, not many works dedicated specifically to Kant's theory of the faculties have been written and agreement among readers on the way of interpreting this central concept has not been reached.[3]

Already a very quick look at some occurrences of the term *Vermögen* in the *Critique of Pure Reason* makes clear how important it is to state what the term exactly means, even though, as for most of Kant's terminology, confusions and misunderstandings are always possible.[4]

---

2 See § 1.3 below.

3 Cf. for instance GILLES DELEUZE, *La philosophie critique de Kant. Doctrine des facultés*, Paris, Presses Universitaires de France 1963 (English translation by Hugh Tomlinson and Barbara Habberjam: *Kant's critical philosophy. The doctrine of the faculties*, London, Athlone Press 1984) and, more recently, STEFAN HESSBRÜGGEN-WALTER, *Die Seele und ihre Vermögen. Kants Metaphysik des Mentalen in der 'Kritik der reinen Vernunft'*, Paderborn, Mentis 2004.

4 In a study dedicated to a linguistic analysis of the first *Critique* (THORSTEN ROELCKE, *Die Terminologie der Erkenntnisvermögen. Wörterbuch und lexikosemantische Untersuchung zu Kants 'Kritik der reinen Vernunft'*, Tübingen, Max Niemeyer 1989) the author notes (p. 9): "Der Gebrauch der Terminologie in der "Kritik der reinen Vernunft" ist sehr vielfältig: Kant verwendet

In the present introductory chapter I show how Kant's critical enterprise can be considered as an investigation of the human mind (*Gemüt*), in that it is dedicated to the analysis of the faculties. I first furnish some well-known examples from the first *Critique* where the term *Vermögen* occurs before I provide, on the basis of these references, a lexicographical analysis of the use of the German term *Vermögen* at Kant's time.

This historical lexicographical study of the term *Vermögen* will eventually serve as an introduction to the analysis of Kant's concept of *Gemüt*, which I present in my study as Kant's unified account of the human mind.[5]

After considering an "epigenetical" reading of Kant's theory of the mental field, I will argue that this interpretive proposal is unsatisfying, if we are to properly understand the meaning of Kant's critical philosophical enterprise.

The fact that these interpretations are not convincing will introduce the consideration of contemporary alternative proposals, such as the one concerning a "transcendental psychological" reading of Kant's mind (*Gemüt*), whose strengths and weaknesses will be analysed in chapter 2.

1.1 Some Occurrences of the Term *Vermögen* from Kant's *Critique of Pure Reason*

In the present section I point at some occurrences of the term *Vermögen* in the Prefaces to the first (1781) and second (1787) edition of the first *Critique* and in the general Introduction to the book, which Kant partially rewrote between 1781 and 1787, in order to show the central role played by the concept of the faculties in Kant's critical enterprise.

In this section I do not develop any systematic account of Kant's concept of "faculty" but I rather aim to give some example of Kant's use of the term *Vermögen* and point out that a more precise terminological analysis of this term is due, in order for confusions and misunderstandings to be avoided.

---

zum einen viele Termini innerhalb der Kritik sehr stark polysem, d. h. unter verschiedene Bedeutungen. Zum anderen gebraucht er viele Termini unter einer entsprechenden Bedeutung synonym. In der "Kritik der reinen Vernunft" wird also die Forderung nach Eindeutigkeit zwischen den bezeichnenden Termini und den bezeichneten Begriffen nicht erfüllt".

5 The English term *mind* in philosophical discussion is usually translated with the German term *Geist* (as in "philosophy of mind" which is rendered "*Philosophie des Geistes*"). Nonetheless, in contemporary English-speaking Kant scholarship, the Kantian term *Gemüt* is translated with the English term *mind*, while the term *Geist* is often rendered as *spirit* (see for instance HOWARD CAYGILL, *A Kant Dictionary*, Oxford/Cambridge (Mass.), Blackwell 1995, entry "*Gemüt*", pp. 210 – 212). For an account of *Gemüt* as Kant's concept of mind see section 1.4 below.

Starting from the Preface to the first edition (1781) of the *Critique of Pure Reason*, at the very beginning of this Preface the reader is told about human reason's "peculiar fate", i.e. that of not being able to answer some questions, which the very same reason asks itself. Kant explains that this is due to the fact that these questions "transcend every faculty of human reason".[6]

The prohibition for reason to go beyond its own boundaries represents a strength and not a limitation of Kant's strategy: as the famous *Prolegomena* example (spread out in §§ 57–60) shows explicitly, the boundaries (*Grenzen*) that we are not allowed to cross in our knowing enterprise do not constitute a constraining and frustrating limitation of our knowledge. On the contrary, they should be considered as a stimulating starting point. To draw the boundaries of experience does not mean to restrict our world to austere limits. Rather, this is the only rigorous way for conducting our research.[7] Aiming to research beyond the boundaries of possible knowledge, we would find ourselves in the case of that "light dove", which "could get the idea that it could do even better in airless space", and thus not realising that the resistance of the air is its only means to keep flying.[8]

The human mental faculties are for human beings what the air is for the dove: they delimit the boundaries of human "mental actions" and, at the same time, make them possible.

This is the picture that we get from the first occurrences of the word *Vermögen* in the first *Critique* as well. As Kant explicitly states, the aim of a critique of pure reason is not an analysis of books or other scholars' systems, but rather a "critique" of the "faculty of reason in general".[9] Kant does not avoid questions

---

6 KrV, A VII/AA 04: 07.02–06: "Die menschliche Vernunft hat das besondere Schicksal in einer Gattung ihrer Erkenntnisse: daß sie durch Fragen belästigt wird, die sie nicht abweisen kann, denn sie sind ihr durch die Natur der Vernunft selbst aufgegeben, die sie aber auch nicht beantworten kann, denn sie übersteigen alles Vermögen der menschlichen Vernunft"; CpR p. 99.
7 Cf. Prol § 57, AA 04: 354. 19–23; but also Prol § 57, AA 04: 352. 21–27; § 57, AA 04: 353. 16–31; Cf. Prol § 57, AA 04: 354. 19–23; but also Prol § 57, AA 04: 352. 21–27; § 57, AA 04: 353. 16–31.
8 KrV, A4–5/B9 – AA 04: 19.06–14/03: 32. 10–13: "Beweis von der Macht der Vernunft [A 5] eingenommen, sieht der Trieb zur Erweiterung keine Grenzen. Die leichte Taube, indem sie im freien Fluge die Luft theilt, deren Widerstand sie fühlt, könnte die Vorstellung fassen, daß es ihr im luftleeren Raum [B 9] noch viel besser gelingen werde"; CpR p. 140.
9 Cf. for instance KrV, A XII/AA 04: 9.11–16: "Ich verstehe [unter Kritik der reinen Vernunft] nicht eine Kritik der Bücher und Systeme, sondern die des Vernunftvermögens überhaupt in Ansehung aller Erkenntnisse, zu denen sie unabhängig von aller Erfahrung streben mag, mithin die Entscheidung der Möglichkeit oder Unmöglichkeit einer Metaphysik überhaupt und die Bestimmung sowohl der Quellen, als des Umfanges und der *Gränzen* derselben, alles aber aus Principien"; CpR p. 101.

addressed by reason "by pleading the incapacity of human reason as an excuse": he rather specifies the questions and, "after discovering the point where reason has misunderstood itself", he answers them.[10]

As in the Preface to the 1781 edition, also in the one to the 1787 edition Kant mentions the term *Vermögen* in close vicinity to the term *Grenze*, as he talks about the way of cognizing *a priori*, starting from "what we ourselves put into things" thanks to our faculty of intuiting objects. What follows is, as Kant puts it, a "deduction" starting from "our faculty of cognizing *a priori*"; however, from this deduction "there emerges a very strange result": by means of this faculty we cannot go "beyond the boundaries of possible experience".[11]

The concept of the faculties delimits the territory of possible experience and traces its boundaries. A faculty corresponds to a boundary and the condition of the possibility of research. The needed reconsideration of the boundaries of our research directly implicates "an antecedent critique of [pure reason's] own capacity":[12] what has to be "criticized", to be brought before "the true court of justice for all controversies of pure reason",[13] is a faculty, i.e. pure reason itself.[14]

The correspondence of Kant's critical enterprise with the analysis of the human faculties is also testified by some passages from the Introduction to the first *Critique*. There, for instance, Kant discusses the metaphysical question raised by the faculty of reason, a faculty which is described as having a natural predisposition to metaphysics.[15]

---

10 KrV, A XII/AA 04: 9.20–24, 10.25: "Ich bin ihren [=der Vernunft] Fragen nicht dadurch etwa ausgewichen, daß ich mich mit dem Unvermögen der menschlichen Vernunft entschuldigte; sondern ich habe sie nach Principien vollständig specificirt und, nachdem ich den Punkt des Mißverstandes der Vernunft mit ihr selbst entdeckt hatte, sie zu ihrer völligen Befriedigung aufgelöst"; CpR p. 101.

11 KrV, B XIX/AA 03: 13.13–18: "Es ergiebt sich aus dieser Deduction unseres *Vermögens a priori* zu erkennen im ersten Theile der Metaphysik ein befremdliches und dem ganzen Zwecke derselben, der den zweiten Theil beschäftigt, dem Anscheine nach sehr nachtheiliges Resultat, nämlich daß wir mit ihm nie über die *Grenze* möglicher Erfahrung hinauskommen können, welches doch gerade die wesentlichste Angelegenheit dieser Wissenschaft ist"; CpR p. 111–112, my italics.

12 Cf. KrV, B XXXV/AA 03: 21.31–32: "das dogmatische Verfahren der reinen Vernunft ohne vorangehende Kritik ihres eigenen Vermögens"; CpR p. 119.

13 KrV, A 751 – B 779/AA 03: 491. 24–25: "Man kann die Kritik der reinen Vernunft als den wahren Gerichtshof für alle Streitigkeiten derselben ansehen"; CpR p. 649. Cf. also KrV, A XI-XII/ AA 04: 09. 04–10; CpR p. 101.

14 Or, as Kant says in the proceeding of the discussion, while speaking about Wolff, an "organ": "Kritik des Organs, nämlich der reinen Vernunft selbst" (KrV, B XXXVI/AA 03: 22.15; CpR p. 119).

15 This text is, as is the preceding fifth section, strongly influenced by the text of the *Prolegomena*. In fact, the first five paragraphs of section V of the 1787-Introduction are copied from

Kant states that, even though the sort of questions concerning metaphysics comes from reason, "one cannot leave it up to the mere natural predisposition to metaphysics", since every time this has been done, "unavoidable contradictions have always been found in all previous attempts to answers these natural questions".[16]

It has to be possible to bring metaphysical questions to some determinate level of certainty regarding:
- either the knowledge/ignorance of objects (which means that we must be able to decide about the objects of metaphysical questioning)
- or else about the capacity/incapacity (*das Vermögen und Unvermögen*) of reason for judging them (the possibility for reason to make meaningful judgements about metaphysics).

It must then be possible to reach a level of certainty, allowing us:
- either to reliably extend our pure reason
- or else to set determinate and secure limits for pure reason itself.[17]

The alternatives Kant proposes are either (1) a secure determination of the objects of metaphysics (and, consequently, an extension of pure reason) or (2) the more modest ambition of analysing the actual possibility reason has to judge about metaphysics within its own specific limits.

Kant decides to go this second way and starts his critical enterprise aiming at founding the conditions of possibility of his philosophical analysis. These conditions of possibility, these boundaries beyond which no analysis is possible, are a limiting barrier and, at the same time, the prolific starting point for a better-founded science. Engaging in a critique means exactly to reach the boundaries

---

the *Prolegomena*: see KrV, B14–17/AA 03: 36.14–03: 38.24 = Prol § 2, AA 04: 268.11–269.37. The first five paragraphs of section VI are also based on the *Prolegomena*, but not directly copied: see KrV, B19–22/AA 03: 39.22–41.14 = Prol § 2, AA 04: 275.24–281.16.

16 KrV, B22/AA 03: 41.15–20; CpR p. 147: "Da sich aber bei allen bisherigen Versuchen, diese natürlichen Fragen, z.B. ob die Welt einen Anfang habe, oder von Ewigkeit her sei u. s. w., zu beantworten, jederzeit unvermeidliche Widersprüche gefunden haben, so kann man es nicht bei der bloßen Naturanlage zur Metaphysik, d. i. dem reinen Vernunftvermögen selbst, woraus zwar immer irgend eine Metaphysik (es sei, welche es wolle) erwächst, bewenden lassen".

17 Kant's text reads as follows: "es muß möglich sein, mit ihr es zur Gewißheit zu bringen, entweder im Wissen oder Nicht-Wissen der Gegenstände, d. i. entweder der Entscheidung über die Gegenstände ihrer Fragen, oder über das Vermögen und Unvermögen der Vernunft in Ansehung ihrer etwas zu urtheilen, also entweder unsere reine Vernunft mit Zuverlässigkeit zu erweitern, oder ihr bestimmte und sichere Schranken zu setzen", KrV, B22/AA 03: 41.21–26; CpR p. 148.

of reason in order to delineate the sources and extent of metaphysics.[18] This undertaking will thus coincide with the analysis of the conditions making that very same research possible.

In this respect, the renewed metaphysics seems to turn out to be not very extensive, in that it "only" deals with reason itself.[19] However, this conclusion is wrong. In effect, in order for this field to be investigated, reason has to become "completely familiar with its own capacity". Once accomplished, this familiarity determines the domain of reason's research and the boundaries of reason's use.[20] The familiarity, i.e. reason's awareness of its own capacity or, in other words, a clearer picture of the faculties, is the condition for easily determining, "completely and securely", the boundaries, i.e. the sphere of reason's proper use.

This might be enough regarding the first occurrences of the term *Vermögen* in the Prefaces and in the Introduction to the *Critique of Pure Reason*. It can be noted that, even though we still do not possess a clear meaning of the term *Vermögen*, this word has been used so far to refer to the mere possibility of performing a "mental act".

Nonetheless, it can also be noted that, by means of the analysis of the faculties, Kant aims to deal with the idea of a special philosophical enterprise. Kant's critique focuses on the examination of reason itself, defined as "the faculty that provides the principles of cognition *a priori*".[21]

As I will show in chapter 2, contemporary English-speaking Kant scholarship in particular tries to interpret the whole of Kant's *Critiques* as an analysis of the human mind (*Gemüt*) that has to be understood by reference to psychology. What I propose instead, in chapter 3, is to read the critical enterprise on the faculties as a "treatise of human nature".

However, both the readings are based on the prior understanding of Kant's concept of the faculties and of Kant's account of the human mind (*Gemüt*). That is why, after having referred to some occurrences of the term *Vermögen* in the first *Critique*, I now aim to more extensively sketch out the philosophical meaning of the term *Vermögen* at Kant's time by referring to some Eighteenth century German dictionaries and lexicons and, after doing so, I aim to relate the analysis

---

18 See KrV, A XII/AA 04: 9.11–16; CpR p. 101.
19 See KrV, B23/AA 03: 41.33–37, 42.01; CpR p. 148.
20 Cf. KrV, B23/AA 03: 42.01–05; CpR p. 148.
21 "Denn Vernunft ist das Vermögen, welches die Principien der Erkenntniß *a priori* an die Hand giebt", KrV, B24/AA 03: 42.30, 43.01–02; CpR p. 149. The passage is different in the A Edition (KrV, A10/AA 04: 22.20–25; CpR p. 132).

of the term *Vermögen* to the analysis of the more general concept of mind, i.e. Kant's concept of *Gemüt*.

1.2 The German Term *Vermögen* during Kant's time

A first account of the way the term *Vermögen* was used at Kant's time can be gained by considering two lexicons, which took into consideration in a very precise way the philosophical use of the term *Vermögen* at Kant's time, namely the one by J. G. Walch (1726)[22] and the one by J. H. Zedler (1732–1754).[23]

In Walch's *Philosophisches Lexicon* the term *Vermögen* is treated in relation to the metaphysical sphere and a parallelism between the German term *Vermögen* and the Latin word *Potentia* is argued for.[24] Most interestingly for the discussion of Kant's faculties, the lexicon mentions a *"potentia transcendentalis"*, which is defined as the sum of all faculties, of the natural as well as the acquired ones, and which possesses an active side, i.e. a *"potentia activa"* or *"wirkendes Vermögen"*, which is what makes one able to perform an act. Walch refers to two finite active faculties, which are predicated of God's creatures, i.e. reason (*Verstand*), identified as the "force of thinking", and will (*Wille*), the "force of willing".[25]

---

22 *Philosophisches Lexicon, Darinnen die in allen Theilen der Philosophie, als Logic, Metaphysic, Physic, Pneumatic, Ethic, natürlichen Theologie und Rechts-Gelehrsamkeit, wie auch Politic fürkommende Materien und Kunst-Wörter erkläret und aus der Historie erläutert; die Streitigkeiten der ältern und neuern Philosophen erzehlet, die dahin gehörigen Bücher und Schrifften aufgeführet und alles nach Alphabetischer Ordnung vorgestellet werden, mit nöthigen Registern versehen und herausgegeben von* JOHANN GEORG WALCH, Leipzig, Verlegts Joh. Friedrich Gleditschens seel. Sohn 1726. For some biographical details about the author see the entry "Walch, Johann Georg (1693–1775)" in the third volume of HEINER F. KLEMME – MANFRED KUEHN (eds.), *Dictionary of Eighteenth-Century German Philosophers*, Bristol, Thoemmes Continuum 2010, pp. 329–333.

23 JOHANN HEINRICH ZEDLER, *Grosses Vollständige Universal-Lexicon Aller Wissenschaften und Künste*, Halle/Leipzig 1732–1754. Notwithstanding the historical importance of Zedler's *Lexicon*, it is now known that many of its philosophical entries have been plagiarized – partly from Walch's *Lexicon* – cf. ULRICH JOHANNES SCHNEIDER (ed.), *Seine Welt wissen. Enzyklopädien in der Frühen Neuzeit. Katalog zur Ausstellung der Universitätsbibliothek Leipzig und der Herzog August Bibliothek Wolfenbüttel*, Darmstadt, Primus 2006 (cf. in particular p. 9).

24 J. G. WALCH, *Philosophisches Lexicon*, cit., column 2662: "Hernach handelt man auch in der Metaphysic von dem Vermögen; oder von der *Potentia*, davon wir die gemeine scholastische Lehre vortragen wollen, damit man die dabey vorkommende Terminos verstehen lerne".

25 The peculiar case of the *"potentia naturalis"* assumes even a neater shape in the prosecution of the lexicon entry, since the distinction necessary/free is added. See J. G. WALCH, *Philosophisches Lexicon*, cit., column 2664.

A similar treatment of the term *Vermögen* is also to be found in Zedler's *Lexicon*, where we read that "Die Facultas rationalis besteht in intellectu et voluntate, im Verstand und Willen".[26]

Moreover, in the dictionary of the German language edited by J. C. Adelung (1774–1786), that is *Grammatisch-kritisches Wörterbuch der Hochdeutschen Mundart*,[27] the word *Vermögen* is analysed as a verb and as a noun. As a verb, the term is defined as polysemantic and refers mainly to the process of arranging, accomplishing something, but also, in broader meaning, to the possession of a power, the capability to generate a certain modification.[28] The second entry of the dictionary, dedicated to *Vermögen* as a noun, deals also with this capability, since *Vermögen* is described as the possibility one possesses for producing a modification.[29] Even though the concept that the term *Vermögen* refers to is defined as a very general one, the entry goes on to stress, interestingly enough, its philosophical usage.[30] In this respect, a list of faculties is given and the peculiarity of using the word in plural forms solely in philosophy is stated.[31] The term is explained primarily as a condition which makes some acts (of perceiving, desiring, willing) possible: we are told of the usage that most notably philosophers make of it, and of a plurality of different faculties referred to with this term.[32]

---

26 J. H. ZEDLER, *Grosses Vollständige Universal-Lexicon Aller Wissenschaften und Künste*, cit., Volume 9, Column 69. However, for the accusation of plagiarism, see note 30 above.

27 *Grammatisch-kritisches Wörterbuch der Hochdeutschen Mundart mit beständiger Vergleichung der übrigen Mundart, besonders aber der Oberdeutschen, von* JOHANN CHRISTOPH ADELUNG, Leipzig, Johann Gottlob Immanuel Breitkopf und Compagnie 1793. First edition 1774–1786; author's last revision (last authorized version): 1793–1801, 4 volumes.

28 J. C. ADELUNG, *Grammatisch-kritisches Wörterbuch*, cit., vol. 4 (Seb-Z), columns 1095–1096: "In weiterer Bedeutung, Kraft, Fähigkeit haben, eine gewisse Veränderung hervor zu bringen, für können".

29 See J. C. ADELUNG, *Grammatisch-kritisches Wörterbuch*, cit., vol. 4 (Seb-Z), column 1096: "*Das Vermögen*, des -s, *plur. Inusit.* das Hauptwort von dem vorigen Zeitworte, die Fähigkeit oder Möglichkeit Veränderungen hervor zu bringen [...] Im weitesten Verstande, wo das Vermögen eine Art der Fähigkeit ist.

30 See J. C. ADELUNG, *Grammatisch-kritisches Wörterbuch*, cit., vol. 4 (Seb-Z), column 1096: "Vermögen ist ein sehr allgemeiner Ausdruck, welcher als ein solcher auch in der philosophischen Schreibart am üblichsten ist".

31 See J. C. ADELUNG, *Grammatisch-kritisches Wörterbuch*, cit., vol. 4 (Seb-Z), column 1096: "*Das Vermögen*, des -s, *plur. Inusit.* [...] Im weitesten Verstande wird es, wie schon gedacht, in der Philosophie gebraucht. [...] In welchem Falle auch von einigen der Plural gebraucht wird. [...] Der doch außer der philosophischen Schreibart ungewöhnlich ist".

32 J. C. ADELUNG, *Grammatisch-kritisches Wörterbuch*, cit., vol. 4 (Seb-Z), column 1097: "Das Vermögen zu begehren, das Begehrungsvermögen, das Vermögen zu wollen, zu erkennen, sich zu erinnern, zu urtheilen u.s.f.".

Without entering into the question of the division of the faculties of the mind (*Gemüt*) and the question of the development of the partition of the mental field in general, since both these questions will be addressed in chapter 4 below, I limit myself to underlining that, by means of this quick terminological analysis, it is easy to testify how the historical German dictionaries and lexica were quite unanimous in stating that *Vermögen* denotes a condition of possibility, a power, capacity, making one able to do something (perceiving, cognizing, willing), and that this term was closely linked to the philosophical sphere.

What should also be noted is the strong interaction between faculty (*Vermögen*) and power (*Kraft*). It is questionable whether these two terms really are synonymous concepts. Both of them have a very wide use in Eighteenth century German philosophy.[33] However, without deepening the debate about the powers of the soul in Eighteenth Century Germany and limiting ourselves to Kant's texts, it can be noted that the term *Kraft* (as well as the term *Vermögen*) plays an important role in the earliest of Kant's texts. For instance, the *Thoughts on the True Estimation of Living Forces*, published in 1749 but already composed in 1746 (which is also the date which appears on the title page – the dedication and preface were added in 1747), deals with the concept of forces and, in partic-

---

33 The *Schulphilosophen* generally bring all the functions of the soul back to a common principle (a power). I will provide later a background of Kant's theory of the faculties of the mind and, then, make some reference to the different philosophical positions on this topic. In the discussion concerning the mental powers in the XVIII Century many fundamental works have to be mentioned, for instance the ones by JOHN LOCKE (*An Essay concerning Humane Understanding*, London 1690), CHRISTIAN WOLFF (for instance the German Metaphysics: *Vernünfftige Gedancken von Gott, der Welt und der Seele des Menschen, auch allen Dingen überhaupt*, Halle 1720), JOHANN HEINRICH LAMBERT (for instance *Neues Organon oder Gedanken über die Erforschung und Bezeichnung des Wahren und dessen Unterscheidung vom Irrthum und Schein*, Leipzig 1764), MOSES MENDELSSOHN (for instance *Phädon oder über die Unsterblichkeit der Seele*, Berlin 1767), JOHANN GEORG SULZER (for instance *Allgemeine Theorie der schönen Künste*, Leipzig 1771–1774), JOHANNES NIKOLAUS TETENS (in particular *Philosophische Versuche über die menschliche Natur und ihre Entwickelung*, Leipzig 1777 – XI. Versuch: "Ueber die Grundkraft der menschlichen Seele und den Charakter der Menschheit", pp. 730 ff.); KARL LEONHARD REINHOLD (for instance *Versuch einer neuen Theorie des menschlichen Vorstellungsvermögen*, Prag und Jena 1789). For an historical reconstruction of the debate cf. MAX DESSOIR, *Geschichte der neueren deutschen Psychologie*, Berlin, Dunker 1902; GIANNA GIGLIOTTI, "'Vermögen' e 'Kraft'. Una rilettura del concetto di 'sintesi' nella *Critica della ragion pura* di Kant", *Rivista di storia della filosofia*, 2/1995, pp. 255–275; GARY HATFIELD, "The Cognitive Faculties", in MICHAEL AYERS – DANIEL GARBER (eds.), *The Cambridge History of Seventeenth Century Philosophy*, Cambridge/New York, Cambridge University Press, 1998; STEFAN HESSBRÜGGEN-WALTER, *Die Seele und ihre Vermögen*, cit.; RAFFAELE CIAFARDONE, "Kraft und Vermögen bei Christian Wolff und Johann Nicolaus Tetens mit Beziehung auf Kant", in JÜRGEN STOLZENBERG – OLIVER-PIERRE RUDOLPH (Hrsg.), *Christian Wolff und die europäische Aufklärung*, Olms, Hildesheim 2007, pp. 405–414.

ular, with what was one of the most discussed scientific problems at the time: the estimation of vital forces.[34] The work, dedicated to a problem of physics, revives some aspects of Leibniz's notion of power in a complete autonomous manner, since Kant adopts the concept of *wirkende Kraft* in order to attack the principles of pre-established harmony and to assess the existence of a real relation between all substances (soul and body included).[35]

However, if we aim to better understand the development of the conceptual difference between *Kraft* and *Vermögen* in Kant's thought, many other texts are relevant. In particular, as Stefan Heßbrüggen-Walter notes, the *Metaphysik Herder*, the *Metaphysik Volkmann*, the *Metaphysik von Schön*, the *Metaphysik Mrongovius* and diverse *Reflections*.[36] In almost all these texts we are often told of a difference between faculty (*Vermögen*) and power (*Kraft*), which consists in the distinction between a mere potentiality-moment and its actuality in the process of the fulfilment of an action.[37]

However, in the context of Kant's published works a definite answer is not easy to be found.[38] The suggested two-level-solution, which considers just the *actus/potentia* dichotomy, does not take into account all the nuances of Kant's proposal. It seems only possible to say that *Kraft* is used by Kant at least to some extent as the term referring to the empirical psychological description of the mind (*Gemüt*) as it is experienced, while *Vermögen* is the term which refers to the pure philosophical level.[39]

---

34 *Gedanken von der wahren Schätzung der lebendigen Kräfte und Beurtheilung der Beweise, deren sich Herr von Leibniz und andere Mechaniker in dieser Streitsache bedient haben, nebst einigen vorhergehenden Betrachtungen, welche die Kraft der Körper überhaupt betreffen*, AA 01: 1– 118. On this writing, cf. for instance AUGUSTO GUERRA, "Metafisica e vita morale nel primo scritto kantiano (1746–1747)", *De homine* 31/32 (1969), pp. 91–118.
35 Cf. A. GUERRA, "Metafisica e vita morale", cit., pp. 109–110.
36 See S. HESSBRÜGGEN-WALTER, *Die Seele und ihre Vermögen*, cit., pp. 136–142 (the section dedicated to "Kraft und Vermögen in den vorkritischen Schriften und Metaphysik-Vorlesungen").
37 Such a thesis seems to be supported by BÉATRICE LONGUENESSE, *Kant et le pouvoir de juger: Sensibilité et discursivité dans l'Analytique de la* Critique de la raison pure, Paris, Presses Universitaire de France 1993, English translation by Charles T. Wolfe, *Kant and the Capacity to Judge: Sensibility and Discursivity in the Transcendental Analytic of the* Critique of Pure Reason, Princeton, Princeton University Press 1998, pp. 7–8.
38 G. GIGLIOTTI, "'Vermögen' e 'Kraft'", cit., p. 265. In assessing her thesis, the author points back to the difference between Kant and Reinhold, who, in his work concerning the representative faculty, neatly distinguishes the two concepts.
39 Or, as Kant says more precisely, *Vermögen* is the term that logic makes use of – see for instance a reflection from 1785–1788 or 1788–1789, i.e. Refl 5864, AA 18: 371.17–19, 372.01–02: "Die logik, welche obiective regeln des Gebrauchs des Erkentnisvermögens vortragt, und die Ethik, die dieses in ansehung des Begehrungsvermögens (das Sollen) thut, setzt zu beydem nur

In my work however, instead of deepening the analysis of these two terms, what deserves a very close look in the context of Kant's description of the human mental field is the difference between the concept of soul (*Seele*) and the concept of mind (*Gemüt*). This theme will be the object of § 1.4 below.

Before starting the analysis of the concept of *Gemüt*, some further considerations about the lively discussion on the faculties are here due. This excursus is important to more deeply appreciate the nuances of the contemporary discussion on the faculties, to which I dedicate chapter two of my study. Here I confine myself to approach a particular case attesting the debate surrounding the faculties during Kant's time, in order to understand how lively the German discussion on these topics was. As already mentioned, I will focus on the particular, exemplifying discussion originated from the question delivered by the Academy of Sciences in Berlin which asked for a more detailed examination concerning two primary faculties of the soul: the faculty of knowing and the faculty of feeling.

1.3 The 1773/1775 Berlin Academy Prize Competition: *Examen des deux facultés primitives de l'ame, celle de connoître et celle de sentir*

The question concerning two basic faculties of the soul, that of knowing and that of feeling, had been announced by the Royal Prussian Academy of Sciences (*Königlich-Preussische Academie der Wissenschaften / Académie Royale des Sciences et des Belles-Lettres*, Berlin) for 1773, and then re-announced for 1775.[40] Questions like the one here analysed have been posed in order to promote the progress of a science at a very particular point or to ascertain the grounding of scientific problems.[41]

Under the patronage of Frederick II of Prussia and in imitation of the Paris Academy of Science and the Royal Society in London, the Prussian Academy held these annual essay contests. Frederick the Great plays a central role in these contests and in the intellectual life in Germany, in that he tries to found

---

Vermögen des Gemüths voraus. Die Psychologie, die das erklart, was geschieht, nicht vorschreibt, was geschehen soll, beschaftigt sich mit Gemüthskräften".

40 Cf. *Nouveaux Mémoires de l'Academie Royale des Sciences et Belles-Lettres. Anné MDCCLXXIII*. Berlin 1775, p. 11ff.

41 Cf. HANS-HEINRICH MÜLLER, *Akademie und Wirtschaft im 18. Jahrhundert. Agrarökonomische Preisaufgaben und Preisschriften der Preußischen Akademie der Wissenschaften. Versuch, Tendenzen und Überblick*, Berlin, Akademie-Verlag 1975, p. 46ff.

a new centre of scientific life during his lifetime (even though he favours the usage of French to the disadvantage of the German language).[42]

The Academy was divided into four "classes": (1) physical/medical, (2) mathematical, (3) philosophical, and (4) philological/literary. These classes took turns submitting the question.[43] During the ages of Frederick the Great, philosophy experiences an improvement worth being mentioned also as a result of the foundation of a new specific class for this discipline inside the Academy.[44]

The questions generally drew about a dozen entries; a number of the questions had to be repeated one or more years before an adequate essay was entered. The Academy printed the prize essay along with the texts that received

---

42 Cf. Cordula Neis, *Anthropologie im Sprachdenken des 18. Jahrhunderts: Die Berliner Preisfrage nach dem Ursprung der Sprache (1771)*, Berlin/New York, de Gruyter 2003, S. 74: "Zwiespalt des zwischen aufklärerischen Grundtendenzen und absolutistischem Machtwillen oszillierenden Königs [Friedrich der Große] kommt auch in seiner Neuschöpfung, der von ihm zu neuem Leben erweckten Berliner *Académie Royale des Sciences et Belles-Lettres* zum Tragen. Inspiriert durch das Vorbild der Pariser Akademie und der Londoner *Royal Society* möchte auch Friedrich II. 1744 durch die Restauration der ehemaligen Preußischen Sozietät in seinem Herrschaftsgebiet ein neues Zentrum geistiger Tätigkeit errichten. Unglücklicherweise paart sich jedoch der Wunsch, durch wissenschaftliche Errungenschaften im intellektuellen Kräftemessen der europäischen Nationen und Kleinstaaten zu Ruhm gelangen, mit einer tiefen Abneigung gegenüber dem deutschen Geistesleben, die in Friedrichs *De la littérature allemande* unverhohlen zum Ausdruck kommt. Das Deutsche gilt Friedrich als eine verwirrte und nur schwer zu verarbeiten Sprache, die wenig Wohllaut habe und arm an Metaphern sei, welche jedoch für die Anmut ausgebildeter Sprachen unverzichtbar wären. Seine Abneigung gegenüber der deutschen Sprache spiegelt sich auch in der stark französisch geprägten Zusammensetzung seiner Akademie wider, zu deren Präsidenten er Maupertuis ernennt, den er aufgrund von dessen Lungenleiden später am liebsten durch d'Alembert ersetzen wollte".

43 A list of the prize questions and winners (up to the year 1788) can be found in Adolf Harnack, *Geschichte der Königlich Preußischen Akademie der Wissenschaften zu Berlin*. 2 volumes, Berlin 1900 – volume 2, pp. 305 – 9. Harnack lists 45 questions. The Academy also printed the prize essay, along with any receiving an *Accessit*.

44 Cf. C. Neis, *Anthropologie im Sprachdenken des 18. Jahrhunderts*, cit., pp. 76 – 77: "In der Tat erlebte die Philosophie unter der Herrschaft Friedrichs II. einen bemerkenswerten Aufschwung, der sich auch in ihrer, für Europa damals einmaligen institutionellen Verankerung im Rahmen der friderizianischen Akademiegründung niederschlug. Neben den drei verschiedenen Klassen der Mathematik, der Naturwissenschaften und der Philologie, welche die *belles-lettres* und Geschichte vereinte, hatte der König nämlich eigens eine Klasse für spekulative Philosophie einrichten lassen und damit der Berliner Akademie ein Novum geschaffen, das an keiner anderen europäischen Akademie dieser Zeit existierte [...] Während im Sinne von Leibniz die Philosophie noch von allen vier verschiedenen Klassen zu betreiben war, wünschte Friedrich ihre Konzentration in der *classe de philosophie spéculative*, die sich ihrerseits in die Disziplinen der Metaphysik, Moral, des *Jus naturale* sowie die *Historie und Critic der Philosophie* untergliederte".

an *Accessit*, that is the texts also worth being mentioned (normally two or three further texts).[45]

The Academy questions play a central role in Europe's cultural life at least until 1786/1787, i.e. until the death of Friedrich II. After his death their importance diminishes considerably.[46] In fact, the questions were considered "the direct and proper way to give an incentive to the progress in the sciences and to keep it in the right direction".[47] Not the answers to the questions, but the questions as such were awaited for with trepidation and the most influential scientists (Euler, Lagrange, d'Alembert, Condorcet, Kant, Rousseau and Herder, among the others) actively participated to the competition from 1744, the first year in which the Academy in Berlin follows the example of the Parisian Academy and publicly announces a contest.[48] Among the 45 themes to which the questions were dedicated in the years of the calls, 20 questions were posed in the physical-medical-mathematical area and 25 in the philosophical and philological-literary area.[49] Philosophy can be considered as the fulcrum of academic life during the Eighteenth Century as representing the compendium of a search

---

45 Cf. C. NEIS, *Anthropologie im Sprachdenken des 18. Jahrhunderts*, cit., p. 83: "Unter Friedrich II. stellte die Akademie insgesamt 45 Preisfragen, von denen einige aber unbeantwortet blieben. Zwischen 1745 und 1900 schrieb die Berliner Akademie 178 Preisfragen aus, zu denen etwa 700 Preisschriften (d.h. ungedruckte Manuskripte) eingegangen sind, ungerechnet die preisgekrönten gedruckten Schriften. Es war nämlich *usus*, nur die gekrönte Preisschrift und noch zwei oder drei weitere Schriften, die das sogenannte *Accessit* erhalten hatten, zu drucken. Bei der offiziellen Preisverleihung wurden die mit dem *Accessit* versehenen Schriften lobend erwähnt und meist mit einer silbernen Medaille ausgezeichnet. Wie sehr die Preisaufgaben das Leben der Akademie im 18. Jahrhundert bestimmten, läßt sich eindrucksvoll anhand der Datenlage dokumentieren. Während die Berliner Akademie zwischen 1745 und 1812 insgesamt 608 Manuskripte erhielt, vermochte sie nach 1812 nur noch 106 Preisbewerbungsschriften anzuregen". Cf. also Hans-Heinrich Müller, *Akademie und Wirtschaft im 18. Jahrhundert. Agrarökonomische Preisaufgaben und Preisschriften der Preußischen Akademie der Wissenschaften. Versuch, Tendenzen und Überblick*, Berlin, Akademie-Verlag 1975, pp. 47–48.

46 Cf. ADOLF HARNACK, *Geschichte der Königlich Preußischen Akademie der Wissenschaften zu Berlin. Band 1,1: Von der Gründung bis zum Tode Friedrich's des Großen*. Berlin, Reichsdruckerei 1900. Cf. in particular Book 2 (*Zweites Buch: Geschichte der Académie Royale des Sciences et Belles-Lettres Friedrich's des Großen 1740–1786*), Chapter 3 (*Drittes Capitel: Die Arbeiten und die wissenschaftliche Bedeutung der Akademie*), pp. 394–421.

47 A. HARNACK, *Geschichte der Königlich Preußischen Akademie der Wissenschaften zu Berlin. Band 1,1*, cit., p. 396.

48 Cf. A. HARNACK, *Geschichte der Königlich Preußischen Akademie der Wissenschaften zu Berlin. Band 1,1*, cit., pp. 396–397.

49 Cf. A. HARNACK, *Geschichte der Königlich Preußischen Akademie der Wissenschaften zu Berlin. Band 1,1*, cit., p. 399.

for the highest principles, in particular with the challenge between English Philosophy and the Leibniz-Wolffian School.[50]

In the light of the capital importance played by the questions of the Academy in Berlin, our attention on the question concerning the faculties gains new relevance. Before the question announced in 1773, another contest is worth mentioning, namely the question posed by the Academy in 1767: "*Si l'on peut détruire les penchans qui viennent de la Nature, ou en faire naître qu'elle n'ait pas produits? Et quels sont les moyens de fortifier les penchans lorqu'ils sont bons, ou de les affoiblir lorsqu'ils sont mauvais, supposé qu'ils soient invincibles?*".[51] This time, the object of the elucidations regards the possibility of destroying natural inclinations (*Neigungen*), and whether it is possible to strengthen the good ones and weaken the bad ones. Leonhard Cochius wins the Academy prize with his study on the inclinations in 1768.[52] In the opinion of the Academy, as well as according to Cochius, the *Neigungen* (*penchants*, inclinations) are presented as capable of reducing the progress of reason.[53] However, what is most noteworthy is the fact that already in these studies dedicated to the inclinations, the role of those states of mind is thought to be properly approached only through the analysis of the more general context of the study of the faculties.

However, as already mentioned, it is in 1773 that the Academy deals with this topic more precisely, given the quest for clarification concerning the relationship between the two basic faculties is asked for the first time and, afterwards, for a second time in 1775. This last time, clearer descriptions of the intended research

---

50 Cf. A. HARNACK, *Geschichte der Königlich Preußischen Akademie der Wissenschaften zu Berlin. Band 1,1*, cit., p. 401.

51 Cf. A. HARNACK, *Geschichte der Königlich Preußischen Akademie der Wissenschaften zu Berlin. Band 2: Urkunden und Actenstücke zur Geschichte der Königlich Preußischen Akademie der Wissenschaften*. Berlin, Reichsdruckerei 1900, p. 307.

52 Cf. the entry Leonhard Cochius the in the first volume of HEINER F. KLEMME – MANFRED KUEHN (eds.), *Dictionary of Eighteenth-Century German Philosophers*, Bristol, Thoemmes Continuum 2010, pp. 211–212: "Cochius became widely known because he won the prize essay competition of the Royal Academy of Sciences in Berlin in 1768. Apart from this treatise about inclinations Cochius only published three essays for the Berlin Academy, of which he had become a member in 1770. His short inaugural address in 1772 deals with Leibnizian philosophy. The prize essay question raised by the Royal Academy of Sciences in Berlin in 1766 was the following: Is it possible to eliminate the natural inclinations or to evoke any inclinations, which are not produced by nature? Furthermore: are there means that can strengthen good inclinations and weaken bad ones?".

53 Also philosophers like Gellert, Garve, Meiners, Mendelssohn, and the same Kant, as we will see in chapters four and five below, dedicate some studies on the topic of the *Neigungen*. Cf. also A. HARNACK, *Geschichte der Königlich Preußischen Akademie der Wissenschaften zu Berlin. Band 1,1*, cit., pp. 411–412.

directions are provided, since no satisfactory answer arrived at the Academy in 1774. Eventually, in 1776 the Academy finds some answers to the question that deserve to be prized.

The question deals more precisely with the analysis of the two original faculties of the human soul, that is the cognitive faculty and the sensitive faculty (*Examen des deux facultés primitives de l'ame, celle de connoître et celle de sentir*).[54] In its completeness, the question is as follows:

"The soul possesses two original abilities (the foundation of all its properties and efficacies): the ability to cognize and the ability of sense. If it exercises the first, it is occupied with an object which it considers as a thing outside itself in which it has curiosity; in this case its entire efficacy seems to be only to see well. If it exercises the other, it is occupied with itself and its condition, and feels well or ill. Its efficacy in this case seems to be solely to want to change the condition if it feels discomfort, or to enjoy the condition if it feels well. Assuming this, we wish:

1. An exact development of the original determinations of both abilities and of the universal laws which they follow.
2. A thorough investigation of the reciprocal dependence of both faculties on each other and of the manner of their influence on each other.
3. Basic principles which make clear how the genius and the character of a human being depends on the degree, strength, and liveliness [of the one or the other of these abilities], and on the steps of progress that one or the other of these abilities has achieved, and on the proportion that holds between them both".[55]

---

54 Cf. A. HARNACK, *Geschichte der Königlich Preußischen Akademie der Wissenschaften zu Berlin. Band 2: Urkunden und Actenstücke zur Geschichte der Königlich Preußischen Akademie der Wissenschaften*. Berlin, Reichsdruckerei 1900, p. 308.

55 JOHANN GOTTFRIED VON HERDER, *Philosophical Writings*, translated and edited by MICHAEL N. FORSTER, Cambridge/New York, Cambridge University Press 2002, pp. 185–186. Cf. also, in particular: *On Cognition and Sensation, the Two Main Forces of the Human Soul* (1775) [preface], pp. 178–186; *On the Cognition and Sensation of the Human Soul* (1778), pp. 187–245. This text is Herder's translation into German of the Berlin Academy's of prize essay task and elucidatory remarks about this task, which were originally in French. The English translation is done from Herder's German, which quotes (from JOHANN GOTTFRIED HERDER, *Vom Erkennen und Empfinden, den zwo Hauptkräften der Menschlichen Seele*, in JOHANN GOTTFRIED HERDER, *Sämtliche Werke*, edited by BERNHARD SUPHAN, Volume 1–33, Berlin 1877–1913 (reprint: Hildesheim, Olms 1968), here volume 8, Berlin 1892, pp. 263–333, here p. 268): "Die Seele besitzt zwo ursprüngliche Fähigkeiten (Grundlage aller ihrer Eigenschaften und Würkungen): die Fähigkeit zu erkennen und zu empfinden. Übet sie die erste: so ist sie mit einem Gegenstande beschäftigt, den sie als Sache außer sich betrachtet, zu dem sie Neugierde hat: ihre ganze Würksamkeit alsdenn scheint nur, wohl zu *sehen*. Übet sie die andere: so ist sie mit sich selbst und ihrem

After the Academy jury finds none of the submitted works worthy of a prize in 1774, the prize is announced one more time in 1775 supported with a more specific clarification of the assignment and the expectations of the jury. The clarifying text of the newly announced question is:

1. In regard to the first question, the Academy wishes to see illuminated the conditions under which a representation only affects the faculty of sensation, and on the other hand to what order those representations belong which only rouse curiosity and occupy the faculty of cognition. In both cases it will be perceived that these conditions depend partly on the representation or on the object itself, partly on the condition of the soul at the time when the representation affects it. 2. Concerning the second question, the Academy wishes a luminous, satisfying explanation of the psychological observation that the heart so often apes the mind, and of the further phenomenon that certain speculative heads sense only weakly. 3. In the case of the third question it is a matter of the requisite

---

Zustande beschäftigt und fühlt sich wohl oder übel. Ihre Würksamkeit dermalen scheint einzig, den Zustand ändern zu wollen, wenn sie sich mißbehaglich, oder zu genießen, wenn sie sich wohl fühlt.

Dies vorausgesetzt wünscht man:

1. Eine genaue Entwicklung der ursprünglichen Bestimmungen beider Fähigkeiten und der allgemeinen Gesetze, denen sie folgen.

2. Eine gründliche Untersuchung der wechselseitigen Abhängigkeit beider Vermögen von einander und der Art ihres Einflusses auf einander.

3. Grundsätze, die in Augenschein bringen, wie das Genie und der Charakter Eines Menschen vom Grad, Stärke und Lebhaftigkeit und von den Fortschritten abhange, die die Eine und andre dieser Fähigkeiten gewonnen, und von dem Verhältnis, das sich zwischen neiden findet".

For the original French text, see *Nouveaux Mémoires de l'Academie Royale des Sciences et Belles-Lettres. Anné MDCCLXXIII.* Berlin 1775, p. 9:"L'ame possède deux facultés primitives qui forment la base de toutes ses opérations; la faculté de connoître, & la faculté de sentir. En exerçant la première, l'ame est occupée d'un objet qu'elle regarde comme une chose hors d'elle & pour lequel elle a de la curiosité: son activité paroit alors se tendre qu'à bien voir. En exerçant l'autre, elle s'occupe d'elle-même & de son état, étant affectée *en bien* ou *en mal*. Alors son activité semble uniquement déterminée à changer d'état, lorsqu'elle se trouve désagréablement affectée, ou à jouir, lorsqu'elle est agréablement affectée. Cela supposé, on demande

1. Un développement exact des déterminations originaires de ces deux facultés et les loìx générales qu'elles suivent.

2. Un examen approfondi de la dépendance réciproque de ces facultés & de la manière dont l'une influe sur l'autre.

3. Des principes qui fervent à faire voir comment le génie & le caractère d'un homme dépendent du degré de force et de vivacité et des progrès de l'une et de l'autre de ces facultés, et la proportion qui se trouve entr'elles".

conditions for a human being having a greater aptitude for exercising the forces of cognition than the faculty of sensation or vice versa.[56]

With no doubt the authorship of this question has to be attributed to Johann Georg Sulzer, since the premises, on which the answer to the question is requested to be based, are the same ones as Sulzer's writings, namely the *Anmerkungen über den verschiedenen Zustand, worinn sich die Seele bey Ausübung ihrer Hauptvermögen, nämlich des Vermögens, sich etwas vorzustellen und des Vermögens zu empfinden, befindet,* a work that has been first published in 1763 and, afterwards, in 1773 in his *Vermischte philosophische Schriften.*[57] In this writing, Sulzer clearly

---

56 JOHANN GOTTFRIED VON HERDER, *Philosophical Writings*, cit., pp. 185–186. And here again Herder's German text (from JOHANN GOTTFRIED HERDER, *Vom Erkennen und Empfinden, den zwo Hauptkräften der Menschlichen Seele*, cit., p. 269): "In Betracht der Ersten Frage wünschet die Akademie die Bedingungen ins Licht gesetzt zu sehen, unter denen eine Vorstellung nur das vermögen zu empfinden trift; und welcher Ordnung gegentheils die Vorstellungen sind, die nur die Neugierde regen und das Vermögen zu erkennen, beschäftigen. In Einem und andern Fall wird man wahrnehmen, daß diese Bedingungen theils von der Vorstellung oder vom Gegenstande selbst, theils vom Zustande der Seele abhangen, in der Zeit, da die Vorstellung sie trift. In Absicht der zweiten Frage, wünscht sich die Akademie eine helle, gnugthuende Erklärung der Psychologischen Wahrnehmung, daß den geist so oft das Herz äffe, und der andern Erscheinung, daß gewiße späkulatice Köpfe nur schwach empfinden. Bei der dritten Frage kommts auf die erforderlichen Bedingungen an, daß ein Mensch mehr Anlage habe, die Erkenntnißkräfte zu üben, als das Vermögen zu empfinden, oder gegenseitig"; and the original French text, (from *Nouveaux Mémoires de l'Academie Royale des Sciences et Belles-Lettres. Anné MDCCLXXIII*, Berlin 1775, p. 20) : "1. Par rapport à la premiere question : quelles sont les conditions sous lesquelles une perception n'affecte que la faculté de sentir, & de quel ordre, au contraire, sont les perceptions qui n'intéressent que la curiosité, & n'occupent que la faculté de connoître ? Dans l'un & dans l'autre cas, on s'appercevra que ces conditions dépendent en partie de la perception ou de l'objet même, & en partie de l'état de l'ame au moment où elle éprouva la perception. 2. Relativement à la seconde question, l'Académie demande une explication claire & satisfaisante du phénomene psychologique qu'on a coutume d'indiquer en disant que *l'esprit est la dupe du cœur*; & d'un autre phénomene qu'on observe dans certains spéculatifs; c'est qu'*ils ne sentent que foiblement*. 3. Par rapport à la troisieme question, on demande les conditions requises pour qu'un homme soit plus disposé à exercer la faculté de connoître que celle de sentir, & celles d'où résulte le cas contraire".

57 Cf. JOHANN GEORG SULZER, *Vermischte Philosophische Schriften: Aus den Jahrbüchern der Akademie der Wissenschaft in Berlin gesammelt*, 2 vols (vol. 1, Leipzig, 1773; vol. 2, Leipzig, 1781; both volumes reprinted in one facsimile, Hildesheim, 1974). For a bio-bibliographical notice, see the entry "Sulzer, Johann Georg (1720–1779)", in HEINER F. KLEMME – MANFRED KUEHN (eds.), *Dictionary of Eighteenth-Century German Philosophers*, Bristol, Thoemmes Continuum 2010, volume 3, pp. 238–244 (p. 238: Sulzer "is best remembered as the author of the *General Theory of the Fine Arts* (*Allgemeine Theorie der schönen Künste*), an enormous encyclopedia of aesthetics and the arts that was first published in two volumes in 1771–4 and which, especially in the

distinguishes between the cognitive faculty (*Erkennen*) and the sensitive faculty (*Empfinden*), by considering them the only two basic faculties of the human soul.[58] According to Sulzer, the sensitive faculty plays no role in man's theoretical insight, which entirely falls under the competence of the cognitive faculty. The cognitive faculty, instead, is excluded from the practical domain, which itself pertains only to the sensitive faculty.[59]

This time, in 1776, three writings gain the *Accessit*. Johann August Eberhard wins the prize with his text: *Allgemeine Theorie des Denkens und Empfindens.*[60]

---

expanded editions by Friedrich von Blankenburg in 1786–7 and 1792–4, remains the most valuable source for the aesthetics of the German Enlightenment and its bibliography. But Sulzer, a long-time member of the Prussian Academy of Sciences, was a typical Enlightenment polymath who made many contributions to areas of philosophy other than aesthetics as well as to psychology and other branches of the natural sciences").

58 "Bey der Ausübung dieser zwei Vermögen scheint die Seele so verschieden von ihr selbst zu sein, daß man in Versuchung geräth, die Meinung der alten Philosophen anzunehmen, daß es zwo Seelen in dem Menschen gebe, eine vernünftige und eine empfindliche", JOHANN GEORG SULZER, *Vermischte Philosophische Schriften: Aus den Jahrbüchern der Akademie der Wissenschaft in Berlin gesammelt*, vol. 1, Leipzig, 1773, p. 227.

59 Cf. PETER GROVE, "Johann August Eberhards Theorie des Gefühls", in HANS-JOACHIM KERTSCHER – ERNST STÖCKMANN (edited by), *Ein Antipode Kants? Johann August Eberhard im Spannungsfeld von spätaufklärerischer Philosophie und Theologie*, Berlin/Boston, de Gruyter 2012, pp. 119–131, here p. 122, and JÜRGEN BRUMMACK – MARTIN BOLLACHER, "Kommentar", in JOHANN GOTTFRIED HERDER, *Werke in zehn Bände*, Volume 4: *Schriften zu Philosophie, Literatur, Kunst und Altertum 1774–1787*, Frankfurt am Main, Deutscher Klassiker Verlag 1994, pp. 795–1407, here pp. 1077–1078.

60 JOHANN AUGUST EBERHARD, *Allgemeine Theorie des Denkens und Empfindens*, Berlin, Voß 1776 (reprint: Hildesheim, Zürich/New York, Olms, 1984). For a bio-bibliographical notice, see the entry "Eberhard, Johann August (1739–1809)", in HEINER F. KLEMME – MANFRED KUEHN (eds.), *Dictionary of Eighteenth-Century German Philosophers*, Bristol, Thoemmes Continuum 2010, volume 1, pp. 262–267 (passim): Johann August Eberhard (1739–1809) "can be deemed one of the most eminent representatives of German popular philosophy in the late eighteenth century. His work and his influence were broad and covered various academic disciplines. His main writings were edited several times during his life, and they are still reprinted today. In opposition to abstract philosophical speculations, his writings are representative of a more empirical approach. He stimulated the contemporary debates in epistemology and metaphysics as well as in anthropology, the theory of emotions, moral philosophy, theology, cultural theory, and the analysis of language. He engaged in the public debates on Enligthenment philosophy, among other things, as an author of the key periodical of German late Enlightenment, the Berlinische Monatsschrift, edited by Johann Erich Biester. [...] In his 1776 *Allgemeine Theorie des Denkens und Empfindens*, he turned, influenced by Mendelssohn, to philosophical-anthropological questions that emerged from Leibnizian positions. For his efforts, Eberhard was awarded the prize of the Berlin Academy and was inducted into their society in 1786. [...] Eberhard also published two periodicals, *Philosophisches Magazin* and *Philosophische Archiv*,

The other two writings are from Johann Gottfried Herder (*Vom Erkennen und Empfinden der menschlichen Seele*)[61] and Joachim Heinrich Campe (*Die Empfindungs- und Erkenntnißkraft der menschlichen Seele: die erstere nach ihren Gesetzen, beyde nach ihren ursprünglichen Bestimmungen, nach ihrem gegenseitigen Einflusse aufeinander und nach ihren Beziehungen auf Character und Genie betrachtet*).[62]

In all these writings, the distinction between the two grounding faculties of the soul has been elucidated starting from psychological grounding theses. However, Campe's text and even more clearly the one by Herder try to make the attempt of using merely physiological-psychological schemes to answer the question. Instead, Eberhard does not criticize the Leibniz-Wolffian School and tries to evaluate the problem merely in a way close to the tradition, even though with some important innovative points.[63] In this way, thanks to his closeness to Sulzer's ideas and the jury's philosophical taste, Eberhard wins the Academy prize. [64]

---

which were significant for the philosophical debates of the time. Specifically, they were important for engaging with Kant's philosophy. [...] Basically, Eberhard criticized Kant for claiming that things in themselves cannot be known. He also struggled with the reproach that Leibniz-Wolffian philosophy is a form of 'general dogmatism', and argued against the assumption that it extends its dominion on all objects, that it excludes all doubt, and that it presumes to know everything with certainty. At its core, Eberhard's criticism is that all that is true in Kant's philosophy can be found in Leibniz already. Eberhard was the Leibniz-Wolffian spokesman who defended the Leibniz-Wolffian school against the Kantian claim that all prior philosophical systems were mistaken".

61 JOHANN GOTTFRIED HERDER, *Vom Erkennen und Empfinden, den zwo Hauptkräften der Menschlichen Seele*, in JOHANN GOTTFRIED HERDER, *Sämtliche Werke*, edited by BERNHARD SUPHAN, Volume 1–33, Berlin 1877–1913 (reprint: Hildesheim, Olms 1968), here volume 8, Berlin 1892, pp. 263–333.

62 JOACHIM HEINRICH CAMPE, *Die Empfindungs- und Erkenntnißkraft der menschlichen Seele: die erstere nach ihren Gesetzen, beyde nach ihren ursprünglichen Bestimmungen, nach ihrem gegenseitigen Einflusse aufeinander und nach ihren Beziehungen auf Character und Genie betrachtet*, Leipzig, Weygandsche Handlung 1776. For a bio-bibliographical notice, see the entry "Campe, Joachim Heinrich (1746–1818)", in HEINER F. KLEMME – MANFRED KUEHN (eds.), *Dictionary of Eighteenth-Century German Philosophers*, Bristol, Thoemmes Continuum 2010, volume 1, pp. 182–186 (passim): "During his time as a student, Campe received a thorough introduction to the history of philosophy. Over the course of his life, he continually engaged with the work of Rousseau, Hobbes, Helvetius, Locke, Hume, Shaftsbury, Leibniz, Spinoza and Mendelssohn".

63 For Eberhard's new points in the argumentation, cf. PETER GROVE, "Johann August Eberhards Theorie des Gefühls", cit., pp. 124–125, who reminds us of the Endlich ist zu betonen, dass diese Argumentation Eberhards der rationalen Psychologie angehört. "Studium des Menschen", "Beobachtung des Menschen", "Selbstbeobachtung" sind zwar bei Eberhard wie in der sonstigen Spätaufklärung häufig auftretende Figuren, und sein Werk ist durchaus im Zusammenhang der anthropologisch orientierten Reflexionskultur der Zeit zu sehen. Dies ist jedoch nur die

The importance of the Academy question is not only exemplary for its central importance in the philosophical discussion concerning the faculties in the 1770s. It assumes more relevance for our interests in the present study if we consider that Kant was also informed about the question and follows the competition with interest. Not only is the Academy question mentioned in Kant's correspondence,[65] moreover it is Kant himself that notes the question in his copy of Baumgarten's *Metaphysica*, so that we can find the entire text of the Academy assignment in the Reflection 184a (in German!).[66]

---

eine Seite seiner philosophischen Methode, wie er sie in der Preisschrift darstellt: Die Methode besteht aus "Theorie" oder "Wissenschaft" auf der einen Seite und "Beobachtung" auf der anderen (JOHANN AUGUST EBERHARD, *Allgemeine Theorie des Denkens und Empfindens. Eine Abhandlung, welche den von den Königl. Akademie der Wissenschaften in Berlin auf das Jahr 1776 ausgesetzten Preis erhalten hat.* Berlin, 1776, S. 4f., 210). Dem entspricht Eberhards tatsächliches Verfahren in dieser Schrift, das damit grundsätzlich mit Wolff übereinstimmt. Überdies ist die genannte Reihenfolge wichtig: Eberhard geht von einer rationalen Psychologie aus und ergänzt im Laufe der Untersuchung empirisch-psychologischen Beobachtungen, so dass diese zur Nachprüfung jener dienen".

64 For Eberhard's closeness to the tradition, cf. DENIS THOUARD, *Schleiermacher: Communauté, Individualité, Communication*, Paris, Vrin 2007, pp. 32–33 (passim): "Eberhard naturalise la métaphysique wolffienne, l'imprègne de psychologie empirique, tout en conservant son cadre. [...] La psychologie est au centre de son enseignement. Eberhard retraduit de grandes parties de la métaphysique wolffienne, qu'il lit d'après les manuels d'Alexander Baumgarten et Georg Friedrich Meier [Eberhard enseigne la logique d'après Meier, la métaphysique d'après Baumgarten et le droit d'après Achenwall, alors qu'il expose l'éthique d'après sa propre *Sittenlehre der Vernunft* (1786), l'esthétique et l'histoire de la philosophie également d'après ses propres ouvrages *Theorie der schönen Wissenschaften* et *Allgemeine Geschichte der Philosophie*], c'est-à-dire les mêmes que ceux qu'employait Kant, dans le langage de la psychologie".

65 Cf. CHRISTIAN JACOB KRAUS, Brief an Kant vom 11. August 1778 (Letter No. 139, AA 10: 239–240, here in particular AA 10: 240. 15–20: "Mein Plan ist also der. Ich bleibe bis künftiges Frühjahr hier in Konigberg; aber nur bis Michael bey Sr Excellz dem Grf Kayserling: arbeite mitlerweile meine Preisschrift für die Academie von Berlin aus und reise im Anfange des Mayes künftigen Iahres mit 100 Ducaten die mir mein Bruder anbietet, nach England, ohne auf andere Empfehlungen als die der Fräumäurerloge zu achten" and the annotations (Anmerkungen) in the Academy Edition concerning this letter (AA 13: 91–92): Diese Preisschrift ist vielleicht dieselbe, von der Hamann bereits am 14. Okt. 1776 an Herder berichtet, "daß sein junger Freund an dem preise über die Urkräfte der Seele Antheil nehmen wollte und glaubte die ganze Arbeit schon im Kopfe fertig zu haben" (Hamanns Schriften Bd. V, S. 191; vgl. ebenda S. 178). Das Thema lautete: *Examen des deux facultés primitives de l'ame, celle de connoître et celle de sentir*. Es wurde 1773 gestellt und 1775 wiederholt. Den Preis erhielt 1776 Eberhard, Pastor in Charlottenburg [...]. Ob Kraus sich beworben hat, läßt sich nach den noch handschriftlich vorhandenen Bewerbungsschriften nicht entscheiden".

66 Here the text of Refl. 158a, AA 15: 57.04–19: "Qvaeritur: Die Seele besitzt zwey ursprüngliche fähigkeiten, die den Grund aller ihrer Eigenschaften und Wirkungen ausmachen: die Fähigkeit

My task in this section was only that of underlining the liveliness of the discussion on the faculties during the second half of the Eighteenth Century in Germany, through a very exemplary event, namely the Academy contest of 1773/1775. The mention of these texts, however, also elucidates that the sensitive faculty come to play a central role in the philosophical analyses of many authors who now try to consider anew the similarities and differences among the grounding abilities of the soul. In my further discussion I will not go deeper into the history nor into possible sources of Kant's thought; I instead limit myself to mentioning that the development of the philosophical considerations concerning the triad of faculties (*Erkennen – Fühlen – Begehren*), as we find it in Kant's text and as I will analyse it in chapter 4 below, is due to a lively discussion in the 1770s, which the Academy question clearly exemplifies.[67]

---

zu erkennen und die zu empfinden. Bey Uebung der ersten ist sie mit etwas außer sich beschaftigt, und wornach sie neugierig ist. Ihre Thatigkeit geht nur darauf, wohl zu sehen. Bey der Zweyten beschaftigt sie sich mit sich selbst und ist gut oder böse gerührt. Ihre Thatigkeit Geht darauf, ihren Zustand allein zu verändern beym unangenehmen, und zu genießen beym angenehmen. Es wird verlangt. 1. Entwikelung der Ursprünglichen bestimmungen dieser zwey Fähigkeiten und ihrer Gesetze. 2. den Wechselseitigen Einflus in einander. 3. Grundsatze, wie das genie und Charakter eines menschen von dem Grade, der Stärke, der Lebhaftigkeit und dem fortgang der einen und der andern dieser Fähigkeiten und der Proportion, die unter ihnen ist, abhängt. (wie die Gefühle Erkentnisse, wie Erkenntnisse Gefühle und dadurch triebfedern werden, wie lebhaftigkeit mit talent vereinigt ist.)". On this point, cf. JÜRGEN BRUMMACK – MARTIN BOLLACHER, "Kommentar", in JOHANN GOTTFRIED HERDER, *Werke in zehn Bände*, Volume 4: *Schriften zu Philosophie, Literatur, Kunst und Altertum Altertum 1774–1787*, Frankfurt am Main, Deutscher Klassiker Verlag 1994, pp. 795–1407, here pp. 1080: "Übrigens hat die Preisaufgabe das Interesse bedeutender Zeitgenossen geweckt. Kant hat sie sich in aller Ausführlichkeit notiert (in sein Handexemplar von Baumgartens *Metaphysica*: AA 15.1, S. 57; vom Herausgeber nicht erkannt".

67 On the evolution of the philosophical role played by the sensitive faculty cf. ERNST STÖCKMANN, "Phänomenologie der Empfindungen – Kultivierung des Gefühlsvermögens. Aspekte der anthropologischen Empfindungstheorie der deutschen Spätaufklärung am Beispiel von Platner und Irwing", in: WALTER SCHMITZ – CARSTEN ZELLE (eds.), *Innovation und Transfer – Naturwissenschaften, Anthropologie und Literatur im 18. Jahrhundert*, Dresden, Thelem 2004, pp. 75–96: Die Wertschätzung der Empfindungen als einer Gemütsqualität sui generis, die in Differenz zu den anderen Gemütsvermögen Erkennen (Vorstellungskraft) und Begehren (Willensvermögen bzw. Affektivität) definiert wird, findet ihren Ausdruck in der Expansion der anthropologischen Gefühlstheorie sowie in der Fixierung des triadischen Schemas der Gemütsvermögen. [...] Zu der ungeklärten Frage nach den "eigentlichen" Pionieren für die Etablierung des dritten Gemütsvermögen vgl. CHRISTIAN HAUSER, *Selbstbewußtsein und personale Identität. Positionen und Aporien ihrer vorkritischen Geschichte*, Stuttgart/Bad Cannstatt, Frommann-Holzboog 1994, S. 141, Anm. 43). [...] Die Theorie der Empfindungen rangiert im letzten Drittel des 18. Jahrhunderts gleichwertig neben der Theorie des Erkenntnis- und Begehrungsvermögens und erhält schließlich wissenschaftsgeschichtlich Sukkurs, so daß Johann Heinrich

In the context of this discussion of the faculties and their partition many other studies should be mentioned, first of all the text by Johann Nicolas Tetens, *Philosophische Versuche über die menschliche Natur und ihre Entwickelung* (Leipzig 1777), which can be considered the "hour of birth of the three-faculties-psychology" in Germany.[68]

However, my aim here was just that of dealing with an exemplary chapter of the philosophical discussion around the faculties by taking into consideration the academy question of 1773/1775 and focusing on the fact that the very idea of delivering this question, the way of attempting to answer it, and the texts written during the second half of the Eighteenth century in Germany show a very variegated debate on the faculties and, in addition, a new trend in the way of considering the sensitive faculty. Furthermore, it is noteworthy is that, what have always been dealt with as mere psychological themes, is now being approached in a new way and the partition of the faculties, as well as the relation between the feeling of the senses and the knowledge of the understanding, has also be interpreted as testifying a new "anthropological turn" in the German discussion on the soul and its faculties.[69] I will deal with the idea of anthropology and

---

Abicht 1801 die "Gefühle" bzw. "Gefühlkraft" als eine "ganz eigene Gattung von Inlagen" bezeichnet (JOHANN HEINRICH ABICHT, *Psychologische Anthropologie*, 1. Abt., Erlangen, Johann Jakob Palm 1801, S. 62). Parallel erfolgt der Ausbau der Dreivermögenslehre im Rahmen des Versuchs einer Gesamtinventarisierung der psychophysischen Ausstattungsmerkmale des Menschen durch Erfahrungsseelenlehre und wissenschaftliche Anthropologie, und zwar unter Anschluß an das von Kant in der *Kritik der Urteilskraft* aufgestellte Gemütskonzeption. [...] Die Geltung der Dreivermögenslehre ist vor Kants Strukturmodell innerhalb der psychophysischen Anthropologie nicht durchgängig zu beobachten. Ihre konsequente Applikation findet sich neben Platner (1790) erstmalig bei dem Kant-Schüler Karl Christian Erhard Schmid (*Empirische Psychologie*, Jena Cröker 1791)". But cf. also BERND OBERDORFER, "Sinnlichkeit und Moral. Zur Bedeutung der Erfahrungstheorie für die 'intellektuelle und moralische Bildung des Menschen' in Eberhards *Allgemeiner Theorie des Denkens und Empfindens*", in HANS-JOACHIM KERTSCHER – ERNST STÖCKMANN (edited by), *Ein Antipode Kants? Johann August Eberhard im Spannungsfeld von spätaufklärerischer Philosophie und Theologie*, Berlin/Boston, de Gruyter 2012, pp. 109–118.
68 For this definition (Geburtsstunde der Dreivermögenspsychologie) and the analysis of Tetens' idea of the tripartite division of the faculties, cf. ERNST STÖCKMANN, *Anthropologische Ästhetik. Philosophie, Psychologie und ästhetische Theorie der Emotionen im Diskurs der Aufklärung*. Tübingen, Niemeyer 2009, in particular pp. 177–199. Two further useful sources are FERNANDO VIDAL, "La psychologie empirique et son historicisation pendant l'Aufklärung", in *Revue d'Histoire des Sciences Humaines*, 2000/2, pp. 29–55 and FERNANDO VIDAL, *The Sciences of the Soul. The Early Modern Origins of Psychology*. Chicago/London, The University of Chicago Press 2011.
69 Cf. LUCAS MARCO GISI, *Einbildungskraft und Mythologie. Die Verschränkung von Anthropologie und Geschichte im 18. Jahrhundert*, Berlin/New York, de Gruyter 2007, who speaks, in this respect,

Kant's new way of treating themes traditionally intended to be psychological in the light of his critical philosophy in the next two chapters. Now it is, instead, time to go back to the analysis of the concept of faculty (*Vermögen*) in general, by treating this concept from a different viewpoint, that is by clarifying the related concept of *Gemüt*, in order to better clarify the term *Vermögen*.

1.4 Kant's Concept of *Gemüt* and the Epigenetical Reading

As I pointed out in my lexicographical analysis, a faculty is, roughly put, the "*X*" which enables one to perform mental actions (i.e. cognizing, willing, feeling).

In the preceding excursus I tried to shed some light on the discussion regarding the faculties during Kant's time. As mentioned, I now focus on some interpretations of the concept of faculty in Kant's philosophy. First of all, it is necessary to remind ourselves that Kant links the term faculty quite generally to the noun "capacity" (*Fähigkeit*) and to the predicates "can" (*können*) and "to make something possible" (*ermöglichen*). Therefore, in speaking about "faculty" we are confronted with a condition of possibility of an action in general.[70]

In Kant's account of mental faculties, along with the word *Vermögen*, words such as *Erkenntnisvermögen*[71], but also the less frequent *Seelenvermögen*[72], *Gemüthsvermögen*[73], *Gemüthsfähigkeiten*[74], *Gemüthsarten*[75], *Seelenkräfte*[76],

---

of an *anthropologische Wende der Aufklärung* and refers to a "culturalisation of anthropology in the Spätaufklärung", pp. 357–359.

70 On the relation between the concept of faculty and Kant's account of action, see VOLKER GERHARDT, "Handlung als Verhältnis von Ursache und Wirkung: Zur Entwicklung des Handlungsbegriffs bei Kant", in GEROLD PRAUSS (ed.), *Handlungstheorie und Transzendentalphilosophie*, Frankfurt a. M., V. Klostermann 1986, pp. 98–131, who notes that already in the essay on the *Negative Magnitudes* (NG, AA 02: 200) and in the *Nova Dilucidatio* (PND, AA 01: 400) Kant connects "action" (*Handlung*) to the concept of faculty ("Alle Handlungen des Menschen wird ein 'Vermögen zu handeln' zugeschrieben", p. 105).

71 Numerous are the occurrences of the word, in a general as well as a technical meaning: the term appears more than half thousand times in Kant's writings.

72 Cf. KU, AA 05: 177.17, 196.23; SF, AA 07: 73.29.

73 Cf. EE, AA 20: 207.09.

74 Kant uses the term only during the pre-critical years: GSE, AA 02: 253.12; *Versuch über die Krankheiten des Kopfes*, AA 02: 264.06.

75 See GSE, AA 02: 218.34; 219.03 and the notes margined by Kant in his copy of the book (Bem. zu GSE, AA 20: 79.11).

76 It is usually mentioned in pre-critical works; afterwards, it appears only in some letters and *Reflexionen*, apart from KU, AA 05, 275.03; MS, AA 06, 445.16; Anth, AA 07: 207.22.

Gemüthskräfte[77], *Gemüthsanlage*[78] are at stake. However, as I will soon show, the most convenient periphrasis is *Vermögen des Gemüts*. All these words denote the broad class to which specific faculties such as sensibility, reason, but also imagination, judgement, sense, will and desire belong.

Apart from *Erkenntnisvermögen*, which is a term taken to denote, at times, a specific class of faculties and, other times, the sole faculty of understanding, all the German words above listed are constituted by a term pertaining to the semantic field of "faculty" / "force" / "capability" / "disposition", preceded by either *Seele* or *Gemüt*. This means that, in most of the cases where Kant refers to the faculties of the human mind, the terms *Seele* and *Gemüt* are taken to be synonymous.

Nonetheless, it has to be emphasized that Kant sometimes also distinguishes sharply between the terms *Seele* and *Gemüt*.[79]

---

77 Mentioned more than 50 times in Kant's writings.

78 See KU, AA 05: 235.34, 307.14; MS, AA 06: 399.11.

79 Cf. in particular the notes of Kant's lectures on anthropology (e.g. *Anthropologie Parow*, *Anthropologie Philippi*, *Anthropologie Friedländer*). Among the many passages, see VParow, AA 25: 247–248: "Wir beobachten aber die Seele aus einem 3fachen GesichtsPunckte, nemlich als *Anima* (Seele) *Animus* (Gemüth) und *Mens* (Geist) – In so fern die Seele in Verbindung mit dem Körper gedacht wird, und also nicht verhindern kann, daß das, was die Sinne afficirt, ihr auch mitgetheilt werde, ist sie Seele und da ist sie bloß leidend. In so fern aber die Seele auf die sinnlichen Eindrüke resignirt und sich thätig beweißt ist sie *animus*, und so weit sie ganz unabhängig von aller Sinnlichkeit sich etwas vorstellt ist sie *Mens*"; VFriedländer, AA 25: 474.02–05: "Wir können bei der Seele unterscheiden Geist und Gemüth. Das Gemüth ist die Art, wie die Seele von den Dingen afficirt wird, es ist das Vermögen über seinen Zustand zu reflectiren, und seinen zustand auf sich selbst und seine Persönlichkeit zu beziehen"; VFriedländer AA 25: 474.25–28: "Das Gemüth ist also ein Vermögen dasjenige zu empfinden, was man empfindet. Dahero ist animus und anima unterschieden. Man nennt auch animus sonst mens, allein mens möchte auch schon Geist bedeuten". Cf. also Refl 4550, AA 17: 590. 21–23: "Die Seele empfindet, das Gemüth urteilt a poster oder schätzt *a posteriori*, der Geist *a priori*". For a discussion of these passages, cf. Claudio La Rocca, "Psicologia", in Stefano Besoli – Claudio La Rocca – Riccardo Martinelli (eds.), *L'universo kantiano. Filosofia, scienze, sapere*, Macerata, Quodlibet 2010, pp. 391–435, who notes that Kant distinguishes *Seele*, *Gemüt* and *Geist* in order to account for different dimensions of "psychological" phenomena (see in particular p. 433). For a distinction between the terms *Geist*, *mens* and *nous*, see Hansmichael Hoenegger, "Geist, mens, nous. Teleologia della filosofia e sistema teleologico delle facoltà in Kant", in Eugenio Canone (ed.), *Per una storia del concetto di mente*, vol. II, Firenze, Olschki 2007, pp. 327–368. For an analysis of the term *Gemüt* see also Pedro Jesús Teruel, "Significato, senso e ubicazione strutturale del termine *Gemüt* nella filosofia kantiana", in Stefano Bacin – Alfredo Ferrarin – Claudio La Rocca – Margit Ruffing (eds.), *Kant and Philosophy in a Cosmopolitan Sense /Kant und die Philosophie in weltbürgerlicher Hinsicht. Akten des XI. Internationalen Kant-Kongresses*, Boston-New York, De Gruyter 2013, volume 4, pp. 507–518.

In addition, an exhaustive exposition of the distinction between soul (*Seele*) and mind (*Gemüt*) can be gained by a reading of the text "To Soemmerring, On the Organ of the Soul".[80] This text, sent by Kant to the author in a letter dated August 10th, 1795, appeared as an afterword in Soemmerring's 1796 published work.[81] Here Kant assimilates *Gemüt* to *animus* and marks the difference between this concept and that of *Seele/anima*; in particular, *Gemüt* is mentioned as the concept under which the representations are brought together.[82]

A treatment of the concept of *Seele* in Kant's critical philosophy would bring me far away from my present aims.[83] Instead, a closer look at the concept of

---

80 "Zu Soemmerring über das Organ der Seele", an appendix to SAMUEL THOMAS VON SOEM-MERRING (also: SÖMMERING), *Über das Organ der Seele*. Königsberg 1796. Kant's letter is on pp. 81–86 of the published work.

81 This *Afterword* and the accompanying letter can be found in AA 12: 30–35. Kant's multiple drafts for this *Afterword* can be found in AA 13: 398–412. For an analysis of the text, see MAURO DI GIANDOMENICO, "Kant, Soemmerring e il dibattito sulla 'sede dell'anima'", in COSTANTINO ESPOSITO – PASQUALE PONZIO – PAOLO PORRO – VENERANDA CASTELLANO (eds.), *Verum et Certum. Studi di storiografia filosofica in onore di Ada Lamacchia*, Bari, Levante 1998, pp. 167– 191; WERNER EULER, "Die Suche nach dem 'Seelenorgan'. Kants philosophische Analyse einer anatomischen Entdeckung Soemmerrings", in *Kant-Studien*, 93 (2002), pp. 453–480; PETER MCLAUGHLIN, "Soemmerring und Kant: Über das Organ der Seele und den Streit der Fakultäten", in *Soemmerring-Forschungen*, 1 (1985), pp. 191–201; PEDRO JESÚS TERUEL, "Das Organ der Seele. Immanuel Kant y Samuel Thomas Sömmerring sobre el problema mente-cerebro", in *Studi kantiani*, XXI (2008), pp. 59–76.

82 Cf. AA 12: 32, note: "Unter Gemüth versteht man nur das die gegebenen Vorstellungen zusammensetzende und die Einheit der empirischen Apperceptionbewirkende Vermögen (*animus*), noch nicht die Substanz (*anima*), nach ihrer von der Materie ganz unterschiedenen Natur, von der man alsdann abstrahirt".

83 As it is well-known, Kant deals with the concept of *Seele* in the Paralogisms section of the first *Critique*. For instance, in the criticism of the first paralogism of pure psychology (as in the A edition) Kant analyses the possibility of denoting the I as thinking being (soul) as substance ["Also bin ich, als denkend Wesen (Seele), Substanz", KrV, A 348 – AA 04: 220.13, CpR p. 416] and concludes that "one can quite well allow the proposition *The soul is substance* to be valid, if only one admits that this concept of ours leads no further, that it cannot teach us any of the usual conclusions of the rationalistic doctrine of the soul" ["man [kann] den Satz: die Seele ist Substanz, gar wohl gelten lassen, wenn man sich nur bescheidet, daß dieser unser Begriff nicht im mindesten weiter führe, oder irgend eine von den gewöhnlichen Folgerungen der ver-nünftelnden Seelenlehre"] A 350 – AA 04: 221.25–28, CpR p. 417. For the possibility of making *a priori* statements about the soul in research on Kant, cf. for instance KARL AMERIKS, *Kant's Theory of Mind. An Analysis of the Paralogisms of Pure Reason*, Oxford/New York, Oxford University Press 1982 (new edition: 2000), who argues for the possibility of making statements on the soul and, in contrast to this reading, HEINER F. KLEMME, *Kants Philosophie des Subjekts. Systematische und entwicklungsgeschichtliche Untersuchung zum Verhältnis von Selbstbewußtsein und Selbsterkenntnis*, Hamburg, Meiner 1996 and, more recently, HEINER F. KLEMME, "Die ra-

Gemüt is necessary for getting a clearer background of Kant's discussion of the faculties.

This concept, as also Kant assesses in the third *Critique*, can be analysed primarily with regard to the biological sphere. From this, however, it does not follow that a biological reading of the concept of faculty is implied. In this regard, before analysing the concept of faculty and the more general concept of *Gemüt* in Kant's pure philosophy, let me first consider the relation between Kant's concept of *Gemüt* and the Eighteenth century epigenetical interpretation of the mind. This relation might be shown by reference to some passages of Kant's first and third *Critiques*. For instance, as it can be read in the third *Critique*, *Gemüt* is a human being's life-principle, whose hindrance and furtherance must be sought outside it, but yet also within the very human being, that is, in connection with the body.[84] Insofar as *Gemüt* is defined as a "life-principle", it is strongly connected to body functions; however, it has to be considered as something within the body and, at the same time, totally independent from the body itself.

At this stage, Soemmerring and Blumenbach seem to play an important role in Kant's considerations on the concept of *Gemüt*. As for what concerns the first author, Soemmerring seeks a similar link between human body and its functional mental structure in his investigations concerning the soul. He was one of the most influential representatives of the studies concerning the "anatomical-functionalist" theory of the mind in Nineteenth-Century Germany and one of the founders of modern neurophysiology.[85] Furthermore, he was acquainted with Johann Friedrich Blumenbach, an important exponent of vitalism.[86] While studying in Göttingen, Soemmerring attended Blumenbach's lectures and remained in contact with him also after having left the city in order to teach in other places in Germany (Kassel, Mainz).[87]

---

tionalistische Interpretation von Kants 'Paralogismen der reinen Vernunft'", in Chotas Jiri – Jindrich Karasek – Jürgen Stolzenberg (eds.), *Metaphysik und Kritik. Interpretationen zur "Transzendentalen Dialektik" der Kritik der reinen Vernunft*, Würzburg, Königshausen & Neumann 2010, pp. 141–157.

84 Cf. KU § 29, AA 05: 278.03–06: "das Gemüth [ist] für sich allein ganz Leben (das Lebensprincip selbst) [...], und Hindernisse oder Beförderungen außer demselben und doch im Menschen selbst, mithin in der Verbindung mit seinem Körper gesucht werden müssen"; CPJ p. 159.

85 See Pedro Jesús Teruel, "Das Organ der Seele. Immanuel Kant y Samuel Thomas Sömmerring sobre el problema mente-cerebro", cit., p. 60.

86 Cf. "Johann Friedrich Blumenbach (1752–1840)" in Klemme, Heiner F. – Kuehn, Manfred (eds.), *Dictionary of Eighteenth-Century German Philosophers*, cit., volume 1, pp. 118–121.

87 See Heiner F. Klemme – Manfred Kuehn (eds.), *Dictionary of Eighteenth-Century German Philosophers*, cit., volume 3, entry "Soemmerring, Samuel Thomas von (1755–1830)", p. 185.

The relation between Soemmerring and Blumenbach is noteworthy insofar as Blumenbach's theses influenced Kant's writings. Kant's acquaintance with Blumenbach's investigations is also testified in his writings concerning human race.[88] However, what is even more remarkable, is Kant's reference to Blumenbach's theory of epigenesis, i. e. the theory which refers to the embryo's gradual development from previously unorganized material.

I am not interested in analysing how correct Kant's understanding of Blumenbach was – and, by the way, Kant's misunderstanding of the actual theory, as Blumenbach proposed it, seems pretty unquestionable.[89] However, what I find noteworthy in relation to my analysis is the use Kant makes of the theory of epigenesis (as he understands it) with regard to his understanding of the concept of *Gemüt*.

In some passages of the first and the third *Critique* Kant quotes Blumenbach's biological theory and seems to make the attempt of approximating his transcendental investigation concerning human knowledge to it. These passages play an important role in the context of the analysis dedicated to the concept of *Gemüt*, since they seem to refer to a possible reading of Kant's theory of the faculties as an epigenetical analysis.

A first reference in this direction comes from the *Critique of Pure Reason* and, more precisely, from the paragraph dedicated to the "Result of the deduction of the concepts of the understanding" (§ 27 of the *Transcendental Deduction*). Here Kant deals with the only "two ways in which a necessary agreement of experience with the concepts of its objects can be thought" and states that "either the experience makes these concepts possible or these concepts make the experience possible".[90] Kant's solution notoriously consists in making experience de-

---

88 See *Von den verschiedenen Racen der Menschen* (1775), AA 02: 427–443; *Bestimmung des Begriffes einer Menschenrace* (1785), AA 08: 89–106.

89 For Blumenbach's concept of *Bildungstrieb*, its role in Kant's works, and Kant's misunderstanding, cf. STEFANO FABBRI BERTOLETTI, *Impulso, formazione e organismo. Per una storia del concetto di Bildungstrieb nella cultura tedesca*, Firenze, Olschki 1990. But see also TIMOTHY LENOIR, "Kant, Blumenbach and Vital Materialism in German Biology", in *Isis*, 71/1 (1980), pp. 71–108; ROBERT J. RICHARDS, "Kant and Blumenbach on the *Bildungstrieb*: A Historical Misunderstanding", in *Studies in History and Philosophy of Biological and Biomedical Sciences*, 31 (2000), pp. 11–32; HEIN VAN DER BERG, "Kant on Vital Forces. Metaphysical Concerns versus Scientific Practice", in ERNST-OTTO ONNASCH (ed.), *Kants Philosophie der Natur. Ihre Entwicklung im Opus postumum und ihre Wirkung*, Berlin/New York, de Gruyter, pp. 115–135.

90 KrV, B 166/AA 03: 128.09–12; CrP p. 264: "Nun sind nur zwei Wege, auf welchen eine nothwendige Übereinstimmung der Erfahrung mit den Begriffen von ihren Gegenständen gedacht werden kann: entweder die Erfahrung macht diese Begriffe, oder diese Begriffe machen die Erfahrung möglich".

pend on the categories, not the other way round.[91] To make the *a priori* concepts depend on experience would correspond to referring to a sort of *"generatio aequivoca"*, on the basis of which a certain thing is made to derive from a completely different one, which has the former as the latter's improper source.[92] Therefore, Kant seems to explain the agreement between the concepts given in our understanding and experience by maintaining that the grounds of experience are to be found in pure reason and, more precisely, in the categories of our understanding. He compares the treatment of the relation between experience and *a priori* concepts with epigenesis. The categories must represent the grounds of the possibility of experience from the side of the understanding and, from this, it follows that Kant also refers experience back to a pure activity of the mind (*Gemüt*). However, with such a theory he thus seems to offer a sort of *"Epigenesis der reinen Vernunft"*. Is this a faithful description of Kant's model?

The epigenetical account of the mental process in Kant is controversial.[93] This way of reading Kant's texts, which finds supporters in contemporary philosophy of mind, as I will show in Chapter 2 below, will show itself inappropriate. In chapter 2 I will propose some arguments against this reading and, in particular, a reference to the so called "transcendental argument", which helps defeat this interpretation. For now, however, it is sufficient to note that the reference to the theory of epigenesis can be simply considered symptomatic of Kant's acquaintance with some of Blumenbach's views, while it is also necessary to underline that the reference to empirical presuppositions for explaining the critical enterprise would give a false account of Kant's pure philosophy. In fact and most notably, Kant refers to Blumenbach's theo-

---

91 KrV, B 167/AA 03: 128.12–19: "Das erstere findet nicht in Ansehung der Kategorien (auch nicht der reinen sinnlichen Anschauung) statt; denn sie sind Begriffe *a priori*, mithin unabhängig von der Erfahrung (die Behauptung eines empirischen Ursprungs wäre eine Art von *generatio aequivoca*). Folglich bleibt nur das zweite übrig (gleichsam ein System der Epigenesis der reinen Vernunft): daß nämlich die Kategorien von Seiten des Verstandes die Gründe der Möglichkeit aller Erfahrung überhaupt enthalten"; CrP pp. 264–265.

92 The editors' example of the English edition of KrV is that of flies apparently generated by rotting meat – see CrP p. 164, note (a). Kant gives a further example of *generatio aequivoca* in the Architectonic-section, where he speaks of maggots and equivocated seed (see KrV, A 835/B 863 – AA 03: 540. 12–23). An extensive explanation concerning the *generatio aequivoca* is given by Kant in KU, § 80, note. AA 05: 419. Kant mentions once again the theory of epigenesis in the following § 81 of KU, as we will see. Interestingly, the two theories occur mostly together in Kant's thought.

93 For this discussion see again STEFANO FABBRI BERTOLETTI, *Impulso, formazione e organismo*, cit.; but see also PHILLIP R. SLOAN, "Preforming the Categories: Eighteenth-Century Generation Theory and Biological Roots of Kant's A Priori", in *Journal of the History of Philosophy*, 40/2 (2002), pp. 229–253.

ries more particularly in all those passages where he takes into consideration the concept of organism and certainly not in order to give a general explanation of the mind (*Gemüt*). For instance, in § 81 of the *Critique of the Power of Judgement*, where Kant takes into consideration the form of causality that enables us to think the possibility of an organised being and suggests that we can explain the internally purposive form of organised beings either by means of the theory of "occasionalism" or through the theory of "prestabilism".[94] However, as he notes, to explain organized beings in terms of occasional production means to say that "all nature is quite lost".[95] Hence, what we are left with is the sole option of prestabilism.

Kant describes two slightly different versions of this theory: prestabilism, he says, could proceed in two ways. According to the first one, each organic being is generated from its own kind as "*educt*". According to the second one, organic beings are described as "*products*". The first explanation refers to the theory of "individual pre-formation" or "evolution". The second one refers to the theory of "epigenesis" or "generic pre-formation". According to this last explanatory strategy, the productive faculty of the progenitor "is still preformed in accordance with the internally purposive predispositions that were imparted to its stock, and thus the specific form was preformed".[96]

Kant seems to incline toward this second explanation. Furthermore, he states that reason already regards it with peculiar favour before any proof is given. Moreover, this explanation has to be preferred since it regards nature as self-producing (with the least expenditure of the supernatural).[97] In this section Kant also praises Blumenbach's role in establishing the principles of the application of this theory and directs very positive judgements toward the scientist.[98] However, he notes finally that Blumenbach leaves too much at the mercy of natural mechanism, namely by referring to an "indispensable *principle* of an original *organisation,* an indeterminable but yet unmistakeable element": the *Bildungstrieb* ("formative impulse").[99] According to Blumenbach's theory, each living being possesses a "formative effort" (also called *nisus formativus*), which makes it differ from all inanimate beings and causes its formation and growth. This active drive has an influence upon unformed material, becomes effective and escorts the bodies of animate being during their whole life. It con-

---

94 KU § 81, AA 05: 422–423, CPJ p. 291 ff.
95 KU § 81, AA 05: 422.32, CPJ p. 291: "so geht alle Natur hiebei gänzlich verloren".
96 Cf. KU § 81, AA 05: 422.36–37, 423:01–08; CPJ p. 291.
97 See KU § 81, AA 05: 424.07–18; CPJ p. 292.
98 Cf. KU § 81, AA 05: 424.19–28, CPJ p. 292.
99 Cf. KU § 81, AA 05: 424.19–34, CPJ p. 292.

stitutes the most important vital power, the one without which no life at all would be possible: it is different and precedes all other powers.[100]

Without overestimating the impact of Blumenbach's theory of the *Bildungstrieb* in Kant's thought, we might limit ourselves to register Kant's interest for the theory of epigenesis and his appraisal of Blumenbach's studies and, with it, Kant's interest for an epigenetical explanation of the processes of the human mind (*Gemüt*). However, this explanation cannot be considered as the founding element of the critical analysis of the mind (*Gemüt*), if we do not want to give an erroneous picture of Kant's pure philosophical analysis: to point out Kant's biological interest is different from trying to associate Kant's name to a peculiar account of innatism or arguing for a possible epigenetic origin of Kant's account of the mind (*Gemüt*), as he proposes it in the critical works.

Such an erroneous interpretation can be deduced, for instance, by the reading of some contemporary scholars who, like Robert Hanna, try to present Kant's theory of the mind (*Gemüt*) as a "doctrine of *capacity innateness*".[101] In Hanna's opinion, what Kant considered innate was "not a mental representation but instead a mental faculty or power for generating representations according to rules".[102] In contrast to a "content innatism" theory, where the mind is described as "a passive recipient or container of divinely caused ideas", Hanna proposes what he calls "Kant's innatist picture", where "the mind is essentially a set of active capacities, each of which contains some determinate formal procedures for the generation of representations".[103]

---

100 See Johann Friedrich Blumenbach, *Ueber den Bildungstrieb und das Zeugungsgeschäft*, several editions, 1781–1792 (here: Göttingen, 1791), p. 31–32.

101 See Robert Hanna, *Kant and the Foundations of Analytic Philosophy*, Oxford, Clarendon Press 2001, p. 33. Hanna uses INNATISM in capitals to refer to the classical rationalist conception of innate ideas, to which his "capacity innateness" wants to be an alternative. Against content innatism, cf. also Patricia Kitcher, "Discovering the Forms of Intuition", in *The Philosophical Review*, XCVI/2 (1987), pp. 205–248, here in particular pp. 219–220: "we should resist the temptation to read Kant's claim that pure process forms lie in the mind *a priori* as a fancy way of saying that they are innate. While Kant uses 'a priori' in various ways, the primordial usage is epistemological: a particular claim is *a priori* if it is knowable by some special means that is independent of experience". See also Philip Kitcher, "A Priori Knowledge", in *The Philosophical Review*, 89 (1980), pp. 3–23.

102 R. Hanna, *Kant and the Foundations of Analytic Philosophy*, cit., p. 33.

103 *Ibidem.* For a similar reading, cf. also Wayne Waxman, *Kant and the Empiricists: Understanding Understanding*, Oxford/New York, Oxford University Press 2005 (in particular pp. 26 ff.) and Wayne Waxman, *Kant's Model of the Mind. A New Interpretation of Transcendental Idealism*, Oxford/New York, Oxford University Press 1991 (in particular pp. 271 ff.).

Even though Hanna's proposal might sound plausible until now, on the basis of his analysis of some of Kant's texts,[104] his suggestion to support this reading by an epigenetic interpretation is not convincing at all. Hanna finds epigenesis very helpful for the understanding of Kant's model of the mind (*Gemüt*), since it contains "an explanation for cognitive content that appeals only to the idea of innate active capacities or faculties containing rules for synthesizing externally supplied sensory information".[105] Creating a strong connection between epigenesis and "capacity innatism", Hanna assesses that the first theory must directly descend from the second one. In this way, the epigenetic account of the origin of the human mind is described as what best supports Kant's "capacity innatism". From this, it follows that the a priority of the concepts and the categories of the understanding can be coherently explained by an epigenetic origin of the mind, in Hanna's opinion.[106] Hanna assesses that "according to Kant's epigenetic model of the mind, the full meaning content and objective reference of *any* mental representation is satisfactorily explained only by appealing to our innate total human capacity for acquiring cognition of the world".[107] Not only does Hanna believe that this capacity is innate, he also describes it as the basis of a "self-guided *a priori* psychological information-processing system".[108]

The problem with Hanna's reading is his assertion that Kant denotes the system of the faculties described in the *Critiques* in a psychological way: this is quite imprecise and rather risky, since it would defeat the whole of Kant's critical enterprise, making Kant's theory depend on empirical psychological basis.

A strong psychological reading of Kant's critical enterprise, which is based on an epigenetical account of the mind, fails to explain Kant's attempt to make the study of the faculties independent from the empirical field in general and that of psychology in particular.

Of course it is possible to focus on the empirical level of Kant's research and then assume a psychological point of view, which permits us to think of Kant's investigation of the faculties as a psychological enterprise. Nonetheless, such an investigation is proposed by Kant in his anthropological studies, which substi-

---

104 Hanna's analysis of Kant's *Über eine Entdeckung, nach der alle neue Kritik der reinen Vernunft durch eine ältere entbehrlich gemacht werden soll* (1790) [ÜE, AA 08: 185–251] is, in this sense, noteworthy.
105 R. HANNA, *Kant and the Foundations of Analytic Philosophy*, cit., p. 33. At this point, he refers to epigenesis in a familiar way and recalls once again the theory of *Bildungstrieb*.
106 R. HANNA, *Kant and the Foundations of Analytic Philosophy*, cit., p. 34.
107 R. HANNA, *Kant and the Foundations of Analytic Philosophy*, cit., p. 35.
108 *Ibidem*.

tute the traditional discipline of empirical psychology.[109] But this is not what Kant aims to do in the critical works: if we read the *Critiques*, we are primarily confronted with the research of the conditions of possibility of knowledge, which are not derived from empirical psychological research but rather analysed *a priori*.

In contrast to a "strong psychological" reading of the theory of the faculties proposed by Kant in the *Critiques*, an attempt has been done in contemporary Kant scholarship to refer to transcendental psychology, in order to explain Kant's investigation of the mind (*Gemüt*) in the context of pure philosophy. A transcendental psychological reading aims to approach the study of the faculties in the *Critiques* as an investigation that is psychological in a "weak" sense.

In the next chapter I will focus on this interpretation.

1.5 The Concept of Human Mental Faculties: Some Concluding Remarks

In this chapter my aim was to illustrate the central role of the concept of "faculty" (*Vermögen*) in Kant's critical enterprise. In order to do so, I first took into consideration some occurrences of this term in the first *Critique*. Afterwards, I proposed a terminological analysis of the term, in order to better identify the meaning of *Vermögen* in Germany in the Eighteenth century and I related this analysis to the concept of power (*Kraft*). Eventually, I analysed Kant's concept of "mind" (*Gemüt*) and I assessed that an epigenetical reading of the theory of the faculties proposed by Kant in his critical enterprise does not succeed in explaining Kant's investigations in pure philosophy, which try to give an account of the faculties independent of the empirical field.

The failure of this interpretive reading gives way to the consideration of an alternative reading, i.e. a transcendental psychological one, which I will now take into consideration. In this way, I will analyse the discussion of "faculty" in contemporary Kant scholarship (at the end of the Twentieth century), and will try to shed some light on this discussion while underlying the differences between the contemporary debate and the debate on the faculties in Germany during the second half of the Eighteenth century, with which I have briefly dealt in the present chapter by pointing to the Academy contest of 1773/1775.

---

109 For a distinction between anthropology and empirical psychology cf. chapter 3.

Chapter 2
The Mind and Its Faculties in Contemporary Kant Scholarship

Almost half a century after Strawson's famously condemning account of Kantian psychology and, more generally, of any kind of successful psychological interpretation of Kant's critical philosophy,[110] is there still room for a positive evaluation of Kant's account of the mental field and of Kant's theory of the human faculties? And where will this room have to be located within pure philosophy? Is there room in Kant's philosophy for a pure, transcendental psychology or anthropology?[111]

In effect, the question whether or not "mental acts" and the faculties that make them possible might be dealt with as a special part of a pure philosophical inquiry is not a new one. Strawson's more specific criticism about the possibility of finding a consistent account of a version of transcendental psychology in Kant's thought is just one part of the story. It seems to come along with other less specific criticism from those scholars who dispute the existence of mental phenomena in general (an example is Gilbert Ryle, who considered mental vocabulary just a different manner of describing action).[112]

Without pretending to answer these questions, which query the very meaningfulness of cognitive science, in what follows I take the analysis of mental life for not frivolous and try to discuss some readings of Kant's account of the mental field in contemporary Kant scholarship.

---

110 Cf. PETER FREDERICK STRAWSON, *The Bounds of Sense. An Essay on Kant's* Critique of Pure Reason, London, Methuen 1966.

111 The question of a supposed psychological foundation of Kant's critical enterprise and, in particular, of the first *Critique*, has a long history, as Hatfield notes (GARY HATFIELD, "Empirical, Rational, and Transcendental Psychology. Psychology as Science and as Philosophy", in PAUL GUYER (ed.), *The Cambridge Companion to Kant*, Cambridge/New York, Cambridge University Press 1992, pp. 200–227, here in particular note 14 pp. 225–226) quoting, among others, KARL LEONARD REINHOLD (*Versuch einer neuen Theorie des menschlichen Vorstellungsvermögens*, Prague 1789, pp. 65–7, and *Briefe über die kantische Philosophie*, 2 vols., Leipzig, 1790–1792, 2:25), JOHANN GOTTLIEB FICHTE ("Zweite Einleitung in die Wissenschaftslehre", 1797, in Fichte's *Sämtliche Werke*, ed. I. H. FICHTE, 8 vols., Berlin, 1845–6, I: 471–9), JAKOB FRIEDRICH FRIES (*Neue oder anthropologische Kritik der Vernunft*, 2nd ed., 3 vols., Heidelberg, 1828, I:20–6, 28–30), JOHAN FRIEDRICH HERBART (*Lehrbuch zur Einleitung in die Philosophie*, Königsberg, 1813, preface, §§126–7, in Herbart's *Sämtliche Werke*, ed. by K. KEHRBACH and O. FLÜGEL, 19 vols., Langensalza, 1887–1912, 4:9–10, 208–13).

112 See GILBERT RYLE, *The Concept of the Mind*, London, Hutchinson 1949.

In particular, I take into consideration those scholars who link their research specifically to Kant's theory of the faculties. A nearly endless list might be drawn up if I were to consider all studies dedicated to Kant and the constitution and functioning of reason as well as the works dealing with his account of the mind in a broad sense. On the contrary, the number of studies dedicated to the connection between Kant's thought and the concept of a faculties-endowed-mind as intended in cognitive science is quite little.

During the first years of the 1990s a small group of scholars (for instance, A. Brook, W. Waxman, G. Hatfield, and P. Kitcher) produced some attempts in that direction. In all these attempts, Kant's model of the mind is considered the dominant one in empirical psychology, but is also influential in cognitive science: Kant (maybe against his own will) is said to have seen "further than anyone else" in this field.[113]

In the present chapter of my study I take into consideration these contemporary interpretations in Kant scholarship. In particular, I first consider two anti-psychologistic readings of Kant's account of the mind, i.e. a functionalist reading of Kant's model of the mind (Brook – section 2.1) and a "faculty-innatist" approach (Hatfield – section 2.2), in order to show how these two accounts might complete each other. Eventually, I take into consideration Kitcher's "transcendental psychological" interpretive proposal together with some criticisms against this reading (section 2.4). This last analysis is followed by a brief overview of the distinction between the two disciplines of rational and empirical psychology (section 2.3).

2.1 Brook's Kantian Mind-Functionalism and the Transcendental Argument

In the present and in the next section I aim to show how two anti-psychologistic readings of Kant's view of the mind, namely Brook's functionalist interpretation

---

113 See ANDREW BROOK, *Kant's View of the Mind*, Cambridge/New York, Cambridge University Press 1994, p.1: "The discoveries he [Kant] made about the mind not only were a contribution in their time, but continue to be important now". See also ANDREW BROOK, "Kant's View of the Mind and Consciousness of Self", *The Stanford Encyclopedia of Philosophy* (Winter 2008 Edition), Edward N. Zalta (ed.), URL = <http://plato.stanford.edu/archives/win2008/entries/kant-mind/>, last accessed on November, 19th, 2011, and, from the same author, "Kant, Cognitive Science and Contemporary Neo-Kantianism", in *Journal of Consciousness Studies (JCS) – Controversies in Science & the Humanities. An International Multi-Disciplinary Journal.* Special number 11/2004 (No. 10 – 11), pp. 1– 25.

and Hatfield's innatist one, might be integrated with one another, in order to give an explanation of how Kant's model of the faculties functions without recurring to a psychological empirical interpretation. In order to do so, I start with the functionalist reading of Kant's model of the mind, as supported by Andrew Brook.[114]

Brook's functionalist reading is based on the idea of what he calls Kant's transcendental method, which he defines as the key to understanding Kant's role in contemporary studies in cognitive science.[115]

According to Brook, the transcendental method serves to answer the question: "how should we study the mind?", which can be answered only "by thinking through what the mind must be like and what capacities it must have to represent things as it does".[116]

In Brook's opinion, the functioning of Kant's transcendental method for furnishing an account of the mental field can be gained by the reading of a passage from the 1781 version of the first *Critique*.[117] Let me briefly recall Kant's strategy in the passage, which Brook takes into consideration. There Kant assesses that it would be a contradiction to borrow the *a priori* elements which make experience possible from experience itself: we must proceed the other way around and begin by considering the "transcendental constitution of the subjective sources that comprise the *a priori* foundations for the possibility of experience".[118] Human beings have to possess a determinate pre-existing "something", in order for their experience in general to be possible. This "something" is described by Kant as subjective sources (*subjektive Erkenntnißquellen*) that permit a threefold synthesis, which manifests itself in human beings as modifications of the mind (*Modificationen des Gemüths*).[119]

---

114 A comprehensive account of this author's perspective can be gained from A. BROOK, *Kant's View of the Mind*, cit.

115 A. BROOK, *Kant's View of the Mind*, cit., p. 12: "Kant's central methodological innovation, the method of transcendental argument, has become a major, maybe the major, method of cognitive science".

116 A. BROOK, "Kant, Cognitive Science and Contemporary Neo-Kantianism", cit., p. 4.

117 Precisely to the second section of the "Deduction of the Pure Concepts of the Understanding" dedicated to the "*a priori* grounds for the possibility of experience", KrV, A 95 ff./AA IV 74 ff.; CpR p. 226 ff.

118 See in particular KrV, A 95–97/AA 04: 75.13–15, 25–30; 76: 04–07; CpR pp. 227–228.

119 The passage in question is that concerning the apprehension of representations in intuition, their reproduction in imagination and their recognition in the concept. See KrV, A 97–98/AA 04: 76.11–21; CpR p. 228.

The subjective sources, which are needed for explaining the process of knowledge, help to furnish a description of the mind, as it should be constituted if cognition is to be at all possible in the way that it is.[120]

In accordance with this exposition, Brook argues that Kant's transcendental method and the corresponding transcendental argument is identical to the argument of inference to the best explanation, which has to be applied in order to gain an account of Kant's theory of the mind, where "unobservable mental mechanisms" must be postulated "in order to explain observed behaviour".[121]

By means of the application of the argument of inference to the best explanation, Brook believes that a number of "substantive claims" about Kant's theory of mind can be made. For instance, Brook affirms that, through the reference to concepts and intuitions, Kant recognizes the functions which are "crucial for knowledge-generating activity" as "processing of sensory inputs and application of concepts to sensory inputs":

> Cognition requires concepts and percepts. As we might say now, to discriminate, we need information; but for information to be of any use to us, we must organize the information. Next, the functions that organize sensory and conceptual raw materials into experiences are different abilities to synthesize.[122]

On the basis of applying the "transcendental argument" in order to give an account of the mind, Brook aims to show that "we *do* know things about the mind": what we know is that the mind "must apply concepts, synthesize, and so on" – in other words, we do know "the mind's functions" (while we lack all knowledge of "its composition and make-up").[123]

This consideration introduces Brook's functionalist reading of Kant's account of the mind:

---

120 For further discussion on this topic see, among others, DIETER HENRICH, "The Proof-Structure of Kant's Transcendental Deduction", in *The Review of Metaphysics*, 22/4 (1969), pp. 640–659; JAAKKO HINTIKKA, "Transcendental Arguments: Genuine and Spurious", in *Noûs*, 6/3 (1972), pp. 274–281; KARL AMERIKS, "Recent Work on Kant's Theoretical Philosophy", in *American Philosophical Quarterly*, 19/1 (1982), pp. 1–24; W. WAXMAN, *Kant's Model of the Mind*, cit., in particular p. 272.
121 A. BROOK, "Kant, Cognitive Science and Contemporary Neo-Kantianism", cit., p. 5.
122 A. BROOK, "Kant, Cognitive Science and Contemporary Neo-Kantianism", cit., p. 5.
123 See A. BROOK, "Kant, Cognitive Science and Contemporary Neo-Kantianism", cit., p. 6.

Kant's conception of the mind is functionalist – to understand the mind, we must study what it does and can do, its functions [...]. According to functionalism, we can gain knowledge of the mind's functions while knowing little or nothing about how the mind is built.[124]

Brook's Kantian mind-functionalism, as well as other contemporary theories of mental functionalism, aims to show that, even though we cannot know anything about the internal constitution of the mind, we do know the way our cognitive system functions, where "mental acts" and the faculties making them possible are identical with the functions which explain the process.[125]

After having analysed Brook's functionalist strategy, I now dedicate the following section to Hatfield's innatist reading, in order to show how the two interpretive proposals can be integrated.

2.2 Hatfield's Innatist Reading of Kant's Faculties

In contrast to most of the innatist readings regarding the mind, Hatfield proposes a new account of innatism in the context of Kant's theory.[126]

According to Hatfield's explanation of Kant's view of the mind, only a few cognitive faculties should be postulated (instead of complex subsystems in the organisation of the human mind) and these faculties are simply cognitive mechanisms which are not to be described as psychological entities but only as innate properties of human mind, at least for what regards the transcendental level of the analysis:

---

124 A. BROOK, "Kant's View of the Mind and Consciousness of Self", cit. See also A. BROOK, "Kant, Cognitive Science and Contemporary Neo-Kantianism", cit., p. 6. On this basis, Brook affirms that "Kant held a functionalist view of the mind almost 200 years before functionalism was officially articulated in the 1960s by Hilary Putnam and others" (*ibidem*). For this last point, see also RALF MEERBOTE, "Kant's Functionalism", in JOHN-CHRISTIAN SMITH (ed.), *Historical Foundations of Cognitive Science*, Dordrecht, Kluwer 1990, pp. 161–188.

125 In this section I limited myself to describing Brook's mind-functionalism. I did not take into consideration Brook's controversial proposal, which talks of the mind as a mere representation: according to Brook, Kant thought of the mind as "a system of representation", namely a "global representation", which is a "single representation within which many of the usual denizens of a system of representations are all contained. The global representation is not something the mind has, it is what the mind is; the mind is a representation" (A. BROOK, *Kant's View of the Mind*, cit., p. 44).

126 See GARY HATFIELD, *The Natural and the Normative: Theories of Spatial Perception from Kant to Helmholtz*, Cambridge (Mass.)/London, MIT Press 1990.

Kant made it quite plain that each faculty – sensibility, imagination, and understanding – has both an empirical and an *a priori* employment, which implies that each faculty may be investigated both in its empirical manifestation and in its transcendental mode.[127]

This way, Hatfield distinguishes between two ways of regarding the faculties: on the one hand, they might be regarded from a psychological point of view, so that their analysis would constitute an empirical investigation of the mind; on the other hand, on the transcendental level of the analysis, if we consider mental activities as they generally occur, we have nonetheless always to presuppose faculties, which make the actions of the mind possible and realizable.[128]

In contrast to the empirical psychological investigation concerning the faculties, which cannot go far enough to argue the innateness of the faculties, on the transcendental level of the analysis the faculties can and must always be given, in order for any sort of mental actions to be possible at all, considering that the process of knowledge happens as it does and without them no mental action would be possible, at least not in the usual way. In Hatfield's opinion, this is exactly the transcendental point Kant is making: call them functions or faculties, in any case we need to presuppose that we can make use of them and, in order to make them function, we first have to be equipped with them. In other words: (1) if it were not possible for us to perform mental actions at all, then we would not perform them either. However, (2) we perform them (as a state of fact). But (3) since "psychology is insufficient to account for our conception of ourselves as beings that have objective knowledge and experience",[129] we better find another explicative strategy. The possible alternative is given by (4) the "transcendental strategy" or, in other words, the method of "inference to the best explanation". This strategy, in this case, leads (5) to call these functions "faculties" and to propose an innatist account of the mind.

In contrast to other innatist views of the mental field in contemporary philosophical scholarship, Hatfield's mental innatism does not refer to an evolutionary theory in order to justify the fact that our mind is constituted in a certain specific way. This investigation, however, does not answer to questions such as: where do the faculties come from? How many are they? How do they cooperate

---

127 G. HATFIELD, *The Natural and the Normative*, cit., p. 84. The Author refers here to KrV, A 94–95/AA 04: 18–29; CpR p. 225.
128 See G. HATFIELD, *The Natural and the Normative*, cit., p. 84: "the transcendental account has its own separate beginning, from which it answers questions about sensibility, imagination, and understanding that are outside the scope of psychology: they are questions that empirically-based psychology cannot answer by its very nature".
129 G. HATFIELD, *The Natural and the Normative*, cit., p.77.

in mental activity? According to Hatfield, this is a task for psychological analysis, where the empirical research comes into the debate.

The faculty-innatist reading *à la* Hatfield and the functionalist explanation *à la* Brook can be combined, so that the faculty-innatist proposal will not be referring to epigenesis or nativism.[130] The two accounts, i. e. mind-functionalism on the one hand and faculty-innatism on the other hand, reveal themselves capable of being combined in a way that together they might be used to propose an alternative to the strong psychological interpretation of Kant's theory of the faculties, such as the above-described epigenetical one.

However, in Kant scholarship another influential proposal has been advanced in recent years. This proposal takes into consideration a particular form of psychology to refer to Kant's account of the mind. This reading is advanced in particular by Patricia Kitcher, who suggests we describe Kant's investigation of the mind as "transcendental psychology."[131] In order to understand the role of transcendental psychology as opposed to the rational and the empirical psychological research concerning the mental field, I find it helpful to briefly refer, first, to the distinction between rational psychology and empirical psychology in Kant's first *Critique*, after having briefly delineated the tradition from where this treatment comes and, second, to refer to the possibility of a Kantian transcendental psychology.

2.3 Some Brief Observations on the Distinction between Rational and Empirical Psychology and the Supposed Place of Psychology within Transcendental Philosophy

Numerous scholars have tried to clarify Kant's psychological discussions.[132] What certainly does not facilitate their enterprise is the fact that Kant uses the

---

130 Against the possibility of bridging the gap between functionalism and faculty innatism, see W. WAXMAN, *Kant's Model of the Mind*, cit., who grounds the transcendental project on psychology (cf. in particular p. 276).

131 PATRICIA KITCHER, *Kant's Transcendental Psychology*, Oxford/New York, Oxford University Press 1990; PATRICIA KITCHER, *Kant's Thinker*, Oxford/New York, Oxford University Press 2011.

132 For a first overview on these topics, a classical work is *Kant's Psychologie. Dargestellt und erörtert von* JÜRGEN BONA MEYER, Berlin, Wilhelm Hertz (Besser'sche Buchhandlung) 1870, pp. 3 – 28, where the Author refers to philosophers such as Johann Gottfried Herder, Carl Leonhard Reinhold, Johann Friedrich Herbart, Jakob Friedrich Fries, Friedrich Eduard Beneke, Arthur Schopenhauer, Hermann Ulrici, Otto Liebmann and Kuno Fischer and deals with their interpretations of the relation between Kant's critical philosophy and psychology. More recently, this discussion has been analysed by THOMAS STURM, *Kant und die Wissenschaften vom Menschen*,

psychological vocabulary of his contemporaries to develop both his pragmatic anthropology and his transcendental model of the possibility and limits of knowledge in order to explain the possibility of experience in the first *Critique* and, in general, in the three *Critiques*.[133]

Even among critics supporting Kitcher's transcendental psychology, no accord on the usefulness of this reading has been reached, also in consideration of the fact that Kant never actually treats this discipline: transcendental psychology is sometimes still considered as "a phrase that for some recognizes Kant as an ally in the development of the natural science of cognition, but for others serves to indicate the opposite conclusion, that Kant's project is distinct from empirical psychology".[134] In other words, one might still ask what the term "transcendental psychology" actually refers to and, in order to answer this question, a prior comprehension of Kant's distinction between rational and empirical psychology is due. It will be shown that, even though neither of the latter two investigations corresponds to transcendental psychology, Kant takes into consideration only these two kinds of psychology and there is no room for a third option.

First of all, one should note that Kant's understanding of psychology is derived from Baumgarten's texts, which are based, in turn, on Wolff's account of psychology. Thus, this last author deserves a closer look.

In Wolff's texts, the discussion concerning psychology as the study of the soul refers back (as it often happens in Wolff's works) to many different philosophical traditions, to rationalism, empiricism, Newtonianism, and scholasti-

---

Bielefeld, Mentis 2009; but see also C. La Rocca, "Psicologia", in S. Besoli et al. (eds.), *L'universo kantiano*, cit.; Soo Bae Kim, *Die Entstehung der Kantischen Anthropologie und ihre Beziehung zur empirischen Psychologie der Wollfschen Schule*, Frankfurt a. M., Lang 1994.

133 G. Hatfield, *The Natural and the Normative*, cit., p. 83: "In developing his account of the possibility and limits of knowledge, Kant adopted the psychological vocabulary of his contemporaries, using such terms as "faculty of sensibility", "inner" and "outer" sense, and "sensory manifold", and he posited a set of activities, those of "synthesis", that allegedly account for the possibility of experience". More generally, for the relation between transcendental philosophy and psychology, cf. also, from the same author, "Empirical, Rational, and Transcendental Psychology. Psychology as Science and as Philosophy", cit., pp. 200–227, and "Kant and Empirical Psychology in the 18th Century", in *Psychological Science*, 9/6 (1998), pp. 423–428; but also Rudolf Makkreel, "Kant on the Scientific Status of Psychology, Anthropology, and History", in Eric Watkins (ed.), *Kant and the Sciences*, Oxford, Oxford University Press 2002, pp. 185–201; Graham H. Bird, "The Paralogism and Kant's Account of Psychology", in *Kant-Studien* 91 (2000), pp. 129–145; Wayne Waxman, "Kant's Psychologism I.", in *Kantian-Review*, 3 (1999), pp. 41–63.

134 G. Hatfield, *The Natural and the Normative*, cit., p. 83.

cism in particular.[135] Nonetheless, the multiplicity of the sources taken into consideration does not condition the continuity of Wolff's account of psychology throughout his works.[136] In fact, if we juxtapose the paragraphs of Wolff's *Deutsche Metaphysik* (the third and fifth part of the *Vernünfftige Gedancken von Gott, der Welt und der Seele des Menschen*, dated 1720) and his "Latin Psychology" (i.e., the two works written in Latin, which Wolff dedicated to psychology: *Psychologia empirica* and *Psychologia rationalis*, dated 1732 and 1734 respectively), we note that they are characterized by a continuity in the way Wolff deals with the topic of the soul. The only consideration to be made here is that in the *Deutsche Metaphysik* the division of the analysis of the soul into two parts, i.e. into empirical and a rational psychology, is still not as marked as it will be in later years,[137] even though the division is still noticeable in the early works.[138] However, it is only in the two Latin volumes dedicated to psychology that the proper dichotomy between empirical and rational psychology is overtly expressed and becomes unmistakeably apparent.[139]

The meaning of this distinction within one and the same science is important in order to illustrate the differences between Kant's theory and Wolff's po-

---

135 See RICHARD J. BLACKWELL, "Wolff's Doctrine of the Soul", in *Journal of the History of Ideas*, 22/3 (1961), pp. 339–354, here in particular p. 339; Cf. also HEINER F. KLEMME, *Kants Philosophie des Subjekts. Systematische und entwicklungsgeschichtliche Untersuchungen zum Verhältnis von Selbstbewußtsein und Selbsterkenntnis*, Hamburg, Meiner [Kant-Forschungen, volume VII] 1996, and UDO THIEL, *The Early Modern Subject. Self-Consciousness and Personal Identity from Descartes to Hume*, Oxford/New York, Oxford University Press, 2011.

136 See MARIANO CAMPO, *Cristiano Wolff e il razionalismo precritico*, 2 volumes, Milan, Vita e pensiero 1939 – both volumes are reprinted in a single one, as part of *Christian Wolff: Gesammelte Werke. Materialen und Dokumente*, edited by J. ÉCOLE – J. E. HOFMANN – M. THOMANN – H. W. ARNDT – CH. A. CORR (ed.), Volume 9, Olms, Hildesheim/New York 1980. See in particular the 10th chapter of the book, dedicated to the distinction between empirical and rational psychology ("La dicotomia in psicologia empirica e razionale", pp. 308–322).

137 Three parts are dedicated to psychology in the *Deutsche Metaphysik*: Part1: *Wie wir erkennen, das wir sind, und was uns diese Erkäntniss nutzet*: §§ 1–9; part 2: *Von der Seele überhaupt, was wir nehmlich von ihr wahrnehmen*: §§ 191–539; part 3: *Von dem Wesen der Seele und eines Geistes überhaupt*: §§ 727–927. For an analysis on this division, see M. CAMPO, *Cristiano Wolff e il razionalismo precritico*, cit., p. 309.

138 See, for instance, § 119, where Wolff manifestly refers to empirical psychology by referring to the study of the soul not as a substance, but rather in the phenomenology of its conscious life.

139 See CHRISTIAN WOLFF, *Psychologia empirica, methodo scientifica pertractata, qua ea, quae de anima humana indubia experientiae fide constant, continentur et ad solidam universae philosophiae practicae ac theologiae naturalis tractationem via sternitur*, Frankfurt/Leipzig 1732; IDEM, *Psychologia rationalis, methodo scientifica pertractata, qua ea, quae de anima humana indubia experientiae fide innotescunt, per essentiam et naturam animae explicantur, et ad intimiorem naturae ejusque autoris cognitionem profutura proponuntur*, Frankfurt/Leipzig 1734.

sition. This distinction is important primarily because the real dissimilarities between the two accounts of psychology are often misunderstood by critics, who misleadingly try to give an account of Wolff's empirical psychology on the basis of Kant's proposal.[140]

According to Wolff, while empirical psychology rests on facts as well as acts of consciousness that describe and classify both phenomena and, by means of description and classification, proximal causes, on the other hand rational psychology directs itself toward the essence and attains the metaphysics of substance, final causes and supreme principles. An account of the faculties is given in rational as well as in empirical psychology. Nonetheless, Wolff considered the empirical psychological analysis more fundamental than rational psychology, since he regarded it more trustworthy and "capable of providing the principles from which rational psychology would derive its demonstrative arguments".[141] Moreover, Wolff maintains that *"Psychologia empirica principia tradit Logicae"* (empirical psychology provides principles for logic).[142]

If we now turn to Kant's works, the differences between his and Wolff's theory (and Baumgarten's as well, which made Kant aware of Wolff's dichotomy between rational and empirical psychology) are evident. Kant still maintains the distinction between *psychologia rationalis* and *psychologia empirica* within the discipline of psychology. At the same time, Kant redefines the Wolffian terminology and, moreover, he makes both these disciplines objects of severe criticism.

First of all, Kant rethinks the relation between the fields of psychology and logic. This is due to the way in which Kant more generally relates the empirical and the scientific levels of pure philosophy. In Wolff's texts, in particular in the *Discursus praeliminaris*, we read that the empirical aspect constitutes an important component of the scientific knowledge of pure philosophy, since a certain level of scientific knowledge can be secured only through the reference to experience.[143]

---

140 See M. CAMPO, *Cristiano Wolff e il razionalismo precritico*, cit., p. 308.
141 G. HATFIELD, *The Natural and the Normative*, cit., p. 73.
142 C. WOLFF, *Psychologia empirica, methodo scientifica pertractata*, § 9 of the *Prolegomena*.
143 CHRISTIAN WOLFF, *Discursus praeliminaris de philosophia in genere*, in *Philosophia rationalis sive logica methodo scientifica pertractata, et ad usum scientiarum atque vitae aptata. Praemittitur discursus praeliminaris de philosophia in genere*, Frankfurt/Leipzig 1740, § 12. Cf. the new edition of the Latin text of Wolff's *Discursus*, comprehensive of a German translation: CHRISTIAN WOLFF, *Einleitende Abhandlung über Philosophie im allgemeinen*, edited, translated and with an introduction by GÜNTER GAWLICK – LOTHAR KREIMENDAHL, Stuttgart/Bad Cannstatt, Frommann-Holzboog 2006. Cf. in particular § 89 (passim): "Quod si in Logica omnia demonstranda, petenda sunt principia ex Ontologia atque Psychologia. [...] Patet igitur porro, quod ad demostrationes regularum Logicae petenda sint ex Psychologia principia"; § 111

In Kant, instead, apriority must characterize the principles of pure philosophy, which do not have to refer back to experience. This also effects the ban of empirical psychology from all pure *a priori* cognition, i.e. from metaphysics, which, as presented in its narrower sense in the Architectonic chapter, is defined as that philosophy which is to present all pure *a priori* cognition in a systematic unity.[144] Pure philosophy contains the *a priori* principles for applied philosophy, to which empirical psychology also belongs. From this, it follows that "empirical psychology must be entirely banned from metaphysics, and is already excluded by the idea of it".[145] However, Kant's strategy is not limited to separating the spheres of transcendental logic and that of psychology, since this delimitation and the ban of psychology from logic also have other important consequences. Maybe the most important one is that Kant finds room for a new discipline, which is similar to empirical psychology but, at the same time, quite different from it in its foundation. This discipline is anthropology. As Kant notes, but also "in accord with the customary scholastic usage", one must concede empirical psychology "a little place in metaphysics", as "a long-accepted foreigner", just until "it can establish its own domicile in a complete anthropology (the pendant to the empirical doctrine of nature)".[146]

(passim): "Quoniam ex Psychologia demonstrationum principia cum in Logica atque arte inveniendi, tum etiam in philosophia practica petuntur [...]".

144 See KrV, A 845/B 873 – AA 03: 546.08–11, CpR p. 698: "Alles reine Erkenntniß *a priori* macht also Vermöge des besonderen Erkenntnißvermögens, darin es allein seinen Sitz haben kann, eine besondere Einheit aus, und Metaphysik ist diejenige Philosophie, welche jene Erkenntniß in dieser systematischen Einheit darstellen soll". On this topic cf. also GABRIEL RIVERO, "Zur Entstehung der Anthropologie Kants. Die Anthropologie in Hinblick auf den kantischen Metaphysikbegriff der 69er und 70er Jahre", in *Methodus. Revista Internacional de Filosofía Moderna/An International Journal for Modern Philosophy*, (forthcoming).

145 See KrV, A 848/B 876 – AA 03: 548.17–19, CpR p. 698: "empirische Psychologie [muß] aus der Metaphysik gänzlich verbannt sein, und ist schon durch die Idee derselben davon gänzlich ausgeschlossen".

146 See KrV, A 848–9/B 876–7 – AA 03: 548.19–21,24–28, CpR p. 698: "Gleichwohl wird man ihr [=empirische Psychologie] nach dem Schulgebrauch doch noch immer (obzwar nur als Episode) ein Plätzchen darin verstatten müssen [...]. Es ist also bloß ein so lange aufgenommener Fremdling, dem man auf einige Zeit einen Aufenthalt vergönnt, bis er in einer ausführlichen Anthropologie (dem Pendant zu der empirischen Naturlehre) seine eigene Behausung wird beziehen können". For an analysis of the passage and the related topic, cf. for instance RICCARDO MARTINELLI, "Ein 'so lange aufgenommener Fremdling'. Kant und die Entwicklung der Psychologie", in CINZIA FERRINI (ed.), *Eredità kantiane (1804–2004). Questioni emergenti e problemi irrisolti*, Napoli, Bibliopolis 2004, pp. 333–355.

The distinction and development of Kant's idea of anthropology from the discipline of empirical psychology deserve a very close look. I dedicate the following chapter, chapter 3, to these topics.[147]

In the remainder of the present chapter, I limit myself to analyzing what transcendental psychology (as a psychological discipline within the boundaries of pure philosophy) consists in, if we try to understand this discipline from the standpoint of the aforementioned passage, where Kant says that some space can be reserved to psychology only outside transcendental philosophy and this space can be dedicated only to the empirical part of psychology (in terms of anthropology).

2.4 Kitcher's Kantian Transcendental Psychology

The theoretical proposal regarding the presence of a transcendental psychology in the context of Kant's pure philosophy is famously advanced, among others, by Patricia Kitcher in a series of works that try to read Kant's first *Critique* in the light of contemporary philosophical approaches in cognitive sciences.[148] Kitcher's attempt comes after a long period during which anti-psychologistic ap-

---

147 For the moment, it might be sufficient to quote some works, which have been quite influential in the discussion dedicated to these topics (and which I will discuss in chapter 3 below): NORBERT HINSKE, "Kants Idee der Anthropologie", in HEINRICH ROMBACH (ed.), *Die Frage nach dem Menschen. Aufriß einer Philosophischen Anthropologie. Festschrift für Max Müller zum 60. Geburtstag*, Freiburg i.Br./München, Alber 1966, pp. 410–427; NORBERT HINSKE, "Wolffs empirische Psychologie und Kants pragmatische Anthropologie. Zur Diskussion über die Anfänge der Anthropologie im 18. Jahrhundert", in NORBERT HINSKE (ed.), *Die Bestimmung des Menschen*, thematic volume of *Aufklärung*, 11/1 (1996), pp. 97–107; REINHARD BRANDT – WERNER STARK, "Einleitung", AA 25 (*Kant's Vorlesungen über Anthropologie*), pp. VII-CLI, and also REINHARD BRANDT, "Kants pragmatische Anthropologie: Die Vorlesung", *Allgemeine Zeitschrift für Philosophie*, 19 (1994), pp. 41–49; cf., in addition, TH. STURM, *Kant und die Wissenschaften vom Menschen*, cit.; HEINER F. KLEMME, "Immanuel Kant", in EIKE BOHLKEN – CHRISTIAN THEIS (eds.), *Handbuch Anthropologie. Der Mensch zwischen Natur, Kultur und Technik*, Stuttgart/Weimar, J. B. Metzler 2009, pp. 11–16; RICCARDO MARTINELLI, "Antropologia", in STEFANO BESOLI ET AL. (eds.), *L'universo kantiano*, cit., pp. 13–52.
148 Cf. in particular P. KITCHER, *Kant's Transcendental Psychology*, cit., and, more recently, P. KITCHER, *Kant's Thinker*, cit. Among the supporters of transcendental psychology has to be remembered, for instance, Ralf Meerbote, who notes that "Kant's transcendental psychology, often maligned, is a cognitive psychology. More specifically, it is a faculty psychology which speaks of capacities and abilities of various sorts which are needed for empirical cognition. The exercise of such capacities and abilities typically consists in mental actions of several types. An activity-characterization of cognitive mental life is the indispensable core element of transcendental psychology" – cf. RALF MEERBOTE, "Kant's Functionalism", cit., p. 161.

proaches were predominant in epistemological studies of the mind and, more generally, in epistemology as a whole.[149]

As the most obvious example of this predominance, Kitcher quotes Gilbert Ryle's case and notes further that philosophy of mind has been strongly anti-psychologistic in its approaches from the 1950s to the 1980s.[150]

In this connection, the case of Strawson also has to be emphasized. He clearly aims to remove psychology from Kant's philosophy and, in this way, defines the entire theory of transcendental psychology as "one of the aberrations into which Kant's explanatory model inevitably led him".[151] Other strong criticisms come from behaviourism.[152] However, in the latter half of the twentieth century behaviourism registered a decrease in importance, since psychologists "have realized that they cannot even explain behaviour without appealing to the cognitive processes that lie behind it".[153]

Even though Kitcher is aware of many commentaries that negate the possibility of Kant having a transcendental psychology, she is also confident in the renaissance we are seeing in psychologistic epistemology and she is convinced that a "careful look at Kant's efforts to provide an abstract description of the constitution of a mind capable of knowledge" is required.[154]

In this way, Kitcher aims to take part to the current debates on psychologistic epistemology and aims to do so by arguing against an anti-psychologistic and for a transcendental psychological reading of Kant's first *Critique*.

To the question "Is Kant doing psychology despite himself?", she answers affirmatively: "I think so, but the issue is controversial".[155]

---

149 See P. KITCHER, *Kant's Transcendental Psychology*, cit., p. 8: "Before the twentieth century, most epistemology was psychologist. [...] Frege attacked psychologism directly only in philosophy of mathematics and in logic. He made these areas central to philosophy, however, through his influence on Russell, Wittgenstein, and Carnap. The three founders of analytic philosophy established logic, philosophy of mathematics – and Fregean philosophy of language – as paradigms of the philosophical enterprise. This model has been so dominant that even recent philosophy of mind has been largely antipsychologistic!".
150 See G. RYLE, *The Concept of the Mind*, cit.
151 P. F. STRAWSON, *The Bounds of Sense*, cit., p. 32.
152 See P. KITCHER, *Kant's Transcendental Psychology*, cit., p. 10, and JOHN B. WATSON, "Psychology as the Behaviorist Views It", in *Psychological Review*, 20 (1913), pp. 158–177.
153 See P. KITCHER, *Kant's Transcendental Psychology*, cit., p. 10.
154 PATRICIA KITCHER, "Kant's Transcendental Psychology", in GERHARD FUNKE (ed.), *Akten des Siebenten Internationalen Kant-Kongresses. Kurfürstliches Schloß zu Mainz 1990* (volume II.1: Sektionsbeiträge. Sektionen A – F), Bonn, Bouvier 1991, pp. 215–225, here in particular p. 224.
155 See P. KITCHER, "Discovering the Forms of Intuition", cit., p. 214. For a clarification of the terms implicated here, see DANIEL C. DENNETT, "Artificial Intelligence as Philosophy and as

We might then ask why this reading is controversial and Kitcher herself answers that, when Kant talks about what is required for a mental task, he is "doing 'transcendental psychology'. The terminology seems apt, because Kant is doing a kind of psychology and because it fits nicely with his characterization of various faculties as 'transcendental'".[156]

This is the aim of Kitcher's interpretive proposal: to show how it is possible to describe Kant's discussion of the faculties as a matter of both transcendental philosophy and psychology at the same time.

In order to explain how the two fields can converge, the first and maybe more difficult problem to be solved has to do with the fact that only two possible meanings of the word psychology are left to readers, if we take seriously Kant's words on this discipline, as we have seen in section 2.3 above. According to the first meaning, psychology denotes the study of the phenomenal self; in this case it cannot be a transcendental discipline but only an empirical discipline. If, however, according to the second meaning, psychology denotes the study of the noumenal self, then it turns out that this discipline is impossible from Kant's point of view, since the noumenal self is unknowable by definition.[157]

However, apart from these two meanings of "psychology", Kitcher believes that a third one can be found, since psychology could also be regarded as the discipline dedicated to the "I" of apperception. As she says, "the two official selves of the *Critique* are joined by a third self, who turns out to be its central character, the 'I' of apperception, or the thinking self"; in this way, transcendental psychology is possible as a discipline in Kant's philosophy and, in particular, as "the psychology of the thinking, or better, knowing, self".[158] Kitcher aims to find a kind of psychology, which corresponds neither to applied logic, for instance, nor, in turn, to empirical psychology: she rather believes that transcendental psychology has its own argumentative procedures.

According to Kitcher, the evidence for these assessments is to be found in the Deduction, where Kant engaged "in transcendental psychology to determine the prerequisites of cognition [and,] on the subjective side, to determine what properties thinking beings must have in order to perform cognitive tasks".[159] Kitcher explains that these prerequisites help the interpreters to understand how "the

Psychology", in IDEM, *Brainstorms*, Cambridge (Mass.), Bradford Books, 1978, pp. 109–126 and ROBERT CUMMINS, "Functional Analysis", in *The Journal of Philosophy*, 72 (1975), pp. 741–765.
156 See P. KITCHER, "Discovering the Forms of Intuition", cit., here in particular p. 214.
157 Cf. P. KITCHER, *Kant's Transcendental Psychology*, cit., p. 21. For a different account, cf. Ameriks' proposal (note 54 above).
158 P. KITCHER, *Kant's Transcendental Psychology*, cit., p. 22.
159 P. KITCHER, *Kant's Transcendental Psychology*, cit., p. 190.

states of thinking beings must be synthetically connected or connectible" and, at the same time, she guards against a mistake that might follow from these considerations, i.e. that of "believing that this type of analysis of the abstract properties or faculties required for cognition provides information about what sort of thing a thinking being is".[160] She warns that, even though the analysis of the faculties which are required in cognition is essential, we must not forget that "Kant realizes clearly that they furnish no serious clues about what the soul is like".[161] Her analysis is particularly clear and helpful in this case: she does not confuse the epistemological and the ontological levels and remarks that "an abstract analysis of the faculties required for a particular cognitive task cannot *by itself* determine the constitution of the faculty that performs the task".[162] As she rightly notes, we can only "move from abstract functional description to claims about particular mechanisms", since we are furnished only with "a functional decomposition of a *task* and further information about what kinds of mechanisms could perform the tasks, and what kinds of mechanisms are available in the brain".[163] Translating this into more Kantian terms, Kitcher argues:

> Kant approached concepts in terms of his general project of transcendental psychology: What must concepts be like, and what faculties must underlie them, for us to be capable of knowledge at all? I argue that his analyses of concepts, and of the faculty of reason, offer a novel suggestion about the kind of mental equipment that underlies concept use.[164]

Are we now able to answer the question concerning the actual nature of the discipline of "transcendental psychology"?

If we follow Kitcher's argumentation, we have to define this discipline as an essential way in which to study human cognition, in that it "seeks to determine the necessary and universal elements of human cognition, and so is of great interest to epistemology, and to cognitive sciences as well".[165] In more detail, however, Kitcher argues that transcendental psychology is not an epistemic analysis (which argues "that we must have a certain faculty *if* knowledge is to be possible") but is an "*analysis of empirical capacities*, which shows that our ability to perform very basic cognitive tasks demonstrates that we actually have one of the faculties noted in epistemic analyses".[166] While analyses of the first sort support

---

160 *Ibidem.*
161 P. KITCHER, *Kant's Transcendental Psychology*, cit., p. 191.
162 P. KITCHER, *Kant's Transcendental Psychology*, cit., note 18 p. 266.
163 *Ibidem.*
164 P. KITCHER, *Kant's Transcendental Psychology*, cit., p. 206.
165 P. KITCHER, "Kant's Transcendental Psychology", in GERHARD FUNKE, cit., p. 220.
166 P. KITCHER, "Kant's Transcendental Psychology", in GERHARD FUNKE, cit., p. 221.

normative assertions, transcendental psychology, as an analysis of empirical capacities, can "only establish the *existence* of faculties, or other mental equipment, specified in the normative argument".[167]

Kitcher's analysis goes even further: in her view, the faculties are also to be considered as "particular aspects of our common wisdom" which are "invariant across peoples and times".[168] They are neither sustained by a metaphysical uniformity nor is continuity of nature assumed in order to explain them. Rather, only what I described in the above section as a transcendental argument can give a detailed account of the faculties: Kant "tried to demonstrate philosophically important invariances throughout the body of human knowledge, by arguing that they reflect the ways in which anyone with our basic mental constitution will be capable of thinking".[169]

Some reflections on and criticisms of Kitcher's proposal are due here. First of all, the risk that derives from Kitcher's reference to "empirical analyses" has to be considered. This way, she aims to bind transcendental to empirical psychology, since it is in the first instance "experience that establishes the presence of a particular cognitive capacity".[170] Nonetheless, this operation is quite risky, since, as her argumentation proceeds, Kitcher's proposal comes closer and closer to empirical psychology and transcendental psychology ends up making "empirical assumptions about cognitive capacities; it has the same basic subject matter; it can guide empirical research",[171] even though "its driving concerns are epistemological" since it aims to "determine what the mind must contribute for various cognitive tasks to be possible".[172]

Eventually, the picture we get is that transcendental psychology belongs neither to philosophy nor to psychology but rather to both of them at the same time,

---

167 P. Kitcher, "Kant's Transcendental Psychology", in Gerhard Funke, cit., p. 222.

168 See Patricia Kitcher, "Kant's Dedicated Cognitivist System", in John-Christian Smith (ed.), *Historical Foundations of Cognitive Science*, Dordrecht, Kluwer 1990, pp. 189–209, here in particular p. 189.

169 See P. Kitcher, "Kant's Dedicated Cognitivist System", cit., p. 189.

170 See P. Kitcher, "Kant's Dedicated Cognitivist System", cit., p. 193.

171 P. Kitcher, *Kant's Transcendental Psychology*, cit., p. 26. The similarities between transcendental and empirical psychology are also underlined by Ralf Meerbote, who, in addition, distinguishes between the two subjects by appealing to the heterogeneity of the faculties they are dedicated to: the former one would represent a psychology of acts of cognitive synthesis, the latter a psychology of sensation and feeling. However, Meerbote notes that the distinction between these two kinds of psychology is "not as clear in Kant's hands as it ideally should have been", Ralf Meerbote, "Kant's Functionalism", cit., p. 165.

172 P. Kitcher, *Kant's Transcendental Psychology*, cit., p. 26.

since the process it analyses seems to be a psychological one but, nonetheless, by means of a closer study, it manifests itself as purely transcendental.[173]

In sum, Kitcher assumes that no reference to "psychology" is appropriate when we analyse the sources of intuitions in Kant's thought. Nonetheless she (1) approximates transcendental psychology to empirical psychology and, in addition, (2) she decides to call Kant's explicative method "transcendental psychology", even if she is aware of her imprecise use of this label.[174]

Are Kitcher's interpretive proposal and her terminological decision correct? I would say: no, she is not. She is incorrect to try and approximate Kant's transcendental study of the faculties to empirical psychology and, in this way, is incorrect to refer to a "weak psychologism"[175] as the foundation of Kant's pure philosophy. I believe this to be the case because the two fields of research, pure philosophy, on the one hand, and empirical psychology, on the other hand, have to be sharply distinguished from one another. Moreover, her terminological choice is incorrect, since the use of the term psychology is very misleading.[176] As Hatfield notes, one might denote Kitcher's strategy not as a psychological but rather, more correctly, as a philosophical strategy: this kind of investigation concerning the conditions for synthetic *a priori* knowledge belongs to the field of philosophy rather than to the psychological one. From this, it follows that "by examining and ruling out on conceptual grounds various candidate explications of the possibility of such knowledge, [...] Kant was right to call his investigation transcendental philosophy rather than "transcendental psychology"".[177]

---

173 Cf. P. KITCHER, "Discovering the Forms of Intuition", cit., pp. 220 – 221.

174 Even though Kitcher considers completely indifferent whether Kant's transcendental method be called "transcendental psychology" or "transcendental logic", she rather prefers the first solution as she finds it somehow less misleading than the latter. See P. KITCHER, *Kant's Transcendental Psychology*, cit., p. 26.

175 P. KITCHER, *Kant's Transcendental Psychology*, cit., p. 9: "Kant's epistemology is clearly weakly psychologistic".

176 Even before Kitcher's proposal, many critics, and also philosophers such as Husserl, noted that such a discipline is still psychology, after all, even if a "transcendental" one. See EDMUND HUSSERL, *Logische Untersuchungen. Erster Teil: Prolegomena zur reinen Logik*, Halle, Max Niemeyer 1900; English translation: *Logical Investigations. Vol. I: Prolegomena to Pure Logic*, translated by JOHN N. FINDLAY, edited by DERMOT MORAN with a preface by MICHAEL DUMMETT, New York, Humanities Press, 1970, p. 172: "For even a transcendental psychology is a psychology". It is also noteworthy that the reference to a "transcendental psychology" is uncommon in Kant's texts and is related (for instance in MPölitz, AA 28: 263) to rational psychology. Cf. PAOLA RUMORE, "La concezione kantiana della psicologia razionale", in S. BACIN ET AL. (eds.), *Kant and Philosophy in a Cosmopolitan Sense*, cit., volume 4, pp. 459 – 472.

177 G. HATFIELD, "Empirical, Rational, and Transcendental Psychology", cit. p. 215.

Similarly, Angelica Nuzzo, proposing a new thesis on the relation between mind and body in her recent book on "transcendental embodiment", attacks the interpretive proposal of transcendental psychology.[178]

Nuzzo starts by noting that "recently, especially in the Anglo-American literature, 'transcendental psychology' has been revived and has come to indicate, in particular, Kant's theory in the transcendental deduction. The expression is meant to characterize an allegedly Kantian psychology and to establish the relation between Kant and, alternatively, philosophy of mind or contemporary cognitive psychology".[179] In contrast to this reading, Nuzzo remarks that Kant's transcendental aesthetic gives the reasons why there is only room for transcendental logic and not for transcendental psychology in critical philosophy.[180] Nuzzo is also against a psychologistic interpretation of Kant's transcendental logic and, after dismissing the possibility of transcendental psychology, she notes that, with it, not the complete study of the faculties is dismissed but, on the contrary, new room should be found for these topics, in order to replace the traditional discipline of psychology "with (1) transcendental philosophy and (2) an anthropology resulting from the principles laid out by his [=Kant's] transcendental philosophy".[181]

Both of the points made by Nuzzo deserve further analysis. According to the first one, the discipline of transcendental philosophy is defined as "a theory of the *a priori* conditions under which cognitive 'experience' is possible for us": Nuzzo notes that "neither materialism nor pneumatology, neither physiology nor (traditional) psychology, but only transcendental philosophy can provide an account of human experience".[182] The objective of the critical enterprise is,

---

178 ANGELICA NUZZO, *Ideal Embodiment. Kant's Theory of Sensibility*, Bloomington/Indianapolis, Indiana University Press 2008.

179 A. NUZZO, *Ideal Embodiment*, cit., p. 331–332, note 3. Apart from Kitcher, Nuzzo quotes scholars who try to deal with some particular form of Kantian psychology. See in particular HANSGEORG HOPPE, *Synthesis bei Kant*, Berlin/New York, De Gruyter 1983; the already quoted A. BROOK, *Kant and the Mind*, cit.; RICHARD E. AQUILA, *Matter and Mind: A Study of Kant's Transcendental Deduction*, Bloomington, Indiana University Press 1989.

180 Cf. A. NUZZO, *Ideal Embodiment*, cit., pp. 47–49.

181 A. NUZZO, *Ideal Embodiment*, cit., note 4 p. 332.

182 A. NUZZO, *Ideal Embodiment*, cit., pp. 48–49. This account of transcendental philosophy helps the author argue for her new interpretative perspective, according to which "transcendental philosophy should rather be understood as the unified (neither empirical nor metaphysical) perspective of both a theory of embodied mind and a theory of the ideality of embodiment", *ibidem*, p. 24. On the sustainability of this reading, see my review of Nuzzo's book in *Kant-Studien*, volume 102/3 (2011), pp. 401–403. For another interpretive proposal concerning Kant's theory of the embodiment of reason, cf. SUSAN MELD SHELL, *The Embodiment of Reason: Kant on Spirit, Generation and Community*, Chicago, University of Chicago Press 1996.

thus, that of searching for and achieving necessary and universal conditions of experience in general: "in order for experience to be possible (experience of one-self as well as objects in general) the two dimensions of sensibility and under-standing must be taken into account as necessary and universal conditions".[183]

We might thus ask: what does Kant's critical enterprise have in common with a particular form of anthropology? Introducing this second point, Nuzzo aims to furnish an alternative to psychology, "to avoid the Scylla and Charybdis of pneumatology and materialism": the alternative is an "anthropology of inner sense, i.e., a cognition of our thinking self *in life*".[184]

In contrast to Nuzzo's suggestion of focusing on the "embodiment" of Kant's transcendental theory, I propose to take into consideration an alternative way to study the faculties in the context of Kant's pure philosophy by suggesting that Kant's system of the faculties of the human mind is a critical investigation dedicated to the knowing, willing, and feeling human being.

2.5 The Mind and Its Faculties in Contemporary Kant Scholarship: Some Concluding Remarks

In this second chapter, my aim was that of illustrating some readings of Kant's theory of the faculties in contemporary scholarship on philosophy and cognitive science.

In order to do so, I first drew my attention to two anti-psychologistic readings of Kant's account of the mental field, i.e. Brook's functionalist reading of Kant's model of the mind and Hatfield's interpretive proposal concerning Kant's faculty-innatism. In this way, I tried to show how these two accounts complete each other.

Eventually, after a brief overview of the distinction between rational and empirical psychology, I considered Kitcher's proposal regarding Kant's transcendental psychology in order to shed light on some of the weaknesses of her interpretive assessments.

This overview of the contemporary debate on Kant's account of the faculties-endowed-mind serves as an introduction to my analysis concerning Kant's theory of human mental faculties. I propose that Kant's theory of human mental faculties is a critical philosophical corpus of studies that deal with the cognizing, willing, and feeling being. To this analysis I dedicate the following chapter of my work.

---

183 A. Nuzzo, *Ideal Embodiment*, cit., p. 49.
184 See A. Nuzzo, *Ideal Embodiment*, cit., p. 47 and KU § 89, AA 05: 461.04–06.

Chapter 3
Anthropology and Kant's Study of the Faculties of the Human Mind

In the previous chapter, I tried to explain why transcendental psychology is not able to answer the question of where the analysis of the faculties belongs within Kant's critical enterprise.

Given that this analysis occurs in the context of pure philosophy, it has to be noted nonetheless that Kant also deals with the faculties by means of empirical investigations and within the limits of a discipline that is derived from the traditional discipline of empirical psychology and which, according to Kant's account in the Architectonic chapter of the first *Critique*, gives way and fades into pragmatic anthropology.[185]

In his lectures on anthropology Kant does not aim to dedicate any room to the ideas concerning pure philosophy that he develops in the *Critiques*. However, from Kant's *Anthropology from a Pragmatic Point of View* (1798) and the notes of Kant's lectures on anthropology collected in volume 25 of the Academy Edition of his works, we get the impression that the acquaintance with Kant's anthropological themes also plays a role in getting a more precise picture of Kant's critical investigation.

Kant wants the difference between the fields of pragmatic anthropology and pure philosophy to remain fairly clear, since anthropology, in contrast to the pure philosophical procedure in the *Critiques*, addresses the empirical level of research and starts from merely empirical cognition. Nonetheless, the delimitation of the fields of pure philosophy and anthropology, as part of the empirical sphere of Kant's system, is nuanced at times even though pragmatic anthropology, as it is analysed in Kant's lectures (AA 25) and in the 1798 text (AA 7), still remains a strongly empirically characterized discipline.

---

185 Among others, cf. S. B. KIM, *Die Entstehung der Kantischen Anthropologie*, cit., p. 74: "Nachdem das Unterfragen der rationalen Psychologie als zum Scheitern verurteilt erwiesen wurde, fährt Kant fort, bleibe nur eine Möglichkeit übrig, nämlich die Seele anhand der Erfahrung zu erforschen [KrV, A 382]. Die empirische Psychologie soll sich mit dem psychologischen Ich als Mannigfaltigkeit des Bewußtseins befassen. [...] Was uns durch innere Beobachtung gegeben wird, ist deswegen kein rein psychologisches Phänomen (im ursprünglichen Sinne), sondern immer mit dem Einfluß des Körpers verbunden. Inwieweit eine innere Erfahrung wirklich innerlich, d.h. rein aus der Seele geschöpft worden ist, wissen wir nicht. Ebenso ist nicht zu bestimmen, 'wie viel bei Handlungen der Seele dem Körper zukomme. An Stelle einer reinen Psychologie bekäme man so nur eine Anthropologie [Metaphysik K 2, AA 28: 740]'".

The aim of this chapter is that of delineating Kant's system of the faculties of the human mind as well as their classification as a model pertaining to a corpus of studies, which Kant analyzes both (a) in his anthropological studies and (b) within his pure philosophical project of critical investigation. In this respect, my aim is to stress that the occasional intersection of these two investigations, that is the pure critical philosophical one and the anthropological one, does not imply an identity of the two disciplines, and the analysis of the three *Critiques* that regards the three fundamental faculties of the human mind will be presented as pertaining neither to a particular anthropological discipline nor to transcendental psychology.

After presenting a brief historical overview of the relationship between pragmatic anthropology and empirical psychology, I discuss the significance of the pragmatic discipline of anthropology and the way it differs from Kant's pure philosophy. I then argue against the possibility of speaking of a "transcendental anthropology" in the context of Kant's work and I deal with some intersections between Kant's critical philosophy and his analysis of the fundamental faculties of the human mind and the discipline of anthropology. In order to illustrate these intersections, I consider some passages concerning Kant's account of sensibility and focus on Kant's classification of the faculties in the 1798 *Anthropology*. In this way, I introduce Kant's classification of the faculties of the human mind as it occurs in the three *Critiques* and in the *Metaphysics of Morals*. To this last topic I will dedicate the next chapter of my study, that is chapter 4 below.

My analysis consists in an attempt to give an alternative to some interpretive proposals in contemporary Kant scholarship, according to which Kant's studies of the faculties of the human mind belong either to some sort of anthropology or to the discipline of transcendental psychology (as analyzed in chapter 2 above).

3.1 A Brief Historical Overview of the Relation between Pragmatic Anthropology and Empirical Psychology

Kant taught his anthropology course twenty-four times over his whole life, from 1772/1773 until his retirement in 1796.[186]

---

186 See EMIL ARNOLDT, "Möglichst vollständiges Verzeichnis aller von Kant gehaltenen oder auch nur angekündigten Vorlesungen nebst darauf bezüglichen Notizen und Bemerkungen", in DERS., *Gesammelte Schriften*, edited by OTTO SCHÖNDÖRFFER, vol. 5 (*Kritische Exkurse im Gebiete der Kantforschung – Teil 2*), Berlin, B. Cassirer 1909, pp. 173–344. The students' notes of Kant's lectures on anthropology are to be found in AA 25 (*Kant's Vorlesungen über Anthropologie*). For an introductory overview on the significance of these lectures see REINHARD BRANDT – WERNER

The manual that Kant uses as a basis for his lectures is Baumgarten's *Psychologia empirica*. Baumgarten's text on empirical psychology is part of his *Metaphysica*.[187] This treatise is reprinted in its 4th edition of 1757 in the Academy Edition of Kant's works. While almost the whole of Baumgarten's *Metaphysica* – the three *Praefationes* and §§ 1–503 (AA 17: 05–130), as well as §§ 700–100 (AA 07: 130–226) – is published in the 17th volume of the Academy Edition as a companion to Kant's *Reflexionen* on metaphysics, the remaining §§ 504–699, which constitute the *Psychologia empirica*, have been reprinted as a companion to Kant's *Reflexionen* on anthropology in the 15th volume of the Academy Edition (AA 15: 05–54).[188]

We can get a picture of Kant's empirical investigation of the faculties both from the students' lectures notes of Kant's anthropology courses and the 1798 published book *Anthropology from a Pragmatic Point of View*.[189] This analysis is much different from the one developed in the context of Kant's critical works. I argue that Kant pursues a different plan when he analyses the faculties of the human mind as the basic mental functions in the context of pure philosophy. This more fundamental project is not confined to a "scholastic" answer to the question: "what is the human being?" and constitutes a link between Kant's pragmatic anthropology as an empirical discipline and the three *Critiques*. Thus,

---

STARK, "Einleitung", AA 25 (*Kant's Vorlesungen über Anthropologie*), pp. VII-CLI, and also REINHARD BRANDT, "Kants pragmatische Anthropologie: Die Vorlesung", in *Allgemeine Zeitschrift für Philosophie* 19 (1994), pp. 41–49.

187 *Metaphysica per Alexandrum Gottlieb Baumgarten, Professorem Philosophiae*. 1st edition: Halae Magdeburgicae – Impensis C. H. Hemmerde 1739. Edition II: 1743; Edition III: 1750; Edition IV: 1757; Edition V: 1763; Edition VI: 1768; Edition VII: 1779.

188 On the history of the publication in AA, cf. GÜNTER GAWLICK – LOTHAR KREIMENDAHL, "Einleitung", in ALEXANDER GOTTLIEB BAUMGARTEN, *Metaphysica – Metaphysik. Historisch-kritische Ausgabe*. Übersetzt, eingeleitet und herausgegeben von GÜNTER GAWLICK – LOTHAR KREIMENDAHL, Stuttgart/Bad Cannstatt, frommann-holzboog 2011, pp. IX-LXXXVII (here in particular pp. LXXX-LXXXIII, "Der Abdruck der *Metaphysica* innerhalb der Akademie-Ausgabe von *Kant's gesammelte(n) Schriften* sowie weitere Editionen auf Datenträgern und im Internet"). Apart from the quoted German translation of Baumgarten's *Metaphysica*, I shall also cite the historical translation by G. F. Meier: ALEXANDER GOTTLIEB BAUMGARTEN, *Metaphysik*, übersetzt von GEORG FRIEDRICH MEIER, Halle im Magdeburgischen, verlegt von Carl Hermann Hemmerde, 1766; Edition II, neue vermehrte Auflage: Halle 1783). A classical commentary to Baumgarten's *Metaphysica* is MARIO CASULA, *La metafisica di A. G. Baumgarten*, Milano, Mursia 1973.

189 Cf. AA 15 (*Reflexionen zur Anthropologie*), AA 25 (*Vorlesungen über Anthropologie*) and *Anthropologie in pragmatischer Hinsicht*, AA 07: 117–334. Interestingly enough, the first time Kant gives a lecture on the topic, he was not obliged to do it: Cf. R. BRANDT, "Kants pragmatische Anthropologie: Die Vorlesung", cit., p. 41: "Im Wintersemester [1772/1773] hielt Kant die Vorlesung über Anthropologie oder empirische Psychologie zum ersten Mal; es war ein Privatkolleg, zu dem er als neu ernannter Ordinarius für Logik und Metaphysik nicht verpflichtet war".

as I will argue, in contrast to pragmatic anthropology, this more fundamental project can be regarded as a study devoted to human nature in general and, in this way, it is very similar to other philosophical treatises on human nature that have been written in the century of the *Aufklärung*.

In consideration of the partial coincidence of some topics analysed by Kant in his pragmatic anthropology, on the one hand, and the ones pertaining to his system of the faculties of the human mind as proposed in the three *Critiques*, on the other hand, a brief reference to Kant's pragmatic anthropology and its historical development from the traditional discipline of empirical psychology is necessary.

Even though some well-researched works have already been dedicated to the partial convergence of empirical psychology and pragmatic anthropology and I do not aim to give any new contribution to this conceptual history debate, I find it nonetheless useful to provide the reader who is unfamiliar with these topics with a concise overview of the themes.[190]

An important stage in the evolution of Kant's anthropology and its relation to the traditional doctrine of empirical psychology is to be found in the Architectonic chapter of the first *Critique* and refers to the ban of empirical psychology from all pure *a priori* cognition. Once Kant has declared this, the search for a space for a new science within his philosophical system follows and anthropology comes into question in the context of the analysis dedicated to pure philosophy.[191] During this time, Kant concedes empirical psychology "a little place in metaphysics", as "a long-accepted foreigner", just until "it can establish its own

---

190 I will not, however, deal with the history and development of the concept and the discipline of anthropology in the eighteenth century. For a first overview, see e.g. ODO MARQUARD, "Zur Geschichte des philosophischen Begriffs 'Anthropologie' seit dem Ende des achtzehnten Jahrhunderts", in *Collegium philosophicum. Studien Joachim Ritter zum 60. Geburtstag*, Basel-Stuttgart, Schwabe 1965, pp. 209–239 and MARETA LINDEN, *Untersuchungen zum Anthropologiebegriff des 18. Jahrhunderts*, Frankfurt a. M., Lang 1976. For what regards Kant's development of the idea of anthropology, one of the most complete sources is TH. STURM, *Kant und die Wissenschaften vom Menschen*, cit. For an introduction to the problem of the difference between Kant's pragmatic anthropology and other anthropological studies in the Eighteenth Century Germany, like Platner's [ERNST PLATNER, *Anthropologie für Aerzte und Weltweise*, Leipzig 1772], cf. R. MARTINELLI, "Antropologia", in S. BESOLI ET AL. (eds.), *L'universo kantiano*, cit., pp. 13–52. For other introductory works on Kant's anthropology (among others, the ones by Hinske and Brandt), cf. chapter 2 above.

191 See above, in particular section 2.3, *Some Brief Observations on the Distinction between Rational and Empirical Psychology and the Supposed Place of Transcendental Psychology*.

domicile in a complete anthropology (the pendant to the empirical doctrine of nature)".[192]

A more detailed exposition of the difference between empirical psychology and anthropology is to be found in the text dedicated to the progress which "metaphysics made in Germany since the time of Leibniz and Wolff", an essay written by Kant for a contest publicly announced in 1790 by the Royal Academy of Sciences in Berlin, which Kant neither ever completed, nor published during his lifetime and which was instead edited afterwards by F. Th. Rink in 1804.[193] Even though the *Fortschritte* are not reliable sources for the history of the development of Kant's point of view on anthropology, it is nonetheless noteworthy to remember what Kant writes in this text. In section 2 of the manuscript, Kant deals with "what has been accomplished, since the age of Leibniz and Wolff, in regard to the objects of metaphysics, i.e. its final goals" and there he distinguishes between rational psychology and empirical psychology. In rational psychology "nothing else but the concept of the immateriality of a thinking substance, that of its change, and that of the identity of person" would represent "*a priori* principles"; "all else" constitutes "empirical psychology, or rather mere anthropology, since it can be shown that it is impossible for us to know whether and what the life-principle in man (the soul) is able to do in thinking without the body, and everything here amounts only to empirical knowledge,

---

192 See KrV, A 848 – 9/B 876 – 7 – AA 03: 548.19 – 21,24 – 28, CpR p. 698. For the precise evolution of anthropology from empirical psychology in the first *Critique*, cf. S. B. KIM, *Die Entstehung der Kantischen Anthropologie*, cit., p. 64: "Was die empirische Psychologie betrifft, hat Kant wenigstens folgende Ansätze entwickelt, die für die Absicht dieser Untersuchung von großer Bedeutung sind. Erstens beschäftige sich die empirische Psychologie (offenbar als die einzig mögliche Psychologie) mit der Seele als Erscheinung des inneren Sinnes und nicht als Substanz [KrV, A 347, 382; Prol. A 141]. Zweitens habe sie nichts 'apodiktisch zu lehren' [KrV, B 406]. Drittens soll die empirische Seelenlehre die Beobachtung zu Hilfe nehmen, nämlich die Beobachtung 'über das Spiel unserer Gedanken und die daraus zu schöpfende Naturgesetze des denkenden Selbst' [KrV, B 405]. Zuletzt geht es um die vorläufige Einordnung der empirischen Psychologie in die Metaphysik [KrV, B 876 f.]. Vorläufig ist diese Einordnung, weil die empirische Psychologie schließlich doch in einer ausführlichen Anthropologie ihren Platz finden soll".

193 "Immanuel Kant über die von der Königl. Akademie der Wissenschaften zu Berlin für das Jahr 1791 ausgesetzte Preisfrage: Welches sind die wirklichen Fortschritte, die die Metaphysik seit Leibnitzens und Wolf's Zeiten in Deutschland gemacht hat, herausgegeben von D. Friedrich Theodor Rink. Königsberg, 1804 bey Goebbels und Unzer" (= FM), AA 20: 253 – 312 ("Beylagen": AA 20: 313 – 332). In addition, cf. also "Lose Blätter zu den Fortschritten der Metaphysik", AA 20: 333 – 351; "Ergänzungen zu den Fortschritten der Metaphysik", AA 23: 469 – 476. On this text and its editorial history, see HERMAN J. DE VLEESCHAUWER, "La Cinderella dans l'ouvre Kantienne", in GERHARD FUNKE (ed.), *Akten des 4. Internationalen Kant-Kongresses, Mainz 6 – 10 April 1974*, Teil I, Berlin/New York, de Gruyter 1975, pp. 304 – 306.

i.e. to a knowledge that we can acquire in life, and hence in a combination of soul with body, and is thus unsuited to the final goal of metaphysics, of attempting to pass over from the sensible to the super-sensible".[194]

This passage illustrates how Kant thinks that it would be better to substitute the discipline of empirical psychology by the one of anthropology, insofar as he states that the life-principle may only be investigated through the reference to empirical knowledge of a human being's own body. Another passage concerning empirical psychology and anthropology occurs in section three of the writing on the progress of metaphysics dedicated to the "Resolution of the Problem Posed by the Academy", where Kant speaks of the "Supposed Theoretico-Dogmatic Advance of Metaphysics in Psychology, in the Epoch of Leibniz and Wolff".[195] At the very beginning of the section, Kant uses clear words to describe how the discipline of anthropology is derived from psychology: "psychology, for human understanding, is nothing more, and can become nothing more, than anthropology, i.e., than a knowledge of man, albeit restricted to the condition: so far as he is acquainted with himself as object of inner sense".[196] Also, many passages from the notes of Kant's lectures on anthropology (AA 25) testify to the change from empirical psychology to Kant's anthropology this way – but one might still ask: how does this conversion occur? Beyond doubt, the simplicity of this passage depends on the closeness and similarity of anthropology's distinguishing features to traditional empirical psychology, as Kant understands it in the philosophical tradition. In particular two names should be mentioned here in order to give an accurate picture of the discipline of empirical psychology at Kant's time: Christian Wolff and Alexander Gottlieb Baumgarten. The derivation of anthropology from *psychologia empirica* is well attested in contemporary Kant scholarship and comes after the neglected older proposal advanced by Erdmann,

---

194 FM, AA 20: 286. 05–20; *Progress-Metaphysics* p. 376.

195 "Vermeynter theoretisch-dogmatischer Fortschritt der Metaphysik in der Psychologie, während der *Leibnitz-Wolfischen* Epoche", FM, AA 20: 308.04–309.35, *Progress-Metaphysics* pp. 395–396. The other two sections are dedicated to the resolution (*Auflösung der academischen Aufgabe*) of other two problems, i.e. the progress of metaphysics in regard to the Super-sensible (Section 1: *Was für Fortschritte kann die Metaphysik in Ansehung des Übersinnlichen thun?*) and the advances in moral theology (Section 2: *Vermeinte theoretisch-dogmatische Fortschritte in der moralischen Theologie während der Leibniz-Wolffischen Epoche*).

196 "Die Psychologie ist für menschliche Einsichten nichts mehr, und kann auch nichts mehr werden, als Anthropologie, d.i. als Kenntniß des Menschen, nur auf die Bedingung eingeschränkt, sofern er sich als Gegenstand des inneren Sinnes kennet", FM, AA 20: 308.07–10, *Progress-Metaphysics* p. 395.

according to which Kant develops anthropology from the disciplines of moral and political geography.[197]

As mentioned, Kant uses Baumgarten's *Metaphysics* as a companion for the lectures on metaphysics and anthropology. Nevertheless, Wolff's importance for Kant's anthropology and, more generally, for the origin of the discipline of anthropology in empirical psychology should not be underestimated. Hinske, for instance, proposes that Wolff can even be defined as the father of *psychologia empirica*.[198] Furthermore, what is not always taken into consideration is the fact that Wolff also plays some role in Kant's thought on anthropology. In fact, even though Kant's first hand reception of Wolff's writings on psychology cannot be taken for granted,[199] signs of Kant's closeness to Wolff rather than Baumgarten, in some particular passages, have been pointed out by some scholars.[200]

---

197 For Erdmann's interpretive proposal, cf. *Reflexionen Kants zur kritischen Philosophie. Aus Kants handschriftlichen Aufzeichnungen herausgegeben von* BENNO ERDMANN, Neudruck der Ausgabe Leipzig 1882/1884, neu herausgegeben und mit einer Einleitung versehen von NORBERT HINSKE, Stuttgart/Bad Cannstatt, frommann-holzboog 1992, here in particular p. 78 [1ˢᵗ edition, Volume I, p. 48, Erdmann's introduction "Zur Entwicklungsgeschichte von Kants Anthropologie"], where Erdmann speaks about an "Entwicklung der Anthropologie [...] aus den Disciplinen der moralischen und politischen Geographie". Against this hypothesis, see the introduction by NORBERT HINSKE in the quoted new edition of Erdmann's *Reflections*, NORBERT HINSKE, "Einleitung zur Neuausgabe", pp. 8–19, in Erdmann's *Reflexionen*, cit., § II (*Erdmanns Herleitung der Anthropologie aus der Geographie*), in particular p. 16: "Nicht die physische Geographie, sondern die empirische Psychologie, eine der erfolgreichsten Neuerungen Christian Wolffs und seiner Schule, hat bei der Ausbildung von Kants Anthropologie Pate gestanden".
198 Cf. N. HINSKE, "Wolffs empirische Psychologie und Kants pragmatische Anthropologie", cit., p. 97, where Hinske speaks of Wolff as "der Urheber einer der erfolgreichsten empirischen Wissenschaften überhaupt, der Urheber der empirischen Psychologie. Bereits in Wolffs deutscher Metaphysik findet sich ein erster Entwurf [...] dieser neuen empirischen Wissenschaft. Das eigentliche Hauptwerk aber ist die *Psychologia empirica* von 1732, ein genialer Entwurf, verbunden freilich mit allen Problemen, die solche 'neuen Würfe' nicht selten mit sich bringen".
199 N. HINSKE, "Wolffs empirische Psychologie und Kants pragmatische Anthropologie", cit., pp. 99–100, argues for the sustainability of this thesis: "Was das Verhältnis von Kant zu Wolff angeht, so gibt es noch ein zusätzliches Problem, nämlich die Frage, ob Kant Wolffs *Psychologia empirica* überhaupt gelesen oder ob er nicht vielmehr nur aus zweiter Hand geschöpft hat. [...] Allem Vermuten nach würde eine detaillierte quellengeschichtliche Untersuchung der Texte zu dem Ergebnis führen, daß Kant zunächst durchaus Wolff selber gelesen hat und nicht nur Baumgarten". For arguments against this thesis, cf. JEAN ÉCOLE, "De la conaissance qu'avait Kant de la métaphysique wolffienne, ou Kant avait-il lu les ouverages métaphysiques de Wolff?", in *Archiv für Geschichte der Philosophie*, 73 (1991), pp. 261–273.
200 Cf. R. BRANDT – W. STARK, "Einleitung", AA 25, cit., who testify the initial influence and later abandonment of Wolff's position. See in particular pp. VIII and X: "Die gegen Baumgarten vollzogene Emanzipation der empirischen Psychologie aus dem Metaphysik-Verbund erfolgt nach dem vorliegenden Material in zwei Schritten. Einmal ist sie vor allem didaktisch motiviert

Nonetheless, as this discussion would take us too far from our original argument, I only wish to mention that the impact of Baumgarten's writings on Kant's anthropology should be taken as the predominant one.[201] If we observe the structure of Kant's lectures published in volume 25 of the Academy edition, on the one hand, and the structure of Kant's 1798 *Anthropology*, on the other hand, Kant's debt to Baumgarten becomes apparent immediately. In particular, this is the case if we take into account the first part of both the lectures and the book. There Kant deals with the three basic faculties of the human mind and the analysis of the cognitive faculty, that of the feeling of pleasure and displeasure and that of the appetitive faculty, starting from the organisation of the material in a triadic structure, as Baumgarten similarly does in the *Psychologia empirica* and, in an even more obvious way, in the *Ethica*.[202] Something different happens

---

und geht in einigen der von Kant geäußerten Gedanken offensichtlich auf Christian Wolffs (1679–1754) *Ausführliche Nachricht von seinen eigenen Schriften* zurück. [...] Der zweite Schritt wird durch die Dissertation *De mundi sensibilis atque intelligibilis forma et principiis* von 1770 erzwungen. In ihr wird Wolffs gleitender Übergang von der sinnlichen zur intellektuellen (und damit nach ihm von der empirischen zur apriorischen) Erkenntnis scharf kritisiert". Cf. also REINHARD BRANDT, *Kritischer Kommentar zu Kants Anthropologie in pragmatischer Hinsicht (1789)*, Hamburg, Meiner 1999 (from now on quoted as *Kommentar*), pp. 10–11.

201 Some useful comments on the topic are R. BRANDT, *Kommentar*, cit., p. 15: "Gemäß den Vorlesungsnachschriften entsteht das Anthropologie-Kolleg 1772 aus der Baumgartenschen empirischen Psychologie; sie ist also eine originär theoretische Disziplin, wenn auch mit praktischer Wichtigkeit. Der Ursprung der Anthropologie ist die empirische Psychologie"; R. BRANDT – W. STARK, "Einleitung", AA 25, cit., pp. VII-VII: "Mit [der Anthropologie] wollte Kant keineswegs eine Grundlagendisziplin bzw. Vorübung für alles Praktische und eine Kenntnis der Welt entwickeln, sondern eine theoretische empirische Psychologie, Anthropologie oder auch 'Naturerkenntniß des Menschen', eine 'Erkenntniß aus Beobachtung und Erfahrung' (AA XXV, Philippi p. 1). Diese nicht praktische, sondern spekulative Ausrichtung entspricht der dem Kolleg zugrunde gelegten Schrift, Alexander Gottlieb Baumgartens (1714–1762) *Metaphysica* (4. Auflage von 1757). Aus ihr wird die "Psychologia empirica" als eine besondere Disziplin ausgegrenzt und in kritischen Kommentaren mit bestimmten Erweiterungen, aber ohne ausdrückliche Änderung der inhaltlichen Zielsetzung vorgetragen"; NORBERT HINSKE, "La psicologia empirica di Wolff e l'antropologia pragmatica di Kant. La fondazione di una nuova scienza empirica e le sue complicazioni", in GIUSEPPE CACCIATORE – VANNA GESSA-KUROTSCHKA – HANS POSER – MANUELA SANNA (eds.), *La filosofia pratica tra metafisica e antropologia nell'età di Wolff e Vico/ Praktische Philosophie im Spannungsfeld von Metaphysik und Anthropologie bei Wolff und Vico*, Napoli, Alfredo Guida Editore 1999, pp. 207–224, here in particular p. 209: "Kant ha chiaramente inteso la psicologia empirica come una sorta di antropologia, cioè come un'antropologia che non ha ancora trovato se stessa [AA 28: 670; AA 29: 757]".

202 R. BRANDT – W. STARK, "Einleitung", AA 25, cit., pp. XXIV-XXV: "Betrachtet man die Struktur der Anthropologie-Vorlesung im ganzen, so ergibt sich eine große Konstanz von den frühesten Nachschriften bis hin zur Buchpublikation von 1798. Kant folgt in lockerer Form im Bereich des (ab der Mitte der siebziger Jahre so bezeichneten) I. Teils den Ausführungen von

in the second part of the lectures and in the second section of the first part of the 1798 published book, which Kant dedicates to his original thoughts and observations, in particular the ones concerning feeling.[203]

But if we stop considering the common characteristics and start looking at the differences between anthropology and empirical psychology, certainly one aspect is particularly striking, that is the alternative place that Kant reserves for the discipline of anthropology within the system of philosophy (at least in 1765/1766): in contrast to the traditional picture, the latter precedes all other disciplines in metaphysics (rather than following them, as empirical psychology does in Baumgarten's model).[204] However, and maybe even more noteworthy, we can notice at once Kant's wish to keep investigating the topics which empirical psychology traditionally dealt with, but which he now aims to examine through theoretical means alternative to the tradition and with a different philosophical goal.[205] In the following sections, my aim is exactly that of analysing

---

Baumgarten in der "Psychologia empirica" seiner Metaphysica (1739(1); von Kant benutzt 1757 (4)). Er ordnet schon in der ersten Vorlesung von 1772/73 das Material deutlicher als Baumgarten nach der Reihenfolge von Erkenntnisvermögen, Gefühl der Lust und Unlust ('voluptas' und 'taedium') und dem Begehrungsvermögen. [...] Die triadische Gliederung von Erkennen, Fühlen und Begehren konnte Kant zwar nicht in völliger Klarheit in der empirischen Psychologie von Baumgarten finden, wohl aber in dessen *Ethica*". Cf. further note 1 p. XXVI: "Die *Ethica philosophica*, die 1740, 1751 und 1763 erschien, erörtert im Bereich der Pflichten gegen sich selbst zuerst die 'cura intellectus' (§§ 221–225), sodann die 'cura voluptatis et taedii' (§§ 226–234) und danach die 'cura facultatis appetitivae' (§§ 235–241) (abgedruckt AA 27: 792–798)".

203 R. BRANDT – W. STARK, "Einleitung", AA 25, cit., p. XXVII: "Mit der Erweiterung der Anthropologie über die Seelenvermögen hinaus (zum späteren Teil II) scheint Kant die Vorlage der Baumgartenschen *Metaphysik* gänzlich zu verlassen und auf seine eigenen *Beobachtungen über das Gefühl des Schönen und Erhabenen* (1764) zurückzugreifen".

204 N. HINSKE, "Kants Idee der Anthropologie", cit., p. 412: "In seiner *Nachricht von der Einrichtung seiner Vorlesungen in dem Winterhalbenjahre 1765–1766* [...] berichtet Kant von gewissen Unterstellungen, die er innerhalb dieser [= Baumgartens] Metaphysik vorgenommen habe; aus den jüngst veröffentlichten Vorlesungsnachschriften Herders läßt sich schließen, daß Kant dieselben schon vor dieser 'Nachricht' ein paar Jahre lang stillschweigend praktiziert hat. Das Auffälligste und für die Zeitgenossen gewiß Revolutionäre der neuen 'Einrichtung' besteht darin, daß die empirische Psychologie an den Anfang der Metaphysik rückt: 'Ich fange demnach nach einer kleinen Einleitung von der empirischen Psychologie an, welche eigentlich die metaphysische Erfahrungswissenschaft vom Menschen ist' (A 9)". Cf. in addition PAUL MENZER, *Kants Lehre von der Entwicklung in Natur und Geschichte*, Berlin 1911, p. 149: "Die Metaphysik halte in sich 1. Anthropologie, 2. Physik, 3. Ontologie, 4. Ursprung aller Dinge, Gott und die Welt, also Theologie".

205 N. HINSKE, "Wolffs empirische Psychologie und Kants pragmatische Anthropologie", cit., p. 98: "Kant [konnte] seine eigene pragmatische Anthropologie als eine Fortsetzung der empirischen Psychologie mit anderen Mitteln verstehen". But cf. also THOMAS STURM, "Kant on

this new contribution of Kant's anthropology and the features, which neatly distinguish this discipline from empirical psychology.

3.2 Anthropology as a Pragmatic Discipline

In order to identify the aim of the discipline of anthropology as Kant presents it in the 1798 published book, we need to understand the meaning of the two central words in its title: "pragmatic" and "anthropology".

In the preface to the book, Kant defines anthropology as "the doctrine of knowledge of the human being, systematically formulated"; this discipline might be regarded from two distinct points of view: a physiological and a pragmatic one.[206] As for the first standpoint, Kant says that "physiological knowledge of the human being concerns the investigation of what *nature* makes of the human being"; as for the second point, he assesses that pragmatic knowledge concerns the "investigation of what *he* [the human being] as a free-acting being makes of himself, or can and should make of himself".[207] In other words, in contrast to physiological anthropology, which aims to shed light on the human being as an object or a product *of* nature *in* natural world, pragmatic anthropology focuses on the human being as a being who is free and capable of giving himself his own ends. The pragmatic aspect of the discipline of anthropology consists in providing the students with some *knowledge of the world* (*Weltkenntnis*), which Kant defines here as the knowledge that has to be useful not merely at school but rather for life.[208]

Empirical Psychology: How Not to Investigate the Human Mind", in ERIC WATKINS (ed.), *Kant and the Sciences*, Oxford/New York, Oxford University Press 2001, pp. 163–184.

206 See Anth, AA 07: 119.09–11: "Eine Lehre von der Kenntniß des Menschen, systematisch abgefaßt (Anthropologie), kann es entweder in physiologischer oder in pragmatischer Hinsicht sein", *Anthropology*, p. 231.

207 See Anth, AA 07: 119.11–14: "Die physiologische Menschenkenntniß geht auf die Erforschung dessen, was die Natur aus dem Menschen macht, die pragmatische auf das, was er als freihandelndes Wesen aus sich selber macht, oder machen kann und soll", *Anthropology* p. 231. This distinction is well analysed, also with reference to the contemporary discussion, by G. HATFIELD, "Kant and Empirical Psychology in the 18th Century", cit., p. 423.

208 It suffices to refer here only to this one meaning of "pragmatic". However, it ought to be noted that ALLEN W. WOOD, in his article "Kant and the Problem of Human Nature", in BRIAN W. JACOBS – PATRICK P. KAIN (eds.), *Essays on Kant's Anthropology*, Cambridge/New York, Cambridge University Press 2003, pp. 38–59, distinguishes between four distinct senses of "pragmatic" (see in particular pp. 40–42). For an introduction on Kant's concept of *Weltkenntnis* in relation to "pragmatic reason", cf. FRIEDRICH KAULBACH, "Weltorientierung, Weltkenntnis und pragmatische Vernunft bei Kant", in FRIEDRICH KAULBACH – JOACHIM RITTER (eds.), *Kritik und*

Two different remarks are due here. The first one concerns the concept of "world" (*Welt*). Kant takes this concept into consideration in several passages in the context of his theoretical philosophy – maybe most notably in the antinomies of pure reason, where he deals with the "First Conflict of the Transcendental Ideas".[209] However, instead of analysing here the many meanings of the word *Welt* in Kant's philosophy, I confine myself to a quotation of a passage from the students' notes of Kant's lectures on anthropology from 1775/76 and 1777/78, where we read an explanation of how anthropology constitutes a *Weltkenntnis*. Here Kant affirms that the world, regarded as the "object of outer sense", corresponds to "nature", while the world considered as the "object of the inner sense" is the human being himself.[210] In this text, Kant clearly identifies one meaning of the word *Welt* (world) with one meaning of "human being".[211]

Moreover, the knowledge of the world (*Weltkenntnis*) has pragmatic relevance: the knowledge of the world as practical knowledge is not merely scholarly knowledge but, rather, practical knowledge, which is helpful in life.[212]

Metaphysik. Studien. Heinz Heimsoeth zum achtzigsten Geburtstag, Berlin, de Gruyter 1966, pp. 60–75.

209 See A 426 ff./B 454 ff., AA 03: 294 ff.: "Die Welt hat einen Anfang in der Zeit und ist dem Raume nach auch in Grenzen eingeschlossen / Die Welt hat keinen Anfang und keine Grenzen im Raume, sondern ist sowohl in Ansehung der Zeit als des Raums unendlich", CpR pp. 470 ff.

210 See *Die Vorlesung des Wintersemesters 1775/76 aufgrund der Nachschrift Friedländer 3.3 (Ms 400), Friedländer 2 (Ms 399) und Prieger*, AA 25: 469.17–19: "Die Welt als ein Gegenstand des äußeren Sinnes ist Natur, die Welt als ein Gegenstand des inneren Sinnes ist der Mensch"; Die Vorlesung des Wintersemesters 1777/78 aufgrund der Nachschrift Pillau], AA 25: 733.25–26: "Zur Welt nehmen wir. 1) Die Natur, 2) Die Menschen". In this respect, cf. also N. HINSKE, "Kants Idee der Anthropologie", cit., who makes use of Kant's *Menschenkunde* [FRIEDRICH CHRISTAN STARKE, i.e.: JOHANN ADAM BERGK, (ed.), *Immanuel Kant's Menschenkunde oder philosophische Anthropologie. Nach handschriftlichen Vorlesungen herausgegeben*, Quedlinburg/Leipzig 1831; 2. edition 1838 / reprint: Olms 1976 – quoted also in the following as *Menschenkunde*) in order to explain the concept of "world" in terms of "human being": "Die philosophische Anthropologie bezweckt Weltkenntnis. [...] Dennoch meint Weltkenntnis für Kant vornehmlich Menschenkenntnis: 'Der Mensch kennt die Welt' heißt 'er kennt den Menschen in allen Ständen. Weltkenntniß im gewöhnlichen Verstande heißt Kenntniß des Menschen' (*Menschenkunde*, p. 2)" (pp. 422–423).

211 For the distinction between many different of the word *Welt*, cf. NESTORE PIRILLO, *L'uomo di mondo fra morale e ceto. Kant e le trasformazioni del Moderno*, Bologna, Il Mulino 1987, and CLAUDIO CESA, "Natura e mondo in Kant", in LUCA FONNESU (ed.), *Etica e mondo in Kant*, Bologna, Il Mulino 2008, pp. 17–34.

212 For the difference between the concept of "pragmatic" and the *Weltbegriff* as practical concept, see CLAUDIO LA ROCCA, "La saggezza e l'unità pratica della filosofia kantiana", in CLAUDIO LA ROCCA, *Soggetto e mondo. Studi su Kant*, Venezia, Marsilio 2003, pp. 217–242; JÜRGEN STOLZENBERG, "'Was jedermann notwendig interessiert'. Kants Weltbegriff der Philo-

Kant speaks of anthropological knowledge of the world (*Kentnis der Welt*) as practical knowledge already in a letter to Marcus Hertz from autumn 1773.[213] In this letter, we read for the first time about Kant's intention to use anthropology "to disclose the sources of all the [practical] sciences, the science of morality, of skill, of human intercourse, of the way to educate and govern human beings, and thus of everything that pertains the practical".[214] Moreover, in these lines, Kant refers to his undertaking concerning the preparations of "a preliminary study for the students out of this very pleasant study,[215] an analysis of the nature of skill (prudence) and even wisdom that, along with physical geography and distinct from all other learning, can be called knowledge of the world" and, with it, he introduces the more specific concept of "pragmatic" and relates it to knowledge of the world as practical knowledge.[216] In this passage knowledge of the world and its being practical are defined in particular on the basis of this knowledge providing something like rules of prudence. This very prudential connotation is often ascribed to the concept of pragmatic that is also in the students' notes of Kant's lectures on anthropology from 1775/76.[217] Finally, Kant identifies the

---

sophie", in HANS FEGER (ed.), *The Fate of Reason. Contemporary Understanding of Enlightenment*, Würzburg, Königshausen & Neumann 2013, pp. 171–179, but also TH. STURM, *Kant und die Wissenschaften vom Menschen*, cit., in particular pp. 291–302 and NORBERT HINSKE, *Kant als Herausforderung an die Gegenwart*, Freiburg/Munchen, Alber 1980, pp. 101 ff.

213 Cf. R. BRANDT, *Kommentar*, p. 63; cf. in particular Brief an Marcus Herz vom Herbst 1773, Br, AA 10: 143–146; *Correspondence*, pp. 139–141.

214 Br, AA 10: 145.29–32: "Die Absicht die ich habe ist durch dieselbe die Qvellen aller Wissenschaften die der Sitten der Geschiklichkeit des Umganges der Methode Menschen zu bilden u. zu regiren mithin alles Praktischen zu eröfnen", *Correspondence*, p. 141.

215 Kant refers here to the study dedicated to the observations of ordinary life, on the basis of which the auditors have the constant occasion to compare their ordinary experience with Kant's remarks – Br, AA 10: 145.36–37, 146.01–04: "Ich bin unabläßig so bey der Beobachtung selbst im gemeinen Leben daß meine | Zuhörer vom ersten Anfange bis zu Ende niemals eine trokene sondern durch den Anlaß den sie haben unaufhörlich ihre gewöhnliche Erfahrung mit meinen Bemerkungen zu vergleichen iederzeit eine unterhaltende Beschäftigung habe", *Correspondence* p. 141.

216 Br, AA 10: 146.04–09: "Ich arbeite in Zwischenzeiten daran, aus dieser in meinen Augen sehr angenehmen Beobachtungslehre eine Vorübung der Geschiklichkeit der Klugheit und selbst der Weisheit vor die academische Iugend zu machen welche nebst der physischen geographie von aller andern Unterweisung unterschieden ist und die Kentnis der Welt heissen kan", *Correspondence*, p. 141.

217 See for instance AA 25: 470.19–22 (Die Vorlesung des Wintersemesters 1775/76 aufgrund der Nachschrift Friedländer 3.3 (Ms 400), Friedländer 2 (Ms 399) und Prieger): "Also nicht speculativ sondern pragmatisch nach Regeln der Klugheit seine Kenntnis anzuwenden, wird der Mensch studirt, und das ist die Anthropologie". Cf. further from this text, AA 25: 471.29–30: "alle pragmatische Lehren sind Klugheits Lehren".

pragmatic field and the one of prudence again in the first *Critique* and in the *Groundwork*.[218]

All of these occurrences concur in showing Kant's initial tendency to explain the concept of "pragmatic" on the basis of its reference to rules of prudence.[219]

However, this is only one part of the story. In fact, firstly, Kant links the reference to the prudential field already in the first *Critique* to the sphere of the empirical, when he defines the concept of pragmatic. Here it is what we find in the Canon chapter: "The first [= the practical law from the motive of happiness – the pragmatic law (rule of prudence)] is grounded on empirical principles; for except by means of experience I can know neither which inclinations there are that would be satisfied nor what the natural causes are that could satisfy them".[220] Secondly, even if the reference to the prudential aspect of "pragmatic" can be considered more preponderant, it is nonetheless not the unique reference possibly linked to the concept of "pragmatic" even earlier in the 1770s. Evidence of it can be found in the text written by Kant on the occasion of the announcement of his lecture activity for the summer semester of 1775, known as *On the Different Races of Human Beings*.[221] In this writing, Kant describes anthropology in terms of a "useful academic instruction" and compares it to physical geography, defining both as "knowledge of the world". Kant further assesses that knowledge of the world serves "to procure the *pragmatic* element for all otherwise acquired

---

218 In the Canon chapter of KrV Kant calls pragmatic (rule of prudence) "the practical law from the motive of happiness"; see CpR p. 677; KrV, A806/B834 – AA 03: 523.27–28: "Das praktische Gesetz aus dem Bewegungsgrunde der Glückseligkeit nenne ich pragmatisch (Klugheitsregel)". In a similar way, in GMS Kant uses the word "pragmatisch" by referring to a moral-practical sense: he names as "pragmatic" those imperatives which belong to welfare (*Wohlfahrt*) and are, furthermore, linked to the concept of prudence (*Klugheit*). See GMS, AA 04. 416.15–29, 417.01–02, 32–37, *Groundwork* p. 69.

219 N. HINSKE, "Kants Idee der Anthropologie", cit., p. 424: "Die anfängliche Erklärung des Begriffs, die Kant gibt, geht von der Klugheit, und zwar von der 'Weltklugheit' aus". On the concept of prudence in Kant's philosophy cf. PIERRE AUBENQUE, *La prudence chez Aristote*, 3. éd. rev. et augm. d'un appendice sur *La prudence chez Kant*, Paris, Presses Univ. de France 1986 and CLEMENS SCHWAIGER, *Kategorische und andere Imperative. Zur Entwicklung von Kants praktischer Philosophie bis 1785*, Stuttgart/Bad Cannstatt, Frommann-Holzboog 1999.

220 A 806/B 834, AA 03: 523.33–35, 524.01–02: "Das erstere [= das praktische Gesetz aus dem Bewegungsgrunde der Glückseligkeit – das pragmatische Gesetz (Klugheitsregel)] gründet sich auf empirische Principien; denn anders als vermittelst der Erfahrung kann ich weder wissen, welche Neigungen dasind, die befriedigt werden wollen, noch welches die Naturursachen sind, die ihre Befriedigung bewirken können", CpR pp. 677–678.

221 *Von den verschiedenen Racen der Menschen zur Ankündigung der Vorlesungen der physischen Geographie im Sommerhalbjahr 1775* (= VvMR), AA 02: 427–443; "On the Different Races of Human Beings", pp. 82–97.

sciences and skills, by means of which they become useful not merely for *school* but rather for *life* and through which the accomplished apprentice is introduced to the stage of his destiny, namely, the world".[222] Here, as already before, the adjective "pragmatic" is primarily used as an antonym for "scholastic", "theoretical", so that the field of the pragmatic does not correspond to the more specific one of the prudential.[223]

In the text published in 1798 Kant still refers to pragmatic anthropology "as a *knowledge of the world*, which must come after our *schooling*"; however, in addition, he notes that this discipline is actually "not yet called *pragmatic* when it contains an extensive knowledge of *things* in the world, for example, animals, plants, and minerals from various lands and climates, but only when it contains knowledge of the human being as a *citizen of the world*".[224]

---

222 VvMR, AA 02: 443.14–19: "Diese Weltkenntniß ist es, welche dazu dient, allen sonst erworbenen Wissenschaften und Geschicklichkeiten das Pragmatische zu verschaffen, dadurch sie nicht bloß für die Schule, sondern für das Leben brauchbar werden, und wodurch der fertig gewordene Lehrling auf den Schauplatz seiner Bestimmung, nämlich in die Welt, eingeführt wird", Engl. transl. cit. p. 97. Cf. also Louden's introduction to *Anthropology*, p. 227–230. Later, Kant spoke about the necessity of acquiring a skill for the good use of sciences and theoretical cognitions many times in his lectures. Cf. for instance his lecture on anthropology (Die Vorlesung des Wintersemesters 1775/76 aufgrund der Nachschrift <u>Friedländer 3.3</u> (Ms 400), <u>Friedländer 2</u> (Ms 399) und Prieger), AA 25: 469.23–25: "Wer viel theoretische Kenntniße hat, der viel weiß, aber keine Geschicklichkeit hat, davon einen Gebrauch zu machen, der ist gelehrt für die Schule nicht aber für die Welt". For the distinction between pure theoretical and cosmopolitan skills and the description of the scholar who possesses only the first skills as a cyclops, see below the sections dedicated to these themes.
223 Cf. also N. Hinske, "Kants Idee der Anthropologie", cit., p. 424: "Kant gebraucht ihn [= den 'Begriff' des Pragmatischen …] als Gegenbegriff zu spekulativ (*Menschenkunde* 5) und theoretisch (*Anth.* B VIf.), zu scholastisch bzw. schulmäßig (*Menschenkunde* 5, Anweisung 1, *Hauptvorl.* 72) und nicht zuletzt auch zu physiologisch (*Anthr.* B IV)".
224 See Anth, AA 07: 120.01–06: "Eine solche Anthropologie, als Weltkenntniß, welche auf die Schule folgen muß, betrachtet, wird eigentlich alsdann noch nicht pragmatisch genannt, wenn sie ein ausgebreitetes Erkenntniß der Sachen in der Welt, z. B. der Thiere, Pflanzen und Mineralien in verschiedenen Ländern und Klimaten, sondern wenn sie Erkenntniß des Menschen als Weltbürgers enthält", *Anthropology* pp. 231–232. The same ideas occur often in the notes of Kant's lectures on anthropology. See, for instance, Kant's lectures of 1777/78 (Die Vorlesung des Wintersemesters 1777/78 aufgrund der Nachschrift <u>Pillau</u>), AA 25: 733.17–24: "Wir können diese Erkenntniß des Menschen auf eine zweifache Art betrachten. 1) Als eine Speculative. Da man blos in der Nachforschung der Wisbegierde dem Verstande ein Gnüge thut. 2) Als eine pragmatische die nicht auf weitere Erkenntniß geht, als in so fern wir davon einen ausgemachten Nutzen ziehen. Wenn sie pragmatisch abgehandelt wird; so ist sie eine Weltkenntniß und bildet einen Weltmann".

In this passage, the idea of a pragmatic teaching as a prudential one is not particularly strong, even though it still remains significant in the 1798 *Anthropology*. Instead, the idea of a discipline delivering an understanding of the human being as a citizen of the world is now rather influential. The fact that the human being needs to be instructed about the world means, on the one hand, that one has to be instructed about the environment in which one lives, but also, at the same time, that one needs to be instructed about oneself: a knowledge of the human being as citizen of the world corresponds to a knowledge useful for human orientation in the world. Even though it is not for the first time that Kant speaks about anthropology as a knowledge of the world, he now describes clearly the knowledge concerning the human being as a sort of reflective knowledge: the human being gets a knowledge concerning itself not exactly by looking at the others but, more essentially, by looking at itself, inside itself.[225]

This new talk of a closer look at the human being's interior must not be interpreted as Kant's attempt to establish pragmatic anthropology as a discipline of pure philosophy. In self-observation, the fact that the human being observes itself does not presuppose the universal validity of the assertions it makes concerning the way it, as human being, is constituted. On the contrary, the link between pragmatic anthropology and the empirical world remains unsolvable. In fact, pragmatic anthropology analyses the way in which human beings relate to each other, the way in which they approach and make use of things in the world, in order to render living together easier. In order to do this, pragmatic anthropology is based on experience; it is a *Beobachtungslehre*, a discipline based on observation.[226] Moreover, pragmatic anthropology can be regarded as a particular, specific, "local" anthropology.[227]

---

225 N. HINSKE, "Kants Idee der Anthropologie", cit., p. 424: "Eine ganz anders gelagerte Begriffserklärung aber gibt Kants Vorrede zu dem gedruckten Werk von 1798. Die pragmatische Anthropologie betrachtet den Menschen hier und nicht mehr – oder jedenfalls nicht mehr primär – in seinem Verhältnis zu anderen Menschen, sondern im Verhältnis zu sich selbst, und zwar zu sich selbst nicht so sehr in seiner faktischen Existenz, sondern vielmehr im Grundzug seines Seins".

226 As N. HINSKE, "Kants Idee der Anthropologie", cit., p. 414, most rightly notes: "Die philosophische Anthropologie ist – ebenso wie die empirische Psychologie – Erfahrungswissenschaft. Sie bildet in der allgemeinen Einteilung der Disziplinen keinen 'rationalen' oder apriorischen, sondern – als "Pendant zu der empirischen Naturlehre" (KrV, B 877) – einen 'empirischen Teil' der Philosophie (GMS B V, vgl. auch B VIIf. 'von allem, was nur empirisch sein mag und zur Anthropologie gehört'; vgl. auch MS, RL A 11 f.). Sie ist 'Beobachtungslehre' (X 146) und gewinnt ihre 'Regeln in den mannigfaltigen Erfahrungen, die wir an den Menschen bemerken' (*Menschenkunde* 5 f.)". But cf. also N. HINSKE, "Wolffs empirische Psychologie und Kants pragmatische Anthropologie", cit., pp. 103 – 104, and REINHARD BRANDT, "Beobachtun-

One of the similarities between pragmatic anthropology and the critical investigation is the fact that, in writing the three *Critiques*, as well as in writing the *Anthropology from a Pragmatic Point of View*, Kant follows the same intention, namely the one contained in the very idea of what Kant calls a "critique" (*Kritik*) and which is also at the bottom of the project of the Enlightenment (*Aufklärung*): this is the idea that the human being needs orientation in the world.

However, from this quest for orientation, it still does not follow that the entire critical philosophy is a sort of anthropology. In the context of pragmatic anthropology, Kant deals with a concept of orientation, which is directed to attain a better understanding of the way of practicing freedom, as we read, for instance, in the Preface of the 1798 published *Anthropology*. In the three *Critiques*, instead, Kant's aim is that of finding grounds and boundaries of knowledge and not primarily that of giving an orientation in the world. This notwithstanding, it has to be noted that the sort of knowledge we get from the *Critiques* serves as a precondition of an orientational knowledge, that is the one discussed in pragmatic anthropology. From this viewpoint, Kant's discussion on the human faculties in the *Critiques* can be neatly separated from the empirical field and can be taken to constitute the precondition of a project for the orientation of the human being in the world. The study of the three fundamental mental faculties and their classification in the context of Kant's critical investigation, which I will analyze in the following chapter, is guided by a general, rational vision of the human being and the three *Critiques* constitute altogether a treatise on human nature.

Still another point connects the three *Critiques* and the discipline of pragmatic anthropology, which is the cosmological meaning of philosophy. In order to focus on this problem, a closer reference to the already analysed pas-

---

gen zur Anthropologie bei Kant (und Hegel)", in FRANZ HESPE und BURKHARD TUSCHLING (eds.), *Psychologe und Anthropologie oder Philosophie des Geistes. Beiträge zu einer Hegel-Tagung in Marburg 1989*, Stuttgart/Bad Cannstatt, Frommann und Holzboog 1991, pp. 75–106.

227 Kant distinguishes a local and a general anthropological knowledge of the world in *Die Vorlesung des Wintersemesters 1777/78 aufgrund der Nachschrift Pillau*, AA 25: 734.03–11, where empirical knowledge of the world, that is the knowledge which the traders usually acquire, is defined as "local", in that it is "bound to a [determinate] place and time and does not furnish any rule for acting in common life. The one who gets to know the world through travel possesses only such a knowledge of the world itself, which, however, lasts some time, since, if the deportment at that place, where he has been, changes, his knowledge of it ceases in the same way" (AA 25: 734.04–11 (passim): "Eine Local Weltkenntniß die die Kaufleute haben, die auch empirisch genannt wird. [...] Die Locale [Weltkenntniß] ist an Ort und Zeit gebunden und giebt auch keine Regeln an die Hand im gemeinen Leben zu handeln. Der welcher die Welt durch Reisen kennen lern, hat nur diese Kenntniß von ihr, die aber auch einige Zeit dauert, denn wenn sich das Betragen an dem Ort wo er gewesen ist ändert, so hört auch seine Kenntniß davon auf").

sage from the writing on human races might be helpful, where Kant mentions *nature* and *the human being* as the subject matters of the disciplines of physical geography and anthropology. There, Kant proposes to consider the two fields not "with respect to the noteworthy details that their objects contain (physics and empirical psychology (*empirische Seelenlehre*)", but, rather, *cosmologically* (*kosmologisch*), i.e. "with respect to what we can note of the relation as a whole in which they stand and in which everyone takes his place".[228] The difference drawn by Kant between the traditional discipline of empirical psychology (called here *empirische Seelenlehre*) and the discipline of anthropology as knowledge of the world is not the only one that is very clearly drawn in the text. Moreover, and more importantly, Kant's reference to the word "cosmological" (*kosmologisch*) is noteworthy and central. This reference recalls the distinction between a scholastic and a worldly, cosmological concept of philosophy.

Such a distinction does not correspond to the one concerning scholastic knowledge and knowledge of the world, since the contexts where the two distinctions are introduced are different. While the pragmatic concept of knowledge of the world refers to the utility of scholastic teaching beyond the academic context and is not only addressed to the human being's world (itself and its environment), but also presupposes a knowledge of the human being's world through empirical observation, the characterization of the difference between a worldly and a scholastic concept of philosophy refers to the scopes of philosophical research. However, even though the two distinctions must not be juxtaposed, their similarities must be taken into consideration. In consideration of this point, a closer treatment of the distinction between a worldly and a scholastic concept of philosophy is now due.

3.3 Anthropology and the Worldly Concept of Philosophy

One of the clearest explanations of Kant's distinction between a worldly and a scholastic concept of philosophy comes from the *Architectonic* chapter of the first *Critique*. The passage in question follows Kant's definition of philosophy

---

228 VvMR, AA 02: 443.19–25: "Hier liegt ein zwiefaches Feld vor ihm, wovon er einen vorläufigen Abriß nöthig hat, um alle künftige Erfahrungen darin nach Regeln ordnen zu können: nämlich die Natur und der Mensch. Seine Stücke aber müssen darin kosmologisch erwogen werden, nämlich nicht nach demjenigen, was ihre Gegenstände im einzelnen Merkwürdiges enthalten (Physik und empirische Seelenlehre), sondern was ihr Verhältniß im Ganzen, worin sie stehen und darin ein jeder selbst seine Stelle einnimmt, uns anzumerken giebt"; "On the Different Races of Human Beings", p. 97.

as "the system of all philosophical cognition".[229] Kant states that "among all rational sciences (*a priori*), therefore, only mathematics can be learned, never philosophy (except historically); rather, as far as reason is concerned, we can at best only learn to philosophize".[230]

The worldly *and* the scholastic concepts of philosophy therefore refer to philosophy as the *a priori*, rational science, which cannot be learned, except historically. The consideration of these two concepts is introduced by Kant's observation that the philosophical analysis of his time has not been able to go beyond a mere scholastic conception of philosophical research: until the time he writes the first *Critique*, "the concept of philosophy has been only a scholastic concept, namely that of a system of cognition that is sought only as a science without having as its end anything more than the systematic unity of this knowledge, thus the logical perfection of cognition".[231] In other words, research has concentrated until that time only on the intrinsic aspects of philosophy itself and has not considered how such cognitions may be applied to the human being's life. In contrast to such self-referentiality, Kant deals with a "cosmopolitan concept (*conceptus cosmicus*)" of philosophy, in whose perspective "philosophy is the science of the relation of all cognition to the essential ends of human reason (*teleologia rationis humanae*)".[232] Kant assesses that it is essential to focus on and determine "what philosophy, in accordance with this cosmopolitan concept, prescribes for systematic unity from the standpoint of ends".[233] He further explains that "a cos-

---

229 KrV, A 838/B 866 – AA 03: 542.03: "Das System aller philosophischen Erkenntniß ist nur Philosophie", CpR p. 694.

230 KrV, A 837/B 865 – AA 03: 541.34–35, 542.01–02: "Man kann also unter allen Vernunftwissenschaften (*a priori*) nur allein Mathematik, niemals aber Philosophie (es sei denn historisch), sondern, was die Vernunft betrifft, höchstens nur philosophiren lernen", CpR p. 694.

231 KrV, A 838/B 866 – AA 542.19–23: "Bis dahin ist aber der Begriff von Philosophie nur ein Schulbegriff, nämlich von einem System der Erkenntniß, die nur als Wissenschaft gesucht wird, ohne etwas mehr als die systematische Einheit dieses Wissens, mithin die logische Vollkommenheit der Erkenntniß zum Zwecke zu haben", CpR p. 694.

232 Here the whole passage from KrV, A 838–839/B 866–867 – AA 03: 542.23–30: "Es giebt aber noch einen Weltbegriff (*conceptus cosmicus*), der dieser Benennung jederzeit zum Grunde gelegen hat, vornehmlich wenn man ihn gleichsam personificirte und in dem Ideal des Philosophen sich als ein Urbild vorstellte. In dieser Absicht ist Philosophie die Wissenschaft von der Beziehung aller Erkenntniß auf die wesentlichen Zwecke der menschlichen Vernunft (*teleologia rationis humanae*), und der Philosoph ist nicht ein Vernunftkünstler, sondern der Gesetzgeber der menschlichen Vernunft", CpR pp. 694–695.

233 KrV, A 839–840/B 867–868 – AA 03: 543.02–06: "da er [=der Philosoph] selbst doch nirgend, die Idee aber seiner Gesetzgebung allenthalben in jeder Menschenvernunft angetroffen wird, so wollen wir uns lediglich an der letzteren halten und näher bestimmen, was Philosophie

mopolitan concept [...] means one that concerns that which necessarily interests everyone".[234]

Philosophical research in the cosmopolitan sense is oriented towards achieving something different from a pure unity of all cognitions. This concept of philosophy aims at dealing with a connection of these cognitions with the human beings' ultimate ends, in contrast to the scholastic philosophy, which, *per se*, does not suffice to answer "existential" human questions. In this attempt of an answer, the cosmopolitan concept of philosophy links philosophical knowledge in its systematic unity to the human being's ends, in a teleology of human reason.

The distinction between a scholastic and a worldly concept of philosophy also occurs in the so-called *Jäsche Logic*, edited by Gottlob Benjamin Jäsche in 1800.[235]

Similarly as in the first *Critique*, here Kant also describes philosophy according to the scholastic concept as "the system of philosophical cognitions or of cognitions of reason from concepts", while, according to the worldly concept, philosophy is regarded as "the science of the final ends of human reason".[236] On the one hand, according to the scholastic concept, philosophy is presented as a science that "involves two things: first, a sufficient supply of cognitions

---

nach diesem Weltbegriffe für systematische Einheit aus dem Standpunkte der Zwecke vorschreibe", CpR p. 695.

234 KrV, A 839/B 867 – AA 03: 543.31–32: "Weltbegriff heißt hier derjenige, der das betrifft, was jedermann nothwendig interessirt", CpR p. 695.

235 Logik, AA 09: 01–150; *Jäsche Logic*, pp. 519–640. It has to be noted that the *Jäsche Logic* was been translated relatively quickly into English by JOHN RICHARDSON: EMMANUEL KANT, *Logic*, London, Simpkin & Marshall 1819; however, the translation is not quite accurate and several mistakes are to be noted (e. g. the translator refers to the editor of the German text calling him Gottlob Benjamin Fesche (!) – ibidem, p. IV in the *Preface*). For the publication of the German text in the Academy edition see NORBERT HINSKE, "Die Jäsche-Logik und ihr besonderes Schicksal im Rahmen der Akademie-Ausgabe", in REINHARD BRANDT – WERNER STARK (eds.), *Zustand und Zukunft der Akademie-Ausgabe von Immanuel Kants Gesammelten Schriften*, Sonderheft: *Kant-Studien*, 91 (2000), pp. 85–93.

236 Logik, AA 09: 23.30–33: "Philosophie ist also das System der philosophischen Erkenntnisse oder der Vernunfterkenntnisse aus Begriffen. Das ist der Schulbegriff von dieser Wissenschaft. Nach dem Weltbegriffe ist sie die Wissenschaft von den letzten Zwecken der menschlichen Vernunft", *Jäsche Logic* p. 537. The XI International Kant Congress, which took place in Pisa (May, 22–26, 2010), was dedicated to these topics (*Kant and Philosophy in a Cosmopolitan Sense*), so that the most recent interpretations of Kant's worldly concept of philosophy can be found in the publication of the conference papers: STEFANO BACIN – ALFREDO FERRARIN – CLAUDIO LA ROCCA – MARGIT RUFFING (eds.), *Kant and Philosophy in a Cosmopolitan Sense / Kant und die Philosophie in weltbürgerlicher Hinsicht. Akten des XI. Internationalen Kant-Kongresses*, Boston-New York, De Gruyter 2013.

of reason, and for the second thing, a systematic connection of these cognitions, or a combination of them in the idea of a whole";[237] on the other hand, according to the worldly concept (*in sensu cosmico*), philosophy is defined as "a science of the highest maxim for the use of our reason, insofar as we understand by a maxim the inner principle of choice among various ends. For philosophy in the latter sense is in fact the science of the relation of all cognition and of all use of reason to the ultimate end of human reason, to which, as the highest, all other ends are subordinated, and in which they must all unite to form a unity".[238]

In both cases Kant underlines the systematic unity of philosophy: on the one hand, in the scholastic concept, as a mere system of cognition; on the other hand, in the worldly, cosmopolitan concept, as this very system teleologically co-ordinated.

The picture we get from this passage is substantially the same as the one we get from the first *Critique*. However, later in the passage Kant further links the cosmopolitan concept of philosophy to the questions concerning the different fields of philosophy, as he conceives of it. Here are the four well-known questions from the *Jäsche Logic*:

> The field of philosophy in this cosmopolitan sense can be brought down to the following questions:
> 1. What can I know?
> 2. What ought I to do?
> 3. What may I hope?
> 4. What is the human being?

---

237 The passage goes on and Kant assesses that "not only does philosophy allow such strictly systematic connection, it is even the only science that has systematic connection in the most proper sense, and it gives systematic unity to all other sciences". Here is the whole passage from Logik, AA 09: 24.20–27: "Zur Philosophie nach dem Schulbegriffe gehören zwei Stücke: Erstlich ein zureichender Vorrath von Vernunfterkenntnissen, für's Andre: ein systematischer Zusammenhang dieser Erkenntnisse oder eine Verbindung derselben in der Idee eines Ganzen. Einen solchen streng systematischen Zusammenhang verstattet nicht nur die Philosophie, sondern sie ist sogar die einzige Wissenschaft, die im eigentlichsten Verstande einen systematischen Zusammenhang hat und allen andern Wissenschaften systematische Einheit giebt"; *Jäsche Logic* p. 537.

238 Logik, AA 09: 24.28–36: "Was aber Philosophie nach dem Weltbegriffe (*in sensu cosmico*) betrifft: so kann man sie auch eine Wissenschaft von der höchsten Maxime des Gebrauchs unserer Vernunft nennen, sofern man unter Maxime das innere Princip der Wahl unter verschiedenen Zwecken versteht. Denn Philosophie in der letztern Bedeutung ist ja die Wissenschaft der Beziehung alles Erkenntnisses und Vernunftgebrauchs auf den Endzweck der menschlichen Vernunft, dem, als dem obersten, alle andern Zwecke subordinirt sind und sich in ihm zur Einheit vereinigen müssen"; *Jäsche Logic* pp. 537–538.

Metaphysics answers the first question, morals the second, religion the third. Fundamentally, however, we could reckon all of this as anthropology, because the first three questions relate to the last one.[239]

In consideration of this passage it seems quite clear that Kant offers anthropology a domicile in the domain of philosophy in its cosmopolitan, worldly concept.

If we now compare the lines in question from the first *Critique* and the *Jäsche Logic*, we arrive at a remarkable result. Let me sum up: Kant assesses (in the *Jäsche Logic*) that (1) the question concerning the human being and the related study of anthropology is part of the field of philosophy in a cosmopolitan sense; he furthermore underlines (in the *Architectonic* chapter of the first *Critique*) that (2) the cosmopolitan concept of philosophy is part of the field of pure philosophy. From these considerations, it seems to follow that (3) anthropology, insofar as it is part of philosophy in its worldly, cosmopolitan concept, must also possess a proper domicile within the field of pure philosophy.

This impression seems to be confirmed by the reading of further passages.

For instance, in the so-called *Metaphysik L2*, Kant refers again to the four questions concerning the subject matter of philosophy.[240] The *Metaphysik L2* consists in the notes of Kant's lectures on metaphysics dedicated to the explan-

---

239 Logik, AA 09: 25.01–10: "Das Feld der Philosophie in dieser weltbürgerlichen Bedeutung läßt sich auf folgende Fragen bringen: 1) Was kann ich wissen? 2) Was soll ich thun? 3) Was darf ich hoffen? 4) Was ist der Mensch? Die erste Frage beantwortet die Metaphysik, die zweite die Moral, die dritte die Religion und die vierte die Anthropologie. Im Grunde könnte man aber alles dieses zur Anthropologie rechnen, weil sich die drei ersten Fragen auf die letzte beziehen"; *Jäsche Logic* (translation slightly modified) p. 538. The passage goes on with the analysis of the philosopher's tasks (Logik, AA 09: 25.11–26: "Der Philosoph muß also bestimmen können 1) die Quellen des menschlichen Wissens, 2) den Umfang des möglichen und nützlichen Gebrauchs alles Wissens, und endlich 3) die Grenzen der Vernunft. Das letztere ist das nöthigste aber auch das schwerste, um das sich aber der Philodox nicht bekümmert. Zu einem Philosophen gehören hauptsächlich zwei Dinge: 1) Cultur des Talents und der Geschicklichkeit, um sie zu allerlei Zwecken zu gebrauchen. 2) Fertigkeit im Gebrauch aller Mittel zu beliebigen Zwecken. Beides muß vereinigt sein; denn ohne Kenntnisse wird man nie ein Philosoph werden, aber nie werden auch Kenntnisse allein den Philosophen ausmachen, wofern nicht eine zweckmäßige Verbindung aller Erkenntnisse und Geschicklichkeiten zur Einheit hinzukommt und eine Einsicht in die Übereinstimmung derselben mit den höchsten Zwecken der menschlichen Vernunft", *Jäsche Logic* p. 538). It has also to be noted that Kant proposes the first three questions in the Canon chapter of the first *Critique* as he asks himself, "whether pure reason is also to be found in practical use" ("ob nämlich auch reine Vernunft im praktischen Gebrauche anzutreffen sei"). Cf. KrV, A 804–5/B 833–4, AA 03: 522.19–34, 523.01–24, CpR pp. 676–677.
240 Metaphysik L2, AA 28: 533.28–39,534.01–06; *Metaphysics L2*, p. 301.

ation of the specific field of ontology (*metaphysica generalis*), published in the Academy Edition (AA 28: 525–610).[241]

The passage concerning the four questions occurs exactly at the beginning of the *Metaphysik L2*, in the introductory section, dedicated to the concept of philosophy in general (*Von der Philosophie überhaupt*).[242] In this passage, in the same way as it happens in the first *Critique*, Kant refers to "two cognitions which are *a priori* but which nevertheless have many noteworthy differences". These cognitions are mathematics and philosophy, which, as "rational cognitions", are "cognitions from principles (*ex principiis*)" and "must thus be *a priori*".[243] In turn, the cognitions pertaining to philosophy are assessed to be of two sorts or, better said, can be used in regard to two different scopes: "in the scholastic sense (*in sensu scholastico*)", which refers to a "system of the philosophical rational cognitions from concepts" or "in the cosmopolitan sense (*in sensu cosmopolitico*)", which refers to "the science of the ultimate ends of human reason". This last concept "gives philosophy dignity, i.e. absolute worth, and it is that which alone has inner worth, and gives worth to all other sciences".[244] The themes and the distinction between a scholastic and a cosmopolitan concept of philosophy, as it already appears in the first *Critique*, occur in these pages exactly in the same terms. However, a section dedicated to the division of the philosophical disciplines (which depends on the four questions) follows now the analysis of the two concepts of philosophy. Here is the passage in its whole length:

> Philosophy in the scholastic concept is merely an instrument (*organon*) of skill. The philosopher in the cosmopolitan sense (*in sensu cosmopolitico*) is he who has maxims of the use of our reason for certain ends. The philosopher must be able to determine:

---

241 According to Erdmann, the manuscript of the *Metaphysik L1* has been written in 1774; in contrast to him, Arnoldt suggests that it comes from the years 1778/1779–1784/1785. The *Metaphysik L2* should instead have been composed between 1788 and 1790/1791. For the editorial history of these two texts see GERHARD LEHMANN, "Einleitung", in AA 28: 1338–1372.
242 Metaphysik L2, AA 28: 531.02.
243 Metaphysik L2, AA 28: 531.33–34, 532.01–02: "Wir haben von Vernunfterkenntnisse geredet, daß sie Erkenntnisse ex principiis sind, sie müssen also *a priori* seyn. Es gibt zwei Erkenntnisse, die *a priori* sind, dennoch aber viele namhafte Unterschiede haben: nämlich Mathematik und Philosophie", *Metaphysics L2*, p. 299.
244 Metaphysik L2, AA 28: 532.29–35: "In sensu scholastico ist also Philosophie das System der philosophischen Vernunfterkenntnisse aus Begriffen; in sensu cosmopolitico aber ist sie die Wissenschaft von den letzten Zwecken der menschlichen Vernunft. Das giebt der Philosophie Würde, d. i. absoluten Werth; und sie ist es, die nur allein innern Werth hat, und allen andern Wissenschaften Werth giebt"; *Metaphysics L2*, p. 300.

1. the sources of human knowledge;
2. the scope of its possible and advantageous use;
3. the boundaries of reason.

The field of philosophy in the cosmopolitan sense (*in sensu cosmopolitico*) can be brought down to the following questions:

1. What can I know? Metaphysics shows that;
2. What should I do? Moral philosophy shows that.
3. What may I hope? Religion teaches that.
4. What is the human being? Anthropology teaches that.

One could call everything anthropology, because the three former questions refer to the last one. Philosophy in the scholastic concept is skill, but philosophy in the eminent sense (*in sensu eminenti*) teaches what this is to serve.[245]

Finally, the four questions occur once again in a well-known letter to Carl Friedrich Stäudlin (1761–1826), professor of theology in Göttingen, dated 4th May 1793.[246] There, Kant mentions the plan, which he already a long time ago described, namely the examination of the field of pure philosophy, and he links this analysis to the solution of three problems: 1. What can I know? 2. What ought I to do? 3. What may I hope? As usual, Kant refers to three different fields of pure philosophy, within which the three questions have to be solved: 1. metaphysics, 2. moral philosophy, and 3. philosophy of religion.[247] However, Kant adds further that "a fourth question ought to follow, finally", that is: "What is the

---

245 Metaphysik L2, AA 28: 533.28–39,534.01–06: "Die Philosophie im Schulbegriff ist blos ein Organon der Geschichtlichkeit. Der Philosoph in sensu cosmopolitico ist der, der die Maxime des Gebrauchs unserer Vernunft zu gewissen Zwecken hat. Der Philosoph muß bestimmen können: 1. Die Quellen des menschlichen Wissens; 2. Den Umfang des möglichen und nützlichen Gebrauchs desselben; 3. Die Grenzen der Vernunft. Das Feld der Philosophie in sensu cosmopolitico läßt sich auf folgende Fragen zurückbringen: 1. Was kann ich wissen? Das zeigt die Metaphysik. 2. Was soll ich thun? Das zeigt die Moral. 3. Was darf ich hoffen? Das lehrt die Religion. 4. Was ist der Mensch? Das lehrt die Anthropologie. Man könnte alles Anthropologie nennen, weil sich die drei ersten Fragen auf die letzere beziehen. – Philosophie im Schulbegriff ist Geschichtlichkeit; wozu aber diese dient, lehrt die Philosophie in sensu eminenti", *Metaphysics L2*, p. 301.
246 Br, AA 11: 429–430, *Correspondence*, pp. 458–459.
247 Br, AA 11: 429. 10–14: "Mein schon seit geraumer Zeit gemachter Plan der mir obliegenden Bearbeitung des Feldes der reinen Philosophie ging auf die Auflösung der drei Aufgaben: 1) Was kann ich wissen? (Metaphysik) 2) Was soll ich thun? (Moral) 3) Was darf ich hoffen? (Religion)", *Correspondence*, p. 458. For an interpretative account of the first three questions see also REINHARD BRANDT, *D'Artagnan und die Urteilstafel. Über ein Ordnungsprinzip der Europäischen Kulturgeschichte 1, 2, 3/4*, new, revised edition: München, dtv 1998, pp. 195–196 (first edition: Stuttgart, Steiner 1991).

human being?". The answer to this question is given by "anthropology, as a subject on which [he has] lectured for over twenty years".[248]

After considering the occurrences of the four questions, we can conclude that anthropology as the discipline answering the question "What is the human being" has to do with the worldly concept of philosophy and is linked to determinate disciplines, which all pertain to the more general examination of pure philosophy.

This still does not mean that Kant aims to deal with a sort of "transcendental anthropology". In order to shed more light on this improbable eventuality, it might be helpful to examine some interpretive attempts concerning a sort of Kantian anthropology in the context of pure philosophy.

3.4 The Cyclops Metaphor and Kant's *anthropologia transscendentalis*

One of the obstacles in considering the possibility of an anthropological investigation in the context of Kant's pure philosophy is constituted by the fact that Kant refers only one time to a "transcendental anthropology", namely in *Reflection* 903 from the years 1776–1778.[249] There we read that, if the scholar is not to fall in the one-eyedness of sterile academic research, which is of no use in everyday life, he has to widen his study through the "self-knowledge of the under-

---

248 Br, AA 11: 429. 14–16: "welcher zuletzt die vierte folgen sollte: Was ist der Mensch? (Anthropologie; über die ich schon seit mehr als 20 Iahren jährlich ein Collegium gelesen habe)", *Correspondence*, p. 458 (translation slightly modified). On this last question cf. also R. Brandt, *Kommentar*, p. 180: "Kant bezieht sich an unserer Stelle vielleicht auf Charles Bonnet zurück, der im Analytischen Versuch über die Seelenkräfte (Übersetzung 1770–1771) leicht pathetisch am Anfang geschrieben hatte: 'Welches ist die Natur unsrer Seelenkräfte? Was haben sie für ein Wachsthum, was für verhältnißmäßige Gränzen, und wie hängen sie von einander ab? Auf welche Art geht der Mensch aus dem Zustande eines Wesens das fähig ist zu empfinden, zu denken, zu wollen, zu handeln, in den Zustand eines Wesens über, das wirklich empfindet, denkt, will, und handelt? [...] Mit einem Worte, was ist der Mensch?' [...]. Die Frage begegnet schon in Platons Theätet 174b3–4 und im Alcibiades Maior 129e9".
249 Refl. 903, AA 15: 395.29–32, written by Kant corresponding to M (abbreviation for: Kants Handexemplar von Baumgartens "Metaphysica") 326'. Erdmann places this reflection among the "Reflexionen Kants zur Kritik der reinen Vernunft" and, more exactly, among the ones pertaining to the "Allgemeine Bedeutung der kritischen Metaphysik". Erdmann chooses the first *Critique* as guideline for the classification of Kant's *Reflections* in his second volume. Cf. Benno Erdmann (ed.), *Reflexionen Kants zur kritischen Philosophie*, cit., Refl. 209 pp. 374–375 – pp. 60–61 of the second volume of the first edition of Erdmann's book. It is Adickes, who dates this reflection back to the years 1776/1778.

standing and reason"; this self-knowledge is called *"anthropologia transscenden-talis"*.[250]

In this *Reflection*, Kant deals with the function of the sciences and the role of scholars and affirms that sciences civilize, in that they "take away the roughness in social intercourse, [...] giving the agreeableness and manners of social intercourse".[251] However, Kant adds that "with regard to the modest judgement about the worth of their own science and the gentle restraint of self-conceit and egoism, which a science gives, if it rules alone in human beings, something is necessary, which would give humanity to the scholar, so that he doesn't lose sight of himself, and [by judging his worth over others] trust his powers too much".[252] Kant compares the scholar who loses sight of himself to a Cyclops: in trusting his powers too much, he would behave as if he only possessed one eye, by whose means the field of sciences were intelligible to him, but which would not suffice in showing him the completeness and profound meaning of human life: the scholar needs "another eye", in order to consider the object of his studies also "from the point of view of other human beings".[253] This second eye allows him to compare himself to others and retain himself to their judgements: "the humanity of the sciences" is grounded upon this second eye, that is, it gives the scholars' capability "the affability of judgement, through which

---

250 Refl. 903, AA 15: 395.29–32: "Nicht die Stärke, sondern das einäugigte macht hier den Cyclop. Es ist auch nicht gnug, viel andre Wissenschaften zu wissen, sondern die Selbsterkentnis des Verstandes und der Vernunft. *Anthropologia transscendentalis*". An English translation of the whole *Reflection*, to which I will refer below, is to be found in HOLLY L. WILSON, *Kant's Pragmatic Anthropology: Its Origin, Meaning, and Critical Significance*, New York, State University of New York Press 2006, pp. 117–118, here in particular p. 118.

251 Refl. 903, AA 15: 395.18–22: "Ausser der Geschiklichkeit ist das, was die Wissenschaften geben, daß (sie) civilisiren, d. i. die Rauhigkeit im Umgange wegnehmen, ob sie gleich nicht immer poliren, d. i. das gefällige und gesittete des Umganges geben, weil die popularitaet aus Mangel des Umgangs mit verschiednen Ständen fehlt", Wilson's translation p. 117.

252 Refl. 903, AA 15: 395.23–26, 396:01–02: "Allein in ansehung des bescheidnen Urtheils über den Werth seiner eignen wissenschaft und der ~~Gelind~~ Mäßigung des Eigendünkels und *egoismus*, den eine Wissenschaft giebt, wenn sie allein im Menschen residirt, ist etwas nöthig, was dem gelehrten humanitaet gebe, damit er | nicht sich selbst verkenne und ~~seinen Werth über andre~~ seinen Kräften zu viel Zutraue", Wilson's translation p. 117.

253 Refl. 903, AA 15: 396.03–05: "Ich nenne einen solchen Gelehrten einen Cyclopen. Er ist ein egoist der Wissenschaft, und es ist ihm noch ein Auge nöthig, welches macht, daß er seinen Gegenstand noch aus dem Gesichtspunkte anderer Menschen ansieht", Wilson's translation p. 117.

one is subjected to the judgement of others".[254] The second eye gains access to "the self-knowledge of human reason, without which we have no measure of the dimensions of our knowledge".[255]

From this perspective, we now better understand the scope of what Kant calls an *anthropologia transscendentalis* in contrast to the one-eyedness of merely scholarly knowledge, which is detached from the context of the world: *anthropologia transscendentalis* serves to illustrate why it is "not enough to know many other sciences" but it is rather necessary to aspire to "the self-knowledge of the understanding and reason".[256]

According to Wilson's interpretation of this *Reflection*, Kant's *anthropologia transscendentalis* helps to understand the function of pragmatic anthropology in shedding new light on "the final end and purpose of knowledge", which "is not theoretical knowledge or speculative knowledge, since that too must come into relationship with the final destiny of the human species".[257] In Wilson's opinion, pragmatic anthropology furnishes the key to the systemic aspect of Kant's philosophical enterprise in terms of a popular philosophy, since "Kant believed that pragmatic anthropology was philosophy", not in the sense of "critical philosophy", but rather in the sense of "popular philosophy" (and, she adds, "calling it popular in no way means that it is not philosophy").[258]

One might wonder, whether Wilson is right and the particular discipline of pragmatic anthropology represents the systematic key to the whole of Kant's philosophy. I do not think so. It does not seem to be the case from many different points of view. Firstly, this thesis does not seem convincing from a philological point of view, since in the quoted passage from *Reflection* 903 Kant does not al-

---

254 Refl. 903, AA 15: 396.06 – 08: "Hierauf gründet sich die humanitaet der Wissenschaften, d. i. die Leutseeligkeit des Urtheils, dadurch man es andrer Urtheil mit unterwirft, zu geben", Wilson's translation p. 117.

255 Refl. 903, AA 15: 396.17 – 19: "Das zweyte Auge ist also das der Selbsterkentnis der Menschlichen Vernunft, ohne welches wir kein Augenmaas der Größe unserer Erkentnis haben", Wilson's translation p. 117.

256 Refl. 903, AA 15: 395.29 – 32: "Nicht die Stärke, sondern das einäugigte macht hier den Cyclop. Es ist auch nicht gnug, viel andre Wissenschaften zu wissen, sondern die Selbsterkentnis des Verstandes und der Vernunft. *Anthropologia transscendentalis*", Wilson's translation p. 118.

257 H. L. WILSON, *Kant's Pragmatic Anthropology*, cit., p. 120.

258 H. L. WILSON, *Kant's Pragmatic Anthropology*, cit., p. 122; cf. also Brandt's thoughts on the connection between anthropology and the "Bestimmung" of the human being in REINHARD BRANDT, "Die Leitidee der Kantischen Anthropologie und die Bestimmung des Menschen", in RAINER ENSKAT (ed.), *Erfahrung und Urteilskraft*, Würzburg, Königshausen und Neumann 2000, pp. 27 – 40and, in addition, Brandt's considerations on popular philosophy in REINHARD BRANDT, *Die Bestimmung des Menschen bei Kant*, Hamburg, Meiner 2007.

lude to pragmatic anthropology as a discipline engaged in empirical investigation, but he rather talks of a "transcendental" aspect of this discipline – and pragmatic anthropology surely does not aim at the "transcendental" level of philosophical research, to *a priori* knowledge and principles.[259] Secondly, Wilson's thesis is destined to fail from a theoretical point of view since, if we consider that Kant generally aims to find new room for a philosophical investigation, which is not based on the empirical world, to say that the whole of Kant's philosophy might be brought back to pragmatic anthropology would make the whole of Kant's philosophical enterprise collapse. Thirdly, if we compare the passage in question with others from Kant's writings, we find clear evidence of the fact that the study defined as *anthropologia transscendentalis* in Reflection 903 can be assimilated to the more general concept of philosophy but there is no evidence of its being linked to the specific discipline of pragmatic anthropology. For instance, in a passage of the published 1798 *Anthropology* the Cyclops' metaphor occurs one more time and we read that "there is also gigantic erudition which is still often cyclopean, that is to say, missing one eye: namely, the eye of true philosophy, by means of which reason suitably uses this mass of historical knowledge, the load of a hundred camels".[260] Moreover, in a passage from the *Jäsche Logic* we read again of Kant's metaphor concerning the Cyclops: "mere polyhistory is cyclopic learnedness, which lacks of one eye, the eye of philosophy, and a Cyclops among mathematicians, historians, natural historian, philologists, and linguists is a learned man who is great in all these matters, but who for all that holds all philosophy to be dispensable".[261] If we consider these two passages,

---

259 Some of Brandt's observations on the cyclops seems to support my thesis. See R. BRANDT, *Kommentar*, p. 17: "Es ist leicht zu sehen, daß wir uns hier in der Theorieebene der Transzendentalphilosophie bewegen. In der KrV selbst wird auf die durch das zweite Auge mögliche Vermessung des menschlichen Erkenntnisvermögens hingewiesen (gegen den Skeptiker Hume) (KrV, A 759; B 787). [...] Der Nomade, der Cyclop, der Skeptiker kann die 'mental geography' nicht leisten. Im ursprünglichen Plan der Kritik stand dieses Problem im Vordergrund, wie der vorgesehene Titel '*Die Grenzen der Sinnlichkeit und der Vernunft*' (an Marcus Herz vom 7. Juni 1771; X 123,2–3; s.a. 129,28–29; vgl. schon in den Träumen eines Geistersehers II 351,32; 368,2; 369,16) zeigt. Diese grundsätzliche Grenzbestimmung setzt sich die empirische Anthropologie nicht zum Ziel. Sie operiert im Feld der möglichen Erfahrung; sie läßt sich in vielerlei Weise apriorische Erkenntnisse und Prinzipien vorgeben und zeigt dann deren empirische Durchführung [...]".
260 AA 07: 227.01–04: "Es giebt aber auch gigantische Gelehrsamkeit, die doch oft cyklopisch ist, der nämlich ein Auge fehlt: nämlich das der wahren Philosophie, um diese Menge des historischen Wissens, die Fracht von hundert Kameelen, durch die Vernunft zweckmäßig zu benutzen"; *Anthropology* p. 331.
261 Logik, 09: 45.28–32: "Die bloße Polyhistorie ist eine cyklopische Gelehrsamkeit, der ein Auge fehlt, das Auge der Philosophie, und ein Cyklop von Mathematiker, Historiker, Natur-

the only thing we may say is that a second eye is "the eye of philosophy" and not the eye of "pragmatic anthropology" (and, we might add, the eye of philosophy in its cosmopolitan rather than scholastic sense).

The last reference from the *Jäsche Logic*, moreover, allows us to move a step further in the attempt to understand the correspondence between the *anthropologia transscendentalis* from Reflection 903 and philosophy in general. In fact, in the *Jäsche Logic* this passage occurs in the section dedicated to explaining the meaning of philosophy in general (*Begriff von der Philosophie überhaupt*). It occurs in that section, precisely where Kant also formulates the four questions concerning philosophy and where he answers, as we already saw, that the fields of metaphysics, morals and religion could all be reckoned "as anthropology, because the first three questions relate to the last one", that is to the question 'what is the human being?'.[262]

If we pay attention to the consequences of Kant's train of thoughts, a noteworthy conclusion seems to follow: an investigation that is in charge of answering the question "what is the human being?" has to be considered also the discipline in charge of dealing with "the concept of philosophy in general".

The correspondence of these two fields again moves us a step forward, so that we might now be willing to ask what kind of question the question concerning the human being is. What are we confronted with here?

This is not a question of "local" anthropology, that is, of a particular, empirical form of anthropology, but it rather involves a discussion concerning a "general knowledge of the world [...], which is not empirical but rather cosmological".[263] In other words, the question concerning the human being is a question concerning knowledge in its generality. Does this more general knowledge, focused on the question of the human being, correspond to a "transcendental anthropology"?

Few scholars have advanced the thesis, according to which the term "transcendental" expressed by Kant in the phrase "*anthropologia transscendentalis*" has to be considered in a very strong sense. According to this thesis, the very *Cri-*

---

beschreiber, Philolog und Sprachkundiger ist ein Gelehrter, der groß in allen diesen Stücken ist, aber alle Philosophie darüber für entbehrlich hält"; *Jäsche Logic*, p. 554.

262 Logik, AA 09: 25.01–10; *Jäsche Logic* (translation slightly modified) p. 538, and the analysis above.

263 Cf. Die Vorlesung des Wintersemesters 1777/78 aufgrund der Nachschrift Pillau, AA 25: 734.04–06: "1) Eine Local Weltkenntniß die die Kaufleute haben, die auch empirisch genannt wird. 2) eine general Weltkenntniß die der Weltmann hat, und die nicht empirisch sondern cosmologisch ist". For a more detailed analysis of this passage and the explanation of the concept of "local" anthropology, cf. the following section.

tique of Pure Reason in particular (but also the three *Critiques* in general) has to be considered the foundation of a "transcendental anthropology". For instance, the study of Simmermacher argues in this direction.[264] In order to show that the first *Critique* corresponds to a "transcendental anthropology", as Kant mentions it in the Latin terms *Anthropologia transscendentalis* in *Reflection* 903, Simmermacher first refers to a passage from the *Opus Postumum* where Kant equates transcendental philosophy to the active self-determinability of subjects.[265] Then, Simmermacher links this activity to the process of self-construction of a transcendental subject and, in turn, he describes this construction as, at the same time, "the self-showing" and the "self-knowing" of the subject to and by himself.[266] In light of these considerations, Simmermacher interprets the passage dedicated to the *anthropologia transscendentalis* as a reference to the self-constructing, self-showing and self-knowing of the transcendental subject in the first *Critique* and defends his thesis by noting that *Reflection* 903 refers to the self-knowledge of understanding and reason.[267]

Patrick R. Frierson, who tends to equate Kant's philosophy of the three *Critiques* and "transcendental anthropology", advances a similar proposal.[268]

---

264 Cf. VOLKER SIMMERMACHER, *Kants Kritik der reinen Vernunft als Grundlegung einer Anthropologia transcendentalis*, Heidelberg, Dissertation 1951. A similar interpretive proposal has been advanced by LEONARDO AMOROSO, *Senso e consenso. Uno studio kantiano*, Napoli, Guida 1984 (cf. in particular pp. 67–87) and by FRANK NOBBE, *Kants Frage nach dem Menschen. Die Kritik der ästhetischen Urteilskraft als transzendentale Anthropologie*, Frankfurt a. M., Lang 1995. For a distinction between different forms of anthropology in Kant's works, cf. CLAUDIA M. SCHMIDT, "Kant's Transcendental, Empirical, Pragmatic, and Moral Anthropology", in *Kant-Studien*, vol. 98 (2007), pp. 156–182.

265 OP, AA 21: 58.11–12: "Es ist hier nicht von einer passiven sondern activen Bestimmbarkeit des Subjects die Rede" (the English translation: IMMANUEL KANT, *Opus Postumum*, edited and translated by ECKART FÖRSTER – MICHAEL ROSEN, Cambridge/New York, Cambridge University Press 1993 represents a selection of the Academy text. The quoted passage from AA 21 is not to be found in the English book). Already now it has to be noted that Simmermacher erroneously equates subject (*Subjekt*) and human being (*Mensch*).

266 Cf. V. SIMMERMACHER, *Kants Kritik der reinen Vernunft als Grundlegung einer Anthropologia transcendentalis*, cit., p. 3: "Das transzendentale Subjekt kommt durch Selbstauslegung in den Blick. Selbstauslegung bedeutet dabei nichts anderes als das Sich-Zeigen seiner selbst, wie es ist, durch sich selbst".

267 Cf. V. SIMMERMACHER, *Kants Kritik der reinen Vernunft als Grundlegung einer Anthropologia transcendentalis*, cit., p. 3: "Die *anthropologia transcendentalis* [muss] als eine Selbsterkenntnis des Verstandes und der Vernunft entwickeln, welche in der Kr. d. r. V. ihren Anfang nimmt".

268 Cf. PATRICK R. FRIERSON, *Freedom and Anthropology in Kant's Moral Philosophy*, Cambridge/New York, Cambridge University Press 2003, and PATRICK R. FRIERSON, *What is the Human Being?*, Abingdon/New York, Routledge 2013. For other contemporary interpretations concerning an idea of transcendental anthropology in Kant's work see also ROSEMARY RIZO-

Another interpretive idea that could be related to the previous ones has an authoritative tradition in other philosophers' reflections, which have their origin in or possess a strong link to Kant's 1798 *Anthropology*. Philosophers such as Heidegger or Foucault propose to consider anthropology as a more fundamental discipline in the context of Kant's critical system.[269] The aims of these interpretations are, however, quite heterogeneous, such that it is better to focus on the thesis advanced by Simmermacher and show how an alternative interpretation of his thesis shows it has some difficulties.

One of the strongest objections against Simmermacher's interpretation refers to the impossibility of anthropology being a transcendental discipline. According to S. B. Kim, "while transcendental philosophy aims to compile the structure of the fundamental human faculties in its purity, anthropology deals with their phenomena in their concrete corporeality",[270] so that it seems impossible to say anything more detailed about a transcendental anthropology "without mixing it with something arbitrarily fictitious".[271]

This objection involves a terminological problem concerning the meaning of the word "transcendental" and the juxtaposition of this adjective with the word "anthropology" and, in this way, involves the identification of two heterogene-

---

PATRÓN DE LERNER – MARÍA JESÚS VÁZQUEZ LOBEIRAS (eds.), *La razón y sus fines. Elementos para una antropología filosófica en Kant, Husserl y Horkheimer*, Hildesheim, Olms 2013, ROBERT B. LOUDEN, *Kant's Human Being: Essays on His Theory of Human Nature*, Oxford/New York, Oxford University Press 2011, and THORSTEN STREUBEL, "Was ist der Mensch? – Das Gehirn-Geist-Problem aus kantischer Sicht. Plädoyer für eine transzendentale Anthropologie", in *Kant-Studien*, vol. 103/3 (2012), pp. 370–377.

269 See, for instance, the proposals by MARTIN HEIDEGGER (*Kant und das Problem der Metaphysik*, vierte, erweiterte Auflage, Frankfurt a. M. 1973; English translation: *Kant and the Problem of Metaphysics*, translated by JAMES CHURCHILL, Bloomington, Indiana University Press 1962) and MICHEL FOUCAULT (*Introduction à l'anthropologie de Kant. Thèse complémentaire pour le doctorat ès Lettres*, Paris 1961; English translation: *Introduction to Kant's Anthropology*, translated by ROBERTO NIGRO – KATE BRIGGS, Los Angeles, Semiotext(e) 2007; cf. also Foucault's French translation of Kant's Anthropology: IMMANUEL KANT, *Anthropologie du point de vue pragmatique*. Traduction par Michel Foucault, Paris, 1994, 7. tirage argumenté d'une table des matières détaillée, 1964).

270 See S. B. KIM, *Die Entstehung der Kantischen Anthropologie*, cit., p. 119: "Während die sogenannte Transzendentalphilosophie die Absicht hat, die Struktur der menschlichen Grundvermögen in ihrer Reinheit herauszuarbeiten, beschäftigt sich die Anthropologie mit den Phänomenen derselben in ihrer konkreten Leibhaftigkeit".

271 See S. B. KIM, *Die Entstehung der Kantischen Anthropologie*, cit., p. 153: "Über die in der Kritik der reinen Vernunft angesprochene ausführliche Anthropologie und den in einer Reflexion verwendeten Begriff 'Anthropologia transzendentalis' [Refl. 903, XV 395; vgl. ferner Refl. 1482, XV 661] scheint man nichts Näheres sagen zu können, ohne dabei auch etwas willkürlich Erdichtetes einzumischen".

ous domains. In regard to this first problem, the proposal of interpreting the whole of Kant's critical system in terms of transcendental anthropology must begin with an analysis of the word "transcendental".[272] The interpretations of the meaning of this word are not univocal.[273] The interpretation is made more difficult by the fact that the meaning of the term shifts throughout Kant's works. However, one generic, constant feature can be registered, namely the fact that the word "transcendental" "is used ubiquitously to qualify nouns such as logic, aesthetic, unity of apperception, faculties, illusion; in each case it signals that the noun it qualifies is being considered in terms of its conditions of possibility".[274] Furthermore, one may also opportunely hold that Kant generally designates with the term "transcendental" the form of knowledge of an object, rather than the object itself.[275] Thus, Kant uses the word "transcendental" to

---

272 See also N. HINSKE, "Kants Idee der Anthropologie", cit., p. 427 (and footnote 32): "Es kann daher trotz aller Inkohärenz der Terminologie auch kaum noch überraschen, wenn in den Reflexionen des handschriftlichen Nachlasses gelegentlich sogar von einer 'Anthropologia transscendentalis' die Rede ist [... Simmermachers] Arbeit krankt vor allem daran, daß sie weder den Begriff des Transzendentalen noch den der Anthropologie im Kantischen Sprachgebrauch einer genaueren Analyse unterzieht".

273 See NORBERT HINSKE, *Kants Weg zur Transzendentalphilosophie. Der dreißigjährige Kant*, Stuttgart/Berlin/Bonn/Mainz, Kohlhammer 1970, here in particular p. 17: "Der Begriff des Transzendentalen hat [...] in der wechselreichen und verschlungenen Geschichte der Kantforschung zu immer neuen Auslegungen, Mißverständnissen und Differenzen Anlaß gegeben", and NORBERT HINSKE, "Transzendental, das Transzendentale, Transzendentalien, Transzendentalphilosophie, V. 18 Jh.", in JOACHIM RITTER – KARLFRIED GRÜNDER (eds.), *Historisches Wörterbuch der Philosophie*, volume 10, Darmstadt 1998, columns 1376–1388.

274 See HOWARD CAYGILL, *A Kant Dictionary*, Oxford/Cambridge (Mass.), Blackwell 1995, entry "Transcendental", pp. 399–400; cf. for instance KrV, A 56/B 80 – AA 04: 51.05–20/AA 03: 78.05–20: "Und hier mache ich eine Anmerkung, die ihren Einfluß auf alle nachfolgende Betrachtungen erstreckt, und die man wohl vor Augen haben muß, nämlich: daß nicht eine jede Erkenntniß *a priori*, sondern nur die, dadurch wir erkennen, daß und wie gewisse Vorstellungen (Anschauungen oder Begriffe) lediglich *a priori* angewandt werden oder möglich sind, transscendental (d. i. die Möglichkeit der Erkenntniß oder der Gebrauch derselben *a priori*) heißen müsse. Daher ist weder der Raum, noch irgend eine geometrische Bestimmung desselben *a priori* eine transscendentale Vorstellung; sondern nur die Erkenntniß, daß diese Vorstellungen gar nicht empirischen Ursprungs sind, und die Möglichkeit, wie sie sich gleichwohl *a priori* auf Gegenstände der Erfahrung beziehen können, kann transscendental heißen. Imgleichen würde der Gebrauch des Raumes von Gegenständen überhaupt auch transscendental sein: aber ist er lediglich auf Gegenstände der Sinne eingeschränkt, so heißt er empirisch. Der Unterschied des Transscendentalen und Empirischen gehört also nur zur Kritik der Erkenntnisse und betrifft nicht die Beziehung derselben auf ihren Gegenstand", CpR p. 196.

275 Cf. KrV, B 25/AA 03: 43. 16–18: "Ich nenne alle Erkenntniß transscendental, die sich nicht sowohl mit Gegenständen, sondern mit unserer Erkenntnißart von Gegenständen, so fern diese *a priori* möglich sein soll, überhaupt beschäftigt", slightly modified from the first edition, A 12/

refer specifically to "transcendental philosophy" as philosophy having to do only with understanding and reason "in a system of all concepts and principles which are related to objects in general, without assuming objects that would be given".[276]

Therefore, Simmarmacher's thesis, which describes anthropology as part of (or equal to) transcendental philosophy, seems to be questionable, if we consider the specific meaning of "transcendental" and the specific scope of transcendental philosophy in theoretical philosophy.

Another different aspect of the possibility of an *anthropologia transscendentalis* is the one concerning the possibility of referring to the domain of pure philosophy for anthropological investigations. This problem is directed to the way of interpreting Kant's treatment of the fundamental faculties as part of pure philosophy and simultaneously as the subject matter of anthropology.

We might then ask ourselves to what extent a theory concerning an anthropological investigation that pertains to the domain of pure philosophy may be coherently defended and whether it is better to speak only of a partial intersection of the topics analysed in the context of the three *Critiques* and the ones analysed in the context of anthropology. In order to find these intersections, we also have to neatly distinguish between the field of pure philosophy and the one of pragmatic anthropology. Let me start, however, with the similarities between these two fields.

AA 04: 23.08 – 09: "Ich nenne alle Erkenntniß transscendental, die sich nicht sowohl mit Gegenständen, sondern mit unsern Begriffen *a priori* von Gegenständen überhaupt beschäftigt", CpR p. 149. According to Erdmann (BENNO ERDMANN, *Beiträge zur Geschichte und Revision des Textes von Kants Kritik der reinen Vernunft*, Berlin, G. Reimer 1900, p. 28), Kant modifies the passage in question, since he aims to refer also to the Transcendental Aesthetic, while according to Hinske (*Kants Weg zur Transzendentalphilosophie*, cit., p. 39), Kant's modified account of the Dialectic is in this case decisive. On these passages, cf. also the Reflection 4851 (from 1776 – 1778), AA 18: 10.01 – 03: "transscendental wird Erkenntnis in Ansehung ihres Ursprungs genannt, transscendent in Ansehung des Obiects, das in keiner Erfahrung angetroffen werden kan".

276 KrV, A 845/B 873 – AA 03: 546.16 – 21: "Die im engeren Verstande so genannte Metaphysik besteht aus der Transscendentalphilosophie und der Physiologie der reinen Vernunft. Die erstere betrachtet nur den Verstand und Vernunft selbst in einem System aller Begriffe und Grundsätze, die sich auf Gegenstände überhaupt beziehen, ohne Objecte anzunehmen, die gegeben wären (*Ontologia*)", CpR p. 698.

3.5 The Boundaries between Kant's Pure Philosophy and His Pragmatic Anthropology

A first, very broad similarity between Kant's critical philosophy and his pragmatic anthropology is their ambition of generality. Arnoldt notes that *pragmatic* anthropology also secures some sort of generality, since it gives an account of "what is common to all human beings under every sky", that is "the original, natural dispositions and capacities of the human soul" or, rather, of the human mind (*Gemüt*).[277] In other words, also pragmatic anthropology aims to furnish an analysis of what is common to all human beings, their cognitive faculties and one may also ascribe to it the character of generality, as Hinske notes.[278] Through the proposal of a theory of the faculties, anthropology "provides the opportunity of classifying all 'phenomena' in an antecedent general schema of the human being, and of understanding in an 'anthropological view' every sort of action".[279] However, Kant's investigations concerning the faculties in the critical works are pure philosophical investigations. While the pragmatic anthropological analysis of human faculties proceeds only on the basis of empirical considerations and focuses on the human being in his singularity in

---

277 See EMIL ARNOLDT, "Verhältnis von Kants physisch-geographischem Kolleg zu seinem anthropologischen", in DERS., *Gesammelte Schriften*, edited by OTTO SCHÖNDÖRFFER, vol. 4 (*Kritische Exkurse im Gebiete der Kantforschung – Teil 1*), Berlin, B. Cassirer 1908, pp. 400 – 420, here in particular p. 404: "die Anthropologie, die Kant zumeist anbaute, d. h. die Anthropologie in pragmatischer Hinsicht, [hat] Menschenkenntnis zu gewähren zunächst in bezug auf das, was allen Menschen unter allen Himmelsstrichen gemeinsam ist, – die Menschenseele, ihre ursprünglichen, natürlichen Anlagen und Fähigkeiten, die dem Menschen als solchen überall eigen sind, sodann aber auch in bezug auf die mancherlei von einander abweichenden Entwicklungen, welche die Menschen ihrer Intelligenz, ihrem Gefühl, ihrem Begehren aus ihrer Willkür heraus gegeben haben, sofern sich die letztere mehr unter der Gesetzgebung der Natur, als unter der Gesetzgebung der Freiheit betätigt".

278 N. HINSKE, "Kants Idee der Anthropologie", cit., p. 415: "Für die philosophische Anthropologie bedeutet 'Menschenkenntnis' primär 'Generalkenntnis': "Die Generalkenntnis geht hierhin immer vor der Lokalkenntnis voraus" (Anthr. B IX, vgl. auch Refl. 1482, AA 15. 659). [...] Als Leitfaden für eine solche 'Generalkenntnis' dient Kant die Vermögenstheorie. Diese zeichnet die Grundbahnen vor, in denen sich das Verhalten des Menschen bewegt, und entwirft damit ein allgemeines Schema, in das sich die verschiedensten 'Beobachtungen' einordnen lassen".

279 N. HINSKE, "Kants Idee der Anthropologie", cit., p. 417: "Diese grundlegende Bestimmung [des Selbstbewußtseins] des Menschen aber, die doch vor allen Vermögen vorhergeht und alle Vermögen des Menschen durchherrscht, gerät in Kants Anthropologie infolge ihres Ansatzes und ihrer 'Gliederung' von Anfang an unter den Oberbegriff des Erkenntnisvermögens. [... p. 418] Die Vermögenstheorie [schafft] die Möglichkeit, alle 'Phänomena' in ein vorgängiges Generalschema vom Menschen einzuordnen (sie unter bestimmte 'Titel' zu bringen) und jede Handlungsweise 'anthropologisch zu verstehen'".

order to furnish a comprehensive account of its inner life, the investigations of the faculties in the critical works are part of critical philosophy. Like anthropology, also these last investigations can be considered as pragmatically relevant, in that they help the human being in the orientation in the world. However, in addition, and in contrast to the empirically based pragmatic anthropology, the investigations of the faculties in the critical works belong to the concept of philosophy as an *a priori*, rational science. These general, pure investigations do not focus on the human being in its empirical singularity and the critical works might be taken to constitute altogether a treatise of human nature, an analysis very similar to the others that have often been conducted in the century of the *Aufklärung*, but which has in addition been thought to be helpful for the human being in its orientation in the world.[280]

The three *Critiques* and the anthropological studies have the object of their investigation in common, namely the human being as cognizing, willing and feeling human being. However, Kant's critical philosophy gives an answer to the question "what is the human being?" by proposing a more fundamental investigation, a "fundamental anthropology",[281] "which is not physiological, empirical, pragmatic, practical or moral" and which rather refers to a "transcendental knowledge on the human being as a thinking, willing and hoping entity".[282]

---

280 For the practical unity of Kant's philosophy and the *conceptus cosmicus* of philosophy, cf. CLAUDIO LA ROCCA, "La saggezza e l'unità pratica della filosofia kantiana", cit., pp. 217–242. For the difference between Kant's anthropology and Hume's science of man cf. THOMAS STURM, "Freedom and the Human Sciences: Hume's Science of Man versus Kant's Pragmatic Anthropology", in *Kant Yearbook 2011 – Anthropology*. Volume 3, pp. 23–42.

281 See also N. HINSKE, "Kants Idee der Anthropologie", cit., p. 427: "In solchen Formulierungen ['Anthropologia transscendentalis'] scheint sich schon bei Kant selber das Projekt einer umfassenden Anthropologie als Fundamentalwissenschaft vorzubereiten". However, in Hinske's opinion, Kant never succeeds in realizing the project of making anthropology a fundamental discipline: "In der Anlage seines Systems freilich und der kritischen Strenge seines Denkens war ein derartiges Projekt nicht zu verwirklichen".

282 HEINER F. KLEMME ("Immanuel Kant", in EIKE BOHLKEN – CHRISTIAN THEIS (eds.), *Handbuch Anthropologie. Der Mensch zwischen Natur, Kultur und Technik*, Stuttgart/Weimar, J. B. Metzler 2009, pp. 11–16) refers to this kind of fundamental anthropology, when he takes into consideration the passage from Reflection 903 dedicated to the *anthropologia transscendentalis*: "In einer Reflexion deutet Kant mit dem Ausdruck 'anthropologia transscendentalis' [...] eine Art von Fundamentalanthropologie an, zu der er sich aber eben falls nicht näher äußert. Eine Anthropologie, die transzendental sein will, kann jedenfalls keine Anthropologie im Sinne der physiologischen, empirischen, pragmatischen, praktischen oder moralischen Anthropologie sein. Sie wäre schlicht ein neuer Name für unser transzendentales Wissen über den Menschen als eines denkenden, wollenden und hoffenden Wesens" (pp. 15–16). Very similar considerations have also been advanced by Buber: "die [Frage] nach dem Wesen des Menschen [...] weist

The fact that Kant's discipline of pragmatic anthropology does not correspond to this investigation is also confirmed by the observation that the question "what is the human being?" represents a guiding problem in neither the 1798 *Anthropology* nor in Kant's lectures on this subject matter.[283]

This is easily recognizable if we consider two further passages where Kant formulates the question on the human being. These passages occur in a text that Kant does not include in the definitive, published version of the 1798 *Anthropology* and can now be found in the Rostock Manuscript.[284] Through these passages, we can find many intersections between Kant's pragmatic anthropology and his pure philosophy.

As in *Reflection* 903, also here the first occurrence follows a section, in which Kant refers to the process of self-observation. In the Rostock Manuscript, Kant distinguishes between the consciousness of self-observing and the self-observed I and specifies that, in contrast to the "consciousness of the one who observes himself", which is "an entirely simple representation of the subject in judgement as such, of which one knows everything if one merely thinks it", innumerous objects come out from self-observation: "the I which has been observed by itself is a sum total of so many objects of inner perception". That is why, in Kant's opinion, "psychology has plenty to do in tracing everything that lies hidden in it", so that, in conclusion, psychology may not even "ever hope to complete this task and answer satisfactorily the question" concerning the human being.[285] As ob-

---

[...] einer Disziplin zu, welche Anthropologie genannt wird, worunter, da es sich um die Grundfragen des menschlichen Philosophierens handelt, nur die philosophische Anthropologie verstanden werden kann. Diese wäre also die fundamentale philosophische Wissenschaft. [...] ...und also ist der Sinn der vierten Frage, auf die die drei ersten zurückgeführt werden können, bei Kant dieser: Was ist das für ein Wesen, das wissen kann, das tun soll, das hoffen darf?" (MARTIN BUBER, *Das Problem des Menschen*, Heidelberg, Lambert Schneider 1948, pp. 11, 14 – German version of Buber's lectures at the Hebrew University of Jerusalem in the summer semester 1938, first published in Hebrew in 1942).

283 Cf. R. BRANDT, *Kommentar*, pp. 16 – 17: "weder die Vorlesungsnachschriften noch die Anthropologie von 1798 [beziehen] sich auf die Frage 'Was ist der Mensch?' als ihr Leitproblem [...]; sie erwähnen sie nicht einmal. Die pragmatische Anthropologie versteht sich also nicht als eine Antwort auf die seit Platon immer wieder erörterte Wesensfrage des Menschen; und das Kolleg, das Kant 1793 tatsächlich über 20 Jahre (nämlich seit dem Wintersemester 1772–1773) gelesen hat, hat zwar die Anthropologie zum Thema, und insofern ist die Feststellung richtig, aber es ist nicht die Anthropologie der vierten Frage".

284 Anth, AA 07: 399.01–03, 400.08. For the editorial history of this text, see section 3.9 below.

285 Here the whole passage from Anth, AA 07: 398.40–43, 399.01–03: "Das Bewußtseyn des sich selbst Beobachtenden ist eine ganz einfache Vorstellung des Subjects im Urtheil überhaupt wovon man alles weis wenn man es blos denkt; aber das von sich selbst beobachtete Ich ist ein Inbegriff von so viel Gegenständen der inneren Warnehmung daß die Psychologie vollauf zu tun

served above, Kant excludes psychology from the task of analysing the result of the subject's self-observation and substitutes the traditional discipline of empirical psychology with pragmatic anthropology. However, in addition, in this particular case it is also noteworthy that psychology is considered insufficient to properly answer the question: "what is the human being?". A second occurrence of the question concerning the human being in the Rostock Manuscript occurs in the context of the analysis of the subject's self-observation. There Kant affirms that "the human being cannot observe himself internally if he is not led by means of a rule, under which perceptions alone must be united, if they are to furnish him with an experience. Therefore they are together only appearances of himself. To cognize himself from them he must take a principle of appearance (in space and time) as a basis, in order to know what the human being is".[286]

The way in which Kant advances the problem concerning the human being in the Rostock Manuscript is a confirmation of the fact that this question alludes to a deeper knowledge of the human being itself, which pragmatic anthropology, with its analysis based merely on observations and developed on the basis of an empirical method, cannot furnish.[287] The answer to this question might rather be given by the whole of critical philosophy, where a pure analysis of the thinking, willing, feeling, hoping human being is given by reference to the fundamental faculties of the human mind.[288]

---

hat um alles darinn im Verborgenen liegende auszuspühren und nicht hoffen darf damit jemals zu Ende zu kommen und die Frage hinreichend zu beantworten: Was ist der Mensch", *Anthropology* p. 253.

286 Anth, AA 07: 400.03–08: "Der Mensch kann sich selbst innerlich nicht beobachten wenn er nicht durch eine Regel geleitet wird unter der allein die Warnehmung verbunden seyn müsse wenn sie ihm eine Erfahrung liefern soll. Daher sind jene insgesammt nur Erscheinung von sich selbst daraus sich selbst zu erkennen muß er das Princip der Erscheinung (in Raum und Zeit) zum Grunde legen um zu wissen was ist der Mensch", *Anthropology* p. 257.

287 Cf. also M. BUBER, *Das Problem des Menschen*, cit., pp. 12–15 and p. 41, who assesses that the answer to the question concerning the human being pertains to a fundamental, philosophical anthropology, about which, however, in Buber's opinion, Kant does not give any elucidation, neither in the pragmatic anthropology nor elsewhere. In fact, in Buber's opinion, Kant's philosophical anthropology would rather have to answer existential problems. Also Volker Gerhardt speaks of an "existential dramatic", which the question concerning the human being causes: VOLKER GERHARDT, *Immanuel Kant. Vernunft und Leben*, Stuttgart, Reclam 2002, p. 295. A similar interpretive suggestion is advanced by FREDERICK VAN DE PITTE, *Kant as Philosophical Anthropologist*, The Hague, Martinus Nijhoff 1971.

288 However, here I do not wish to claim that the whole of Kant's philosophy corresponds to the discipline of anthropology, nor that a "philosophical anthropology" is given or should be given in the context of Kant's pure philosophy (both options are criticised in TH. STURM, *Kant und die Wissenschaften vom Menschen*, cit., pp. 389–390; on the difficulties of a Kantian

This explains why the analysis of the faculties pertaining to the field of pure philosophy and the analysis of the faculties in the 1798 *Anthropology* might sometimes link but do not correspond. This happens because both the investigation of the faculties of the human mind in the critical works and the empirical investigation of the faculties in the 1798 published work have a similar subject matter and a similar practical scope but, nonetheless, they proceed by means of very different methods. Only by bearing this in mind it is possible to allude to the fact that the boundary between Kant's pure philosophy and his pragmatic anthropology is sometimes nuanced.[289]

In order to show this, we can start already with a letter to Marcus Hertz from the autumn of 1773, where Kant positions anthropology in the context of the plan of his work as a whole and refers to it after speaking about his projects concerning transcendental philosophy, metaphysics of nature and metaphysics of morals.[290] Anthropology is taken into account since Kant intended to make it a proper academic discipline.[291] However, it is decisive that this discipline does not have to do with "the foundations of the possibility of human thinking in general" but is rather focused on the discussion concerning "phenomena and their laws" and the empirical field of philosophical analysis.[292]

"philosophical anthropology", cf. also N. HINSKE, "La psicologia empirica di Wolff e l'antropologia pragmatica di Kant", cit., pp. 207–224, here in particular p. 217, who quotes the work by FRIEDRICH CHRISTIAN STARKE [alias JOHANN ADAM BERGK] (ed.), *Immanuel Kant's Menschenkunde oder philosophische Anthropologie*, Quedlinburg/Leipzig 1831).

289 Cf. also N. HINSKE, "Kants Idee der Anthropologie", cit., pp. 426–427: "Die philosophische Anthropologie ist eine Disziplin, deren Territorium nur unsicher abgesteckt ist. [...] Die philosophische Anthropologie ist eine Disziplin, die die Grenzen einer Disziplin zu sprengen sucht und auf Totalität aus ist", and E. ARNOLDT, "Verhältnis von Kants physisch-geographischem Kolleg zu seinem anthropologischen", cit., pp. 405 ff.

290 Br, AA 10: 145.17–22: "Ich werde froh seyn wenn ich meine Transscendentalphilosophie werde zu Ende gebracht haben welche eigentlich eine Critik der reinen Vernunft ist alsdenn gehe ich zur Metaphysik die nur zwey Theile hat: die Methaphysik der Natur und die Metaph. der Sitten wovon ich die letztere zuerst herausgeben werde und mich darauf zum voraus freue", *Correspondence* p. 141.

291 Br, AA 10: 145.26–28: "Ich lese in diesem Winter zum zweyten mal ein collegium privatum der Anthropologie welches ich ietzt zu einer ordentlichen academischen disciplin zu machen gedenke", *Correspondence* p. 141.

292 The whole passage from Kant's letter, where he constantly refers to the phenomenal, empirical field, reads – Br, AA 10: 145.32–37, 146.01–04: "Da suche ich alsdenn mehr Phänomena u. ihre Gesetze als die erste Gründe der Möglichkeit der modification der menschlichen Natur überhaupt. Daher die subtile u. in meinen Augen auf ewig vergebliche Untersuchung über die Art wie die organe des Korper mit den Gedanken in Verbindung stehen ganz wegfällt. Ich bin unabläßig so bey der Beobachtung selbst im gemeinen Leben daß meine Zuhörer vom ersten Anfange bis zu Ende niemals eine trokene sondern durch den Anlaß den sie haben unaufhörlich

This is also the aim of the 1798 *Anthropology*, where Kant conducts his analysis on a merely empirical basis. Nonetheless, these programmatic and methodological premises do not prevent Kant from at times almost converging empirical, *a posteriori* disciplines, such as the one treated in the 1798 book is, and the *a priori* field of pure philosophy. The reader of the 1798 published *Anthropology* (AA 07) and of the students' notes of Kant's lectures on anthropology (AA 25) witnesses Kant sometimes going beyond the boundaries of mere experience and approaching points which belong to the debate in pure philosophy.

As already noted, the strong interconnection of the topics that Kant presents in the 1798 published *Anthropology* and the ones that he treats in his three *Critiques* is the cause of this episodic mixture. That some of the differences between the discipline of anthropology and pure philosophy are nuanced can be recognized by a quick look at the index of this work. One can easily see that the whole discussion of the first part of the 1798 book (Part I – *Anthropological Didactic*) is dedicated to the three grounding faculties of the human mind (*Gemüt / animus*), namely the faculty of cognition (*Erkenntnisvermögen*), the feeling of pleasure and displeasure (*Gefühl der Lust und Unlust*), and the faculty of desire (*Begehrungsvermögen*). Each of these faculties has been at the centre of one of the three *Critiques*. This tripartition is also emphasized in the introduction and the so called "first introduction" to the third *Critique*, as well as in the introduction to the second *Critique* and the general introduction to the *Metaphysics of Morals*.[293]

Trespassing the boundary between an empirical point of view and Kant's particular one, that is to his critical approach, is well testified in § 7 of the 1798 *Anthropology*, emblematically titled *On Sensibility in Contrast to Understanding* (*Von der Sinnlichkeit im Gegensatz mit dem Verstande*).[294]

This section begins with a very precise description of the difference between two aspects of the mind (*Gemüt – animus*). Kant stresses that the mind is either "active" (*handelnd*) or "passive" (*leidend* – maybe, more properly: "enduring") in regard to the state of its representations. In the first respect, the mind presents

---

ihre gewöhnliche Erfahrung mit meinen Bemerkungen zu vergleichen iederzeit eine unterhaltende Beschäftigung habe", *Correspondence* p. 141.

293 I already referred to this tripartition. The passages quoted will be at the centre of my discussion in chapter 4 below.

294 Kant, Anthr, AA 07: 140.15 – 143.13 and the relevant *Ergänzungen* in AA 07: 396.21 – 399.33 – *Anthropology* pp. 251 – 256.

itself as a faculty (*Vermögen / facultas*). In the second respect, it consists in receptivity (*Empfänglichkeit / receptivitas*).[295]

In accordance with the heading of the section in question, this difference has to be put on the same level as the difference between sensibility (*Sinnlichkeit*) and understanding (*Verstand*). This classification recalls a distinction Kant already made in the Transcendental Aesthetic of the first *Critique*. There he states that an object "affects the mind in a certain way", such that in this process of affection we can distinguish between

1. sensibility (*Sinnlichkeit*), which Kant defines in the first *Critique* as a capacity (*Fähigkeit*), which consists in receptivity (*Receptivität*), through which we as human beings are affected by the object, and
2. understanding (*Verstand*), by which the objects are thought and from which concepts arise.[296]

When comparing this passage from the first *Critique* and the previous one from the 1798 published *Anthropology*, at first sight it looks as if we are confronted with nothing new. Kant overtly refers to the distinction between the two aspects of the mind (*Gemüt*), the "active" (*handelnd*) and the "passive / enduring" (*leidend*), in both texts. However, in regard to these passages at least two observations ought to be made. Firstly, it is noteworthy that the distinction between a faculty's "spontaneity" and the "passivity" of receptivity recurs in the context of anthropology, such that a distinction pertaining to pure philosophy is now incorporated into Kant's empirical study on the human being. This means that in the first *Critique* Kant classifies these aspects of the mind as pertaining to pure philosophy and there he takes them to be valid *a priori*. However, such a classi-

---

295 AA 07: 140.16–18: "In Ansehung des Zustandes der Vorstellungen ist mein Gemüth entweder handelnd und zeigt Vermögen (*facultas*), oder es ist leidend und besteht in Empfänglichkeit (*receptivitas*)", *Anthropology* p. 251.
296 KrV, A 20 (AA 04: 19.06–16)/B 34 (03: 49.06–16): "Auf welche Art und durch welche Mittel sich auch immer eine Erkenntniß auf Gegenstände beziehen mag, so ist doch diejenige, wodurch sie sich auf dieselbe unmittelbar bezieht, und worauf alles Denken als Mittel abzweckt, die Anschauung. Diese findet aber nur statt, sofern uns der Gegenstand gegeben wird; dieses aber ist wiederum [in the B-Edition Kant adds: 'uns Menschen wenigstens', which casued some scholars to talk about an "anthropological" turn in the second edition of the first *Critique* – see FRANÇOIS-XAVIER CHENET, *L'assise de l'ontologie critique: l'esthétique transcendantale*, Lille, Presses Univ. de Lille, 1994] nur dadurch möglich, daß er das Gemüth auf gewisse Weise afficire. Die Fähigkeit (Receptivität), Vorstellungen durch die Art, wie wir von Gegenständen afficirt werden, zu bekommen, heißt Sinnlichkeit. Vermittelst der Sinnlichkeit also werden uns Gegenstände gegeben, und sie allein liefert uns Anschauungen; durch den Verstand aber werden sie gedacht, und von ihm entspringen Begriffe"; CpR 153/172.

fication finds a new place within the corpus of anthropology, such that it can further be incorporated in a study that is grounded on self-observation and *a posteriori* assumptions.

Secondly, a slightly different distinction between the two aspects of the mind is evidenced by Kant's terminology in the 1798 *Anthropology*. In the first *Critique* Kant describes the capacity of sensibility as receptive while he defines understanding as a means for thinking ideas and from which concepts arise. Now, in the 1798 *Anthropology* the two terms sensibility and understanding are mentioned only in the title of the section while in the body of the text we are confronted only with the more generic distinction between capacity (*Fähigkeit*) and faculty (*Vermögen*).

The distinction between the "spontaneity" of a faculty and the "passivity" of receptivity occurs in the same way in Baumgarten's *Metaphysica*.[297] Kant is aware of this distinction, since he uses Baumgarten's book as a companion for his lectures on metaphysics and anthropology.[298] The Latin terms *"facultas"* and *"receptivitas"*, used by Kant in the passage of the *Anthropology*, are respectively translated as *Vermögen* (faculty) and *Empfänglichkeit* (receptivity) in Baumgarten's treatise as well as in Kant's quoted passage.[299]

One only apparent oddity is that Baumgarten deals with this distinction in the first section of the *Metaphysica*, namely the one dedicated to ontology. One might have expected to find a reference to the relation between faculty and receptivity in the section of the book dedicated to empirical psychology, where the study of human mind belongs. Nonetheless, there is no trace of it in the corresponding third section of the book. This apparent incongruity dissolves once we consider (1) that Baumgarten analyses receptivity and faculty as relations between a subject and himself or the external world and that traditionally analyses concerning "relations" belong to ontology, and (2) that the dis-

---

297 See BAUMGARTEN, *Metaphysica*, § 216 (AA 17: 72.27–31) and the following notes.

298 See R. BRANDT, *Kommentar*, cit., but also REINHARD BRANDT – WERNER STARK, "Einleitung", in AA 25 (*Kant's Vorlesungen über Anthropologie*), pp. VII-CLI. In addition, cf. S. B. KIM, *Die Entstehung der Kantischen Anthropologie*, cit., the article by H. F. KLEMME, "Immanuel Kant", in EIKE BOHLKEN – CHRISTIAN THEIS (eds.), *Handbuch Anthropologie*, cit., pp. 11–16, and N. HINSKE, "Kants Idee der Anthropologie", cit. Kant's notes on Baumgarten's *Metaphysics* can be found in AA 15.

299 Baumgarten also uses the word "Fähigkeit" (capacity) in order to translate the Latin term "receptivitas". See Baumgarten, *Metaphysica*, II. Tractatio, 1. Ontologia, β) disiunctivis, ɣ) substantia et accidens, B) de statu, § 216 (AA 17: 72.27–31): "Omnis substantia exsistens agit, §. 210, 199, hinc habet possibilitatem agendi seu FACULTATEM*) (potentiam activam, vim, cf. §. 197), §. 57, si patitur, habet possibilitatem patiendi, i.e. (potentiam passivam, capacitatem) RECEPTIVITATEM**). §. 57. [translation in the footnote: *) Vermögen. **) Fähigkeit, Empfänglichkeit]".

tinction between faculty and receptivity is also taken for granted in Baumgarten's empirical psychology.

One might then wonder where this distinction belongs in Kant's philosophy. One can consider the historical background of this distinction and then be tempted to say that it is just a heritage of empirical psychology, which now rightly flows into Kant's pragmatic anthropology.[300]

However, this is only a part of the story, since, as I said, Kant's attempt to remain within the boundaries of his empirical research clashes with the need to be constantly referring to the architectonical classification of the mind in pure philosophy: the same distinctions at stake here are also part of the analyses of the *Critiques*.

In order to better understand the nuances of this discussion, it is opportune to delineate more clearly the boundaries between the pure philosophical investigation into the constitution of the human mind and empirical, anthropological research.

3.6 The Boundaries between Pure and Empirical Philosophy

In an already quoted passage from the *Architectonic* of the first *Critique*, Kant wonders where empirical psychology ought to be placed, since it "must be entirely banned from metaphysics, and is already excluded by the idea of it".[301] Kant's answer to this question is unequivocal: empirical psychology "comes in where the proper (empirical) doctrine of nature must be put, namely on the side of applied philosophy, for which pure philosophy contains the *a priori* principles, which must therefore be combined but never confused with the former".[302] At this stage of the analysis Kant still concedes empirical psychology

---

300 For the differences between Kant's 1798 *Anthropology* and Baumgartens' *psychologia empirica* see the analysis of the meaning of "pragmatic" above and also the historical review dedicated to the transition from empirical psychology to pragmatic anthropology.

301 See KrV, A 848/B 876 – AA 03: 548.17–19: "empirische Psychologie [muß] aus der Metaphysik gänzlich verbannt sein, und ist schon durch die Idee derselben davon gänzlich ausgeschlossen"; CpR p. 698.

302 See KrV, A 848/B 876 – AA 03: 548.13–17: "sie kommt dahin, wo die eigentliche (empirische) Naturlehre hingestellt werden muß, nämlich auf die Seite der angewandten Philosophie, zu welcher die reine Philosophie die *Principien a priori* enthält, die also mit jener zwar verbunden, aber nicht vermischt werden muß"; CpR p. 698.

"a little place in metaphysics", until it will be able to establish "its own domicile in a complete anthropology (the pendant to the empirical doctrine of nature)".[303]

What is at stake here is the relation between the new discipline of anthropology and the traditional discipline of empirical psychology and, moreover, the place of anthropology in the field of applied philosophy. Nevertheless, Kant grants temporary refuge to empirical psychology in metaphysics, i.e. within the boundaries of pure philosophy, since, in this case, Kant uses the term metaphysics in its wide sense, as the name that "can also be given to all of pure philosophy"[304].

Kant's distinction between pure and empirical philosophy is clear: "All philosophy [...] is either cognition from pure reason or rational cognition from empirical principles. The former is called pure philosophy, the latter empirical".[305] However, Kant allows an applied, empirical discipline – in this case: empirical psychology – to have a temporary refuge in pure philosophy. In regard to this, one might wonder whether an applied study can also (just temporarily) be treated as if it were a pure investigation.

Kant's project develops over time, such that pragmatic anthropology originates from the discipline of empirical psychology and becomes a new discipline, which has quite different aims and whose sphere of relevance is defined in more precise and more accurate terms. Empirical psychology should have its new domicile within the boundaries of the new discipline of pragmatic anthropology. However, the topics with which Kant's pure philosophy and his pragmatic anthropology intend to deal remain partially identical. This identity helps explain the intersections between the two disciplines that Kant conceives, however, as neatly separated from one another. It is easy to furnish some examples of this difficulty. For instance, firstly, the already mentioned fact that both in pure phi-

---

303 See KrV, A 848–9/B 876–7 – AA 03: 548.19–21,24–28: "Gleichwohl wird man ihr [=der empirischen Psychologie] nach dem Schulgebrauch doch noch immer (obzwar nur als Episode) ein Plätzchen darin verstatten müssen [...] Es ist also bloß ein so lange aufgenommener Fremdling, dem man auf einige Zeit einen Aufenthalt vergönnt, bis er in einer ausführlichen Anthropologie (dem Pendant zu der empirischen Naturlehre) seine eigene Behausung wird beziehen können"; CpR p. 698.
304 KrV, A 841/B 869 – AA 03: 543.02–03, CpR p. 696.
305 KrV, A 840/B 868 – AA 03: 543.24–26: "Alle Philosophie aber ist entweder Erkenntniß aus reiner Vernunft, oder Vernunfterkenntniß aus empirischen Principien. Die erstere heißt reine, die zweite empirische Philosophie"; CpR p. 695. Kant clearly distinguishes pure and empirical philosophy already in the *Dissertatio*. Cf. MSI (*De mundi sensibilis atque intelligibilis forma et principiis*), §. 8, AA 02: 395.15–23, but also MSI, §. 23, AA 02: 411.05–11. Here I do not take into consideration Kant's relation to the (Wolffian) tradition regarding this topic as this would lead away from my central question. But cf. also GMS, AA 04: 388.04–14, *Groundwork* p. 43–44.

losophy and in anthropology Kant deals with the gap between "receptivity" and "activity", but also with the topic of the faculties in their lower and higher classification and with their tripartition: the conformity of the topics is undeniable. However, what has to be noted is that the points of view from which the analyses are conducted are quite heterogeneous, and the means used in the two analyses (on the one hand, empirical recognitions, on the other hand, *a priori* assessments), are also fairly distinct; this notwithstanding, it is difficult to demonstrate their complete separation from one another.

Another example of the difficulty in distinguishing between the enterprise of pure philosophy and the empirical discipline of pragmatic anthropology can be found if we consider the more restricted field of ethical theory and, in particular, the distinction between metaphysics of morals and moral anthropology.

This distinction is most clearly illustrated in the general introduction to the *Metaphysics of Morals*, where we read that "a metaphysics of morals cannot dispense with principles of application", which means that the pure part of philosophical reflection must always relate to the applied one as well.[306] This happens in the same way as in a metaphysics of nature, where we must find principles "for applying those highest universal principles of nature in general to objects of experience".[307] From this, it thus follows that also in the case of a metaphysics of morals we have to consider experience and refer to the applied part of philosophical analysis; furthermore, in the context of a metaphysics of morals we "shall often have to take as our object the particular nature of human beings, which is cognized only by experience, in order to show in it what can be inferred from universal moral principles or cast doubt on their *a priori* source".[308]

These premises do not prevent Kant from being quite firm in assessing that pure and applied philosophy should not interfere, also in the case of ethics, for "a metaphysics of morals cannot be based upon anthropology", even though it

---

306 See MS, AA 06: 216.37–217.01, MM p. 372. The distinction between pragmatic and moral anthropology is, nonetheless, not completely clear. On this subject see, for instance, S. B. KIM, *Die Entstehung der Kantischen Anthropologie*, cit., p. 151, but also E. ARNOLDT, "Verhältnis von Kants physisch-geographischem Kolleg zu seinem anthropologischen", cit., in particular pp. 407–418; and, in addition, cf. also MARY J. GREGOR, *Laws of Freedom: A Study of Kant's Method of Applying the Categorical Imperative in the "Metaphysik der Sitten"*, Oxford, Blackwell 1963, pp. 5–9; UWE JUSTUS WENZEL, *Anthroponomie: Kants Archäologie der Autonomie*, Berlin, Akademie Verlag 1992; MONIKA FIRLA, *Untersuchungen zum Verhältnis von Anthropologie und Moralphilosophie bei Kant*, Frankfurt a. M., Lang 1981; CLAUDIA M. SCHMIDT, "The Anthropological Dimension of Kant's Metaphysics of Morals", in *Kant-Studien*, 96 (2005), pp. 66–84.
307 See MS, AA 06: 216.34–37, MM p. 372.
308 See MS, AA 06: 216.34–37, 217.01–06, MM p. 372.

"can still be applied to it".[309] In this way, Kant confirms the line adopted in the *Architectonic* chapter of the first *Critique* and maintains that the two spheres of philosophical analysis must be kept sharply distinct from one another.

Even though Kant has a clear idea of two distinct studies that are heterogeneous in scope and different in method, the limits between the empirical and the pure field of Kant's investigation are nonetheless not always neat, since Kant often handles one and the same subject matter in both fields of research. In a passage from the general introduction to the *Metaphysics of Morals*, which follows the one just mentioned, the risk of mixing the scopes of the analyses is once again embodied in Kant's talk of moral anthropology. Kant defines this discipline as "the counterpart of a metaphysics of morals, the other member of the division of practical philosophy as a whole".[310] He assesses that moral anthropology deals only with "the subjective conditions in human nature that hinder people or help them in *fulfilling* the laws of a metaphysics of morals".[311] Moreover, he says that moral anthropology should be concerned with "the development, spreading, and strengthening of moral principles (in education in schools and in popular instruction), and with other similar teachings and precepts based on experience".[312]

Such statements leave us with numerous unanswered questions and doubts. The first question regards the "subjective conditions in human nature", which are here said to be the subject matter of moral anthropology, but which are, later, nonetheless analysed in the context of a metaphysics of morals, as "preconditions of the mind's receptivity to the concepts of duty" in the introduction to the *Doctrine of Virtue*.[313] A second question concerns education and teaching, which should both be analysed in the context of a moral anthropology, but which are also treated in a metaphysics of morals, namely in the second part of the *Doctrine of Virtue*, i.e. the *Doctrine of the Methods of Ethics*.[314]

---

309 MS, AA 06: 217.06–08, MM p. 372: "Das will so viel sagen als: eine Metaphysik der Sitten kann nicht auf Anthropologie gegründet, aber doch auf sie angewandt werden".
310 MS, AA 06: 217.09–11, MM p. 372: "Das Gegenstück einer Metaphysik der Sitten, als das andere Glied der Eintheilung der praktischen Philosophie überhaupt, würde die moralische Anthropologie sein".
311 MS, AA 06: 217.11–13, MM p. 372: "[Die moralische Anthropologie würde] nur die subjective, hindernde sowohl als begünstigende Bedingungen der Ausführung der Gesetze der ersteren [= einer Metaphysik der Sitten] in der menschlichen Natur [enthalten]".
312 MS, AA 06: 217.13–16, MM p. 372: "die Erzeugung, Ausbreitung und Stärkung moralischer Grundsätze (in der Erziehung, der Schul- und Volksbelehrung) und dergleichen andere sich auf Erfahrung gründende Lehren und Vorschriften".
313 MS, TL, § XII, AA 06: 399–403.
314 MS, TL, AA 06: 475–485.

At first sight, Kant seems to justify the recurrence to the empirical study of the human being in pure philosophy, since he says that we cannot do without moral anthropology. But at the same time he confirms that to say moral anthropology "cannot be dispensed with" is not the same as saying that a mixture of the two fields is allowed. Kant surely recognizes that a mixture of applied and pure philosophy (in this case, of moral anthropology and metaphysics of morals) is no sustainable solution. He emphasizes that moral anthropology "must not precede a metaphysics of morals or be mixed with it".[315] If this happened, the consequences for the autonomy of ethics would be catastrophic, since

> one would then run the risk of bringing forth false or at least indulgent moral laws, which would misrepresent as unattainable what has only not been attained just because the law has not been seen and presented in its purity (in which its strength consists) or because spurious or impure incentives were used for what is itself in conformity with duty and good. This would leave no certain moral principles, either to guide judgement or to discipline the mind in observance of duty, the precepts of which must be given *a priori* by pure reason alone.[316]

This notwithstanding, some of the previously examined points bring us in the direction of illuminating a sort of interchange between the two fields of pure and applied philosophy. In fact, even though Kant aims to keep the fields separate in the most precise way possible, these disciplines share some topics, such as the study of the faculties, which are analysed with very distinct methods.

The boundaries between the empirical study of pragmatic anthropology and the investigations dedicated to the faculties in the critical works seem to be nuanced at times. However, it must be emphasized that Kant strongly aims to avoid the two disciplines of pure philosophy and pragmatic anthropology intermingling with one another. And, by the way, he is also successful in defining their scopes and methods as completely distinct.

---

315 MS, AA 06: 217.16–18, MM p. 372: "[Die moralische Anthropologie kann] nicht entbehrt werden [...], aber [sie muß] durchaus nicht vor jener vorausgeschickt, oder mit ihr vermischt werden [...]".
316 MS, AA 06: 217.18–27, MM p. 372: "weil man alsdann Gefahr läuft, falsche oder wenigstens nachsichtliche moralische Gesetze herauszubringen, welche das für unerreichbar vorspiegeln, was nur eben darum nicht erreicht wird, weil das Gesetz nicht in seiner Reinigkeit (als worin auch seine Stärke besteht) eingesehen und vorgetragen worden, oder gar unächte oder unlautere Triebfedern zu dem, was an sich pflichtmäßig und gut ist, gebraucht werden, welche keine sichere moralische Grundsätze übrig lassen, weder zum Leitfaden der Beurtheilung, noch zur Disciplin des Gemüths in der Befolgung der Pflicht, deren Vorschrift schlechterdings nur durch reine Vernunft *a priori* gegeben werden muß".

With this in mind, let me now consider some other passages, which further testify the interchange of topics and doctrines between pragmatic anthropology and pure philosophy. These passages come from the already quoted § 7 of the 1798 *Anthropology*.

3.7 The Mind's Activity: *Anthropology*, § 7

If we now go back to the lines in § 7, where Kant analyses sensibility and understanding and considers the status of cognition, we note that Kant states that a cognition (*ein Erkenntniß*) contains "joined together" both states of mind (*Gemüt*), the "active" (*handelnd*) one, which presents itself as a faculty, but also the "passive" (*leidend*) one, consisting in receptivity. Kant denotes "the possibility of having such a cognition" by the term "cognitive faculty" (*Erkenntnißvermögen*) and justifies the choice of this term by assessing that it refers firstly to the "most distinguished part of this faculty, namely, the activity of mind (*Thätigkeit des Gemüths*) in combining or separating representations from one another".[317]

Something noteworthy is expressed in this passage, which also helps to clarify why Kant is able to speak of "cognitive faculties" in many different ways also in the various classifications of the faculties, which he gives in the third *Critique* and elsewhere. It is crucial that Kant, when he provides the definition of the term "cognitive faculty", introduces new characteristics at the same time, which go beyond the distinction between spontaneity and passivity, on the one hand, and receptivity, on the other hand. According to this characterisation, the mind (*Gemüt*) is "active" (*tätig*) both (a) in the case that the sensuous capacities (the ones grouped under the general name of sensibility – *Sinnlichkeit*) are activated and (b) in the case that the properly-cognitive faculties (the ones grouped under the general name of understanding – *Verstand*) are at stake. The active character unites lower and higher cognitive faculties (*untere / obere Erkenntnißvermögen*), which are further characterized by the reference to two different kinds of representations (*Vorstellungen*):

---

317 Here is the complete passage in question: "Ein Erkenntniß enthält beides verbunden in sich, und die Möglichkeit eine solche zu haben führt den Namen des Erkenntnißvermögens von dem vornehmsten Theil derselben, nämlich der Thätigkeit des Gemüths Vorstellungen zu verbinden, oder von einander zu sondern", Anth, AA 07: 140. 18 – 22; *Anthropology* p. 251.

1. Representations "in regard to which the mind (*Gemüt*) behaves passively, and by means of which the subject is therefore *affected* (whether it *affects* itself or is *affected* by an object)";[318]
2. Representations "that comprise a sheer *doing* (thinking)";[319]

These two kinds of representations belong, respectively, to:
a) "the sensuous (*sinnlich*) cognitive faculty", which is also called "lower cognitive faculty" (*das untere Erikenntnißvermögen*) and is described as having "the character of *passivity* of the inner sense of sensations, [...] *that* [=character of passivity of the inner sense / inner sense] belongs to psychology (a sum of all inner perceptions under laws of nature) and establishes inner experience";[320]
b) "the intellectual (*intellectuell*) cognitive faculty", which is also called "higher cognitive faculty" (*das obere Erikenntnißvermögen*) and is described as having the character of "spontaneity of apperception, that is, of pure consciousness of the action, that constitutes thinking", *which* [spontaneity / apperception] belongs "to logic (a system of rules of the understanding)".[321]

---

318 Anth, AA 07: 140. 23–25: "Vorstellungen, in Ansehung deren sich das Gemüth leidend verhält, durch welche also das Subject afficirt wird (dieses mag sich nun selbst afficiren oder von einem Object afficirt werden)", *Anthropology* p. 251.
319 Anth, AA 07: 140. 26–27: "diejenigen [Vorstellungen], welche ein bloßes Thun (das Denken) enthalten, zum intellectuellen Erkenntnißvermögen", *Anthropology* p. 251. In the English translation of this sentence, the translator adds the words "ideas" ("But ideas that comprise a certain activity (thinking) belong to..."), not present in Kant's text (the discussion is concentrated, as before, more generally on representations) and translates "Thun" as "activity", a term used before for rendering "Thätigkeit".
320 Anth, AA 07: 140. 26–28, 141. 01–06 (passim – my italics): "[Diese Vorstellungen] gehören zum sinnlichen [Erkenntnißvermögen] [...]. Jenes wird auch das untere [...] Erkenntnißvermögen genannt. Jenes hat den Charakter der Passivität des inneren Sinnes der Empfindungen. [...] *Jener* [= Charakter der Passivität/innerer Sinn] [gehört] zur Psychologie (einem Inbegriff aller innern Wahrnehmungen unter Naturgesetzen) [...] und [begründet] innere Erfahrung", *Anthropology* p. 251.
321 Anth, AA 07: 140. 26–28, 141. 01–06 (passim – my italics): "Diejenigen [Vorstellungen gehören] [...] zum intellectuellen Erkenntnißvermögen [...]. Dieses [wird] aber [auch] das obere Erkenntnißvermögen genannt. [...] Dieses [hat den Charakter] der Spontaneität der Apperception, d.i. des reinen Bewußtseins der Handlung, *welche* [= Spontaneität / Apperception] das Denken ausmacht und zur Logik (einem System der Regeln des Verstandes) [...] gehört", *Anthropology* p. 251 (the translation of "Handlung" as activity is also misleading, since, as I already said, Louden already used the term for rendering the terms "Thätigkeit" and "Thun").

It has to be noted that the references of the two pronouns (in italics in my translation) are not completely clear. Here, as well as below, I do not agree with Louden's translation, which is partly misleading and which in any case neither helps one understand the reference here of the pronoun "jener" (AA 07: 141.04), nor below that of the pronoun "welche" (AA 07: 141.03). As for the first case, Kant speaks of something, "that" (=*jener*, pronoun, singular, nominative, masculine) belongs to psychology and establishes inner experience.[322] The pronoun might refer either to the character (*der Charakter*, singular masculine) of passivity of the inner sense or to inner sense itself (*innerer Sinn*, singular masculine). In both cases we are confronted with aspects of the lower cognitive faculty: this is the determining point. On the other hand, as for the second case, Kant speaks of something, "which" (=*welche*, pronoun, singular, nominative, feminine) constitutes thinking and belongs to logic. This time, the pronoun might refer either to spontaneity (= *Spontaneität*, singular feminine) of apperception or to apperception itself (=*Apperception*, singular feminine). Also in this case, it does not make a big difference, since, in the end, we are confronted with aspects of the higher cognitive faculty.[323] If we want to read the "jener" as referring to "the character of passivity", then it makes more sense to interpret "welche" as referring to "spontaneity". This is in my opinion the most sensible reading, and this would also mean that Kant generally aims to distinguish between spontaneity and passivity. If we decided instead to have "jener" refer to "inner sense", it would be more plausible to refer "welche" to "Apperception" and, in this way, we must intend Kant's point of view to be directed to particular capacities.

Let the translation and interpretation of this passage be as it may, the difficulty in finding the grammatical reference of the two pronouns does not really influence the important conclusion reached by Kant. To sum it up:

1. The lower cognitive faculty allows us to get access to the "sensuous" (*sinnlich*) part of our representations; it is passive and consists in receptivity (*Empfänglichkeit*). The discipline to which its study belongs is *psychology*;
2. The higher cognitive faculty allows us to get access to the "intellectual" (*intellectuell*) part of our representations; it is spontaneous and presents itself as a faculty (*Vermögen*). The discipline to which its study belongs is *logic*.

If we constitute a parallel between the just traced distinction and the title of the section in question ("On sensibility in contrast to understanding" / *Von der Sinn-*

---

322 Anth, AA 07: 141.04.
323 A third option, according to which "welche" refers to "Handlung" is also possible, but, for interpretation's sake, not really attractive.

lichkeit im Gegensatz mit dem Verstande), it will be quite clear that Kant refers to *sensibility* (*Sinnlichkeit*) when he analyses the "lower cognitive faculty", while he speaks of *understanding* (*Verstand*) when he analyses the "higher cognitive faculty". Both sensibility and understanding are defined as "cognitive faculties", since both of them are necessary in order to cognize (and with this verb I do not refer to the specialistic meaning of scientific knowledge, but only to cognition in a very broad sense). Moreover, both of these aspects of the mind (*Gemüt*) are "active" (*tätig*), since the *"activity" of the mind* (*Thätigkeit des Gemüths*) constitutes the most distinguished part of both of them: this activity enables us to combine or separate representations from one another. From this consideration it seems to follow that sensibility is not to be regarded as pure passivity, since Kant considers both the higher and the lower faculties of the mind (*Gemüt*) to be "active" (*tätig*). However, each of them is active in quite a different way: sensibility is "active" (*tätig*) only in that it can participate in the "mental process" and it does so through its receptive role, that is, sensibility is only receptive and not active in the specific sense used by Kant in the first *Critique* to denote the spontaneity of the higher faculty of understanding.[324]

The analysed passage is interesting in many respects but, first of all, in that it shows one more time that pragmatic anthropology and pure philosophy oft share themes and doctrines. In the proceedings of this text and, in particular, in that part of the text not included in the published book, Kant himself seems to wonder whether such kinds of distinctions can coherently belong to anthropology as well. Let me continue with the analysis of this text, which has not been included in the final version (the one edited) of the 1798 *Anthropology*.

3.8 A Significant Passage from the Rostock Manuscript

The remark following § 7 of the *Anthropology* treats in more detail, on the one hand, the parallels between the higher cognitive faculty and understanding and, on the other hand, the parallels between the lower cognitive faculty and sensibility. As already noted, part of the remark and, in particular, the one dedicated to this distinction, has been crossed out and not included in the published book. Nonetheless, the text is available to us thanks to the fact that the manu-

---

324 For a different interpretation of this point cf. also MATTHIAS WUNSCH, "The Activity of Sensibility in Kant's Anthropology. A Developmental History of the Concept of the Formative Faculty", in *Kant Yearbook 2011 – Anthropology*. Volume 3, pp. 67–90.

script prepared for the publication of the book is preserved at the University of Rostock.[325]

The answer to the question: "by whom was the remark crossed out?" seems, at first sight, to remain unanswered. Some scholars believe that it is impossible to know how many of the changes between the hand-written manuscript and the first (and second) edition of Kant's *Anthropology* were approved by Kant himself, such that the role played by Kant in preparing the publication remains unknown to a certain extent.[326]

Nonetheless, it is possible to reconstruct with a certain precision the history of the publication of the book.[327] For instance, it has been ascertained that Christian Gottfried Schütz was entrusted in the proofreading of the text of the *Anthropology*.[328] Besides this, according to Brandt, it was not Kant himself that crossed

---

325 These supplementary texts will from now on be quoted as *Ergänzungen* and the manuscript at the University of Rostock Library as *H*. The *Anthropology* is Kant's only published book for which we have a complete hand-written manuscript prepared by Kant himself, which is conserved at the University of Rostock Library. See R. BRANDT, *Kommentar*, pp. 20–21: "Die <u>Anthropologie in pragmatischer Hinsicht</u> ist das einzige gedruckte Buch Kants, von dem – mit Ausnahme geringer Textbestände (Vorrede, Inhaltsverzeichnis, Titelblatt von Teil 1) – ein vollständiges fortlaufendes Manuskript existiert. Die Handschrift umfaßt 150 Folioseiten; die Prüfung der Wasserzeichen durch das 'Buch- und Schriftmuseum Deutsche Bücherei Leipzig' 1991 führte zu keinen datierungsrelevanten Erkenntnissen. Für das Rostocker Manuskript gilt, was Vittorio Mathieu im Hinblick auf das <u>Opus postumum</u> festgehalten hat: Kant bevorzugt es, neue Kapitel oder Paragraphen auf neuen Blättern zu beginnen; dadurch entstehen einerseits Leerstellen, andererseits gedrängte Schriftpassagen am Ende der vorhergehenden Abschnitte mit dem Ziel, den Schluß dieses Teils möglichst noch auf derselben Seite unterzubringen". For a more detailed account concerning the manuscript, cf. WERNER STARK, *Nachforschungen zu Briefen und Handschriften Immanuel Kants*, Berlin, Akademie Verlag 1993 (zugleich Marburg, Dissertation, 1992), pp. 48–52.

326 See R. BRANDT, *Kommentar*, p. 20 ff., and Louden's introduction to *Anthropology*, pp. 228–229.

327 See R. BRANDT, *Kommentar*, pp. 20–31 (*Die Entstehung des Buches*) – in particular: "Die Zeit der Abfassung von H [Manuscript at the University of Rostock Library] läßt sich nur durch Indizien erschließen. Die Handschrift ist so verfaßt, daß sie nicht als Druckvorlage dienen kann; es mußten in eine Abschrift von H Ergänzungen (z. B. offengelassene Paragraphenziffern) eingetragen werden. Die anzunehmende Abschrift wurde von einer bislang unbekannten Person erstellt, Kant vorgelegt und dann an den Verleger Nicolovius gesandt, der sie seinerseits an eine Druckerei in Jena weiterschickte. Über das Erscheinen des Buches im Herbst 1798 wird in Briefen und Anzeigen berichtet", p. 20

328 See for example Schütz' letter to Kant, dating 22nd May 1800, where Schütz wishes also for the publication of a book on physical geography, AA 12: 307.24–27: "Das angenehme Geschäft, was ich übernommen hatte die letzte Correctur der 2ten Ausgabe Ihrer Anthropologie zu besorgen, hat in mir den Wunsch erneuert, auch die physische Geographie von Ihnen, Verehrungswürdigster Mann, gedruckt zu sehn".

out the *Ergänzungen*, which are now to be found at the end of the seventh volume of the Academy edition, since Kant himself wanted to eliminate from his 1798 *Anthropology* all the references to metaphysics in general and, in particular, the ones pertaining to his own critical theory, which he now aims to keep fairly distinct from the scholastic, academic subject matter of anthropology, as he newly conceives of it.[329] The description of the faculties belongs to pure philosophy in that they are defined as the necessary and *a priori* conditions of the possibility of mental action. Nonetheless, the treatment of the faculties is also part of empirical studies, insofar as Kant analyses them on the basis of empirical observations.

The first shorter annotation from the *Ergänzungen* consists in a piece of writing, which could have appeared without any problem in the critical works.[330] In this annotation, Kant assesses that the cognition of objects of the senses can take place in no other way, than that in which the objects "appear to us", rather than "according to what they are in themselves".[331] Furthermore, Kant remarks that we are "concerned only with those things that can be given to our senses".[332] This reference constitutes only the first of a long list in the *Ergänzungen*, where Kant deals with distinctions, to which he already dedicated a lot of space in pure philosophy.

The longer text that follows in the manuscript distinguishes between metaphysics and anthropology.[333] At the beginning of the remark, Kant tries to apply

---

329 See R. BRANDT, *Kommentar*, p. 176: "Der Grund der Streichung dieser langen Passage dürfte nicht in der Ablehnung des Inhalts liegen (es findet sich wohl kein Gedanke, der nicht in publizierten Schriften ebenfalls zu belegen wäre), sondern in der Meinung, daß hier die Grenze von der Anthropologie zur Transzendentalphilosophie überschritten wurde, kombiniert vielleicht mit der Feststellung, daß alles hier Vorgetragene schon vielfältig seit 1787 (der 2. Auflage der <u>KrV</u>) gesagt wurde".
330 Anth, AA 07: 396.21–33.
331 Anth, AA 07: 396. 24–26: "Diese [Eindrücke] stellen uns die Gegenstände der Sinne nur vor wie sie uns erscheinen nicht nach dem was sie an sich selbst sind". Louden's translation in *Anthropology* (p. 251) is quite mistaken, since the translator does not explain, which term "diese" refers to (I would say, "Eindrücke") and he misleadingly translates in singular the German "stellen" (in Louden's translation: "this [who? What?] presents objects of the senses to us").
332 Here the whole passage from the *Ergänzungen*, Anth, AA 07: 396. 30–33: "[das Erkenntnis (von Gegenständen der Sinne) kann] für uns keine Kenntnisse geben [...] als von Dingen die unseren Sinnen vorgelegt werden können so mag es immer in der Vernunftidee Begriffe geben welche über jene ihre Grentze hinaus aber nur in practischer Absicht (der Freiheitsidee) objective Realität haben; uns gehen hier nur diejenige an welche unseren Sinnen gegeben werden können".
333 On these passages of the *Ergänzungen* see also R. BRANDT, *Kommentar*, pp. 176–177: "Auch die vorhergehenden Bemerkungen des gestrichenen Textes gehören nicht zur Anthropologie,

to the cognition of the self the just mentioned principle, according to which human beings cognize only on the basis of what is given to their senses. From this, it follows that a human being's self-recognition provides no cognition of the self as it absolutely is.[334] However, Kant notes at once that this sentence "cannot be dealt with in anthropology" and has to be taken merely as "a bold *metaphysical proposition (paradoxon)*".[335] Let us have a closer look at this passage, firstly clarifying that, in general, a paradox consists primarily in carrying out as far as possible an inner experience, so that the human being who "pursues this investigation as far as he can" will "have to confess that self-knowledge would lead to an unfathomable depth, to an abyss in the exploration of his nature".[336] Kant's strategy for passing over this paradox and partly understanding this abyss consists in distinguishing between two approaches to the analysis of inner experience. The first approach is the purely logical one; the second approach is a "physiological" one, which Kant also calls the "psychological" or "anthropological" approach. We are confronted here with a duplication of the analysis, since Kant distinguishes between the study on sensibility and the one on understanding.

In order to see how these two disciplines relate to one another and, by so doing, clarify why the boundaries between anthropology and pure philosophy are so nuanced, it may be helpful to group the keywords recurring in Kant's remark from the 1798 *Anthropology* into two sets.[337] Here is my proposal:

1. (A) "understanding" [*Verstand*, e.g. AA 07: 397.03,07,11,12, 398.17,36, 399.04,10,16], "faculty of spontaneity" [*Vermögen der Spontaneität*, AA 07: 397.11], "higher cognitive faculty" [*oberes Erkenntnisvermögen*, AA 07: 397.12],

---

und es ist zugleich signifikant für die prekäre Grenzbestimmung, daß sie [...] in die <u>Anthropologie</u> eingeführt werden".

334 Anth, AA 07: 396.36–39: "Daß dieser Satz [d. i., in my opinion (A. F.), the reference is here to the already quoted sentence: 'Diese (Eindrücke) stellen uns die Gegenstände der Sinne nur vor wie sie uns erscheinen nicht nach dem was sie an sich selbst sind', Anth, AA 07: 396. 24–26] so gar vom inneren Selbst gelte und daß der Mensch wenn er sich innerlich nach den Eindrücken die gewisse Vorstellungen aus welchen Ursachen sie auch entspringen mögen beobachtet er sich auch dadurch [[doch]] nur erkennen könne wie er sich erscheint nicht wie er schlechthin ist", *Anthropology* p. 252.

335 Anth, AA 07: 396.36–39: "das ist ein kühner metaphysischer Satz (*paradoxon*), der in einer Anthropologie gar nicht zur Frage kommen kann", *Anthropology* p. 252.

336 Anth, AA 07: 396.41–43, 397.01–02: "Daß [[er]] aber wenn er innere Erfahrungen [[von]] an sich selbst [[mache]] anstellt [[daß]] wenn er [[durch]] diese Nachforschung [[auch noch]] so weit verfolgt als er kann er doch gestehen müsse das Selbsterkentnis führe zu unergründlicher Tiefe zum Abgrunde in der Erforschung seiner Natur gehört zur Anthropologie", *Anthropology* p. 252 (modified translation).

337 I consider here Anth, AA 07: 397.03–399.22.

"faculty which submits representations to a certain *a priori* rules" [*Vermögen, das die Vorstellungen gewissen Regeln a priori unterwirft*, AA 07: 397.12–13]; (B) "logic" [*Logik*, AA 07: 398.03,38]; (C) "consciousness of the I" as "mere thinking" [*Bewußtsein des Ich – des bloßen Denkens*, AA 07: 398.01], "discursive apperception" [*discursive Apperception*, AA 07: 398.02–03], "pure apperception of the understanding" [*reine Apperception des Verstandes*, AA 07: 398.03], "apperception" as "intellectual self-consciousness" [*Apperception als intellektuelles Selbstbewußtsein*, AA 07: 398.32–33];

2. (A1) "sensibility" [*Sinnlichkeit*, AA 07: 399.05, 09], "affectability" [*Affectibilität*, AA 07: 397.31]; (B1) "theoretical (physiological) cognition of nature" [*ein theoretisches (physiologisches) Erkentnis der Natur des Menschen*, AA 07: 397.28], "psychology" [*Psychologie*, AA 07: 397.29, 398.43], "anthropology (as physiology)" [*Anthropologie (als Physiologie)*, AA 07: 398.03–04], "empirical cognition of the inner sense (inner experience)" [*empirisches Erkentnis seiner selbst (innere Erfahrung)*, AA 07: 398.26; *innere Erfahrung*, AA 07: 397.14, 399.19]; (C1) "consciousness of the I as inner perception" [*Bewußtsein des Ich – der inneren Wahrnehmung*, AA 07: 398.01–02], "intuitive apperception" [*intuitive Apperception*, AA 07: 398.03], "empirical apperception of sensibility" [*empirische Apperception (der Sinnlichkeit)*, AA 07: 399.04–05], "inner sense" as "empirical self-consciousness" [*innerer Sinn – empirisches Selbstbewußtsein*, AA 07: 398.31–32].

A consideration of the two groupings (and their three subgroups) gives us the opportunity to clarify Kant's attempt. Thus, one may draw the following considerations:

(1) Kant firstly proposes two levels for the operations of the mind (*Gemüt*) and describes, on the one hand, understanding (*Verstand*) as a faculty of spontaneity (*Vermögen der Spontaneität*) and, on the other hand, sensibility (*Sinnlichkeit*) as affectability (*Affectibilität*). This distinction parallels the one between lower cognitive faculty (*unteres Erkenntnisvermögen*) and higher cognitive faculty (*oberes Erkenntnisvermögen*), which, as discussed above, he already treats in the body of § 7.

(2) Secondly, Kant makes two different disciplines correspond to these two aspects of the mind (*Gemüt*): on the one hand, the analysis of the understanding is logic [*Logik*]; on the other hand, Kant refers to psychology (*Psychologie*) / physiology (*Physiologie*) / anthropology (*Anthropologie*) in connection with sensibility. In the published text, Kant assessed that the study concerning understanding belongs to logic, which is a "system of rules of the understanding" (*System der Regeln des Verstandes*).[338] Now, while assimilating understanding to "a higher

---

338 Anth, AA 07: 141. 03–04, *Anthropology* p. 251.

cognitive faculty", to a "faculty of spontaneity", he states in addition that this faculty "submits representations to certain *a priori* rules and itself makes experience possible".[339] It makes sense to say that "all cognition presupposes understanding".[340] Psychology, instead, is presented as a discipline, which aims at "theoretical (physiological) cognition" (*ein theoretisches – physiologisches – Erkentnis*) of a human being's nature.[341] Psychology has "plenty to do in tracing everything that lies hidden" in the "I which has been observed by itself" and which is therefore constituted by "a sum total of so many objects of inner perception".[342] Furthermore, Kant equates physiology with anthropology,[343] such that, conclusively, we are allowed to state in this case that the field of psychology may also coincide with that of physiology which, in turn, coincides with the field of anthropology.

(3) Thirdly, both the disciplines of logic and anthropology (/ physiology / psychology) descend from and apply to a "doubled consciousness of [the] I", that is, respectively, on the one side, the rational consciousness of mere thinking (*Bewusstsein des bloßen Denkens*, also identified with the intellectual self-consciousness and with apperception), which does not furnish any content (that is, matter of cognition); on the other side, the empirical consciousness of inner perception (*Bewusstsein der inneren Wahrnehmung*, also identified with empirical self-consciousness and with inner sense), which provides a content (by inner sense).[344] In addition to this, the fact that the distinction parallels

---

339 Anth, AA 07: 397. 11–13: "der Verstand [ist] ein Vermögen der Spontaneität in unserem Erkentnis ein oberes Erkentnisvermögen weil es die Vorstellungen gewissen Regeln *a priori* unterwirft und selbst die Erfahrung möglich macht", *Anthropology* p. 252.
340 Anth, AA 07: 397. 03: "Alles Erkentnis setzt Verstand voraus", *Anthropology* p. 252.
341 Anth, AA 07: 397. 28 – 29: "Ein theoretisches (physiologisches) Erkenntnis seiner Natur [...], worauf die Psychologie eigentlich ausgeht", *Anthropology* p. 252.
342 That is also why, as we have already seen, the discipline of psychology "may not ever hope to complete this task and satisfactorily answer the question: 'What is the human being?'". Here is the whole passage from Anth, AA 07: 398.42 – 43, 399.01 – 03: "das von sich selbst beobachtete Ich ist ein Inbegriff von so viel Gegenständen der inneren Warnehmung daß die Psychologie vollauf zu tun hat um alles darinn im Verborgenen liegende auszuspühren und nicht hoffen darf damit jemals zu Ende zu kommen und die Frage hinreichend zu beantworten: Was ist der Mensch". *Anthtopology*, p. 253.
343 Anth, AA 07: 398. 02– 05: "... discursive und intuitive Apperception wovon die erste zur Logik die andere zur Anthropologie (als Physiologie) gehört jene ohne Inhalt (Materie des Erkentnisses) diese von dem inneren Sinne mit einem Inhalte versehen ist", *Anthropology* p. 253.
344 Anth, AA 07: 398.01– 05: "ein doppeltes Bewußtseyn dieses Ich, einmal das des bloßen Denkens dann aber auch der inneren Warnehmung (ein rationales und empirisches) gebe d.i. discursive und intuitive Apperception wovon die erste zur Logik die andere zur Anthropologie (als Physiologie) gehört jene ohne Inhalt (Materie des Erkentnisses) diese von dem inneren

the one between understanding and sensibility as well, as Kant separates "pure apperception (of the understanding) from empirical apperception (of sensibility)", has to be noted.[345] The text manifests a more precise account of the concept of sensibility and its subjective condition: sensibility "brings representations to consciousness";[346] these representations are, in turn, "in conformity with each other, according to the form of their relation, the subjective and the formal condition of sensibility [...] and not merely according to rules of the understanding".[347]

This definition will become important later in my analysis in chapter 4 and, more in particular, in chapter 5 below.

Sinne mit einem Inhalte versehen ist", *Anthropology* p. 253. The passage seems to constitute the basis for further discussion about concepts normally pertaining to pure philosophy, as the ones of appearance (*phaenomenon*) and experience, with which Kant deals in the *Critiques*. See Anth, AA 07: 398.06–08: "Ein Gegenstand des (äußeren oder inneren) Sinnes so fern er wargenommen wird heißt Erscheinung (*phaenomenon*). Das Erkentnis eines Gegenstandes in der Erscheinung (d.i. als Phänomens) ist Erfahrung"; Anth, AA 07: 398.12–16: "Also ist Erfahrung die Handlung (der Vorstellungskraft) wodurch Erscheinungen unter den Begriff von einem Gegenstande derselben gebracht werden und Erfahrungen werden gemacht dadurch daß Beobachtungen (absichtliche Warnehmungen) angestellt und über die Vereinigung derselben unter Einem Begriffe nachgedacht (reflectirt) wird"; *Anthropology* p. 253.

345 Anth, AA 07: 399. 04–17: "Man muß also die reine Apperception (des Verstandes) von der empirischen (der Sinnlichkeit) unterscheiden bey welcher letzteren wenn das Subject aus sich attendirt es sich dadurch auch zugleich afficirt und so [[Erscheinungen]] Empfindungen in sich aufruft d.i. Vorstellungen zum Bewußtseyn bringt die der Form ihres Verhältnisses nach untereinander der subjectiven formalen [[Bedingungen]] Beschaffenheit der Sinnlichkeit nämlich der Anschauung in [[Raum und]] der Zeit (zugleich oder nacheinander zu sein) nicht blos den Regeln des Verstandes gemäs sind. Da nun [[diese letzteren Bedingungen]] jene Formen nicht als für jedes Wesen überhaupt das sich seiner bewußt ist geltend angenommen werden kann so wird das Erkentnis was den inneren Sinn des Menschen zum Grunde hat diesen bey der inneren Erfahrung nicht vorstellen wie er an sich selbst ist (weil die Bedingung nicht für alle denkende Wesen gültig ist denn sonst wäre eine Vorstellung des Verstandes) sondern ist blos ein Bewußtseyn der Art wie der Mensch [[sich selber]] in der inneren Beobachtung [[sich]] ihm selbst erscheint", *Anthropology* p. 253–254.

346 Anthr, AA 07: 399.07: "Vorstellungen zum Bewußtseyn bringt", *Anthropology* p. 253.

347 Anthr, AA 07: 399.07–11: "die der Form ihres Verhältnisses nach untereinander der subjectiven formalen [[Bedingungen]] Beschaffenheit der Sinnlichkeit nämlich der Anschauung in [[Raum und]] der Zeit (zugleich oder nacheinander zu sein) nicht blos den Regeln des Verstandes gemäs sind", *Anthropology* p. 253.

3.9 The Published Remark to § 7 of the 1798 *Anthropology*

In the 1798 published *Anthropology* a different text substitutes the one just analysed.[348] In the published remark to § 7 Kant does not refer primarily to the difference between understanding and sensibility; he rather deals with the topic afterwards in sections 8–11, where he composes an apology to sensibility and a defence of it against three accusations.[349] In the remark, Kant tackles themes which he himself defines as metaphysical, so that anthropology and pure philosophy once again approximate each other. A first clear proof of the contiguity of metaphysical themes to the empirical discipline of pragmatic anthropology is the reference to the distinction between objects as they appear to us and objects as they are, that is, the distinction between *phenomena* and *noumena* proposed in the first *Critique*. Kant determines that "all experience (empirical cognition), inner no less than outer, is only the cognition of objects as they appear to us, not as they are (considered in themselves alone)".[350] The reference to the subject's inner constitution (*Beschaffenheit des Subjects*) has to be noted, with its reference to "receptivity (*Empfänglichkeit*), after which thinking (*das Denken*) (the concept of the object) follows" and on whose basis depends "what kind of sensible intuition there will be". This theory contrasts the view according to which the human being's sensible intuitions depend rather "merely on the constitution of the object of the representation".[351] In relation to this form of receptivity (*Empfänglichkeit*), Kant notes that the "formal constitution of this receptivity (*Receptivität*) cannot in turn be borrowed from the senses, but rather must (as intuition) be given *a priori*".[352] Furthermore, he refers to this sensible intuition as something "which remains even after everything empirical (comprising sense experi-

---

348 Anthr, AA 07: 141.07–143.12, *Anthropology* pp. 254–256.

349 Anthr, AA 07: 143.13–146.25, *Anthropology* pp. 256–259.

350 Anthr, AA 07: 141.09–11: "Der Gegenstand der Vorstellung, der nur die Art enthält, wie ich von ihm afficirt werde, kann von mir nur erkannt werden, wie er mir erscheint, und alle Erfahrung (empirische Erkenntniß), die innere nicht minder als die äußere, ist nur Erkenntniß der Gegenstände, wie sie uns erscheinen, nicht wie sie (für sich allein betrachtet) sind", *Anthropology* p. 254.

351 Here the whole passage from Anthr, AA 07: 141.12–15: "Denn es kommt alsdann nicht blos auf die Beschaffenheit des Objects der Vorstellung, sondern auf die des Subjects und dessen Empfänglichkeit an, welcher Art die sinnliche Anschauung sein werde, darauf das Denken desselben (der Begriff vom Object) folgt", *Anthropology* p. 254.

352 Anthr, AA 07: 141.15–17: "Die formale Beschaffenheit dieser Receptivität kann nun nicht wiederum noch von den Sinnen abgeborgt werden, sondern muß (als Anschauung) *a priori* gegeben sein", *Anthropology* p. 254.

ence) is omitted" and, as he already noted in the first *Critique*, Kant here remembers that "in inner experiences this formal element of intuition is time".[353]

The consideration of what in receptivity still remains when everything empirical is omitted points to a knowledge which goes beyond the empirical, that is the field of pure philosophy, to which Kant's considerations on the I also refer, in so far as Kant identifies two different ways of referring to the I: "I as a thinking being" and the I "as a sensing being". Kant first excludes the possibility of becoming acquainted with the I as a *noumenon*, in that he emphasizes that I "cognize myself only as I appear to myself, not as a thing in itself". Afterwards, he refers to the thinking and sensing I, in that he assesses that the subject comes up to self-cognition only by means of his own receptivity, of the passive role of the faculty of ideas: "for this cognition still depends on the temporal condition, which is not a concept of the understanding (consequently not mere spontaneity); as a result it depends on a condition with regard to which my faculty of ideas is passive (and belongs to receptivity)".[354]

These two different functions of the I serve also to introduce the distinction between a psychological analysis of inner sense as applied consciousness and a merely logical analysis of apperception as pure consciousness. This contrast recalls the already mentioned distinction between anthropological analyses, as a sort of "empirical psychological" analysis, based on the lower cognitive faculties, i.e. on sensibility in general, on the one hand, and logical analyses, as pure rational analyses based on the higher cognitive faculties, i.e. on understanding in its most general meaning, on the other hand.[355] Pure and empirical

---

353 Kant's reference to time, in order to institute this connection, is surely tempting for many Heideggerrian readers of Kant, Anthr, AA 07: 141.17–20: "d.i. es muß eine sinnliche Anschauung sein, welche übrig bleibt, wenn gleich alles Empirische (Sinnenempfindung Enthaltende) weggelassen wird, und dieses Förmliche der Anschauung ist bei inneren Erfahrungen die Zeit", *Anthropology* p. 254.

354 Here is the whole passage from Anthr, AA 07: 142.03–19: "Ich, als denkendes Wesen, bin zwar mit Mir, als Sinnenwesen, ein und dasselbe Subject; aber als Object der inneren empirischen Anschauung, d.i. so fern ich innerlich von Empfindungen in der Zeit, so wie sie zugleich oder nach einander sind, afficirt werde, erkenne ich mich doch nur, wie ich mir selbst erscheine, nicht als Ding an sich selbst. Denn es hängt doch von der Zeitbedingung, welche kein Verstandesbegriff (mithin nicht bloße Spontaneität) ist, folglich von einer Bedingung ab, in Ansehung deren mein Vorstellungsvermögen leidend ist (und gehört zur Receptivität)", *Anthropology* pp. 254–255.

355 As we read in Anthr, AA 07: 142.20–24: "The cause of these errors [subjective causes are regarded as objective] is that the terms inner sense and apperception are normally taken by psychologists to be synonymous, despite the fact that the first alone should indicate a psychological (applied) consciousness, and the second merely a logical (pure) consciousness" – "Daß die Wörter innerer Sinn und Apperception von den Seelenforschern gemeinhin für

analyses are thus kept apart from one another, even though topics which apparently pertain also to anthropological studies (as the one dedicated to receptivity) are dealt with also by means of pure philosophy, as well as topics already treated in the context of pure philosophy (as the discussion concerning the faculties in the *Critiques*) find a place in the context of the discipline of pragmatic anthropology as well. Pure philosophical investigations, even though they do not pertain to the field of an empirical discipline, share with it topics such as the one of the faculties. Even the conclusion to the published remark just analysed can be read in light of this consideration:

> This note does not really belong to anthropology. In anthropology, experiences are appearances united according to laws of understanding, and in taking into consideration our way of representing things, the question of how they are apart from their relation to the senses (consequently as they are in themselves) is not pursued at all; for this belongs to metaphysics, which has to do with the possibility of *a priori* cognition.[356]

Eventually, Kant himself acknowledges that the observations advanced in the remark in question, which occurs in the context of his pragmatic anthropology, still belong to the domain of critical philosophy.[357]

In my present work I do not aim to deal with the analysis of the faculties in the 1798 *Anthropology*; I rather aim to concentrate on the pure philosophical aspect of Kant's investigations of the faculties and, in this way, I will present Kant's classification of the faculties as it is proposed in the critical works (in chapter 4 below).

Nonetheless, before turning to this classification, I still intend to mention some observations made by Kant on some aspects of the concept of "sensibility" in the 1798 *Anthropology*, since in this case we also find further references to the domain of pure philosophy and since the concept of sensibility plays a central part in the next two chapters of my work.

---

gleichbedeutend genommen werden, unerachtet der erstere allein ein psychologisches (angewandtes), die zweite aber blos ein logisches (reines) Bewußtsein anzeigen soll, ist die Ursache dieser Irrungen", *Anthropology* p. 255.

356 Anthr, AA 07: 142.31–143.02: "Diese Anmerkung gehört eigentlich nicht zur Anthropologie. In dieser sind nach Verstandesgesetzen vereinigte Erscheinungen Erfahrungen, und da wird nach der Vorstellungsart der Dinge, wie sie auch ohne ihr Verhältniß zu den Sinnen in Betrachtung zu ziehen (mithin an sich selbst) sind, gar nicht gefragt; denn diese Untersuchung gehört zur Metaphysik, welche es mit der Möglichkeit der Erkenntniß *a priori* zu thun hat", *Anthropology* p. 255.

357 Cf. R. BRANDT, *Kommentar*, p. 184: "Kant meidet es in der <u>Anthropologie</u>, von seiner eigenen Transzendentalphilosophie zu sprechen. Deren Lehre wird hier generell zur Metaphysik gerechnet".

3.10 The Concept of Sensibility: *Anthropology*, §§ 8 – 11

The guideline of sections 8 – 11 is the defence of sensibility (*Sinnlichkeit*) against three accusations: that it (1) confuses, (2) has command over the understanding and (3) deceives.[358] The need to defending sensibility is caused by the fact that it "is in bad repute", in contrast to the understanding.[359] As Kant says, "everyone shows the greatest respect for the understanding, as is already indicated by the very name *higher* cognitive faculty" attributed to it,[360] while the opposite happens in the case of sensibility. Kant identifies "the cause of all the evil said about it" in "the passive element in sensibility, which we after all cannot get rid of".[361]

Let me briefly refer to Kant's defence of sensibility. We remember that at the beginning of § 7, "On sensibility in contrast to understanding", Kant refers to sensibility (*Sinnlichkeit*) as the "lower cognitive faculty" and to understanding (*Verstand*) as the "higher cognitive faculty" and calls both "cognitive faculty" from the "most distinguished part" of these two faculties, which is the "activity of mind (*Thätigkeit des Gemüths*)". The mind (*Gemüt*) is "active" (*tätig*) both with respect to the sensuous capacities (collectively grouped under *Sinnlichkeit*) and to the properly-cognitive faculties (collectively grouped under *Verstand*).[362]

---

358 Cf. Anthr, AA 07: 143.20 – 24: "Man sagt ihr viel Schlimmes nach: z. B. 1) daß sie die Vorstellungskraft verwirre; 2) daß sie das große Wort führe und als Herrscherin, da sie doch nur die Dienerin des Verstandes sein sollte, halsstarrig und schwer zu bändigen sei; 3) daß sie sogar betrüge und man in Ansehung ihrer nicht genug auf seiner Hut sein könne", and, more generally, AA 07: 144.09 – 146.25, *Anthropology* pp. 256 – 259.

359 Anthr, AA 07: 143.19: "die Sinnlichkeit ist in üblem Ruf", *Anthropology* p. 256. These accusations come from the rationalists. For an analysis of the accusations, see R. Brandt, *Kommentar*, pp. 184 – 186.

360 Anthr, AA 07: 143.15 – 16: "Dem Verstande bezeigt jedermann alle Achtung, wie auch die Benennung desselben als oberen Erkenntnißvermögens es schon anzeigt", *Anthropology* p. 256.

361 Anthr, AA 07: 144.01 – 02: "Das Passive in der Sinnlichkeit, was wir doch nicht ablegen können, ist eigentlich die Ursache alles des Übels, was man ihr nachsagt", *Anthropology* p. 256.

362 Anthr, AA 07: 140.15 – 28: "*Von der Sinnlichkeit im Gegensatz mit dem Verstande* / § 7. / In Ansehung des Zustandes der Vorstellungen ist mein Gemüth entweder handelnd und zeigt Vermögen (*facultas*), oder es ist leidend und besteht in Empfänglichkeit (*receptivitas*). Ein Erkenntniß enthält beides verbunden in sich, und die Möglichkeit eine solche zu haben führt den Namen des Erkenntnißvermögens von dem vornehmsten Theil derselben, nämlich der Thätigkeit des Gemüths Vorstellungen zu verbinden, oder von einander zu sondern. Vorstellungen, in Ansehung deren sich das Gemüth leidend verhält, durch welche also das Subject afficirt wird (dieses mag sich nun selbst afficiren oder von einem Object afficirt werden), gehören zum sinnlichen; diejenigen aber, welche ein bloßes Thun (das Denken) enthalten, zum intellectuellen Erkenntnißvermögen. Jenes wird auch das untere, dieses aber das obere Erkenntnißvermögen genannt", *Anthropology* p. 251.

In the published § 8 Kant confirms this position and writes that "understanding should rule without weakening sensibility (which in itself is like a mob, because it does not think), for without sensibility there would be no material that could be processed for the use of legislative understanding".³⁶³ A human being's inner perfection (*innere Vollkommenheit*) does not consist in the supremacy of the higher faculties over the lower ones, but rather in "having in his power the use of all of his faculties, in order to subject them to his free choice".³⁶⁴

As the defence of sensibility goes on, in particular in § 10, Kant clarifies that neither of the senses have to command over understanding nor the latter over the senses. In order to support this assertion, Kant refers to the false assumption according to which "there are judgements which one does not bring formally before the tribunal of understanding in order to pronounce sentence on them, and which therefore seem to be directly dictated by sense".³⁶⁵ Kant dismisses this deceptive supposition by noting that these sort of judgements "do not come from the senses" but rather "come from the real, though obscure, reflections of understanding".³⁶⁶ From this, it follows that "the senses do not deceive" in that "they do not judge at all".³⁶⁷

Altogether, the defence sheds light on the inconsistency of the charges against sensibility and, as this last observation also stresses, on the different, but at the same time substantial, roles of both the higher and lower faculties in a subject's mental actions. Nonetheless, Kant advances a further fundamental consideration that stresses the weaknesses of a kind of cognition based either

---

363 Anthr, AA 07: 144.05–08: "Dazu aber wird erfordert, daß der Verstand herrsche, ohne doch die Sinnlichkeit (die an sich Pöbel ist, weil sie nicht denkt) zu schwächen: weil ohne sie es keinen Stoff geben würde, der zum Gebrauch des gesetzgebenden Verstandes verarbeitet werden könnte.", *Anthropology* pp. 256–257.

364 Anthr, AA 07: 144.02–05: "Die innere Vollkommenheit des Menschen besteht darin: daß er den Gebrauch aller seiner Vermögen in seiner Gewalt habe, um ihn seiner freien Willkür zu unterwerfen", *Anthropology* p. 256.

365 Anthr, AA 07: 145.16–19: "Zwar giebt es Urtheile, die man eben nicht förmlich vor den Richterstuhl des Verstandes zieht, um von ihm abgeurtheilt zu werden; die daher unmittelbar durch den Sinn dictirt zu sein scheinen"; Kant also adds a reference to the *Genius Socratis* in Anthr, AA 07: 145.19–21: "Dergleichen enthalten die sogenannten Sinnsprüche oder orakelmäßigen Anwandlungen (wie diejenigen, deren Ausspruch Sokrates seinem Genius zuschrieb)", *Anthropology* p. 258, which appears in very similar terms e.g. in the *Doctrine of Virtue* in the context of a discussion on moral feeling (see MS, TL 06: 387.12–13); but see also Anth, AA 07: 139: 26–34; 203.22–29), which will become very important in the following.

366 Anthr, AA 07: 145.24–25: "Aber sie kommen in der That nicht aus den Sinnen, sondern aus wirklichen, obzwar dunkelen Überlegungen des Verstandes", *Anthropology* p. 258.

367 Anthr, AA 07: 146.03,06: "Die Sinne betrügen nicht [...] weil sie gar nicht urtheilen", *Anthropology* p. 258.

solely on sensibility or on understanding alone. In the last paragraph of the defence, we read that "a reproach which logic throws against sensibility is that in so far as cognition is promoted by sensibility, one reproaches it with superficiality (individuality, limitation to the particular)", while, on the other hand, "understanding, which goes up to the universal and for that reason has to trouble itself with abstractions, encounters the reproach of dryness".[368]

In order to avoid the Scylla of understanding's dryness and the Charybdis of sensibility's superficiality, Kant suggests appealing to an *ästhetische Behandlung* of this matter, that is an "aesthetic treatment, whose first requirement is popularity", which "adopts a method by which both errors can be avoided".[369]

One might ask what exactly the word "aesthetic" refers to in this case and in what an "aesthetic" treatment, which avoids the two extremes of dryness and superficiality, consists. According to this passage, only three alternative ways of acquiring cognition in general seem to be given. Let me sum up these alternatives: (1) logic, which is defined as the discipline investigating understanding and which, however, reaches abstractions in its way to universality, so that it eventually results in a dry discipline; (2) the analyses of cognition deriving exclusively from the materials furnished by sensibility alone: this cognition is condemned to remain superficial, Kant does not define it more accurately in the passage; nonetheless, it can be identified with a set of anthropological observations (we are allowed to do so if we take into consideration the already analysed crossed out remark where Kant juxtaposes sensibility and understanding and respectively identifies anthropology and logic as the disciplines in charge of studying these concepts); (3) the "aesthetic treatment", which seems to succeed in summing up the characteristics of both analyses mentioned and, in this way, furnishes a comprehensive cognition, which result is neither dry nor superficial.

One might wonder how Kant aims to make the two fields of logic and anthropology accessible to each other. An interpretation advanced, among others, by John Zammito, may perhaps help our comprehension of what the expression "aesthetic treatment" means. According to this reading a "very anthropological sense" of the word "aesthetic" should be considered, so that the concept of "aes-

---

368 Anthr, AA 07: 146.19 – 23: "Ein Tadel, den die Logik der Sinnlichkeit entgegen wirft, ist der: daß man dem Erkenntniß, so wie es durch sie befördert wird, Seichtigkeit (Individualität, Einschränkung aufs Einzelne) vorwirft, da hingegen den Verstand, der aufs Allgemeine geht, eben darum aber zu Abstractionen sich bequemen muß, der Vorwurf der Trockenheit trifft", *Anthropology* pp. 258 – 259.

369 Anthr, AA 07: 146.23 – 25: "Die ästhetische Behandlung, deren erste Forderung Popularität ist, schlägt aber einen Weg ein, auf dem beiden Fehlern ausgebeugt werden kann", *Anthropology* p. 259.

thetics" would also denote "the study of human response, and not [...just] an inquiry into principles of beauty (or the sublime) along the lines of the later *Critique of Judgement*".[370] Zammito advances his suggestion on the basis of his interpretation of Kant's *Observations on the Feeling of the Beautiful and Sublime*,[371] since he intends to take part in the controversy whether this text represents a contribution to ethical themes or is purely an inquiry into the principles of beauty.[372] Nonetheless, if we apply this interpretation more generally and intend "aesthetic" as an adjective also denoting *human* responses in general in Kant's philosophy, it seems to follow that two of the three considered alternatives, i.e. number (2) and (3), should have to do with anthropology. Nonetheless, alternative (2) refers to the account of anthropology based on merely empirical considerations, while alternative (3) refers to an anthropological treatment only in that it refers to an "aesthetic" treatment (where "aesthetic", according to Zammito's suggestion, has to do with anthropology as well). This means that an "anthropological", "aesthetic treatment" would furnish a syncretic account of logical (= pertaining to the field of understanding) and empirical (= pertaining to the field of sensibility) cognition.

Unfortunately, this is Kant's only reference to an "aesthetic treatment" which brings logic closer to the "dry" analysis of cognition derived from understanding and the "superficial" analysis of cognition derived from sensibility: no other passage in Kant's works helps us solving this question. In any case, let the interpretation of the "aesthetic treatment" be what it may, what remains noteworthy is Kant's suggestion that something which has to do with "aesthetic" furnishes a complete cognition and brings the analyses on the higher and the lower cogni-

---

370 JOHN H. ZAMMITO, *Kant, Herder, and the Birth of Anthropology*, Chicago/London, The University of Chicago Press 2002, p. 110. In a footnote (note 170, p. 395) he further adds that "Schiller launched such criticism in a letter to Goethe, February 19, 1795: 'The exposition is merely anthropological, and one learns nothing from it about the ultimate principles of the beautiful" (*Briefwechsel Schiller-Goethe*, Frankfurt a. M., Insel 1966, p. 87)'. He concludes: "once we have made such a generous interpretation of what 'aesthetic' offers, there seems little left to Schmucker's discrimination: Kant clearly considered anthropological inquiry a propaedeutic to fundamental moral philosophical inquiry", p. 110.

371 See *Beobachtungen über das Gefühl des Schönen und Erhabenen* (1764), GSE, AA 02: 205 – 256; *Observations*, pp. 23 – 62.

372 Cf. PAUL MENZER, "Der Entwicklungsgang der Kantischen Ethik in den Jahren 1760 bis 1785", in *Kant-Studien*, 2 (1898), pp. 290 – 322; 3 (1899), pp. 41 – 104; PAUL ARTHUR SCHILPP, *Kant's Pre-Critical Ethics*, Evaston (Ill.), Northwestern University Press 1970; JOSEF SCHMUCKER, *Die Ursprünge der Ethik Kants in seinen vorkritischen Schriften und Reflektionen*, Meisenheim am Glan, A. Hain 1961, in particular pp. 102, 104. An analysis of these points of view is offered in J. H. ZAMMITO, *Kant, Herder, and the Birth of Anthropology*, cit., p. 110 and respective notes.

tive faculties closer to each other, ultimately bridging the gap between two apparently quite heterogeneous studies. What is noteworthy is the fact that this thesis, which is central in pure philosophy, specifically in the Transcendental Aesthetic of the first *Critique*, now finds room in the context of the investigations of pragmatic anthropology.

There are still some other passages from the 1798 published *Anthropology* left, which take into consideration the affinity of some themes dealt with both in pragmatic anthropology and in pure philosophy. In order to introduce the discussion concerning Kant's classification of the mental faculties in 1798, I shall go back to the analysed sections and more closely analyse one last time a few references which I deliberately avoided before. The analysis of these passages might provide us with a better understanding of Kant's system of the faculties.

3.11 Sensibility as Strength

The first passage comes from a marginal note to § 9 in the Rostock manuscript. In section 9 of the 1798 *Anthropology* Kant aims to defends sensibility from the accusation that the senses confuse. In the passage that I now take into consideration, Kant refers to perception as "an empirical intuition" of which the subject has consciousness and he states that one may also call it "merely appearance of inner sense" which, nonetheless, needs a rule in order to be accessible to human consciousness: if a perception has to become inner experience, "the law must be known which determines the form of this connection in a consciousness of the object".[373] This law (*Gesetz*) which constitutes the form of the connection (*Form der Verbindung*) is the rule (*Regel*) on whose basis the human being observes himself. Kant calls it the principle of appearance (*Princip der Erscheinung*). This principle is, in turn, the basis for answering the question "what is the human being?" (*Was ist der Mensch?*). As Kant notes, "the human being cannot observe himself internally if he is not led by means of a rule, under which perceptions alone must be united, if they are to furnish him with an experience. Therefore they are together only appearances of himself. To cognize himself

---

373 Anthr, AA 07: 399.42–43, 400.01–02 (marginal note at § 9, AA 07: 144.25 ff.): "Die Warnehmung (empirische Anschauung mit Bewußtseyn) könne nur Erscheinung des inneren Sinnes genannt werden. Damit sie aber innere Erfahrung werde muß das Gesetz bekannt sein welches die Form der Verbindung in einem Bewußtseyn des Objects bestimmt", *Anthropology* p. 257.

from them he must take a principle of appearance (in space and time) as a basis, in order to know what the human being is".[374]

In the Rostock Manuscript, section 9 ends wit the uncompleted sentence: "Sensibility as strength or weakness" (which is not to be found in the published text).[375] As noted above, Kant already refers to sensibility as both a strength or a weakness for human cognition. We remember: when we gain cognition exclusively on the basis of the perceptions deriving from sensibility, we become subject to superficiality (that is sensibility as weakness) while, when these materials are linked to cognition deriving from understanding, sensibility shows itself as strength, from which one should conclude that "understanding should rule without weakening sensibility".[376] The fact that, in the present case, the reference to sensibility's strength or weakness occurs in the marginal note right after the mention of a necessary rule for perceptions is to be linked to these considerations. In fact, both in the case of (1) perceptions subsumed under a principle and in the case of (2) sensibility considered as strength, a necessary subsumption under rules is at stake. In the first case, Kant mentions this subsumption first-hand by referring to a "principle of connection". In the second case, this subsumption becomes apparent once we consider that the capacity of sensibility has to be regarded (1) as a weakness if the cognition that it furnishes is not linked to the domain of logic (the rules of understanding) and (2) as a strength if we subsume its materials under these rules.

To sum up, two subsumptions under rules are at stake here: (A) the subsumption of the perceptions under a principle of appearance and (B) the right use of sensibility as a strength, which involves the subsumption of sensibility under the rules of logic (as the domain of understanding). Both these subsumptions refer to the link between the fields of rules (a pure philosophical enterprise which sheds light on the domain of understanding) and appearances (an empirical philosophical enterprise which sheds light on the domain of sensibility). This link seems to point at the investigation of the faculties in pure philosophy. The conjunct treatment of both the lower faculties ("sensibility") and the higher

---

374 Anthr, AA 07: 400.03–08 (marginal note at § 9, AA 07: 144.25 ff., not crossed out): "Der Mensch kann sich selbst innerlich nicht beobachten wenn er nicht durch eine Regel geleitet wird unter der allein die Warnehmung verbunden seyn müsse wenn sie ihm eine Erfahrung liefern soll. Daher sind jene insgesammt nur Erscheinung von sich selbst daraus sich selbst zu erkennen muß er das Princip der Erscheinung (in Raum und Zeit) zum Grunde legen um zu wissen was ist der Mensch", *Anthropology*, p. 257.

375 Anthr, AA 07: 400.09 (marginal note at § 9, AA 07: 144.25 ff.): "Die Sinnlichkeit als Stärke oder Schwäche", *Anthropology*, p. 257.

376 Anthr, AA 07: 144.05–06: "Dazu aber wird erfordert, daß der Verstand herrsche, ohne doch die Sinnlichkeit [...] zu schwächen", *Anthropology*, p. 256.

faculties ("understanding" in its broad sense) corresponds to the investigation of the faculties in Kant's critical works.

Thus, I now propose to consider Kant's classification of the mental faculties in the critical works from this point of view and, before taking a closer look at the three *Critiques*, I conclude my reading of some passages of the 1798 *Anthropology* by referring to Kant's classification of the faculties in the pragmatic anthropology.

3.12 Kant's Classification of the Faculties in the 1798 *Anthropology* and in the Rostock Manuscript

The classification of the faculties occurring in the Rostock manuscript at § 8 chronologically represents one of the last passages where Kant deals with the faculties in the works he himself published. Kant probably planned to place the division at the beginning of the published sections dedicated to sensibility (§§ 8–11), but he eventually substituted it with the observation that some topics treated do not really belong to anthropology but rather to metaphysics as the idea of pure philosophy which he expresses in the *Critiques*.

The classification of the mental faculties is to be found at the beginning of the unpublished section entitled "Of the field of sensibility in relation to the field of understanding".[377] This title closely reminds one of the one given to the published section 7, which reads: "On sensibility in contrast to understanding".[378] In the published section 7, we remember, Kant describes the distinctive traits of the concept of faculty and that of receptivity and links this differentiation with a further distinction between higher and lower cognitive faculties.[379]

The different way of introducing the discussion on sensibility and understanding in both sections, in the published section 7 as well as in section 8 from the *Ergänzungen*, must be emphasized. In the published text Kant does not mention a relation but rather a divergence between understanding and sensibility, in that he entitles the section "On sensibility in contrast to understanding". The new title may be due to the fact that Kant decides to eliminate the paragraph regarding the illustration of the faculties' mutual relations, i.e. their classification.

---

377 *Von dem Felde der Sinnlichkeit im Verhältnis zum Felde des Verstandes*, Anth, AA 07: 399.24–33, *Anthropology* p. 254.
378 *Von der Sinnlichkeit im Gegensatz mit dem Verstande*, Anth, AA 07: 140.15, *Anthropology* p. 251.
379 Cf. Anth, AA 07: 140.15–141.06, *Anthropology* p. 251.

As we notice when reading the text in the Rostock manuscript, Kant institutes a clear relation between two different domains of the mind (*Gemüt*): on the one hand, sensibility, on the other hand, intellectuality. These two spheres concern in turn three parts, that is the tripartite classification of the higher and lower faculties. The description of these reciprocal relations occurs in section 8 of the manuscript, entitled "Of the field of sensibility in relation to the field of understanding", while in the previous section 7, entitled "On sensibility", Kant defines in particular the lower faculties and introduces many distinctions which, we remember, pertain more properly to metaphysics as pure philosophy rather than anthropology as an empirical discipline. In the published text, not only do these distinctions nearly disappear, but, moreover, a section dedicated to sensibility as such (*Von der Sinnlichkeit*) is missing. The observations dedicated to the lower faculties are directly presented in the published section 7 under the title: "On sensibility in contrast to understanding", which straight away follows Kant's analysis of consciousness in §§ 1–6 and directly introduces the comparison of sensibility and understanding without first clearly defining the concept of sensibility in a separate section.[380]

As noted above, in the published § 7 of the 1798 *Anthropology* Kant defines the mind (*Gemüt*) as either "active" (*handelnd*) or "enduring" (*leidend*) in regard to the state of its representations and he states that, in the first respect, it presents itself as a faculty (*Vermögen / facultas*), while, in the second respect, it consists in receptivity (*Empfänglichkeit / receptivitas*).[381] Furthermore, in the published § 7 the term "cognitive faculty" (*Erkenntnißvermögen*) refers to "the possibility of having a cognition" and that Kant chooses this term in reference to the "most distinguished part of this faculty, namely, the activity of mind (*Thätigkeit des Gemüths*)".[382] From these considerations, it follows that both (a) sensuous capacities (grouped under the general name of sensibility – *Sinnlichkeit*) and (b) properly-cognitive faculties (grouped under the general name of understanding – *Verstand*) belong to the mind (*Gemüt*), i.e. both lower and higher cognitive faculties (*untere / obere Erkenntnißvermögen*).

The dichotomy between higher and lower cognitive faculties in the mental context occurs in very similar terms once more when Kant proposes his division of the mental faculties in the crossed out text from the Rostock manuscript. The paragraph in question reads as follows:

---

380 Anth, AA 07: 127–140, *Anthropology*, pp. 130–251.
381 AA 07: 140.16–18: "In Ansehung des Zustandes der Vorstellungen ist mein Gemüth entweder handelnd und zeigt Vermögen (*facultas*), oder es ist leidend und besteht in Empfänglichkeit (*receptivitas*)", *Anthropology* p. 251.
382 Cf. Anth, AA 07: 140. 18–22; *Anthropology* p. 251.

Of the field of sensibility in relation to the field of understanding
§ 8
Division
The mind (*animus*) of the human being, as the sum total of all representations that have place within it, has a domain (*sphaera*) which concerns three parts: the faculty of cognition, the feeling of pleasure and displeasure, and the faculty of desire. Each of these has two divisions, the field of sensibility and the field of intellectuality. (the field of sensible or intellectual cognition, pleasure and displeasure, and desire or abhorrence).[383]

This is the passage in the manuscript where Kant switches from the preliminary studies on consciousness to the analyses of each single faculty, which are dealt with in detail in the following sections of the 1798 *Anthropology*.[384] Neither the contrast between the field of sensibility and that of intellectuality, which corresponds to the one between "passivity" and spontaneity in the human mind, nor the underlying tripartition among the faculties, are new acquisitions in Kant's thought.[385] However, in this text it is very clear how Kant relates the three faculties both to the lower (the one subsumed under sensibility) and the higher (the one subsumed under understanding) field of cognition and how clearly he refers them all to the concept of mind (*Gemüt*).

---

383 Anthr, AA 07: 399.24–33: "Von dem Felde der Sinnlichkeit im Verhältnis zum Felde des Verstandes / § 8 / Eintheilung / Das Gemüth (*animus*) des Menschen, [[als der]] als Inbegriff aller Vorstellungen die in demselben Platz haben hat einen Umfang (*sphaera*) der die drey [[Abtheilungen]] Grundstücke Erkentnisvermögen, Gefühl der Lust und Unlust und Begehrungsvermögens befaßt deren jedes in zwey Abtheilungen dem Felde der Sinnlichkeit und der Intellectualität zerfällt. (dem der sinnlichen oder intellectuellen Erkenntnis, Lust oder Unlust, und des Begehrens oder Verabscheuens). / Die Sinnlichkeit kann als Schwäche oder auch als Stärke betrachtet werden", *Anthropology* p. 254.
384 Cf. R. BRANDT, *Kommentar*, p. 181: "Die Einteilung des Erkenntnis-, aber auch des Begehrungsvermögens in eine 'facultas inferior' und eine 'facultas superior' kennt auch die empirische (!) Psychologie Baumgartens (s. §624; §676; §689); vgl. auch Wolff 1962ff., II 5, 33. – Die Einteilung an diesem Ort zeigt, daß die Bewußtseinspräliminarien hier zu Ende gehen und jetzt die Vermögen im einzelnen erörtert werden". Brandt further notes that Kant does not always consequently follow his partition: "Kant beachtet jedoch nicht durchgängig die Zweiteilung; sie erscheint im Hinblick auf die Erkenntnisvermögen in den §§40–42; beim Gefühl der Lust und Unlust in der 'Eintheilung' 230, 3–8 [...] und fehlt beim Begehrungsvermögen". I dedicate the following chapter to a close analysis of Kant's inconstancy in the classification of the faculties, not only in the context of the 1798 *Anthropology*.
385 See Refl 202, AA 15: 78.10–13, κ? [1769?], λ? [Ende 1769 – Herbst 1770?], (ζ? [Um 1764–1766?]), M 180'; E I 31.62: "Die Sinnlichkeit ist die passibilitaet meiner Vermögen, die intellectualitaet ist die spontaneitaet derselben: des Erkenntnis, Gefuehls und des Begehrens" and my analysis in chapter 4 below.

The terms *Gemüt* and *animus*, as we remember from chapter 1 above, are used for describing a sum total of a human being's faculties in the context of pure philosophy. Starting from these terminological considerations, some other conclusions may be drawn. Given that (1a) Kant speaks in the crossed out § 8 about the concept of human mind (*Gemüt*) and given that (1b) this concept of mind (*Gemüt*) pertains to pure philosophy, the fact that (3) Kant does not deal with this concept in his published text on pragmatic anthropology seems appropriate, if we remember that (2) the 1798 published *Anthropology* is a book dedicated to an empirically based discipline. Furthermore, if (1b) the concept of mind (*Gemüt*) to which Kant here refers pertains to pure philosophy, then (4) so does the classification of the domain (*Umfang – sphaera*) of this concept of the human mind (*Gemüt*) given by Kant in the crossed out § 8, i.e. the classification which analyses the domain of the mental pertains to pure philosophy. From this perspective, it appears appropriate that Kant does not introduce this classification in the 1798 *Anthropology* but limits himself, in the entire book, to generally presenting each faculty in the context of empirical analysis. Instead, as we will see in chapter 4 below, a classification that pertains to pure philosophy occurs in the third *Critique* and in the *Metaphysics of Morals*.

If we consider that the classification of the mental faculties, as presented in § 8 from the Rostock manuscript, pertains to the domain of pure philosophy, consequently one must emphasize Kant's clear reference to the fact that the three different parts (*Grundstücke*) of the mental domain singularly fall, in turn, into two distinct divisions (*Abteilungen*) of a particular field, the field of sensibility and that of intellectuality. Let us then consider the scheme presented by Kant. We first note that there are the "fundamental parts" previously mentioned, namely:
(A) the faculty of cognition (*Erkenntnisvermögen*);
(B) the feeling of pleasure and displeasure (*Gefühl der Lust oder Unlust*);
(C) the faculty of desire (*Begehrungsvermögen*).

Each of these parts falls into the divisions of
(1) the field of sensibility (*Feld der Sinnlichkeit*);
(2) the field of intellectuality (*Feld der Intellectualität*).

The following double tripartition of the human being's states of mind results, thus, from the combination of parts (A), (B) and (C) with the mental partitions (1) and (2), such that we eventually get:
(A1) sensible cognition (*sinnliche Erkenntnis*) / (A2) intellectual cognition (*intellectuelle Erkenntnis*)

(B1) sensible pleasure or displeasure (*sinnliche Lust oder Unlust*) / (B2) intellectual pleasure or displeasure (*intellectuelle Lust oder Unlust*);
(C1) sensible desire or abhorrence (*sinnliche Begehren oder Verabscheuen*) / (C2) intellectual desire or abhorrence (*intellectuelles Begehren oder Verabscheuen*).

In this passage, Kant suggests to apply the faculties to both fields of sensibility and intellectuality. Sensibility (*Sinnlichkeit*), in this case, denotes also "what is sensuous", i.e. the sum total of the "materials" (empirical perceptions – *Empfindungen*) coming from the receptive capacity of sensibility, so that the word denotes, in this context, both the capacity of sensibility and the "materials" acquired by this very capacity of sensibility; in the same way, intellectuality (*Intellektualität*) means "what is intellectual" and refers to the sum total of what descends (*a priori* concepts and principles – *apriorische Begriffe und Grundsätze*) from understanding (*Verstand* in its general meaning).

A further consideration is also due to the six different "mental states", which result from the application of the three faculties to both these fields.[386] Eventually, we obtain: two different kinds of cognition, two different sorts of feeling and two different sorts of desire. In particular, if we apply the faculty of cognition to the field of sensibility, i.e. to the sensible "materials" furnished by sensibility, we acquire sensible cognitions (*phenomena*);[387] accordingly, if we apply the feeling of pleasure or displeasure and the faculty of desire to the field of sensibility, we acquire, respectively, a sensible pleasure or displeasure (a pleasure or displeasure introduced by the senses)[388] and a sensible desire or abhorrence (affects, inclinations, passions)[389]. Conversely, if we apply each of the three mental faculties to the field of intellectuality, that is, on the intellectual field offered by the activity of understanding, we attain three different mental states. In the case of the application of the cognitive faculty to the field of intellectuality, we attain intellectual cognitions, which are not the *noumena* (defined by Kant intellectual cog-

---

386 The analysis of these topics in the context of pure philosophy will follow in chapter 4 below. Cf. Also S. HESSBRÜGGEN-WALTER, *Die Seele und ihre Vermögen*, cit.
387 Cf. e.g. KrV, A41–42/B59, AA 04: 42.23–36/AA 03: 65.02–16; CpR p. 168, 185; Prol, AA 04: 290.17–20; *Prolegomena*, p. 85.
388 Cf. e.g. Anth, AA 07: 230.04–08 (The beginning of the second book on the *Gefühl der Lust oder Unlust*): "1) Die sinnliche, 2) die intellectuelle Lust. Die erstere entweder A) durch den Sinn (das Vergnügen), oder B) durch die Einbildungskraft (der Geschmack); die zweite (nämlich intellectuelle) entweder a) durch darstellbare Begriffe oder b) durch Ideen, – und so wird auch das Gegentheil, die Unlust, vorgestellt", *Anthropology*, p. 333.
389 Cf. e.g. AA 07: 251. 05, 15–19; *Anthropology*, p. 353; but also AA 07. 265:27–30; *Anthropology*, p. 367.

nitions, e.g. in the fifth section of the *Dissertatio*),[390] since only God, if anybody, could acquire them, but they are rather the elements that give formal unity to human cognition, that is the cognition's formal unity coming from the self-determining act of understanding's spontaneity.[391] Finally, in the cases of the application of the faculties of feeling and the faculty of desire to the field of intellectuality, we attain, respectively, intellectual pleasure or displeasure (a pleasure or displeasure introduced by the contemplation of concepts or ideas, as a mental state which occurs in concomitance of a realised interest of reason)[392] and intellectual desire or abhorrence (that is a pure act of willing which corresponds to the moral law given by the pure practical reason as the free will, the higher faculty of desire in its pure application).[393]

In this classification of the faculties and the consequent classification of the mental states acquired by means of the faculties, Kant's attempt to cover the two fields of pure and empirical philosophy is apparent, in that he proposes to distinguish between two different (a sensible and an intellectual) fields of application for the three faculties. However, this division is not to be found in the published book and Kant's treatment of the faculties in the 1798 published *Anthropology* is not focussed on their application to the intellectual field.

As a first look at the table of contents of the book testifies,[394] Kant dedicates the whole of part I (Part I. Anthropological Didactic: On the way of cognizing the

---

390 Cf. MSI, AA 02: 385–419, here in particular § 5 (AA 02: 393–394); *Inaugural dissertation*, pp. 385–386.

391 On that I agree with Engstrom when he says: "in both theoretical and practical cognition, the distinction between the sensible and the intellectual is drawn in terms of the contrast between the two representational powers that cooperate in discursive cognition – externally determined and self-determining spontaneity", STEPHEN ENGSTROM, "Reason, desire, and the will", in LARA DENIS (ed.), *Kant's Metaphysics of Morals. A Critical Guide*, Cambridge/New York, Cambridge University Press 2010, p. 28–50, here in particular p. 42.

392 Cf. the already quoted passage from Anth, AA 07: 230.04–08; *Anthropology*, p. 333; but cf. also MS, AA 06: 212.23–26; 27–31; 213: 01–08; MM pp. 212–213.

393 The possibility of an intellectual desire and its identification with the will will become clear once we deal with Kant's assimilation of the concept of pure practical reason with that of will and, in turn, the distinction between the concept of will and capacity of choice, as it is presented in the general introduction to the *Metaphysics of Morals* (in particular AA 06: 211–214, MM p. 373–376) – cf. chapter 4 below.

394 Anth, AA 07: 124–125, *Anthropology*, 234–237. It has to be noted that the English translation of the table of contents (*Anthropology* pp. 234–237) shows many small inaccuracies, such as the omission of some of punctuation as well as of prepositions and the way the same German word is rendered in two distinct ways (e.g. "Art" once as "art", another time as "way"). In particular, some omissions could lead to the consideration that Kant aimed in some way to distinguish the analyses of the different faculties (the name of each faculty is introduced in Kant's text by the

interior as well as the exterior of the human being – *Von der Art, das Innere sowohl als das Äußere des Menschen zu erkennen*)[395] to the three faculties and, respectively, the first book to the cognitive faculty (Book I. On the cognitive faculty – *Erstes Buch. Vom Erkenntnißvermögen*)[396], the second book to the faculty of feeling (Book II. On the feeling of pleasure and displeasure – *Zweites Buch. Vom Gefühl der Lust und Unlust*)[397] and the third book to the faculty of desire (Book III. On the faculty of desire – *Drittes Buch. Vom Begehrungsvermögen*)[398]. Nonetheless, as will become apparent from a quick look inside the book, in each single chapter Kant mostly refers to the sensible application of these three faculties and mentions only briefly their intellectual application. In particular, he mentions a "correct" application of the cognitive faculties just twice: these two instances may remind us of the domain of intellectuality. This happens a first time in the context of his defence of sensibility, when he notes that both the rules of understanding and the "materials" furnished by sensibility to the human mind (*Gemüt*) are indispensable in order to reach "concise expressions for the concept, emphatic expressions for the feeling, and interesting ideas for determining the will".[399] This happens then a second time, in the context of the "Anthropological comparison of the three higher cognitive faculties with one another",[400] where Kant affirms that "correct understanding, practical

---

preposition 'von', while in the English table of contents the translator rendered the titles as follows: "'Book I. On the cognitive faculty'; 'Book II. The feeling of pleasure and displeasure'; Book III On the faculty of desire'").

395 Anth AA 07: 125–282, *Anthropology*, pp. 07: 238–382.

396 Anth AA 07: 129–229, *Anthropology*, pp. 239–333.

397 Anth AA 07: 230–250, *Anthropology*, pp. 333–353.

398 Anth AA 07: 251–282, *Anthropology*, pp. 353–382. A second part follows: Part II. Anthropological Characteristics: On the way of cognizing the interior of the human being from the exterior – *Von der Art, das Innere des Menschen aus dem Äußeren zu erkennen*, Anth AA 07: 283–333, *Anthropology*, pp. 383–429.

399 In this context Kant notes: "Die sinnlichen Vorstellungen kommen freilich denen des Verstandes zuvor und stellen sich in Masse dar. Aber desto reichhaltiger ist der Ertrag, wenn der Verstand mit seiner Anordnung und intellectuellen Form hinzukommt und z.B. prägnante Ausdrücke für den Begriff, emphatische für das Gefühl und interessante Vorstellungen für die Willensbestimmung ins Bewußtsein bringt". Anthr, AA 07: 144.25–30; *Anthropology* p. 257.

400 *Anthropologische Vergleichung der drei oberen Erkenntnißvermögen mit einander* – cf. Anth, AA 07: 197–201, §§ 41–44, *Anthropology* pp. 304–309. This section is followed by the subsection *On the weakness and illnesses of the soul with respect to its cognitive faculty* – *Von den Schwächen und Krankheiten der Seele in Ansehung ihres Erkenntnißvermögens*, Anth, AA 07: 202–217, §§ 45–52; *Anthropology*, pp. 309–322.

judgement, and thorough reason constitute the entire range of the intellectual cognitive faculty".[401]

However, these two passages do not directly analyse the faculties' application to the intellectual field. Indeed, Kant deals directly with this topic only once in the published text of the 1798 *Anthropology*, namely in the context of the analysis of "The cognitive faculty, in so far as it is based on understanding".[402]

This section (§ 40), introduced by the subtitle "Division", is the text that comes closest to section 8 from the Rostock manuscript. It functions as an introduction to a comparison of the three higher cognitive faculties and is dedicated to the way in which the higher cognitive faculties are applied to the intellectual domain.

This reference to the application of the higher cognitive faculty leads the discussion beyond the domain of a merely empirically founded discipline, such as the one of pragmatic anthropology, and makes its way towards the field of pure philosophy. This becomes evident right from the beginning of section 40, where Kant refers to understanding as "the faculty of thinking (representing something by means of concepts)" or "the faculty of concepts", which "contains the universality of representations, the rule to which the manifold of sensuous intuitions must be subordinated in order to bring unity to the cognition of the object" and distinguishes it, as "the higher cognitive faculty", from the lower cognitive faculty, that is from sensibility, since the latter, as "the faculty of intuition (pure or empirical), contains only the singularity in objects".[403]

Both understanding (the higher cognitive faculty, the faculty of concepts) and sensibility (the lower cognitive faculty, the faculty of intuition) also refer to the domain of pure philosophy; however, if in the case of sensibility Kant briefly mentions pure intuition, in the case of understanding this reference to pure philosophy is even more overt, since Kant states that understanding fur-

---

401 Anth, AA 07: 198.07–08: "Ein richtiger Verstand, geübte Urtheilskraft und gründliche Vernunft machen den ganzen Umfang des intellectuellen Erkenntnißvermögens aus", *Anthropology* p. 305.

402 Anthr, § 40, AA 07: 196–197:01–07: *Vom Erkenntnißvermögen, so fern es auf Verstand gegründet wird. Eintheilung* (*Anthropology* pp. 303–304).

403 Here the whole passage from Anthr, AA 07: 196.17–24: "Verstand, als das Vermögen zu denken (durch Begriffe sich etwas vorzustellen), wird auch das obere Erkenntnißvermögen (zum Unterschiede von der Sinnlichkeit, als dem unteren) genannt, darum weil das Vermögen der Anschauungen (reiner oder empirischer) nur das Einzelne in Gegenständen, dagegen das der Begriffe das Allgemeine der Vorstellungen derselben, die Regel, enthält, der das Mannigfaltige der sinnlichen Anschauungen untergeordnet werden muß, um Einheit zur Erkenntniß des Objects hervorzubringen", *Anthropology* p. 303.

nishes the rules subordinating the manifolds of sensuous intuitions. This notwithstanding, as Kant affirms in his defence of sensibility, understanding cannot alone gain a complete cognition, since its higher rank does not imply its self-sufficiency in the process of the acquisition of human knowledge: "understanding certainly is of higher rank than sensibility, with which irrational animals can manage provisionally, following implanted instincts, like a people without a sovereign. But a sovereign without a people (like understanding without sensibility) is not able to do anything at all. Therefore between the two there is no dispute about rank, though the one is addressed as higher and the other as lower".[404]

In this passage, the allusion to the necessity of bringing together the two "mental actions" pertaining to the fields of understanding and sensibility also testifies to the indispensability of a joint account of these two levels. Only by means of such a joint examination does it become possible to shed light on an overall account of the cognitive faculties.

To the analysis of this joint examination of the two levels of the application of the faculties I dedicate the next chapter of my study.

3.13 Anthropology and Kant's Study of the Faculties of the Human Mind: Some Concluding Remarks

In this third chapter of my work I aimed to show the intersections between Kant's pragmatic anthropology and pure philosophy. My aim was that of explaining how, even if the study of the faculties constitutes a central topic of Kant's pragmatic anthropology, it is nonetheless noteworthy that Kant also analyzes these very topics and doctrines in the context of his critical philosophy when he presents an analysis of the fundamental faculties of the human mind, which aims at shedding light on the thinking, willing, and feeling human being. In this sense, Kant's analysis of the faculties of the human mind and their classification in the critical works has to be read, notwithstanding the many similarities between the anthropological studies and the *Critiques*, as a corpus of studies that is distinguished from the empirically based discipline of anthropology and which is rather dedicated to the pure philosophical study of the human being and its nature.

---

404 Anthr, AA 07: 196.24–30: "Vornehmer ist also zwar freilich der Verstand als die Sinnlichkeit, mit der sich die verstandlosen Thiere nach eingepflanzten Instincten schon nothdürftig behelfen können, so wie ein Volk ohne Oberhaupt; statt dessen ein Oberhaupt ohne Volk (Verstand ohne Sinnlichkeit) gar nichts vermag. Es ist also zwischen beiden kein Rangstreit, obgleich der eine als Oberer und der andere als Unterer betitelt wird", *Anthropology* pp. 303–304.

This reading is an alternative to the interpretations of contemporary philosophical scholarship dedicated to Kant's account of the faculties, according to which a reference either to transcendental psychology or to anthropology is always necessary if we intend to explain Kant's concepts of the faculties (*Vermögen*) and of the mind (*Gemüt*). Against these two interpretive proposals, in this chapter of my work I aimed to show that Kant's analysis of the faculties of the human mind in the three *Critiques* is a constitutive part of the critical investigation, which should not be confused either with psychology or with anthropology.

On the basis of this reading, in the following chapter of my study I aim to illustrate Kant's system of the faculties of the human mind as Kant present it in his critical works.

Chapter 4
Kant's System of the Faculties of the Human Mind

After shedding some light on the concept of "faculty" and on some contemporary interpretations of the role played by this concept in Kant's philosophy (chapters 1 and 2), and after rejecting the idea of reading Kant's classification of the faculties in the *Critiques* in the light of his anthropological studies (chapter 3), in the present chapter my aim is to present Kant's division of the faculties in his critical works.

In this chapter, I limit myself to a description of the different classifications that can be gained from the three *Critiques*, the 'First Introduction' to the third *Critique*, and the *Metaphysics of Morals*. In this presentation I aim to show, in particular, the role played by the faculty of feeling pleasure and displeasure in the context of Kant's division of the faculties. I will thus emphasize how Kant increasingly focuses his attention on the faculty of feeling and on the *a priori* character of the component of pleasure and displeasure by also suggesting that Kant's acknowledgement of the role of moral feeling of respect in the *Groundwork* and in the second *Critique* is also evidence of this orientation of his attention.

In the present chapter my aim is only that of furnishing a description of the faculties, as Kant proposes in some of his critical project, since the study of the role of the faculties in Kant's philosophy has often been considered solely in the context of a psychological or anthropological reading of Kant's philosophy and is underestimated for this reason.

After presenting some controversies regarding the way in which the classification of the faculties is read in Kant scholarship, I will make some brief comments concerning Kant's division of the faculties in the first *Critique* before proceeding to Kant's account of the faculties in the second *Critique*, which I present with a particular focus on the concepts of "desire" and "pleasure". This description will be followed by one of Kant's treatment of the faculties in the 'First Introduction' to the third *Critique* and in the published introduction to the *Critique of the Power of Judgement*.

Eventually, I will present the division of the faculties advanced by Kant in the general introduction to the *Metaphysics of Morals*. This last description will introduce the last chapter of my work, i. e. chapter 5 below, which I will dedicate to interpreting only one of the faculties analysed in this study so far, namely the faculty of feeling, and its role in the context of Kant's theory of moral action.

4.1 The Classification of the Mental Faculties in Kant Scholarship

Before describing the way in which Kant seems to classify the faculties in his critical works (in particular, in the three *Critiques* and in the *Metaphysics of Morals*), some considerations concerning the interpretive and philological work on Kant's faculties in philosophical scholarship are first due.

It first has to be noted that, for a long time, the sole study of the role of the faculties in Kant's philosophy has been underestimated and treated as a topic of secondary interest, always subordinated to what have been considered more important themes. This way, the faculties have mostly been considered in the context of a psychological reading of Kant's transcendental philosophy.

The (1) psychological reading of Kant's theory of the faculties has been advanced most influentially by Jürgen Bona Meyer (1869) in a book dedicated to what the author has understood as Kant's psychology.[405] A more general overview of Kant's faculties was also given in treatises on the history and development of the discipline of psychology in Germany; the two best-known works of this kind are by Robert Sommer (1892) and Max Dessoir (1902).[406]

In contrast to the lack of interest on these themes at the beginning of the last century, a renaissance of the study dedicated to the role played by psychology in Kant's philosophy occurred in the last fifty years. Thus, especially in English speaking countries a very lively discussion concerning Kant's (2) "transcendental psychology" can be seen (as I already mentioned in the first two chapters of this work).[407]

In the context of a treatment of Kant's theory of the faculties as connected to psychological studies, works that deal with the (3) historical origins of Kant's "psychology" have to be remembered.[408] Such works aim to give an overview of the evolution of Kant's theory of the faculties on the basis of Kant's debts

---

405 JÜRGEN BONA MEYER, *Kant's Psychologie. Dargestellt und erörtert von*, Berlin, Wilhelm Hertz (Bessersche Buchhandlung) 1870.

406 ROBERT SOMMER, *Grundzüge einer Geschichte der Deutschen Psychologie und Aesthetik von Wolff-Baumgarten bis Kant-Schiller. Nach einer von der königlich preußischen Akademie der Wissenschaften in Berlin preisgekrönten Schrift des Verfassers*, Würzburg, Staehl 1892; MAX DESSOIR, *Geschichte der neueren deutschen Psychologie*, Berlin, Dunker 1902.

407 Cf. for instance the already quoted works by P. Kitcher, G. Hatfield, A. Brook, W. Waxman.

408 Cf. for instance MAX DESSOIR, "Kant und die Psychologie", in *Kant-Studien*, 29 (1924), pp. 98–120; GIORGIO TONELLI, *Kant, dall'estetica metafisica all'estetica psicoempirica. Studi sulla genesi del criticismo (1754–1771) e sulle sue fonti*, Torino, V. Bona 1955; LEWIS WHITE BECK, *Early German Philosophy. Kant and His Precedessors*, Cambridge (Mass.), The Belknap Press of Harvard University Press 1969, especially the parts dedicated to Tetens (pp. 412–425).

to and relationships with his contemporaries. Among other works, the studies that deal with (4) the historical evolution of Kant's theory of the faculties with particular regard to Kant's classification of the faculties from the 'First Introduction' and the published introduction to the third *Critique* deserve to be mentioned.[409]

In contrast to the studies dedicated to Kant's faculties as part of a psychological discussion in particular, many works appeared in the last half of the twentieth and the beginning of the new century. These are the works dealing with (5) Kant's anthropology, which, by means of their focus on this discipline, have contributed to the revitalization of studying Kant's system of the faculties.[410]

As can be noted, the analysis of Kant's system of the faculties has mostly been subordinated to the attention paid to either psychology or anthropology. That is why the works dedicated (6) solely and particularly to the investigation of Kant's tripartite division of the mental faculties can be considered exceptional, notwithstanding the fundamental role played by this system in the evolution of Kant's philosophical work.[411]

In this direction, the most recent and complete work dedicated solely to the topic of Kant's faculties is (7) Heßbrüggen-Walter's book, which closely deals

---

409 HELGA MERTENS, *Kommentar zur Ersten Einleitung in Kants Kritik der Urteilskraft. Zur systematischen Funktion der Kritik der Urteilskraft für das System der Vernunftkritik*, Berchmans, München 1975; JOHN H. ZAMMITO, *The Genesis of Kant's Critique of Judgment*, Chicago, The University of Chicago Press 1992 (see in particular pp. 53–63).

410 Apart from the already mentioned works by N. Hinske, R. Brandt, Th. Sturm, and K. Bae Soo, cf. also the studies by Jeanine M. Grenberg (JEANINE M. GRENBERG, "Anthropology from a Metaphysical Point of View", in *Journal of the History of Philosophy*, 37/1 (1999), pp. 91–115), Patrick R. Frierson (PATRICK R. FRIERSON, "Kant on the Causes of Human Actions: A Brief Sketch", in VALERIO ROHDEN – RICARDO R. TERRA – GUIDO A. DE ALMEIDA – MARGIT RUFFING (eds.), *Recht und Frieden in der Philosophie Kants. Akten des X. Internationalen Kant-Kongresses*, Band 5, Berlin/New York, de Gruyter 2008, pp. 33–44), and Fiorella Battaglia (FIORELLA BATTAGLIA, "Leben als Erleben. Sechs Funktionen des phänomenalen Erlebens bei Kant", in MATTHIAS JUNG – JAN-CHRISTOPH HEILINGER (eds.), *Funktionen des Erlebens*, Berlin-New York, de Gruyter 2009, pp. 253–284; FIORELLA BATTAGLIA, *Il sistema antropologico. La posizione dell'uomo nella filosofia critica di Kant*, Pisa, Plus 2010).

411 KURT BURCHARDT, *Kants Psychologie im Verhältnis zur transzendentalen Methode*, Dissertation, Bonn 1911; G. DELEUZE, *La philosophie critique de Kant: doctrine des facultés*, cit.; HEINZ JANSOHN, *Kants Lehre von der Subjektivität. Eine Systematische Analyse des Verhältnisses von transzendentaler und empirischer Subjektivität in seiner theoretischen Philosophie*, Bonn, Bouvier 1969; and, more recently, G. GIGLOTTI, ""Vermögen" e "Kraft". Una rilettura del concetto di "sintesi"", cit.; GIANNA GIGLIOTTI, "Il rispetto del tulipano. Riflessioni sul sistema kantiano delle facoltà", *Rivista di storia della filosofia*, 1 (2001), pp. 25–61.

with the history of the development of Kant's system of mental faculties on the basis of a reference to Kant's contemporaries and without any aspiration to read the critical works in a psychological way.[412]

In the context of a revaluation of the analysis of the system of the faculties as a study which deserves closer attention *per se* and, in particular, in contrast to the psychological and anthropological readings that were furnished to explain this system, I tried to show that Kant's study of the system of the faculties is a fundamental part of pure philosophy as a tripartite critical enterprise. But it is so in a way that the analysis of the faculties forms a comprehensive study of the human being in its cognizing, willing, and feeling actions. Through pure philosophy, Kant reaches a comprehensive picture of the human mind (*Gemüt*) and, in this way, of the acting human being.

In the light of this consideration, I now begin my description of Kant's proposal concerning the faculties of the human mind and follow the development of Kant's proposal over the course of his philosophical career.

4.2 Some Brief Considerations Concerning Kant's Division of the Faculties in the First *Critique*

Let me start with some observations concerning Kant's classification of the faculties in the first *Critique*. [413] The centrality of the role played by this classification is clear from a quick look at the table of contents. As is well-known, the Transcendental Doctrine of Elements (*Transscendentale Elemetarlehre*) consists of two parts: the first one is dedicated to the study of what Kant calls a "Transcendental Aesthetic", which he defines as "a science of all principles of *a priori* sensibility"[414] and that deals with the concepts of space and time as "two pure

---

412 S. HESSBRÜGGEN-WALTER, *Die Seele und ihre Vermögen*, cit. But see now also the studies by THOMAS HÖWING, *Praktische Lust. Kant über das Verhältnis von Fühlen, Begehren und praktischer Vernunft*, Berlin/Boston, de Gruyter 2013 and HEINER F. KLEMME, "Fühlen, Begehren, Erkennen – Selbstbesitz. Reflexionen über die Verbindung der Vermögen in Kants Lehre vom Kategorischen Imperativ", in INGA RÖMER (ed.), *Affektivität und Ethik bei Kant und in der Phänomenologie*, Berlin/Boston, de Gruyter 2014 (forthcoming).

413 For a more detailed analysis of the classification of the faculties in the first *Critique* cf. ANGELICA NUZZO, *Kant and the Unity of Reason*, West Lafayette, Indiana, Purdue University Press 2008, pp. 23–44.

414 KrV, A 21/B35, AA 04: 20.23–24/AA 03: 50.28–29: "Eine Wissenschaft von allen Principien der Sinnlichkeit *a priori* nenne ich die transscendentale Ästhetik"; CpR 156/173.

forms of sensible intuition as principles of *a priori* cognition".[415] A second part, which Kant names "Transcendental Logic", follows the transcendental aesthetic and "contains the principles of pure thinking".[416]

This bipartition into 'Transcendental Aesthetic' and 'Transcendental Logic' should remind one of the general distinction, with which we are acquainted from the previous chapter, i. e. the distinction in the Rostock manuscript between the two disciplines of aesthetic and logic, which followed the bipartition into the faculty of sensibility (*Sinnlichkeit*) and the faculty of understanding in its broad sense (*Verstand* generally as *oberes Erkenntnisvermögen*) in the manuscript.

Kant also distinguishes clearly between these two faculties at the beginning of the first *Critique*; in the introduction, both in its 1781 version as well as its second one, published in 1787. In the A-Edition, Kant titles the section where the distinction occurs 'Division of Transcendental Philosophy'.[417] In the B-edition, Kant writes a longer section where he aims to explain his plan concerning transcendental philosophy and gives the section a new title: 'The Idea and Division of a Special Science under the Name of a Critique of Pure Reason'.[418] Nevertheless, the passage concerning the distinction between sensibility and understanding remains practically unchanged in both editions.

This paragraph concerns the division of the first *Critique* into two doctrines (*Transscendentale Elemetarlehre* / *Transscendentale Methodenlehre*). In particular, the subdivisions pertaining to the 'Doctrine of Elements' are now to be noted.

Kant's discussion advances hypothetically: "Now if one wants to set up the division of this science [=transcendental philosophy] from the general viewpoint of a system in general, then the one that we will now present must contain first a Doctrine of Elements and second a Doctrine of Method of pure reason".[419] Even

---

415 KrV, A 22/B36, AA 04: 31.09 – 12/AA 03: 51.10 – 13: "Bei dieser Untersuchung wird sich finden, daß es zwei reine Formen sinnlicher Anschauung als Principien der Erkenntniß *a priori* gebe, nämlich Raum und Zeit"; CpR 156/173.
416 KrV, A 21/B35 – 6, AA 04: 30.24 – 25,31.01 – 02/AA 03: 50. 29, 51.01 – 03: "Es muß also eine solche Wissenschaft geben, die den ersten Theil der transscendentalen Elementarlehre ausmacht, im Gegensatz mit derjenigen, welche die Principien des reinen Denkens enthält und transscendentale Logik genannt wird"; CpR 156/173. For a first introduction to the division of the first *Critique* and the immense literature on the topics that I briefly treat in the present section, cf. IMMANUEL KANT, *Kritik der reinen Vernunft (Klassiker Auslegen)*, edited by GEORG MOHR – MARCUS WILLASCHEK, Berlin, Akademie Verlag 1998 and the relative bibliographical sources.
417 *Eintheilung der Transscendental-Philosophie*, KrV, A13 – 16, AA 04: 24 – 28; CpR pp. 134 – 135.
418 *Idee und Eintheilung einer besonderen Wissenschaft unter dem Namen einer Kritik der reinen Vernunft*, KrV, B24 – 30, AA 03: 42 – 48; CpR pp. 149 – 152.
419 KrV, A 15/B29, AA 04: 26.05 – 08/AA 03: 46.01 – 05: "Wenn man nun die Eintheilung dieser Wissenschaft aus dem allgemeinen Gesichtspunkte eines Systems überhaupt anstellen will, so

though Kant, at this preliminary stage of the work, does not aim to go into detail, he refers nonetheless to the fact that his research is based on the analysis of "two stems (*Stämme*) of human cognition, which may perhaps arise from a common but to us unknown root, namely sensibility and understanding".[420]

The two "stems" mentioned are the two fundamental faculties, through which human beings may attain cognition, in a way that "through the first [... i. e., sensibility] objects are given to us" and "through the second [... i. e., understanding] they are thought".[421]

Due to the fact that Kant starts with a hypothetical form at the beginning of the paragraph ("if one wants to set up the division of this science...") and he now goes on with the hypothetical periphrasis and, in this way, refers to the first of the faculties, which he analyses in the 'Transcendental Aesthetic of the Doctrine of Elements'. This fundamental faculty is sensibility.

Let me sum up Kant's line of thought: relative to the 'Doctrine of Elements', we find two stems of human cognition; the first one, sensibility, is the faculty containing "*a priori* representations, which constitute the conditions under which objects are given to us", studied in the 'Transcendental Aesthetic' (also called "transcendental doctrine of the senses"), which belongs "to the first part of the science of elements".[422] The fact that the transcendental study of sensibility precedes the one dedicated to understanding would then be justified by the fact that "the conditions under which alone the objects of human cognition are given precede those under which those objects are thought".[423]

---

muß die, welche wir jetzt vortragen, erstlich eine Elementar=Lehre, zweitens eine Methoden= Lehre der reinen Vernunft enthalten"; CpR 135/151.

420 KrV, A 15/B29, AA 04: 26.10 – 13/AA 03: 46.06 – 09: "Nur so viel scheint zur Einleitung oder Vorerinnerung nöthig zu sein, daß es zwei Stämme der menschlichen Erkenntniß gebe, die vielleicht aus einer gemeinschaftlichen, aber uns unbekannten Wurzel entspringen"; CpR 135/152. For concision's sake I do not take into consideration here the immense bibliography referring to the hypotheses on the mentioned "gemeinschaftliche Wurzel".

421 KrV, A 15/B29, AA 04: 26.13 – 15/AA 03: 46.09 – 11: "...Sinnlichkeit und Verstand, durch deren ersteren uns Gegenstände gegeben, durch den zweiten aber gedacht werden"; CpR 135/152.

422 KrV, A 15/B29 – 30, AA 04: 26.15 – 19/AA 03: 46.11 – 15: "Sofern nun die Sinnlichkeit Vorstellungen *a priori* enthalten sollte, welche die Bedingung ausmachen, unter der uns Gegenstände gegeben werden, so würde sie zur Transscendental=Philosophie gehören. Die transscendentale Sinnenlehre würde zum ersten Theile der Elementarwissenschaft gehören müssen"; CpR 135/152.

423 KrV, A 16/B30, AA 04: 26.19 – 21/AA 03: 46.15 – 17: "Weil die Bedingungen, worunter allein die Gegenstände der menschlichen Erkenntniß gegeben werden, denjenigen vorgehen, unter welchen selbige gedacht werden"; CpR 135/152. Cf. also KrV A 21/B 35 – 36, AA 04: 30.23 – 25, 31.01 – 02/AA 03: 50.28 – 29, 51.01 – 03 CpR 156/173.

The just mentioned reference to the distinction between the fundamental faculties of sensibility and understanding furnishes the first distinctive elements of the two basic aspects of Kant's *Gemüt*.

The distinction between sensibility and understanding is more closely analysed at the beginning of the 'Transcendental Aesthetic'. Two elements of this text in particular should be stressed: first, the fact that the "capacity" (*Fähigkeit*) of sensibility is defined as receptivity (*Receptivität*) and is said to afford intuitions (*Anschauungen*), through which objects are given to us; second, Kant's reference to the understanding, which is presented as the faculty that enables the human being to think objects (by means of the concepts (*Begriffe*) that arise from this faculty).

The two fundamental faculties can be more precisely characterised by the reference to the mental elements, which they afford: intuitions and concepts. As we read in Kant's words, intuition (*Anschauung*)

> takes place only insofar as the object is given to us; but this in turn, [ADDED IN B: at least for us humans] is possible only if it affects the mind (*Gemüt*) in a certain way. The capacity (receptivity) to acquire representations through the way in which we are affected by objects is called sensibility. Objects are therefore given to us by means of sensibility, and it alone affords us intuitions; but they are thought through the understanding, and from it arise concepts.[424]

Sensibility has a role that cannot be substituted in order to gain knowledge, since "all thought, whether straight away (*directe*) or through a detour (*indirecte*), must ultimately be related to intuitions, thus, in our case, to sensibility, since there is no other way in which objects can be given to us".[425]

It is essential, in relation to my further analyses in the present and next chapter, to keep in mind that in these passages from the first *Critique* both sensibility and the understanding are considered in relation to objective cognition, while, as I note below, in the development of Kant's considerations of the facul-

---

424 KrV, A19/B33, AA 04: 29.09 – 16/AA 03:49.09 – 16: "Diese [= die Anschauung] findet aber nur statt, sofern uns der Gegenstand gegeben wird; dieses aber ist wiederum [ADDED IN B: uns Menschen wenigstens] nur dadurch möglich, daß er das Gemüth auf gewisse Weise afficire. Die Fähigkeit (Receptivität), Vorstellungen durch die Art, wie wir von Gegenständen afficirt werden, zu bekommen, heißt Sinnlichkeit. Vermittelst der Sinnlichkeit also werden uns Gegenstände gegeben, und sie allein liefert uns Anschauungen; durch den Verstand aber werden sie gedacht, und von ihm entspringen Begriffe"; CpR 155/172.
425 KrV, A19/B33, AA 04: 29.16 – 19/AA 03: 49.16 – 20: "Alles Denken aber muß sich, es sei gerade zu (*directe*) oder im Umschweife (*indirecte*), zuletzt auf Anschauungen, mithin bei uns auf Sinnlichkeit beziehen, weil uns auf andere Weise kein Gegenstand gegeben werden kann"; CpR 155/172.

ties, sensibility, in particular, will be afterwards analysed in relation to the subjective aspect of the representations.

Kant describes his analysis of transcendental aesthetic more closely and states that "we will [...] first isolate sensibility by separating off everything that the understanding thinks through its concepts, so that nothing but empirical intuition remains. Second, we will then detach from the latter everything that belongs to sensation, so that nothing remains except pure intuition and the mere form of appearances, which is the only thing that sensibility can make available *a priori*".[426]

Kant uses similar words at the beginning of the "Transcendental Logic" as well, where, in section 1, he speaks "On Logic in General" and calls the two fundamental faculties two "fundamental sources in the mind" (*Grundquellen des Gemüths*). There we read that "our cognition arises from two fundamental sources in the mind, the first of which is the reception of representations (the receptivity of impressions), the second the faculty for cognizing an object by means of these representations (spontaneity of concepts); through the former an object is given to us, through the latter it is thought in relation to that representation (as a mere determination of the mind)".[427]

In this passage from the "Transcendental Logic", once again the concepts of "receptivity" and "intuitions" occur, which refer to sensibility, and the concepts of "spontaneity" and "concepts" occur as well, which pertain to the sphere of understanding. Moreover, in the same way as in the 'Transcendental Aesthetic', Kant also in this passage from the 'Transcendental Logic' refers to the necessity of taking into consideration the role of both these faculties of our mind in the cognitive process, in order for an objective cognition to be gained: "these two faculties or capacities cannot exchange their functions. The understanding is

---

426 KrV, A 22/B 36, AA 04: 31.03–09/AA 03: 51.04–10: "In der transscendentalen Ästhetik also werden wir zuerst die Sinnlichkeit isoliren, dadurch daß wir alles absondern, was der Verstand durch seine Begriffe dabei denkt, damit nichts als empirische Anschauung übrig bleibe. Zweitens werden wir von dieser noch alles, was zur Empfindung gehört, abtrennen, damit nichts als reine Anschauung und die bloße Form der Erscheinungen übrig bleibe, welches das einzige ist, das die Sinnlichkeit *a priori* liefern kann"; CpR 157/174. The reference to *a priori* intuition introduces the analysis concerning space and time. Cf. KrV, A 22/B 36, AA 04: 31.09–12/AA 03: 51.10–13; CpR 157/174.
427 KrV, A50/B74, AA 04: 47.09–14/AA 03: 74.09–14: "Unsre Erkenntniß entspringt aus zwei Grundquellen des Gemüths, deren die erste ist, die Vorstellungen zu empfangen (die Receptivität der Eindrücke), die zweite das Vermögen, durch diese Vorstellungen einen Gegenstand zu erkennen (Spontaneität der Begriffe); durch die erstere wird uns ein Gegenstand gegeben, durch die zweite wird dieser im Verhältniß auf jene Vorstellung (als bloße Bestimmung des Gemüths) gedacht"; CpR p. 193. But see also KrV A51/B75, AA 04: 48.04–11/AA 03: 75.05–12, CpR 193.

not capable of intuiting anything and the senses are not capable of thinking anything".[428]

What Kant aims to emphasize is, again, the necessity that both the faculties play a role in the process of cognition: it is "only from their unification" that cognition can arise. The necessary conjoined use of both of them does not, in turn, imply any possible use of one of them singularly, since "one must not mix up their roles, rather one has great cause to separate them carefully from each other and distinguish them. Hence we distinguish the science of the rules of sensibility in general, i. e. aesthetic, from the science of the rules of understanding in general, i. e. logic".[429]

What we have gained up until this point from the consideration of Kant's division of the 'Transcendental Logic of Elements' into a 'Transcendental Aesthetic', on the one hand, and a 'Transcendental Logic', on the other hand, has, as a consequence, the bipartition of the mind into two different fundamental faculties: the faculty of sensibility, on the one hand, and the faculty of understanding in the broad sense, on the other hand.[430]

Kant presents further differences between the faculty of understanding and the faculty of sensibility, among others, at the beginning of the "Transcendental Analytic" (A64 ff./B89 ff.), where we read again that understanding "separates itself completely not only from everything empirical, but even from all sensibility".[431] In this case, apart from judging that the sphere of sensibility does not uniquely correspond to the empirical domain, Kant denotes pure understanding as the entire pure, higher faculty of cognition, to which transcendental logic is generally dedicated. This faculty is analysed with respect to two different aspects: once in accordance with concepts, and again according to the principles which arise from it, such that the "Analytic" section of the "Transcendental

---

428 KrV, A51–52/B75–76, AA 04: 48.17–19/AA 03: 75.18–21: "Beide Vermögen oder Fähigkeiten können auch ihre Functionen nicht vertauschen. Der Verstand vermag nichts anzuschauen und die Sinne nichts zu denken"; CpR 194.

429 KrV, A51–52/B75–76, AA 04: 48.19–25/AA 03: 75.21–26: "Nur daraus, daß sie sich vereinigen, kann Erkenntniß entspringen. Deswegen darf man aber doch nicht ihren Antheil vermischen, sondern man hat große Ursache, jedes von dem andern sorgfältig abzusondern und zu unterscheiden. Daher unterscheiden wir die Wissenschaft der Regeln der Sinnlichkeit überhaupt, d. i. Ästhetik, von der Wissenschaft der Verstandesregeln überhaupt, d. i. der Logik"; CpR 194.

430 For the relation between sensibility and the understanding in the first *Critique*, cf. the recent work by JOHANNES HAAG, *Erfahrung und Gegenstand. Das Verhältnis von Sinnlichkeit und Verstand*, Frankfurt a. M., Klostermann 2007.

431 KrV, A65/B89, AA 04: 56.18–20/AA 03: 83.18–19: "Der reine Verstand sondert sich nicht allein von allem Empirischen, sondern sogar von aller Sinnlichkeit völlig aus"; CpR p. 201.

Logic" "consists of two books, the first of which contains the concepts of pure understanding, the second its principle".[432] Thus, Kant uses the term "understanding" in the first *Critique* to refer only to the higher faculty of cognition in the broad sense and, as it can be noted in a passage at the beginning of the 'Analytic of Concepts', Kant stresses that he does not aim to analyse "the content of concepts that present themselves" and to bring them "to distinctness", but aims rather to focus, first, on "the much less frequently attempted analysis of the faculty of understanding itself, in order to reach the possibility of *a priori* concepts by seeking them only in the understanding as their birthplace and analysing its pure use in general".[433]

From such considerations, it follows that, in the first *Critique*, the distinction between a use of the understanding in a broad sense (as faculty of cognition in general – *Erkenntnisvermögen überhaupt*) and a use of it in the narrow sense (*Verstand stricto sensu*) is not so distinct as it will be in the third *Critique*, where Kant clearly distinguishes between the more general, fundamental faculty of cognition (understanding in the broad sense) and the faculty of cognition in its strictly theoretical use (understanding in the narrow sense).[434] This is due to the philosophical function of the first *Critique* and Kant's different philosophical interest in this text.

On this basis, one can also explain why in the Transcendental Dialectic, specifically in the section of the introduction entitled 'On Reason in General', Kant does not deepen the discussion of the practical use of the faculty of reason (*Vernunft*) and rather confines himself to the genesis of a "dialectic" application of the faculty of reason in the context of its theoretical use, by focusing only on

---

432 KrV, A65/B90, AA 04: 56.26–28/AA 03: 83.25–26: "Es besteht aber dieser ganze Theil der transscendentalen Logik aus zwei Büchern, deren das eine die Begriffe, das andere die Grundsätze des reinen Verstandes enthält"; CpR p. 201.

433 Here the whole passage of KrV, A65–66/B90–91, AA 04: 56.33–34, 57.01–05/AA 03: 83.32–33, 84.01–05: "Ich verstehe unter der Analytik der Begriffe nicht die Analysis derselben, oder das gewöhnliche Verfahren in philosophischen Untersuchungen, Begriffe, die sich darbieten, ihrem Inhalte nach zu zergliedern und zur Deutlichkeit zu bringen, sondern die noch wenig versuchte Zergliederung des Verstandesvermögens selbst, um die Möglichkeit der Begriffe *a priori* dadurch zu erforschen, daß wir sie im Verstande allein, als ihrem Geburtsorte, aufsuchen und dessen reinen Gebrauch überhaupt analysiren"; CpR p. 202.

434 For Kant's distinction between the understanding in its broad and narrow sense and the relation between Kant's concept of the understanding and the philosophical tradition cf. among others WAYNE WAXMAN, *Kant and the Empiricists. Understanding Understanding*, Oxford / New York, Oxford University Press 2005.

an erroneous use of this faculty, which may cause what Kant calls "transcendental illusion".[435]

From these brief considerations on the classification of the faculties in the first *Critique*, one can notice that the distinction between sensibility and theoretical reason (i.e. understanding in general) is marked very clearly, while the classification within the field of the "higher cognitive faculties" is less clear as the one we find in the third *Critique*. This does not mean that Kant does not yet think of a tripartite division of the fundamental cognitive faculties: as we will see in the sections below, the idea of a tripartite division of the fundamental faculties is already testified in a letter addressed to Karl Leonhard Reinhold and dated 28th-31st December 1787.[436] Nonetheless, the pair of concepts 'sensibility / understanding (i.e. reason in its theoretical use)' is the one to which Kant dedicates his attention at this point in time in the first *Critique*. Furthermore, even though Kant speaks of "a science of all principles of *a priori* sensibility"[437] in the first *Critique* and thereby refers to an *a priori* application of the faculty of sensibility, only later in the published works does Kant include sensibility, in its particular form of the faculty of feeling, within a more stringent tripartite division of the fundamental faculties and proposes a tripartite division among (1) the faculty of cognition in the narrow sense (*oberes Erkenntnisvermögen*), (2) the feeling of pleasure and displeasure (*Gefühl der Lust und Unlust*), and (3) the faculty of desire (*Begehrungsvermögen*). In order to follow the developments, which give rise to this change, I now consider Kant's division of the faculties in the second *Critique*.

4.3 Towards Kant's Tripartite Division of the Faculties in the third *Critique*

Two changes in Kant's interest concerning the theory of the faculties are most noteworthy in the second *Critique*. First is the fact that Kant focuses on the faculty of reason in its practical use and makes this faculty correspond to the higher faculty of desire. Second, Kant's interest in a further faculty, i.e. the faculty of feeling pleasure and displeasure, and its *a priori* application. The focus on the

---

435 Cf. the section *Von der Vernunft überhaupt* (KrV, A298–302/B355–359, AA04:191–193/ AA03:237–239, CpR pp. 387–389) and the following ones.
436 Cf. Letter 313, Br, AA 10: 514.24–37, 515.01–05; *Correspondence*, pp. 271–273. This letter is quoted in the middle of my analysis in the following sections.
437 KrV, A 21/B35, AA 04: 20.23–24/AA 03: 50.28–29: "Eine Wissenschaft von allen Principien der Sinnlichkeit *a priori* nenne ich die transscendentale Ästhetik"; CpR 156/173.

latter faculty is a central transition in the evolution of Kant's general mapping of the mind, since it introduces also the analysis of a particular aspect of sensibility within the set of higher faculties.

I propose to read this stronger focus on the faculty of feeling with regard to Kant's consideration of the *a priori* application of the faculty of sensibility, as well, in the particular form of the faculty of feeling pleasure and displeasure, which is devoid of all reference to objective cognition and refers to a merely subjective relation. Such an application gives way to the consideration of a new tripartite division of all the faculties of the human mind, such that in the third *Critique* Kant refers to (1) the cognitive faculty in the narrow sense, (2) the faculty of feeling pleasure and displeasure, and (3) the faculty of desire as the three fundamental faculties of the human mind, as this table (derived from the introduction to the third *Critique*)[438] shows:

All the faculties of the mind:		
(a) Cognitive faculty in the narrow sense	(b) Feeling of pleasure and displeasure	(c) Faculty of desire
which corresponds to the cognitive faculty of	which corresponds to the cognitive faculty of the	which corresponds to the cognitive faculty of
(a1) Understanding in the narrow sense, i. e., higher cognitive faculty in its *a priori* use	(b1) Power of judgement, i.e. feeling of pleasure and displeasure in its *a priori* use	(c1) Reason, i.e. faculty of desire in its *a priori* use

In considering the divisions of the faculties in the first and in the third *Critique*, one should note, first of all, that in the classification that occurs in the *Critique of the Power of Judgement* Kant deals with all the faculties of the human mind but he does not divide them into two big groups, as he seems to do in

---

438 Cf. KU, AA 05: 198, CPJ p. 83 and the sections dedicated to the analysis of the faculties in the third *Critique*.

the first *Critique*. There, in fact, he gives importance primarily to the distinction between sensibility, on the one hand, and understanding in the broad sense, on the other hand. As already noted, this depends on the fact that, in contrast to the first *Critique*, in the *Critique of the Power of Judgement* Kant aims to deal not only with the analysis of theoretical philosophy and objective cognition, but with all the actions of the human mind and the faculties which are responsible for them. Consequently, while (1) the reference to sensibility in the first *Critique* aims to clarify what the source of the materials of objective human cognition is and (2) the reference to the understanding aims to clarify the sources of its form, in the classification of the faculties coming from the introduction to the third *Critique* Kant takes into consideration all the faculties in general.

In this last classification, to the concept of reason according to its theoretical meaning (i.e. the concept of reason analysed in the *Critique of Pure Reason* as the understanding – in the broad sense of faculty of theoretical cognition) and to the concept of reason according to its practical meaning (i.e. the concept of reason analysed in the *Critique of Practical Reason* as the faculty of desire), a third concept is added: the concept of the feeling of pleasure and displeasure, which is now presented as the third fundamental faculty.

In contrast to the presentation of the first *Critique*, the mention of the faculty of feeling in the third *Critique* as a fundamental faculty is very clear. This can also be due to the fact that feeling, as a special determination of the faculty of sensibility, becomes central in the context of the critical analysis dedicated to practical reason, where Kant considers an *a priori* use of a particular aspect of sensibility which is not linked to the *a priori* intuitions of space and time.

Thus, in the following section I aim to underline Kant's interest in the concept of feeling in the context of practical philosophy and to consider his acknowledgement of the possibility of an *a priori* use of the faculty of feeling pleasure and displeasure in moral action (by referring to respect for the moral law).

4.4 The Correspondence between (Pure) Reason and the (Higher) Faculty of Desire, as well as (Pure) Reason and (Autonomous) Will

In order to illustrate how, in particular in the second *Critique*, Kant's discussion of the faculties is focused on desire (which corresponds to the faculty of reason in its practical use) and feeling, I shall start this section with Kant's considerations on the concept of feeling in a footnote in the Preface of the *Critique of Practical Reason*.

After clarifying (in the main text) that in the second chapter of the Analytic of the second *Critique* he aims to deal with the objection advanced by a "certain reviewer", who "is devoted to truth and astute",[439] in this footnote Kant considers a further objection, which could have been put to him in relation to the *Groundwork of the Metaphysics of Morals*. This objection could have read as follows: "why have I not previously explicated the concept of the faculty of desire (*Begehrungsvermögen*) or of the feeling of pleasure (*Gefühl der Lust*)".[440]

---

439 KpV, AA 05: 08.25–26; CprR p. 143. Kant refers here to Hermann Andreas Pistorius, who wrote an anonymous review of the *Grundlegung* for the *Allgemeine deutsche Bibliothek*: "Grundlegung zur Metaphysik der Sitten von Immanuel Kant. Riga 1785.", in *Allgemeine deutsche Bibliothek*, Volume 66/2 (1786), pp. 447/463. Cf. also the others reviews by H. A. Pistorius on Kant's philosophy: (PISTORIUS, HERMANN ANDREAS,) "Erläuterungen über des Herrn Professor Kant Critik der reinen Vernunft von Joh. Schultze, Königl. Preußischem Hofprediger. Königsberg 1784.", in *Allgemeine deutsche Bibliothek*, Volume 66/1 (1786), pp. 92–123; (PISTORIUS, HERMANN ANDREAS,) "Critik der reinen Vernunft von Immanuel Kant, Prof. in Königsberg, der Königl. Akademie der Wissenschaften in Berlin Mitglied. Zweyte hin und wieder verbesserte Auflage, Riga 1787.", in *Allgemeine deutsche Bibliothek*, Volume 81/2 (1788), pp. 343/354; (PISTORIUS, HERMANN ANDREAS,) "Prüfung der Mendelssohnschen Morgenstunden, oder aller spekulativen Beweise für das Daseyn Gottes in Vorlesungen von Ludwig Heinrich Jakob, Doktor der Philosophie in Halle. Nebst einer Abhandlung vom Herrn Professor Kant. Leipzig 1786.", in *Allgemeine deutsche Bibliothek*, Volume 82/2 (1788), pp. 427–470; (PISTORIUS, HERMANN ANDREAS,) "Critik der praktischen Vernunft, von Immanuel Kant. Riga 1788.", in *Allgemeine deutsche Bibliothek*, Volume 117/1 (1794), pp. 78–105. Pistorius' reviews are partially reprinted in ALBERT LANDAU (ed.), *Rezensionen zur Kantischen Philosophie, 1781–1787,* Bebra (Landau) 1991 and, more recently, in BERNWARD GESANG (ed.), *Kants vergessener Rezensent. Die Kritik der theoretischen und praktischen Philosophie Kants in fünf frühen Rezensionen von Hermann Andreas Pistorius,* Hamburg, Meiner 2007. On the role of Pistorius in Kant's philosophy, cf. HEINER F. KLEMME, "Spontaneität und Selbsterkenntnis. Kant über die ursprüngliche Einheit von Natur und Freiheit im Aktus des Denkens (1785–1787/88)", in MARIO BRANDHORST – ANDREE HAHMANN – BERND LUDWIG (eds.), *Sind wir Bürger zweier Welten? Freiheit und moralische Verantwortung im transzendentalen Idealismus,* Hamburg, Meiner 2012, pp. 195–222; BERND LUDWIG, "Die 'consequente Denkungsart der speculativen Kritik'. Kants radikale Umgestaltung seiner Freiheitslehre im Jahre 1786 – und die Folgen für die Kritische Philosophie als Ganze", in *Deutsche Zeitschrift für Philosophie*, 58/4 (2010), pp. 595–628; BERND LUDWIG, "Was weiß ich vom Ich? Kants Lehre vom Faktum der reinen praktischen Vernunft, seine Neufassung der Paralogismen und die verborgenen Fortschritte der Kritischen Metaphysik im Jahre 1786", in MARIO BRANDHORST – ANDREE HAHMANN – BERND LUDWIG (eds.), *Sind wir Bürger zweier Welten? Freiheit und moralische Verantwortung im transzendentalen Idealismus,* Hamburg, Meiner 2012, pp. 155–194.
440 KpV, AA 05: 09 (Fußnote): "Man könnte mir noch den Einwurf machen, warum ich nicht auch den Begriff des Begehrungsvermögens, oder des Gefühls der Lust vorher erklärt habe"; CprR p. 143 (note).

Kant first assesses that "this reproach would be unfair because this explication as given in psychology could not reasonably be presupposed".[441] Successively, he notes that the definition of these two faculties "could admittedly be so framed that the feeling of pleasure would ground the determination of the faculty of desire (as is in fact commonly done), and thus the supreme principle of practical philosophy would necessarily turn out to be empirical, although this has to be settled first and in the present *Critique* altogether refuted".[442]

Kant argues against the traditional doctrine, according to which the faculty of desire is motivated exclusively by the feeling of pleasure. In order to understand his objections, Kant believes that a preliminary explanation of the traditional concepts is due and he starts off with the following definitions:

(a) the concept of "life (*Leben*)" is defined as "the faculty of a being to act in accordance with laws of the faculty of desire";[443]

(b) the "faculty of desire (*Begehrungsvermögen*)" is said to be "a being's faculty to be by means of its representations the cause of the reality of the objects of these representations";[444]

(c) the concept of "pleasure (*Lust*)" is defined as "the representation of the agreement of an object or of an action with the subjective conditions of life, i.e. with the faculty of the causality of a representation with respect to the reality of its object (or with respect to the determination of the powers of the subject to action in order to produce the object)".[445]

---

441 KpV, AA 05: 09 (Fußnote): "Obgleich dieser Vorwurf unbillig sein würde, weil man diese Erklärung, als in der Psychologie gegeben, billig sollte voraussetzen können"; CprR p. 143 (note).

442 KpV, AA 05: 09 (Fußnote): "Es könnte aber freilich die Definition daselbst so eingerichtet sein, daß das Gefühl der Lust der Bestimmung des Begehrungsvermögens zum Grunde gelegt würde (wie es auch wirklich gemeinhin so zu geschehen pflegt), dadurch aber das oberste Princip der praktischen Philosophie nothwendig empirisch ausfallen müßte, welches doch allererst auszumachen ist und in dieser *Kritik* gänzlich widerlegt wird"; CprR pp. 143–144 (note).

443 KpV, AA 05: 09 (Fußnote): "Leben ist das Vermögen eines Wesens, nach Gesetzen des Begehrungsvermögens zu handeln"; CprR p. 144 (note).

444 KpV, AA 05: 09 (Fußnote): "Das Begehrungsvermögen ist das Vermögen desselben, durch seine Vorstellungen Ursache von der Wirklichkeit der Gegenstände dieser Vorstellungen zu sein"; CprR p. 144 (note).

445 KpV, AA 05: 09 (Fußnote): "Lust ist die Vorstellung der Übereinstimmung des Gegenstandes oder der Handlung mit den subjectiven Bedingungen des Lebens, d. i. mit dem Vermögen der Causalität einer Vorstellung in Ansehung der Wirklichkeit ihres Objects (oder der Bestimmung der Kräfte des Subjects zur Handlung es hervorzubringen)"; CprR p. 144 (note). For an analysis of the relation between the concepts of pleasure and the one of desire, in particular in Kant's lectures on anthropology, cf. HEINER F. KLEMME, "Fühlen, Begehren, Erkennen", cit.

Kant acknowledges that these concepts are "borrowed from psychology" and, as we remember from the chapters above, it is not uncommon to describe the concepts of the faculties as flowing from the traditional discipline of empirical psychology into Kant's critical enterprise. Nonetheless, what Kant aims to underline is, first of all, that "the question whether pleasure must always be put at the basis of the faculty of desire or whether under certain conditions pleasure only follows upon its determination, is left undecided" for now in the context of his critical enterprise, for the first *Critique* does not shed any light on such topics.[446] It is rather up to the *Critique of Practical Reason* to supply the analysis of the process of (moral) volition and, this way, to explain how it happens that not only pleasure succeeds in motivating the faculty of desire but also, the other way round, how the faculty of feeling is moved by the faculty of desire, i.e. by reason.

Kant makes the first steps towards the clarification of these "mental processes" and of the functioning of the faculties of desire and feeling in the preface to the second *Critique*. He states that, "when it is a matter of determining a particular faculty of the human soul as to its sources, its contents, and its limits, then, from the nature of human cognition, one can begin only with the *parts*, with an accurate and complete presentation of them".[447] Nonetheless, Kant further recognizes, as a second step, that in our research we should also "grasp correctly the *idea of the whole*" and consequently, from this idea, we should also pass "to see all those parts in their mutual relation by means of their derivation from the concept of that whole in a pure rational faculty".[448]

---

446 Here the whole passage of KpV, AA 05: 09 (Fußnote): "Mehr brauche ich nicht zum Behuf der *Kritik* von Begriffen, die aus der Psychologie entlehnt werden, das übrige leistet die Kritik selbst. Man wird leicht gewahr, daß die Frage, ob die Lust dem Begehrungsvermögen jederzeit zum Grunde gelegt werden müsse, oder ob sie auch unter gewissen Bedingungen nur auf die Bestimmung desselben folge, durch diese Erklärung unentschieden bleibt"; CprR p. 144 (note). On this point, cf. HANS-MARTIN GERLACH, "Gefühl – Sinnlichkeit – Verstand. Bemerkungen zu einem erkenntnistheoretisch-psychologischen Problem in der Philosophie der Aufklärung", in *Deutsche Zeitschrift für Philosophie* (Berlin), 32/11 (1984), pp. 991–999, but also MANFRED BAUM, "Gefühl, Begehren und Wollen in Kants praktischer Philosophie", in *Jahrbuch für Recht und Ethik/Annual Review of Law and Ethics*, 14 (2006), pp. 125–139.

447 KpV, AA 05: 10.03–08: "Wenn es um die Bestimmung eines besonderen Vermögens der menschlichen Seele nach seinen Quellen, Inhalte und Grenzen zu thun ist, so kann man zwar nach der Natur des menschlichen Erkenntnisses nicht anders als von den Theilen derselben, ihrer genauen und [...] vollständigen Darstellung anfangen"; CprR p. 144.

448 KpV, AA 05: 10.08–13: "Aber es ist noch eine zweite Aufmerksamkeit, die mehr philosophisch und architektonisch ist: nämlich die Idee des Ganzen richtig zu fassen und aus derselben alle jene Theile in ihrer wechselseitigen Beziehung auf einander vermittelst der Ableitung derselben von dem Begriffe jenes Ganzen in einem reinen Vernunftvermögen ins Auge zu fassen"; CprR p. 144.

In these passages from the preface to the second *Critique* Kant describes a procedure, which could be used for comprehending how each faculty is generally constituted: not only the single function of every single faculty has to be taken into consideration, but also the way in which each of them architectonically relates to all the other ones. However, in particular in the context of the second *Critique*, through this procedure Kant aims to arrive at "the *a priori* principles of two faculties of the mind (*Gemüt*), the faculty of cognition and that of desire", which "would be found and determined as to the conditions, extent, and boundaries of their use", so that "a firm basis would thereby be laid for a scientific system of philosophy, both theoretical and practical".[449]

In this context, as I will also note below in the analysis dedicated to the 'First Introduction' of the *Critique of the Power of Judgement*, Kant juxtaposes what he considers the two fundamental parts of his philosophical system (theoretical and practical philosophy) to the two fundamental faculties of cognition and of desire (even though he still does not mention the intermediate faculty of feeling, nor does he refer to the power of judgement, as he does in the third *Critique*). In this passage we thus see the faculty of cognition in the narrow sense, i.e. understanding *stricto sensu*, on the one hand, which gives access to that part of the system that Kant dedicates to the field of theoretical philosophy, and the faculty of desire, on the other hand, which is said to be giving access to the field of practical philosophy.

Kant's interest in this bipartition between two fundamental faculties seems to be confirmed also in some passages from the introduction to the second *Critique*, occurring in the section 'On the Idea of a Critique of Practical Reason'.[450] There Kant refers to:

(a) a pure cognitive faculty;
(b) the practical use of reason as determining the will;
(c) pure reason as unconditionally practical.

The pure cognitive faculty occurs in the discussion concerning the theoretical use of reason. The analysis of the pure faculty of cognition is necessitated, in the first *Critique*, by the fact that this pure faculty *per se* "might easily lose itself

---

449 KpV, AA 05: 12.01–05: "Auf diese Weise wären denn nunmehr die Principien *a priori* zweier Vermögen des Gemüths, des Erkenntniß=und Begehrungsvermögens, ausgemittelt und nach den Bedingungen, dem Umfange und Grenzen ihres Gebrauchs bestimmt, hiedurch aber zu einer systematischen, theoretischen sowohl als praktischen Philosophie als Wissenschaft sicherer Grund gelegt"; CprR pp. 145–146.
450 Cf. *Von der Idee einer Kritik der praktischen Vernunft*, KpV, AA 05: 15–16; CprR pp. 148–149.

beyond its boundaries, among unattainable objects or even among contradictory concepts".[451]

As to what concerns the successive use of reason, Kant affirms that, in its practical application, "reason is concerned with the determining grounds of the will".[452]

The analysis of the concept of the will is fundamental in the context of the second *Critique*, for the faculty of the will in its pure application corresponds to pure practical reason (even though, at least at this stage, Kant seems to distinguish between pure will and pure practical reason). At another place, Kant defines the will as "the faculty either of producing objects corresponding to representations or of determining itself to effect such objects (whether the physical power is sufficient or not), that is, of determining its causality".[453] If the will does not only produce objects corresponding to representations, but it may also determine its causality, then it follows that

(a) it is not only empirical determinations succeed in motivating human action and, furthermore,

(b) it could also be possible for reason to "suffice to determine the will".[454]

The aim of Kant's explanation is, thus, to show that "pure reason can be practical", that "it alone, and not reason empirically limited, is unconditionally practical"[455] and, consequently, that not only empirically conditioned reason, "alone

---

451 Here the whole passage of KpV, AA 05: 15.03–08: "Der theoretische Gebrauch der Vernunft beschäftigte sich mit Gegenständen des bloßen Erkenntnißvermögens, und eine Kritik derselben in Absicht auf diesen Gebrauch betraf eigentlich nur das reine Erkenntnißvermögen, weil dieses Verdacht erregte, der sich auch hernach bestätigte, daß es sich leichtlich über seine Grenzen unter unerreichbare Gegenstände, oder gar einander widerstreitende Begriffe verlöre"; CprR p. 148.

452 KpV, AA 05: 15.08–10: "Mit dem praktischen Gebrauche der Vernunft verhält es sich schon anders. In diesem beschäftigt sich die Vernunft mit Bestimmungsgründen des Willens"; CprR p. 148.

453 KpV, AA 05: 15.10–14: "welcher [= der Wille] ein Vermögen ist, den Vorstellungen entsprechende Gegenstände entweder hervorzubringen, oder doch sich selbst zu Bewirkung derselben (das physische Vermögen mag nun hinreichend sein, oder nicht), d. i. seine Causalität, zu bestimmen"; CprR p. 148.

454 Kant goes even further and states that reason "always has objective reality insofar as volition alone is at issue" ("Denn da kann wenigstens die Vernunft zur Willensbestimmung gelangen und hat so fern immer objective Realität, als es nur auf das Wollen ankommt"), KpV, AA 05: 15.14–16; CprR p. 148.

455 KpV, AA 05: 15.23–26: "...so wird dadurch nicht allein dargethan, daß reine Vernunft praktisch sein könne, sondern daß sie allein und nicht die empirisch=beschränkte unbedingterweise praktisch sei"; CprR p. 148.

and exclusively, furnishes the determining ground of the will".[456] The defence of these theses is fundamental in the second *Critique*.

By analysing the passages from the preface and the introduction to the *Critique of Practical Reason*, we made the first steps towards the comprehension of the functioning of the (pure application of the) faculty of desire as (pure) practical reason. A further step for the presentation of this faculty is the analysis of its functioning in relation to the faculty of feeling. Kant explains this relation in the third section (Theorem II) of the first chapter ('On the Principles of Pure Practical Reason')[457] of the first book of the second *Critique*, in the context of 'The Analytic of Pure Practical Reason'.[458] In this third section, Kant specifies the way in which feeling works on the faculty of desire. Furthermore, he there refers to the empirical moving force of feeling through the analysis of the concept of pleasure:

> Pleasure arising from the representation of the existence of a thing, insofar as it is to be a determining ground of desire for this thing, is based on the *receptivity* (*Empfänglichkeit*) of the subject, since it depends upon the existence of an object; hence it belongs to sense (feeling) and not to the understanding, which expresses a relation of a representation *to an object* by concepts, not to the subject by feeling. It is, then, practical only insofar as the feeling of agreeableness that the subject expects from the reality of an object determines the faculty of desire.[459]

In this passage, we note again that:
(a) Kant refers to a particular aspect of sense, i. e. feeling, as receptivity, i. e. by the same term that he also uses for the more general faculty of sensibility, as we remember from the first *Critique* and the 1798 *Anthropology*;

---

456 KpV, AA 05: 16.03 – 06: "Die Kritik der praktischen Vernunft überhaupt hat also die Obliegenheit, die empirisch bedingte Vernunft von der Anmaßung abzuhalten, ausschließungsweise den Bestimmungsgrund des Willens allein abgeben zu wollen"; CprR p. 148.

457 *Erstes Hauptstück. Von den Grundsätzen der reinen praktischen Vernunft*, KpV, AA 05: 19 – 57; CprR pp. 153 – 186.

458 Cf. *Erstes Buch. Die Analytik der reinen praktischen Vernunft*, KpV, AA 05: 19 – 106; CprR pp. 153 – 225.

459 KpV, AA 05: 22.09 – 17: "Die Lust aus der Vorstellung der Existenz einer Sache, so fern sie ein Bestimmungsgrund des Begehrens dieser Sache sein soll, gründet sich auf der Empfänglichkeit des Subjects, weil sie von dem Dasein eines Gegenstandes abhängt; mithin gehört sie dem Sinne (Gefühl) und nicht dem Verstande an, der eine Beziehung der Vorstellung auf ein Object nach Begriffen, aber nicht auf das Subject nach Gefühlen ausdrückt. Sie ist also nur so fern praktisch, als die Empfindung der Annehmlichkeit, die das Subject von der Wirklichkeit des Gegenstandes erwartet, das Begehrungsvermögen bestimmt"; CprR pp. 155 – 156.

(b) pleasure determines the faculty of desire by expressing a particular relation of a representation to the subject. Feeling makes this relation possible: the feeling of agreeableness expected by the subject from the reality of an object that determines the faculty of desire.

From these considerations and particularly from the second point, it follows that feeling is a faculty which pertains to the more general faculty of sensibility and, at the same time, whose functioning is not always necessarily explained only by reference to the empirical field. Consequently, Kant is now in a position to state that not only pleasure or displeasure deriving from an empirical object can succeed in motivating the faculty of desire. With this assertion, he contrasts the traditional reading, as it is presented in the preface to the second *Critique*, according to which only pleasure, of empirical origin, may determine the will. Certainly, merely from this consideration, it does not follow that there must exist a non-empirical determination of the faculty of desire, which does not have to do with the empirical motivating force of feeling. The possibility for the faculty of desire to be determined by a non-empirical motive is now to be found.

In order to do so, in the corollary that follows the theorem just analysed (II), Kant observes that a higher faculty of desire would not exist if there were no formal law of the will by means of which the higher faculty of desire might be determined: "All material practical rules put the determining ground of the will in the *lower faculty of desire*, and were there no *merely formal* laws of the will sufficient to determine it, then neither could *any higher faculty of desire* be admitted".[460]

And afterwards Kant assesses that such a law does exist: this is the moral law. We can read Kant's solution in Remark I, following the just quoted corollary: "Only insofar as reason of itself (not in the service of the inclinations) determines the will, is reason a true *higher* faculty of desire, to which the pathologically determinable is subordinate".[461] In this way, Kant states that reason by itself successes in determining the will without any reference to the empirical forces of inclinations and he makes reason correspond to the higher faculty of desire.

---

460 KpV, AA 05: 22.27–31: "Alle materiale praktische Regeln setzen den Bestimmungsgrund des Willens im unteren Begehrungsvermögen, und, gäbe es gar keine blos formale Gesetze desselben, die den Willen hinreichend bestimmten, so würde auch kein oberes Begehrungsvermögen eingeräumt werden können"; CprR p. 156.

461 KpV, AA 05: 24.40, 25.01–02: "Alsdann allein ist Vernunft nur, so fern sie für sich selbst den Willen bestimmt (nicht im Dienste der Neigungen ist), ein wahres oberes Begehrungsvermögen, dem das pathologisch bestimmbare untergeordnet ist"; CprR p. 158.

Thus, Kant now presents a distinction within the faculty of desire between a lower part, which is influenced by the impulses, and a higher part, which operates without external influences: reason is, in this case, "really, and indeed *specifically*, distinct from the latter [the pathologically determinable one], so that even the least admixture of the latter's impulses infringes upon its strength and superiority".[462] The existence of a higher faculty of desire, which corresponds to pure practical reason, is proven by the givenness of the moral law to human beings: "In a practical law reason determines the will immediately, not by means of an intervening feeling of pleasure or displeasure, not even in this law; and that it can as pure reason be practical is what alone makes it possible for it *to be lawgiving*".[463]

Reason itself in its pure practical application is *per se* lawgiving, without the intervention of a feeling, that is, the higher faculty of desire can alone motivate the human being to a moral action. No feeling whatsoever and, in particular, no empirically determined feeling is here called into question, which means that the lower faculty of desire, which would render the validity and obligating force of the moral law dependent on heterogeneous factors, is not called into question either. Only the purity of the higher faculty of desire and the autonomy of the law are taken here into consideration. From this, it follows that pure reason "can be regarded as a faculty immediately determining the will".[464]

At this stage, some closer observations concerning the relation between the above assessments and the classification of the faculties are due. Kant here seems to identify the higher faculty of desire most of the time with the concept of pure practical reason, even though, sometimes, as for instance in the last quotation, he also says that the faculty of pure reason in its practical application determines the will and he distinguishes between the two faculties. This partial identification of the will and practical reason is overtly testified also by another

---

462 KpV, AA 05: 25.02–04: "[Vernunft ist ein wahres oberes Begehrungsvermögen, das das pathologisch bestimmbare untergeordnet ist], und wirklich, ja spezifisch von diesem unterschieden, so daß sogar die mindeste Beimischung von den Antrieben der letzteren ihrer Stärke und Vorzuge Abbruch thut"; CprR p. 158.

463 KpV, AA 05: 25.06–10: "Die Vernunft bestimmt in einem praktischen Gesetze unmittelbar den Willen, nicht vermittelst eines dazwischen kommenden Gefühls der Lust und Unlust, selbst nicht an diesem Gesetze, und nur, daß sie als reine Vernunft praktisch sein kann, macht es ihr möglich, gesetzgebend zu sein"; CprR p. 158. For the motivating force of pure practical reason, the role of respect, and the problem in Kant scholarship on these topics, see more in particular chapter 5 below.

464 KpV, AA 05: 46.34–36: "die Vernunft durch dieselbe Causalität in einem vernünftigen Wesen hat, d. i. reine Vernunft, die als ein unmittelbar den Willen bestimmendes Vermögen angesehen werden kann"; CprR p. 177.

passage, which sheds light on a further lack of sharpness in the distinction between these faculties and, in turn, adds further information concerning the relation between the faculty of understanding and that of reason in its practical application. Let us consider this passage, which reads as follows:

> besides the relation in which the *understanding* stands to object (in theoretical cognition) it has also a relation to the faculty of desire, which is therefore called the will and is called the pure will insofar as the pure understanding (which in this case is called reason) is practical through the mere representation of a law.[465]

Here, Kant uses the word "understanding" (*Verstand*) both in its broad and its narrow sense: he first refers to (1) understanding (*Verstand*) in its theoretical application, i.e. understanding in the narrow sense, which is directed to objects and is applied by human beings in order to get cognition; then he states that understanding as a theoretical faculty has a relation to (2) the faculty of desire (*Begehrungsvermögen*), which Kant makes here completely correspond to (2a) the will (*Wille*). In addition, he assesses that the will can be called a (3) pure will (*reiner Wille*) only in the case where (3a) pure understanding (*reiner Verstand*) is practical, i.e. in the case where (3b) reason (*Vernunft*) is practical. If we aim to get a sense of this last assertion, we should intend the term "understand" to be used (3a) in the broad sense of "higher faculty", which corresponds to reason.

Kant considers the reality of the correspondence of pure practical reason to pure will, as a fact (*Factum*) given *a priori* in the moral law, as we read in the following passage from the second *Critique:* "the objective reality of a pure will or, what is the same thing, of a pure practical reason is given *a priori* in the moral law, as it were by a fact – for so we may call a determination of the will that is unavoidable even though it does not rest upon empirical principles".[466] According to Kant, we identify the will's determination through the moral law as an undeniable fact.

This is Kant's theory of the "fact of reason", which plays a fundamental role in Kant's moral foundation and which I will consider more closely in the next

---

465 KpV, AA 05: 55.11–15: "Außer dem Verhältnisse aber, darin der Verstand zu Gegenständen (im theoretical Erkenntnisse) steht, hat er auch eines zum Begehrungsvermögen, das darum der Wille heißt, und der reine Wille, so fern der reine Verstand (der in solchem Falle Vernunft heißt) durch die bloße Vorstellung eines Gesetzes praktisch ist"; CprR p. 184.
466 KpV, AA 05: 55.15–19: "Die objective Realität eines reinen Willens oder, welches einerlei ist, einer reinen praktischen Vernunft ist im moralischen Gesetze *a priori* gleichsam durch ein Factum gegeben; denn so kann man eine Willensbestimmung nennen, die unvermeidlich ist, ob sie gleich nicht auf empirischen Principien beruht"; CprR p. 184.

chapter.[467] At this stage I shall limit myself to briefly mentioning this doctrine, since there is no need to deal with it more closely in the present context of the analysis of Kant's classification of the mental faculties. Instead, I shall continue with the presentation of another essential element of Kant's account of the faculties in the second *Critique*, namely the concept of pleasure, to which the faculty of feeling is indivisibly linked.

4.5 The Concept of Pleasure and the Role of Feeling in the *Critique of Practical Reason*

In the *Critique of Practical Reason*, Kant's treatment of the concept of "feeling" differs from the one in the first *Critique*, as can be noted when confronting the two works. To begin with, we can refer to a passage from the first *Critique:* at the end of the introduction to the *Critique of Pure Reason*, both in the first and in the second edition, after explaining what belongs to a critique of the faculty of reason and to transcendental philosophy, Kant notes that "the chief target in the division of such a science [=transcendental philosophy] is that absolutely no concept must enter into it that contains anything empirical, or that the *a priori* cognition be entirely pure".[468] From this consideration it follows that morality cannot find a proper place in the context of transcendental philosophy, for "although the supreme principles of morality and the fundamental concepts of it are *a priori* cognitions, they still do not belong in transcendental philosophy".[469] The passage concerning the justification of the ban of morality from transcendental philosophy is slightly different in the second edition of the first *Critique*.

In the first edition Kant assesses that morality is banned from transcendental philosophy "since the concepts of pleasure and displeasure, of desire and inclinations, of choice (*Willkür*), etc., which are all of empirical origin, must there

---

467 For an introduction to the central topic of the *Faktum der Vernunft* in the second *Critique* and for a first overview of the bibliography of this theme, see PAULINE KLEINGELD, "Moral Consciousness and the 'Fact of Reason'", in ANDREWS REATH – JENS TIMMERMANN (eds.), *Kant's Critique of Practical Reason. A Critical Guide*, Cambridge/New York, Cambridge University Press 2010, pp. 55–72.

468 KrV, A14/B28, AA 04: 24.29–32/AA 03: 45.18–21: "Das vornehmste Augenmerk bei der Eintheilung einer solchen Wissenschaft ist: daß gar keine Begriffe hineinkommen müssen, die irgend etwas Empirisches in sich enthalten, oder daß die Erkenntniß *a priori* völlig rein sei"; CpR pp. 134/151.

469 KrV, A14–15/B28, AA 04: 24.32–34/AA 03: 45.21–23: "Daher, obzwar die obersten Grundsätze der Moralität und die Grundbegriffe derselben Erkenntnisse *a priori* sind, so gehören sie doch nicht in die Transscendental-Philosophie"; CpR p. 151.

be presupposed".[470] This means that moral philosophy does not belong to transcendental philosophy, for it always implies a reference to concepts which are not of *a priori* origin and can, instead, only be attained through a reference to the field of the empirical.

Among these concepts, Kant quotes not only desire and inclination, but also the power of choice and the concepts of "pleasure" and "displeasure". Nonetheless, as I will show soon, Kant afterwards includes both the faculty of choice and a particular form of pleasure among those concepts that pertain to an *a priori* undertaking.

In the 1787 edition of the *Critique of Pure Reason* Kant modifies the passage in question regarding the concepts of choice and feeling. The passage from the second edition, which aims to justify the ban of morality from transcendental philosophy, reads differently. Kant assesses that the principles of morality and the fundamental concepts of it "do not, to be sure, take the concepts of pleasure and displeasure, of desire and inclinations, etc., which are all of empirical origin, as the ground of their precepts" and, this time, he also adds that, however, the moral concepts "still must necessarily include them in the composition of a system of pure morality in the concept of duty, as the hindrance that must be overcome or the attraction that ought not to be made into a motive (*zum Bewegungsgrunde*)".[471]

In this passage, we first note the absence of the reference to the power of choice (*Willkür*) as a concept of empirical origin. Nevertheless, pleasure and displeasure, desire and inclination are still considered to be concepts of empirical origin. However, in contrast to the 1781 edition, Kant notes that pleasure and displeasure must still be included in the concept of duty, even though only as an hindrance that must be overcome and never as motives (*Bewegungsgründe*) for an action that can be judged as moral. In fact, as Kant states afterwards in the critical works, only reason succeeds in motivating moral action, when it provides the human being with the moral law in its form of the categorical imperative. The term motive (*Bewegungsgrund*) refers, in fact, only to the proper moti-

---

470 KrV, A14–15, AA 04: 24.34–36: "Weil die Begriffe der Lust und Unlust, der Begierden und Neigungen, der Willkür etc., die insgesammt empirischen Ursprunges sind, dabei vorausgesetzt werden müßten"; CpR pp. 134–135.

471 Here the whole passage of KrV, B28–29, AA 03: 45.23–29: "weil sie die Begriffe der Lust und Unlust, der Begierden und Neigungen etc., die insgesammt empirischen Ursprungs sind, zwar selbst nicht zum Grunde ihrer Vorschriften legen, aber doch im Begriffe der Pflicht als Hinderniß, das überwunden, oder als Anreiz, der nicht zum Bewegungsgrunde gemacht werden soll, nothwendig in die Abfassung des Systems der reinen Sittlichkeit mit hineinziehen müssen"; CpR p. 151.

vation of the action and, in the moral case, only the moral law in its form of the categorical imperative can be an agent's determining motive (*Bestimmungs-grund*).[472] In contrast to the concept of (determining) motive (*Bewegungsgrund / Bestimmungsgrund*), the word incentive (*Triebfeder*) is dedicated to the subjective incentives, which help realize (concur in the realization of) an action, but which do not suffice by themselves to furnish the agent with the necessary force to act. In conclusion, while the power of choice is not considered among the empirical concepts anymore, pleasure is still considered in this way, i. e. as a hindrance, in contrast to the pure motive which has to cause moral action, i. e. the law.

This consideration of the determining motive and the incentives of moral action is not limited to the lines mentioned. In fact, a further switch in Kant's way of considering practical philosophy from the first (1781) to the second (1787) edition of the first *Critique* can be seen in the conclusion of the paragraph in question, where we read (practically unvaried in both versions, except for a fundamental change):

> Hence transcendental philosophy is a philosophy of pure, merely speculative reason. For everything practical, insofar as it contains motives (*Bewegungsgründe*) [SUBSITUTED IN THE 1787 EDITION WITH: incentives / *Triebfedern*], is related to feelings, which belong among empirical sources of cognition.[473]

In the version of this passage from the 1781 *Critique of Pure Reason* Kant still talks of the motives (*Bewegungsgründe*) which have a role in practical philosophy and which are always of empirical origin. Instead, in the version of this passage from the 1787 edition, Kant does not refer to determining motives any more as the empirical elements that cause the ban of morality from pure philosophy, but rather of the incentives (*Triebfedern*) of an action, which are always of empirical origin. In this way, he leaves the domain of morality outside the field of research dedicated to pure philosophy.

---

472 Already in the *Groundwork* Kant uses the term *Bestimmungsgrund* instead of *Bewegungsgrund* in order to refer to the determining ground of the action and in the second *Critique* he uses nearly exclusively (and more than a hundred times) the term *Bestimmungsgrund* instead of *Bewegungsgrund*. For this discussion, cf. the following chapter of my study (in particular: note 682).

473 KrV, A15/B29, AA 04: 24.36, 25.01–04/AA 03: 45.29–32: "Daher ist die Transscendental=Philosophie eine Weltweisheit der reinen, bloß speculativen Vernunft. Denn alles Praktische, so fern es Bewegungsgründe [IN B: Triebfedern] enthält, bezieht sich auf Gefühle, welche zu empirischen Erkenntnißquellen gehören"; CpR pp. 135/151.

In these years Kant is working on and re-elaborating his theory of moral motivation, in particular while preparing the *Groundwork*.[474] The terms that Kant chooses to denote the moral concepts pertaining to the field of motivation in the quoted passages seem also to testify his reflection on this topic: he does not mention the determining motives of a moral action as an empirical source of cognition anymore; nonetheless, he still mentions all the incentives (*Triebfedern*) as empirical in their sources.

Even though Kant refers to the concept of respect already in the *Groundwork*, it is then in the third chapter of the 'Analytic of Pure Practical Reason', namely 'On the Incentives of Pure Practical Reason',[475] where these changes are testified, in that Kant most closely takes into consideration the new role played by feeling in the context of a moral action. Kant's considerations on the faculties, which until now have been concentrated on the higher faculty of desire and, consequently, on the functioning of pure practical reason, switch now, in this chapter, to the concept of the feeling of pleasure and displeasure and, in particular, to the notion of moral feeling (*moralisches Gefühl*).[476]

Nearly at the beginning of the so called *Triebfedern-Kapitel*, the chapter dedicated to analysing the incentives of pure practical reason, Kant assesses that "what we shall have to show *a priori* is [...] not the ground from which the moral law in itself supplies an incentive but rather what it effects (or, to put it better, must effect) in the mind (*im Gemüthe*) insofar as it is an incentive (*eine Triebfeder*)".[477] According to Kant, it is a fact that reason succeeds, through the moral law, in motivating to act morally. What has to be found out is, instead, the effect of the lawgiving activity of reason in the human mind (*im Gemüthe*), an activity which releases a certain effect in the form of an incentive for action. In fact, Kant notes that, when the will is moved by the law, it is moved solely by the law and nothing else.[478] It is, however, most interesting, with regard to my actual

---

474 On Kant's theory of moral motivation and its development cf. Heiner F. Klemme – Manfred Kuehn – Dieter Schönecker (eds.), *Moralische Motivation: Kant und die Alternativen*, Hamburg, Meiner 2006.

475 Cf. *Drittes Hauptstück. Von den Triebfedern der reinen praktischen Vernunft*, KpV, AA 05: 71–89; CprR pp. 198–211.

476 I dedicate closer attention to this topic in the following chapter 5, to which I also add a bibliographical report on these themes.

477 KpV, AA 05: 72.24–28: "Also werden wir nicht den Grund, woher das moralische Gesetz in sich eine Triebfeder abgebe, sondern was, so fern es eine solche ist, sie im Gemüthe wirkt (besser zu sagen, wirken muß), *a priori* anzuzeigen haben"; CprR pp. 198–199.

478 Cf. KpV, AA 05: 72.34, 73.01–02 [passim]: "Das Wesentliche aller Bestimmung des Willens durchs sittliche Gesetz ist: daß er als freier Wille [...] blos durchs Gesetz bestimmt werde"; CprR p. 199.

analysis of Kant's classification of the faculties of the human mind, to read what follows Kant's last assessment.

The passage in question reads as follows:

> So far, then, the effect of the moral law as incentive is only negative, and as such this incentive can be cognized *a priori*. For, all inclination (*Neigung*) and every sensible impulse (*sinnlicher Antrieb*) is based on feeling (*Gefühl*), and the negative effect on feeling (*die negative Wirkung aufs Gefühl*) (by the infringement upon the inclinations that takes place) is itself feeling (*Gefühl*).[479]

Kant observes that the negative incentive produced by reason through the moral law, which is here in question, can be cognized *a priori*. Nonetheless, in that it humiliates all inclination and sensible impulse, which are based on feeling, this negative incentive is itself feeling. Thus, at the same time, the effect of the moral law as the negative incentive:

(a) is based on feeling;
(b) is itself a feeling;
(c) can be cognized *a priori*.

Through these considerations, Kant's analysis of feeling is enriched by many details. For instance, Kant affirms that feeling can be cognized *a priori* and, in this way, allows for a different consideration of the concept of feeling in the context of pure philosophy.

Moreover, with regard to the case of this negative incentive, Kant notes that we are confronted with the fact that "the negative effect on feeling [...] is itself feeling (*die negative Wirkung aufs Gefühl ist selbst Gefühl*)".[480] In the *Triebfedern-Kapitel*, Kant aims to show *a priori* what the moral law "effects (or, to put it better, must effect) in the mind (*Gemüt*) insofar as it is an incentive".[481] Now we come to see that the moral law is both the objective incentive of moral action and, at the same time, what effects a change in the mind, i.e. a particular feeling, and is what the subjective incentive of the moral action consists in.[482] This effect on the mind (a) can be perceived *a priori*, (b) results from the modification of feeling,

---

479 KpV, AA 05: 72.32–34, 73.01–02: "So weit ist also die Wirkung des moralischen Gesetzes als Triebfeder nur negativ, und als solche kann diese Triebfeder *a priori* erkannt werden. Denn alle Neigung und jeder sinnliche Antrieb ist auf Gefühl gegründet, und die negative Wirkung aufs Gefühl (durch den Abbruch, der den Neigungen geschieht) ist selbst Gefühl"; CprR p. 199.
480 KpV, AA 05: 73.01–02; CprR p. 199.
481 KpV, AA 05: 72.24–28; CprR pp. 198–199.
482 On the discussion concerning the motivational force of reason and of respect see chapter 5 below.

and (c) is itself a negative effect on feeling (*die negative Wirkung aufs Gefühl*). In other words, this state of mind results from the modification of the faculty of feeling pleasure and displeasure and is itself feeling in that it is the effect (as feeling of displeasure, of humiliation of all inclination) of the moral law on this faculty of feeling (as the faculty of feeling pleasure and displeasure).

In this case, a particular fundamental faculty of the human mind, namely the faculty of feeling, i. e. the faculty through which the human being feels pleasure and displeasure, is modified in a way that the human being perceives as a sort of pain in its mind.

As Kant clearly adds,

> we can see (*einsehen*) a priori that the moral law, as the determining ground of the will, must by thwarting all our inclinations produce a feeling that can be called pain; and here we have the first and perhaps the only case in which we can determine *a priori* from concepts the relation of a cognition (*Verhältniß eines Erkenntnisses*) (here the cognition of a pure practical reason) to the feeling of pleasure and displeasure (*Gefühl der Lust oder Unlust*).[483]

In the case of the effect of the moral law on the human mind, the relation between the faculty of cognition and the faculty of feeling is determined *a priori* by concepts.

What is noteworthy here is the fact that Kant sees the possibility to take into consideration such kinds of relation between the two faculties and to refer to an *a priori* determination of the faculty of feeling pleasure and displeasure.

Thanks to the preceding analysis concerning the subjective motivation of moral action Kant finds an important confirmation of the fact that a connection between the two faculties of cognition and of feeling is possible, i. e. a connection which is central for the third *Critique*. As I will show in the sections below, this may also constitute the key for better comprehending the organisation of Kant's classification of the mental faculties, which occurs in the third *Critique*.

However, before turning to such analyses, a last consideration concerning the mentioned negative incentive, i. e. the feeling of displeasure as the effect of the law on the human mind, is due. Namely, it has to be noted that the law does not change the mind only through the production of a negative feeling,

---

483 KpV, AA 05: 73.02–08: "Folglich können wir *a priori* einsehen, daß das moralische Gesetz als Bestimmungsgrund des Willens dadurch, daß es allen unseren Neigungen Eintrag thut, ein Gefühl bewirken müsse, welches Schmerz genannt werden kann, und hier haben wir nun den ersten, vielleicht auch einzigen Fall, da wir aus Begriffen *a priori* das Verhältniß eines Erkenntnisses (hier ist es einer reinen praktischen Vernunft) zum Gefühl der Lust oder Unlust bestimmen konnten"; CprR p. 199.

since it also produces a positive, subjective incentive. As we remember from the title of the *Triebfedern*-section, Kant assesses that his goal there is to analyse the incentives (*von den Triebfedern*) of pure practical reason – i.e. he declines the word not in singular but in plural and, in this way, suggests that his analysis does not focus only on this one incentive, the negative one: he also analyses a positive incentive. As I will note in the next chapter of my work, this negative incentive, which Kant defines as humiliation, is only one aspect of one and the same feeling of respect for the law, which the human mind feels along with the positive effect of the moral law itself on the very same human mind. The positive effect is also a feeling, which "contains something elevating (*Erhebung*)" and, thus, can be called "self-approbation" (*Selbstbilligung*).[484]

The concept of respect for the moral law and the twofold subjective incentive of a moral action are the fundamental themes of the final chapter of my work. That is why, for now, I limit myself to emphasizing the centrality of the feeling of pleasure and displeasure in Kant's interest concerning the faculties in the second *Critique* and, furthermore, I will stress that the increasing interest in the concept of "feeling" causes Kant to identify more precisely the *a priori* determination from concepts of "the relation of a cognition (here the cognition of a pure practical reason) to the feeling of pleasure and displeasure",[485] i.e. to find the way for *a priori* relating the faculty of feeling to the faculty of reason.

Such considerations are now helpful to propose a comprehensive scheme of Kant's classification of the faculties of the mind in the second *Critique*.

4.6 Kant's Classification of the Faculties in the *Critique of Practical Reason*: Some General Remarks

We can derive a more comprehensive account of the faculties in the second *Critique* from the chapter dedicated to the 'Critical Elucidation of the Analytic of Pure Practical Reason' (*Kritische Beleuchtung der Analytik der reinen praktischen*

---

484 Here the whole passage of KpV, AA 05: 80.33–37, 81.01–03: "Es enthält also, als Unterwerfung unter ein Gesetz, d. i. als Gebot (welches für das sinnlich afficirte Subject Zwang ankündigt), keine Lust, sondern so fern vielmehr Unlust an der Handlung in sich. Dagegen aber, da dieser Zwang blos durch Gesetzgebung der eigenen Vernunft ausgeübt wird, enthält es auch Erhebung, und die subjective Wirkung aufs Gefühl, so fern davon reine praktische Vernunft die alleinige Ursache ist, kann also blos Selbstbilligung in Ansehung der letzteren heißen"; CprR p. 205
485 Cf. KpV, AA 05: 73.02–08; CprR p. 199.

Vernunft).[486] In this chapter, on the basis of a parallel with the first *Critique*, Kant aims to explain his way of dividing the *Critique of Practical Reason*. He first clarifies that both the first and the second *Critique* aim to analyse one and the same faculty, since "practical reason has as its basis the same cognitive faculty as does speculative reason so far as both are *pure reason*".[487] Thus, one might also say that both the first and the second *Critique* deal with the higher cognitive faculty, which Kant now calls reason and which he sometimes has also called understanding in its broad sense.

For what concerns practical reason in particular, Kant assesses that, insofar as it has to do "only with its own faculty" to make objects real, practical reason provides "only a law" for the object which is to be realized and, hence, it has to do "with a will", i. e. with "a causality" whose "determining ground" is contained in reason itself.[488] Practical reason, as the lawgiving faculty, triggers a certain causality. This causality corresponds to the faculty of the will, which is determined by the ground provided by reason. According to Kant, from this, "it follows that a critique of the Analytic of reason, insofar as it is to be a practical reason [...], must begin from the possibility of practical principles *a priori*",[489] or, in other words, that this Analytic starts with the analysis of the fact that the moral law is binding on human actions.

Kant gives clear information about the fact that, in contrast to the first *Critique*, in the *Critique of Practical Reason* the Analytic section precedes the "Aesthetic" (i. e. the *Triebfedern-Kapitel*) and this can also be noted now, when we consider that he first analyses the higher faculty of volition as pure practical reason or pure will as the lawgiving faculty. Afterwards, he moves on to the analyses

---

486 Cf. KpV, AA 05: 89–106; CprR pp. 211–225. On this section, cf. in particular REINHARD BRANDT, "Kants 'Paradoxon der Methode'", in ROLF W. PUSTER (ed.), *Veritas filia temporis? Philosophiehistorie zwischen Wahrheit und Geschichte*, Berlin / New York, de Gruyter 1995, pp. 206–216.

487 KpV, AA 05: 89.15–17: "Nun hat praktische Vernunft mit der speculativen so fern einerlei Erkenntnißvermögen zum Grunde, als beide reine Vernunft sind"; CprR p. 211.

488 Here the whole passage of KpV, AA 05: 89.25–33: "weil praktische Vernunft es nicht mit Gegenständen, sie zu erkennen, sondern mit ihrem eigenen Vermögen, jene (der Erkenntniß derselben gemäß) wirklich zu machen, d. i. es mit einem Willen zu thun hat, welcher eine Causalität ist, so fern Vernunft den Bestimmungsgrund derselben enthält, da sie folglich kein Object der Anschauung, sondern (weil der Begriff der Causalität jederzeit die Beziehung auf ein Gesetz enthält, welches die Existenz des Mannigfaltigen im Verhältnisse zu einander bestimmt) als praktische Vernunft nur ein Gesetz derselben anzugeben hat"; CprR p. 212.

489 KpV, AA 05: 89.33–35, 90.01: "So muß eine Kritik der Analytik derselben, so fern sie eine praktische Vernunft sein soll (welches die eigentliche Aufgabe ist), von der Möglichkeit praktischer Grundsätze *a priori* anfangen"; CprR p. 212.

of the concepts deriving from this faculty, which are the fundamental concepts of moral good and evil.[490] Conclusively, he switches to the analysis of a particular form of the faculty of sensibility in the *Triebfedern-Kapitel*, i.e. to the analysis of moral feeling as the moral application of the faculty of feeling pleasure and displeasure in moral actions: "only then could the last chapter conclude this part, namely the chapter concerning the relation of pure practical reason to sensibility and about its necessary influence upon sensibility to be cognized *a priori*, that is, about moral feeling (*moralisches Gefühl*)".[491]

These divisions are complementary to Kant's explanation of the division between the Aesthetic-section and the Logic-section both in the first and in the second *Critique:*

> Thus the Analytic of practical reason divides the whole sphere of all the conditions of its use quite analogously with that of theoretical reason, but in reverse order. The Analytic of theoretical pure reason was divided into transcendental Aesthetic and transcendental Logic; that of practical reason, reversely, into Logic and Aesthetic of pure practical reason [...]; the Logic in turn was there divided into Analytic of concepts and Analytic of principles, here into that of principles and concepts.[492]

Even though Kant aims to shed light on the similarities between the first two *Critiques* and their systems, an important difference between the divisions of the two works has to be noted. This difference pertains to the section devoted to the Aesthetic, which in the first *Critique* "had two parts, because of the twofold kind of sensible intuition", while in the second *Critique* is not divided into subsections: "here sensibility is not regarded as a capacity for intuition at all but

---

490 Cf. KpV, AA 05: 90.01–04: "Von da konnte sie allein zu Begriffen der Gegenstände einer praktischen Vernunft, nämlich denen des schlechthin Guten und Bösen, fortgehen, um sie jenen Grundsätzen gemäß allererst zu geben"; CprR p. 212.
491 KpV, AA 05: 90.06–09: "nur alsdann konnte allererst das letzte Hauptstück, nämlich das von dem Verhältnisse der reinen praktischen Vernunft zur Sinnlichkeit und ihrem nothwendigen, *a priori* zu erkennenden Einflusse auf dieselbe, d. i. vom moralischen Gefühle, den Theil beschließen"; CprR p. 212.
492 KpV, AA 05: 90.09–18: "So theilte denn die Analytik der praktischen reinen Vernunft ganz analogisch mit der theoretischen den ganzen Umfang aller Bedingungen ihres Gebrauchs, aber in umgekehrter Ordnung. Die Analytik der theoretischen reinen Vernunft wurde in transscendentale Ästhetik und transscendentale Logik eingetheilt, die der praktischen umgekehrt in Logik und Ästhetik der reinen praktischen Vernunft [...]; die Logik wiederum dort in die Analytik der Begriffe und die der Grundsätze, hier in die der Grundsätze und Begriffe"; CprR p. 212.

only as feeling (which can be a subjective ground for desire), and with respect to it pure practical reason admits no further division".[493]

In contrast to the analyses of the first *Critique*, where the Transcendental Aesthetic is dedicated to the study of sensibility in general, as the faculty which attains intuitions, the Aesthetic-chapter of the second *Critique*, i.e. the *Triebfedern-Kapitel*, is, instead, treated in the context of the "Analytic of the Pure Practical Reason", in contrast to the first *Critique* where the 'Transcendental Aesthetic' is a section *per se*. Moreover, this "Aesthetic-chapter" in the second *Critique* focuses only on the analysis of the concept of feeling and, in particular, of moral feeling, as a particular aspect of the faculty of sensibility or, more precisely, as a peculiar application of the faculty of feeling pleasure and displeasure, which is, in turn, a more peculiar application of the faculty of sensibility.

While the objective ground of desire, i.e. the objective motive which determines the higher faculty of desire, is the *a priori* causality of pure practical reason in the form of the moral law, Kant speaks now in this passage of a "subjective ground for desire", which is the subjective incentive that is able to subjectively motivate the human being. As we remember, this subjective ground is moral feeling, i.e. respect for the moral law. Respect consists in the modification caused by the moral law in the human mind: the faculty of feeling pleasure and displeasure, which is a particular form of the faculty of sensibility, is modified in a way that the human being feels displeasure (in the form of a humiliation of the sensible inclinations) and, at the same time, pleasure (in the form of self-approbation for being an autonomous agent).

Through the preceding considerations we may now compose a schema regarding Kant's classification of the faculties in the second *Critique:*

---

493 KpV, AA 05: 90.18–22: "Die Ästhetik hatte dort noch zwei Theile wegen der doppelten Art einer sinnlichen Anschauung; hier wird die Sinnlichkeit gar nicht als Anschauungsfähigkeit, sondern blos als Gefühl (das ein subjectiver Grund des Begehrens sein kann) betrachtet, und in Ansehung dessen verstattet die reine praktische Vernunft keine weitere Eintheilung"; CprR p. 212.

Critique of Practical Reason			
(a) Higher cognitive faculties = Understanding in the broad sense = Reason in the broad sense			(b) Sensibility as Moral Feeling
(a1) Understanding in the narrow sense, in its theoretical application (only mentioned; properly analysed in the first *Critique*)	(a2) Reason in the narrow sense = Pure Practical Reason = Higher Faculty of Desire = Pure Will	(a3) Practical Judgement (cf. the *Typic of the Pure Practical Power of Judgement*)	Feeling of Pleasure and Displeasure, in its moral application = Moral Feeling (as analysed in the *Triebfedern-Kapitel*; it is a priori connected to pure practical reason)

If we confront the present classification of the faculties with Kant's treatment of this topic in the first *Critique*, it is easy to notice that, in this classification from the second *Critique*, the faculty of understanding in the narrow sense, i.e. the faculty of reason applied to the theoretical domain, appears only marginally: in the *Critique of Practical Reason* Kant does not focus on the theoretical application of reason since he deals specifically with the practical use of this faculty.

Moreover, we note that the division between two fundamental faculties, i.e. the faculty of understanding in its broad sense (which corresponds to the higher faculties) on the one hand, and the sensible faculty (be it sensibility in general as in the first *Critique*, or feeling in particular, as in the second *Critique*), on the other hand, still holds.

Nevertheless, the order of considering the faculties is inverted, as Kant himself admits, such that in the first *Critique* the first faculty analysed is that of sensibility and the consideration of understanding in the broad sense follows this analysis.[494] In the second *Critique*, instead, the analysis of the faculty of feeling pleasure and displeasure, which occurs in relation to the treatment of moral feeling in the *Triebfedern-Kapitel*, follows the analyses dedicated to the higher faculty of desire, i.e. pure reason in its practical use, which is the higher cognitive faculty at the centre of the second *Critique*.

---

494 Cf. also R. BRANDT, "Kants 'Paradoxon der Methode'", cit.

Eventually, Kant's reference to a "practical judgement" (*praktische Urtheil-skraft*) is also to be considered. I still have not referred to the passages where Kant mentions it. They occur in the section 'Of the Typic of the Pure Practical Power of Judgement',[495] which precedes the *Triebfedern-Kapitel* in the Analytic of the Pure Practical Reason. There, Kant affirms that "whether an action possible for us in sensibility is or is not a case that stands under the rule requires practical judgement (*praktische Urtheilskraft*), by which what is said in the rule universally (*in abstracto*) is applied to an action *in concreto*".[496]

Through the reference to the practical application of the power of judgement, Kant seems to find a link between the lawgiving faculty of reason which provides the moral law and the concrete realization of moral action. In fact, for the moral law's concrete realization in the world, pure reason has to be confronted with the concreteness of the situation of the agent in the world, which is made accessible through sensibility. This way, the moral law is rendered concrete through a judgement which also takes into consideration the particular situation of the agent in the world through a reference to the faculty of sensibility. The power of judgement mediates, so to speak, between the purity of the law given by practical reason and the concreteness of the information given by sensibility. This role played by the power of judgement in its practical application was sometimes underestimated in Kant scholarship, but has been reassessed in recent years.[497]

However, in order to consider Kant's discussion of the faculties in the critical investigation, it is now useful to briefly confront the table of Kant's classification of the faculties from the second *Critique* with the already mentioned classification from the third *Critique*. Let me thus propose once again the table derived from the third *Critique*, before analysing more closely this classification in the following sections.

---

495 Cf. *Von der Typik der reinen praktischen Urtheilskraft*, KpV, AA 05: 67–71; CprR pp. 194–198.
496 KpV, AA 05: 67.28–32: "Ob nun eine uns in der Sinnlichkeit mögliche Handlung der Fall sei, der unter der Regel stehe, oder nicht, dazu gehört praktische Urtheilskraft, wodurch dasjenige, was in der Regel allgemein (*in abstracto*) gesagt wurde, auf eine Handlung *in concreto* angewandt wird"; CprR pp. 194–195.
497 Cf. for instance BARBARA HERMAN, *The Practice of Moral Judgment*, Cambridge (Mass.)/ London, Harvard University Press 1993, but also ALFREDO FERRARIN, *Saggezza, immaginazione e giudizio pratico. Studio su Aristotele e Kant*, Pisa, ETS 2004. The underestimation of this theme might also be due to the fact that the concept of maxim plays a more important role of mediation between the purity of the law and the concreteness of action in Kant's account of moral action. On the concept of maxim in Kant's moral philosophy see, for instance, URS THURNHERR, *Die Ästhetik der Existenz. Über den Begriff der Maxime und die Bildung von Maximen bei Kant*, Tübingen, Francke 1994.

Critique of the Power of Judgement		
All the faculties of the mind:		
(a) Cognitive faculty in the narrow sense	(b) Feeling of pleasure and displeasure	(c) Faculty of desire
which corresponds to the cognitive faculty of	which corresponds to the cognitive faculty of the	which corresponds to the cognitive faculty of
(a1) Understanding in the narrow sense, i. e., higher cognitive faculty in its *a priori* use	(b1) Power of judgement, i.e. feeling of pleasure and displeasure in its *a priori* use	(c1) Reason, i.e. faculty of desire in its *a priori* use

It can be immediately noted that Kant, in the third *Critique*, abandons the more general bipartition between understanding in the broad sense, as a higher faculty, on the one hand, and sensibility/feeling, on the other hand – a distinction which was still quite clear in the first *Critique* and which was already more nuanced in the second *Critique*. This is due, in particular, to the fact that, in the classification in the third *Critique*, Kant does not mention the faculty of sensibility and, instead, refers only to the more specific faculty of feeling pleasure and displeasure (even though there he aims to propose a classification of "all the faculties of the mind" (*Gesamte Vermögen des Gemüths*).[498]

In contrast to both the first and the second *Critique*, in the *Critique of the Power of Judgement* Kant pairs the faculty of feeling with the cognitive faculty of the power of judgement and, in turn, he pairs the cognitive faculty of understanding in the narrow sense with the cognitive faculty of theoretical cognition, on the one hand, and the cognitive faculty of reason with the faculty of desire, on the other hand. This does not mean that Kant does not take into consideration the "sensible" aspect anymore in its discussion of the faculties. On the contrary, Kant specifies his concepts of "power of choice" and, in particular, "understanding", which in the third *Critique* is intended only as *Verstand stricto sensu*, to which sensibility is obviously strictly connected (so strongly, that there is no need to mention it anymore). Moreover, the faculty of feeling is now definitely introduced as a higher faculty also in the context of Kant's published critical works and the tripartite division among the theoretically cognitive, the appeti-

---

498 Cf. KU, *Einleitung*, § IX, AA 05: 198, CPJ p. 83.

tive, and the sensitive part of the mind is firmly acknowledged.[499] And this firm acknowledgement is probably also due to the consideration of the treatment of an *a priori* relation between reason and feeling and of the *a priori* application of the faculty of feeling, which the theory of respect confirms.

In the light of the preceding considerations, it is now time to analyse those pages, where Kant most precisely presents his classification. The texts I refer to are to be found in the definitive, published introduction to the *Critique of the Power of Judgement* as well as in the so called 'First Introduction', that is, the firstly written but then not published introduction to the third *Critique*.

4.7 The System of the Higher Cognitive Faculties and Its Relation to the Distinction between "Philosophy as a System" and "Critique" in the So-Called 'First Introduction' to the *Critique of the Power of Judgement*

Kant compiles the 'First Introduction' to the *Critique of the Power of Judgement* (the so called *Erste Einleitung*, to which I will refer, from now on, as 'First Introduction') up until the beginning of October 1789 and probably revises it between October 1789 and January 1790.[500] The published introduction is composed, instead, between January and March 1790,[501] with the aim of shortening the ver-

---

499 Kant's attempt of introducing this tripartite division is as old as at least 1787 (cf. Kant's letter of 28th-31st December 1787 to Karl Leonhard Reinhold – Letter 313, Br, AA 10: 513–516 – this letter is at the centre of my analysis in the following section). For the historical origin of this tripartite division see the works by S. HESSBRÜGGEN-WALTER (*Die Seele und ihre Vermögen*, cit.) and TH. STURM (*Kant und die Wissenschaften vom Menschen*, cit., in particular pp. 370–394); but cf. also L. W. BECK, *Early German Philosophy*, cit., pp. 412–425; H.-M. GERLACH, "Gefühl – Sinnlichkeit – Verstand", cit., pp. 991–999; M. BAUM, "Gefühl, Begehren und Wollen in Kants praktischer Philosophie", cit.

500 For a detailed history of the genesis of the *Erste Einleitung* see IMMANUEL KANT, *Erste Einleitung in die Kritik der Urteilskraft. Faksimile und Transkription*, edited by NORBERT HINSKE – WOLFGANG MÜLLER-LAUTER – MICHAEL THEUNISSEN, Stuttgart/Bad Cannstatt, Frommann-Holzboog 1965. This edition comprises the facsimile of the text of the 'First Introduction' and its transcription, i. e. the text written by Kant's literary assistant Johann Gottfried Karl Kiesewetter with the corrections and amendments written by Kant himself. On the genesis of the *Erste Einleitung* cf. also GIORGIO TONELLI, "La formazione del testo della *Kritik der Urteilskraft*", in *Revue internationale de philosophie*, volume 8 (1954), pp. 423–448; GIORGIO TONELLI, *Kant, dall'estetica metafisica all'estetica psicoempirica. Studi sulla genesi del criticismo (1754–1771) e sulle sue fonti*, Torino, V. Bona 1955.

501 See HEINER F. KLEMME, "Einleitung" to "Erste Einleitung in die Kritik der Urteilskraft [=EE]", pp. 473–483, in IMMANUEL KANT, *Kritik der Urteilskraft – Beilage: Erste Einleitung in die*

sion already written.[502] Nonetheless, in the end, instead of it, Kant composes a completely new introduction.[503]

The 'First Introduction' has to be considered closely in my analysis dedicated to the faculties of the human mind, since there Kant deals in detail with this topic.

Right at the beginning of section 1 'On Philosophy as a System' (*Von der Philosophie als einem System*), Kant aims to clarify the difference between the concepts of "critique of pure reason" and "philosophy". He states that, "if philosophy is the *system* of rational cognition through concepts, it is thereby already sufficiently distinguished from a critique of pure reason, which, although it contains a philosophical investigation of the possibility of such cognition, does not belong to such a system as a part, but rather outlines and examines the very idea of it in the first place".[504] This means that the critique is needed in order to examine the idea of philosophy, which is defined as a system of rational cognition through concepts; nonetheless, the critique itself does not belong to that very system.

Kant characterizes the system of philosophy by means of a clear bipartition between a formal part and a material part, which he respectively calls logic, on the one hand, and "the real part" of the system, on the other hand. The formal part, i.e. logic, "concerns merely the form of thinking in a system of rules"; the second part, instead, i.e. the real part, "systematically takes under consideration the objects which are thought about, insofar as a rational cognition of them from concepts is possible".[505]

Kritik der Urteilskraft, edited by HEINER F. KLEMME, with explanatory notes by PIERO GIORDANETTI, Hamburg, Meiner 2006 (cf. here, in particular p. 475).

502 See the letter to the publisher François Théodore de la Garde, dated March 9th, 1790, where Kant writes about his decision to abbreviate the introduction to the work in particular (AA 11: 143.16 – 23).

503 For the main reasons for this change of mind, see H. F. KLEMME, "Einleitung" to the EEKU, cit., p. 476 – 477.

504 EEKU, AA 20: 195.04 – 09: "Wenn Philosophie das System der Vernunfterkenntniß durch Begriffe ist, so wird sie schon dadurch von einer Kritik der reinen Vernunft hinreichend unterschieden, als welche zwar eine philosophische Untersuchung der Möglichkeit einer dergleichen Erkenntniß enthält, aber nicht als Theil zu einem solchen System gehört, sondern so gar die Idee desselben allererst entwirft und prüfet"; CPJ, p. 3.

505 Here the whole passage of EEKU, AA 20: 195.10 – 14: "Die Eintheilung des Systems kann zuerst nur die in ihren formalen und materialen Theil seyn, davon der erste (die Logik) blos die Form des Denkens in einem System von Regeln befaßt, der zweyte (reale Theil), die Gegenstände, darüber gedacht wird, so fern ein Vernunfterkenntniß derselben aus Begriffen möglich ist, systematisch in Betrachtung zieht", CPJ p. 3.

The distinction introduced by Kant here in section 1 of the 'First Introduction' reminds us the distinction occurring in the Rostock Manuscript and in the 1798 *Anthropology* concerning the division of philosophical studies into (1) merely "logical", (2) merely "sensible" disciplines and, eventually, the reference to (3) an "*aesthetic treatment*" (*ästhetische Behandlung*), which allows for a joint application of both these disciplines.[506]

However, the distinction between the "logical" and the "real" part of philosophy here in the third *Critique* is different and, in a way, even more structured. Kant brings his systematisation further and makes a distinction within the real part of the system. He notes that

> this real system of philosophy itself, given the original distinction of its objects and the essential difference, resting on them, of the principles of a science that contains them, cannot be divided except into theoretical and practical philosophy; thus, the one part must be the philosophy of nature, the other that of morals, the first of which is also empirical, the second of which, however (since freedom absolutely cannot be an object of experience), can never contain anything other than pure principles *a priori*.[507]

---

506 We remember that Kant defined there (1) logic as the discipline investigating only understanding and that reaches abstractions in its way to universality, such that it eventually results in a dry discipline, from (2) the analyses of cognition deriving exclusively from the materials furnished by sensibility alone, which is condemned to remain superficial. Kant juxtaposes there to these two treatments and (3) "aesthetic treatment" [*ästhetische Behandlung*], which sums up the characteristics of both analyses mentioned. Cf. section 3.11 above and Anthr, AA 07: 145 ff.; *Anthropology* pp. 258 ff.

507 EEKU, AA 20: 195.15–22: "Dieses reale System der Philosophie selbst kann nun nicht anders als nach dem ursprünglichen Unterschiede ihrer Objecte und der darauf beruhenden wesentlichen Verschiedenheit der Principien einer Wissenschaft, die sie enthält, in theoretische und practische Philosophie eingetheilt werden; so, daß der eine Theil die Philosophie der Natur, der andere die der Sitten seyn muß, von denen die erstere auch empirische, die zweyte aber (da Freyheit schlechterdings kein Gegenstand der Erfahrung seyn kann) niemals andere als reine Principien *a priori* enthalten kann", CPJ p. 3.

From what precedes, we gain the following table:

Philosophy (System of rational cognition through concepts)		
Logic (formal part)	Real Part (material part)	
	Theoretical Philosophy Philosophy of Nature	Practical Philosophy Philosophy of Morals
	A priori / Empirical	*A priori*

In the context of philosophy, Kant organizes into big groups the system built up by reason, such that only the discipline of logic proceeds on the basis of merely formal means, while all other analyses are also based on (not precisely specified) materials. This does not mean that the real part of philosophy, since it is also material philosophy, must proceed only empirically. On the opposite, both theoretical philosophy and practical philosophy investigate the field of the *a priori*.

If we want to apply to this passage the already mentioned distinction between a "logical" or "sensible" philosophical analysis, we may then suppose that logic, as presented here, has to do merely with the understanding and its formal rules (we remember: logic "concerns merely the form of thinking in a system of rules"[508]), while the real part of the system of philosophy has to do with the conjunct analysis of both the faculties of understanding and sensibility, since it investigates objects in accordance with both the "forms" coming from understanding and the "materials" coming from sensibility (we remember: the real part of the system "systematically takes under consideration the objects which are thought about, insofar as a rational cognition of them from concepts is possible"[509]). From this joint consideration of both fundamental faculties, we thus derive the complete system of the "real part" of philosophy.

This parallel between the system of the faculties and the system of philosophy is not at all new if we remember, for instance, the analyses of the Architec-

---

508 EEKU, AA 20: 195.11–12: "[Die Logik befaßt] blos die Form des Denkens in einem System von Regeln, der zweyte (reale Theil), die Gegenstände, darüber gedacht wird, so fern ein Vernunfterkenntniß derselben aus Begriffen möglich ist, systematisch in Betrachtung zieht"; CPJ p. 3.
509 EEKU, AA 20: 195.13–14.

tonic chapter from the first *Critique* or the ones dedicated to anthropology. However, even though Kant bases his system of philosophy on the system of the mental faculties, he repeatedly underlines in the 'First Introduction' as well as in the passage concerning the faculties and the pure system of philosophy both from the Architectonic of Pure Reason and from the Rostock Manuscript, that he does not aim to bring the whole of his philosophical system back to empirical psychology: his reference to the faculties does not, as a consequence, imply a reference to something empirical, but rather pertains to pure philosophy.

The independence from the empirical field holds true for both parts of real philosophy: as in a science of nature "the principles in accordance with which we set up experiments must themselves always be derived from the knowledge of nature, hence from theory". In the same way in the philosophy of morals, "the same is true of practical precepts, which concern the voluntary production of a certain state of mind in us".[510]

In accordance with the former considerations, Kant also excludes the possibility of considering a pure analysis dedicated to psychology as that part of practical philosophy that aims to explain human nature ("there is no practical psychology as a special part of the philosophy of human nature"), for "the principles of the possibility of its state by means of art must be borrowed from those of our determinations from the constitution of our nature and, although the former consist of practical propositions, still they do not constitute a practical part of empirical psychology, because they do not have any special principles, but merely belong among its scholia".[511] Practical philosophy always remains only a part of pure philosophy. Even the practical propositions, which are formed by borrowing concepts from empirical psychology in that they aim to clarify the determination of the constitution of human nature, remain only an additional, accessory part of pure practical philosophy but no essential part of the philosophy of morals. This is also the case for a moral anthropology, as I have already mentioned in chapter 3 above.

---

510 EEKU, AA 20: 199.01– 05: "[In der Wissenschaft der Natur müssen] die Principien, wornach wir Versuche anstellen, [...] immer selbst aus der Kenntniß der Natur, mithin aus der Theorie, hergenommen werden. Eben das gilt von den practischen Vorschriften, welche die willkührliche Hervorbringung eines gewissen Gemüthszustandes in uns betreffen"; CPJ p. 6.
511 EEKU, AA 20: 199.07– 14: "Es gibt keine practische Psychologie, als besondern Theil der Philosophie über die menschliche Natur. Denn die Principien der Möglichkeit seines Zustandes vermittelst der Kunst, müssen von denen der Möglichkeit unserer Bestimmungen aus der Beschaffenheit unserer Natur entlehnt werden, und, obgleich jene in practischen Sätzen bestehen, so machen sie doch keinen practischen Theil der empirischen Psychologie aus, weil sie keine besondere Principien haben, sondern gehören blos zu den Scholien derselben"; CPJ p. 6.

At this stage, a further consideration is due: what Kant calls here the system of philosophy unites the forms coming from the understanding and the materials coming from sensibility in order to compose a Philosophy of Nature and a Philosophy of Morals – the three *Critiques*, which are also all structured in a system, are not part of the system of Philosophy in this sense.

I have been concerned so far with the classification of the philosophical system that Kant proposes in the 'First Introduction'. I now pass from this classification to the analysis of the system of Kant's critical enterprise. This transition seems to be made possible also by the consideration that the tripartite division of the higher cognitive faculties of the human mind corresponds to the tripartite division of Kant's critical enterprise (i. e. by the parallel between the triad of the *Critiques* and the triad of the faculties).[512] That is why, after having distinguished between Kant's two concepts of "critique" and "system" in the last table and having focused on the latter concept, in the following table I now focus on Kant's critical works and try to illustrate how the analysis of the faculties gives us a further key for the comprehension of the whole of Kant's critical enterprise. I thus get the following table:

Critique of pure reason			System of Philosophy		
			Logic	Real Part	
Critique of Pure Theoretical Reason (1781/1787)	*Critique of Practical Reason* (1787)	*Critique of the Power of Judgement* (1790)		Theoretical Philosophy	Practical Philosophy
				Metaphysical Foundations of Natural Science (1786)	*Metaphysics of Morals* (1797/8)

My aim is thus to focus on the left-hand side of the table and try to shed light on the correspondence between the tripartite division of Kant's critical works and the division of the fundamental cognitive faculties of the human mind, as Kant presents them in the *Critique of the Power of Judgement*.

Kant even entitles the second section of the 'First Introduction': 'On the System of the Higher Cognitive Faculties, Which Grounds Philosophy'.[513] He assesses that the founding of the very system of philosophy is to be found in the system of the higher cognitive faculties. Nonetheless, this section does not only take into consideration philosophy as a the system of *a priori* cognition through concepts

---

512 However, on the controversial nature of this view, see Brandt's proposal concerning a "fourth *Critique*": R. BRANDT, *Die Bestimmung des Menschen bei Kant*, cit., pp. 497–533.
513 *Von dem System der obern Erkenntnisvermögen, das der Philosophie zum Grunde liegt*, EEKU, AA 20: 201.12–13, CPJ p. 8.

but also the complex of the critiques of each faculty of *a priori* cognition through concepts. As Kant notes at the beginning of the section:

> If the issue is not the division of a philosophy, but of our faculty of *a priori* cognition through concepts (of our higher faculty of cognition), i.e, of a critique of pure reason, but considered only with regard to its faculty for thinking (where the pure kind of intuition is not taken into account), then the systematic representation of the faculty for thinking is tripartite: namely, first, the faculty for the cognition of the general (of rules), the understanding; second, the faculty for the subsumption of the particular under the general, the power of judgement; and third, the faculty for the determination of the particular through the general (for the derivation from principles), i.e. reason.[514]

Rather than presenting the partition of the system of philosophy, which, however, he has already presented in the first section of the 'First Introduction', and rather than immediately focusing on the foundation of this system on the tripartite division of the higher cognitive faculties, Kant shows instead how the tripartite division of the higher cognitive faculties, i.e. the tripartite division of the faculty of reason in the broad sense, is the basis of his critical enterprise. Kant notes that "the *a priori* principles for the whole of philosophy already seem to have been completely treated" after (1) a "critique of pure theoretical reason" ("which was dedicated to the sources of all cognition *a priori*" and "yielded the laws of nature") and after (2) a "critique of practical reason" (which yielded "the laws of freedom, and so the *a priori* principle for the whole of philosophy").[515] Nonetheless, as we further read in section 2 of the 'First Introduction', there is room also for a third *Critique*. However, this does not imply a necessary reconfiguration of the system of philosophy. As Kant notes, at this stage one would expect that from the consideration of the power of judgement a further part of philosophy could be formed. In fact, one might have expected that the power of judgement, which is the faculty mediating "the connection between

---

514 EEKU, AA 20: 201.14–24: "Wenn die Rede nicht von der Eintheilung einer Philosophie, sondern unseres Erkenntnißvermögens *a priori* durch Begriffe (des oberen) ist, d.i. von einer Kritik der reinen Vernunft, aber nur nach ihrem Vermögen zu denken betrachtet (wo die reine Anschauungsart nicht in Erwägung gezogen wird), so fällt die systematische Vorstellung des Denkungsvermögens dreyteilig aus, nämlich erstlich in das Vermögen der Erkenntniß des Allgemeinen (der Regeln), den Verstand, zweytens das Vermögen der Subsumtion des Besondern unter das Allgemeine, die Urtheilskraft, und drittens das Vermögen der Bestimmung des Besonderen durch das Allgemeine (der Ableitung von Principien), d.i. die Vernunft"; CPJ p. 8.
515 EEKU, AA 20: 202.01–06: "Die Kritik der reinen theoretischen Vernunft, welche den Quellen alles Erkenntnisses *a priori* (mithin auch dessen, was in ihr zur Anschauung gehört) gewidmet war, gab die Gesetze der Natur, die Kritik der practischen Vernunft das Gesetz der Freyheit an die Hand, und so scheinen die Principien *a priori* für die ganze Philosophie jetzt schon vollständig abgehandelt zu seyn"; CPJ p. 8.

the two faculties" of understanding in the narrow sense and reason in the narrow sense, would, just like the other faculties of understanding and reason, "add its own special principles *a priori* and perhaps ground a special part of philosophy, even though philosophy as a system can have only two parts".[516] But, as Kant firmly states, this is not the case. According to Kant, the system of philosophy (and here Kant intends the system of the real part of philosophy) remains bipartite; it is still composed only by the philosophy of nature, on the one hand, and the philosophy of morals, on the other hand, as Kant assesses in the first section of the 'First Introduction'.[517] The power of judgement does not add any special principles *a priori*, for even though it is "a special faculty of cognition", it is nonetheless "not at all self-sufficient", that is, "it provides neither concepts, like the understanding, nor ideas, like reason, of any object at all, since it is a faculty merely for subsuming under concepts given from elsewhere".[518] The only concept arising from the power of judgement is "that of nature as art, in other words that of the technique of nature with regard to its particular laws".[519] This concept "does not enrich the knowledge of nature by any particular objective law, but rather only grounds a maxim for the power of judgement, by which to observe nature and to hold its forms together".[520] The system of philosophy is not enriched with a further part and the bipartition between philosophy of nature and philosophy of morals still holds: we can gain no further cog-

---

516 Here the whole passage of EEKU, AA 20: 202.07–13: "Wenn nun aber der Verstand *a priori* Gesetze der Natur, dagegen Vernunft Gesetze der Freyheit an die Hand giebt, so ist doch nach der Analogie zu erwarten: daß die Urtheilskraft, welche beider Vermögen ihren Zusammenhang vermittelt, auch ebensowohl wie jene ihre eigenthümliche Principien *a priori* dazu hergeben und vielleicht zu einem besonderen Theile der Philosophie den Grund legen werde, und gleichwohl kann diese als System nur zweytheilig seyn"; CPJ p. 8.

517 We will see in the section below dedicated to the published introduction to the third *Critique* that the bipartite constitution of the real system of philosophy is due to the reference of this system to concepts a priori: on the one hand, with regard to the philosophy of nature, to the pure concepts of nature; on the other hand, with regard to the philosophy of morals, to the pure concept of freedom. Cf. KU, AA 05: 13–15, CPJ p. 59.

518 Here the whole passage of EEKU, AA 20: 202.14–18: "Allein Urtheilskraft ist ein so besonderes, gar nicht selbständiges Erkenntnißvermögen, daß es weder, wie der Verstand, Begriffe, noch, wie die Vernunft, Ideen von irgend einem Gegenstande giebt, weil es ein Vermögen ist, blos unter anderweitig gegebene Begriffe zu subsumiren"; CPJ p. 8.

519 EEKU, AA 20: 204.12–15: "Der ursprünglich aus der Urtheilskraft entspringende und ihr eigenthümliche Begrif ist also der von der Natur als Kunst, mit andern Worten der Technik der Natur in Ansehung ihrer besonderen Gesetze"; CPJ p. 10.

520 EEKU, AA 20: 205.01–04: "Hierdurch aber wird die Kenntniß der Natur mit keinem besondern obiectiven Gesetze bereichert, sondern nur für die Urtheilskraft eine Maxime gegründet, sie darnach zu beobachten und die Formen der Natur damit zusammen zu halten"; CPJ p. 10.

nition, other than the one of nature and that of morals. Rather, there is a new idea of nature, which we are confronted with in art.[521]

Nonetheless, the two fundamental faculties of understanding and reason in the narrow sense, on which philosophy of nature and that of morals are respectively based, are brought closer to each other by a reference to the power of judgement, which works as a medium between the two fundamental faculties. This means that, even though there is no new partition in the system of philosophy, since there is no further cognition gained by means of the use of the power of judgement, there is still a faculty that also needs a critique, i.e. the power of judgement, since this faculty also disposes of an a priori application. As Kant himself stressed in a passage which, however, has afterwards been crossed out in the 'First Introduction', "philosophy, as a real system of cognition of nature *a priori* through concepts, thus does not acquire a new part; for that consideration belongs to its theoretical part. But the critique of the pure faculties of cognition does indeed acquire such a new part, and indeed one that is very necessary".[522] In the text substituting this crossed out passage Kant explains more precisely the lack of a new part in philosophy: "philosophy, as a doctrinal system of the cognition of nature as well as freedom, does not hereby acquire a new part; for the representation of nature as art is a mere idea, which serves as a principle, merely for the subject, for our investigation of nature".[523]

The real part of the system of philosophy does not acquire a new partition since it is grounded only on the two fundamental faculties of understanding and reason, which gain objective cognition of nature and freedom. The power of judgement has to be considered, with regard to the cognition it gains, merely as a specific application of the higher cognitive faculty of understanding in the narrow sense. The bipartition between philosophy of nature and philosophy of

---

521 On the idea of "nature as art" cf. JULIET FLOYD, "Heautonomy: Kant on Reflective Judgment and Systematicity", in HERMAN PARRET (ed.), *Kants Ästhetik / Kant's Aesthetics / L'esthétique de Kant*, Berlin / New York, de Gruyter 1998, pp. 192–218. More generally, on the central topics of art and nature in the third *Critique*, cf. PAUL GUYER, *Kant and the Claims of Taste*, Cambridge / New York, Cambridge University Press, 1997 (second edition).
522 EEKU, AA 20: 205.27–30: "Die Philosophie, als reales System der Naturerkenntniß *a priori* durch Begriffe, bekömmt also dadurch keinen neuen Theil: Denn jene Betrachtung gehört zum theoretischen Theile derselben. Aber die Critik der reinen Erkenntnißvermögen bekömmt ihn wohl und zwar einen sehr nöthigen Theil"; CPJ p. 10.
523 EEKU, AA 20: 205.05–08: "Die Philosophie, als doctrinales System der Erkentniß der Natur sowohl als Freyheit, bekommt hiedurch nun keinen neuen Theil; denn die Vorstellung der Natur als Kunst ist eine bloße Idee, die unserer Nachforschung derselben, mithin blos dem Subiecte, zum Princip dient"; CPJ p. 10.

morals still holds since both understanding and the power of judgement apply to nature: a "third realm" of cognition is not given.

By contrast, Kant's critical enterprise is enriched by a third part: the new tripartite division of the critique is not due to a reference to a new form of objective cognition but to a subjective representation of nature.[524] The analysis of the power of judgement, as the faculty of the mind, which attains this subjective representation, does not cause any further partition in the system of philosophy but does found a new partition within the critique.

That is why Kant, after clarifying the relation between the system of philosophy and the system of the higher cognitive faculties in section 2 of the 'First Introduction', passes to the comprehensive treatment of all the faculties of the human mind and to their relation to the critical enterprise in section 3, which he entitles 'On the System of All the Faculties of the Human Mind',[525] and, later, he further completes this picture in section 11, which he dedicates to an 'Encyclopaedic Introduction of the Critique of the Power of Judgement into the System of the Critique of Pure Reason'.[526]

These two sections together furnish a particularly precise picture of Kant's classification of all the faculties of the human mind, as Kant described it in the 'First Introduction', and it is to these sections that I will now refer in my analysis.

4.8 Kant's Classification of All the Faculties of the Human Mind in the 'First Introduction' to the *Critique of the Power of Judgement*

Kant gives a very clear division of all the faculties of the human mind right at the beginning of section 3 of the 'First Introduction':

---

524 Cf. EEKU, AA 20: 205.11–19: "Dagegen wird unser Begriff von einer Technik der Natur, als ein hevristisches Princip in Beurtheilung derselben, zur Kritik unseres Erkentnißvermögens gehören, die anzeigt, welche Veranlassung wir haben, uns von ihr eine solche Vorstellung zu machen, welchen Ursprung diese Idee habe und ob sie in einer Qvelle *a priori* anzutreffen, imgleichen welches der Umfang und die Grentze des Gebrauchs derselben sey: mit einem Wort eine solche Untersuchung wird als Theil zum System der Kritik der reinen Vernunft, nicht aber der doctrinalen Philosophie gehören"; CPJ pp. 10–11.
525 *Von dem System aller Vermögen des menschlichen Gemüths*, EEKU, AA 20: 205–208; CPJ pp. 11–13.
526 *Enzyklopädische Introduktion der Kritik der Urteilskraft in das System der Kritik der reinen Vernunft*, EEKU, AA 20: 241–247; CPJ pp. 41–48.

we can trace all faculties of the human mind without exception back to these three: the faculty of cognition, the feeling of pleasure and displeasure, and the faculty of desire.[527]

In contrast to all the already analysed passages from the first two *Critiques* and from the previous sections of the 'First Introduction', Kant now states the comprehensiveness of the already mentioned tripartite division. As I have already noted, the distinction between philosophy of nature and philosophy of morals is traced back to the distinction between the faculty of cognition (*Erkenntnißvermögen*) and the faculty of desire (*Begehrungsvermögen*), respectively, and these two faculties were already defined as fundamental and were also at the centre of the first and the second *Critique*. Nonetheless, Kant now introduces an intermediate element between them: the fundamental faculty of feeling pleasure and displeasure (*Gefühl der Lust und Unlust*).

In order to emphasize the impossibility of tracing all the faculties back to a single one, Kant first refers to the "great difference" between representations.[528] Kant considers

(A) the "representations belonging to cognition, insofar as they are related merely to the object and the unity of the consciousness of it"[529] and, in this way, he refers to the role played by the higher cognitive faculty of understanding in the narrow sense in the process of forming representations. He then passes on to

(B) the "objective relation" of the representations "where, considered at the same time the cause of the reality of this object, they are assigned to the faculty of desire".[530] He underlines the functioning of the higher faculty of reason in the narrow sense, as pure practical reason. Finally, he considers

(C) the relation of these representations "merely to the subject, where they are considered merely as grounds for preserving their own existence in it and to

---

527 EEKU, AA 20: 205.23–24, 206.01–02: "Wir können alle Vermögen des menschlichen Gemüths ohne Ausnahme auf die drei zurückführen: das Erkenntnißvermögen, das Gefühl der Lust und Unlust und das Begehrungsvermögen"; CPJ p. 11. Due to its fundamental role, in the present section I will analyse, step by step, the section 3 from the 'First Introduction' in its entirety.
528 EEKU, AA 20: 206.08–09: "Denn es ist immer ein großer Unterschied zwischen Vorstellungen"; CPJ p. 11.
529 EEKU, AA 20: 206.09–11: "...so fern sie, blos aufs Object und die Einheit des Bewußtseyns derselben bezogen, zum Erkenntniß gehören"; CPJ p. 11.
530 EEKU, AA 20: 206.11–13: "...imgleichen zwischen derjenigen objectiven Beziehung, da sie, zugleich als Ursach der Wirklichkeit dieses Objects betrachtet, zum Begehrungsvermögen gezählt werden"; CPJ p. 11.

this extent in relation to the feeling of pleasure".[531] Kant remarks that the relation between representations and subject through the faculty of feeling "is absolutely not a cognition, nor does it provide one, although to be sure it may presuppose such a cognition as a determining ground".[532]

The difference between
(A) the relation between representations and the faculty of feeling and
(B1) on the one hand, the relation between representations and the faculty of cognition and
(B2) on the other hand, the relation between representations and the faculty of desire
needs further explanation, which Kant provides. He notes that a common opinion is basically true and the "connection between the cognition of an object and the feeling of pleasure and displeasure in its existence, or the determination of the faculty of desire to produce it, is certainly empirically knowable".[533] In this way, he defends the commonly accepted explanation of mental process, according to which the faculty of feeling and the faculty of desire are connected to each other by means of an empirically conditioned process. Thus, considering that "this interconnection is not grounded in any principle *a priori*", it follows that in this mental process regarding the faculty of feeling "the powers of the mind constitute only an aggregate and not a system",[534] i.e. the faculty of feeling and the faculty of desire seem to be connected only in a way that cannot be included into Kant's philosophical system.

Nonetheless, Kant assesses that these two faculties can also be connected in such a way as to form a philosophical system, i.e. in a way that deserves to be analysed in the context of his critical enterprise. The faculty of feeling gains new relevance in Kant's critical enterprise. The necessity of undertaking a new critique, this time dedicated to the faculty of feeling, is shown by the reference to the *a priori* connection between the faculty of feeling and the faculty of rea-

---

531 EEKU, AA 20: 206.13–16: "…und ihrer Beziehung blos aufs Subject, da sie für sich selbst Gründe sind, ihre eigene Existenz in demselben blos zu erhalten und so fern im Verhältnisse zum Gefühl der Lust betrachtet werden"; CPJ p. 11.

532 EEKU, AA 20: 206.16–17: "…welches letztere schlechterdings kein Erkenntniß ist, noch verschaft, ob es zwar dergleichen zum Bestimmungsgrunde voraussetzen mag"; CPJ p. 11.

533 EEKU, AA 20: 206.18–21: "Die Verknüpfung zwischen dem Erkenntniß eines Gegenstandes und dem Gefühl der Lust und Unlust an der Existenz desselben, oder die Bestimmung des Begehrungsvermögens, ihn hervorzubringen, ist zwar empirisch kennbar gnug"; CPJ p. 11.

534 EEKU, AA 20: 206.12–23: "Aber, da dieser Zusammenhang auf keinem Princip *a priori* gegründet ist, so machen sofern die Gemüthskräfte nur ein Aggregat und kein System aus"; CPJ p. 11.

son, which the rational concept of freedom allows. In order to make sense of the assertion that the concept of freedom institutes the a priori connection between the faculty of feeling and the faculty of desire, we shall go back to the theory concerning moral feeling.

This reading is supported by three-step argument, which can be extracted from some passages of the 'First Introduction'. Let me start with the first argument, which reads as follows:

> (A)
> Now it is surely enough to produce a connection *a priori* between the feeling of pleasure and the other two faculties if we connect a cognition *a priori*, namely the rational concept of freedom, with the faculty of desire as its determining ground, at the same time subjectively finding in this objective determination a feeling of pleasure contained in the determination of the will.[535]

Among other things, Kant states that an *a priori* connection between the faculty of feeling and the higher faculty of desire is based on the rational concept of freedom. In this case, the faculty of pure practical reason determines the faculty of feeling (and not, as it usually happens, the other way round) through a reference to an *a priori* cognition, so that, as we remember from the above analysis of some passages from the second *Critique*, the human being experiences a modified state of mind, i. e. feels respect. In this way, as Kant further explains in the second part of his argument,

> (B)
> the faculty of cognition is not combined with the faculty of desire by means of the pleasure or displeasure, for this does not precede the latter faculty, but either first succeeds the determination of it, or else is perhaps nothing other than the sensation of the determinability of the will through reason itself, thus not a special feeling and distinctive receptivity that requires a special section under the properties of the mind.[536]

---

535 EEKU, AA 20: 206.23–27, 207.01–02: "Nun gelingt es zwar, zwischen dem Gefühle der Lust und den andern beiden Vermögen eine Verknüpfung *a priori* herauszubringen, und wenn wir ein Erkenntniß *a priori*, nämlich den Vernunftbegriff der Freyheit, mit dem Begehrungsvermögen als Bestimmungsgrund desselben verknüpfen, in dieser obiectiven Bestimmung zugleich subiectiv ein in der Willensbestimmung enthaltenes Gefühl der Lust anzutreffen"; CPJ p. 11.

536 EEKU, AA 20: 207.02–09: "Aber auf die Art ist das Erkenntnißvermögen nicht vermittelst der Lust oder Unlust mit dem Begehrungsvermögen verbunden; denn sie geht vor diesem nicht vorher, sondern folgt entweder allererst auf die Bestimmung des letzteren, oder ist vielleicht nichts anders, als die Empfindung dieser Bestimmbarkeit des Willens durch Vernunft selbst, also gar kein besonderes Gefühl und eigenthümliche Empfänglichkeit, die unter den Gemüthseigenschaften eine besondere Abtheilung erforderte"; CPJ pp. 11–12.

In the second part of the argument, Kant explains the functioning of the process that links the two mental faculties of desire and feeling: the change of the state of the human mind, which occurs during, or rather, before the performance of moral action, i.e. the perception of the feeling of respect, does not precede the determination of the faculty of desire. It rather occurs at the same time as the cognition of the rational concept of freedom, so that the awareness of reason's influence on the will immediately corresponds to this feeling of respect.

However, as Kant notes in the last part of his argument, the particular *a priori* connection between the faculties of feeling and desire, which is shown by the moral case, implies that also the faculty of feeling rests on an *a priori* principle for its application and, consequently, the necessity of dedicating a critique to the faculty of feeling is also implied:

> (C)
> Now since in the analysis of the faculties of the mind in general a feeling of pleasure which is independent of the determination of the faculty of desire, which indeed is rather able to supply a determining ground for that faculty, is incontrovertibly given, the connection of which with the other two faculties in a system nevertheless requires that this feeling of pleasure, like the other two faculties, not rest on merely empirical grounds but also on *a priori* principles, there is thus required for the idea of philosophy as a system (if not a doctrine then still) a critique of the feeling of pleasure and displeasure insofar as it is not empirically grounded.[537]

Thus, in contrast to what was most commonly maintained in the philosophical tradition of Kant's time, there is also room for an *a priori* principle which guides the faculty of feeling. This means that the critical enterprise has not yet reached a conclusion after the publication of the first and the second *Critique:* as the moral case of the feeling of respect has shown, since the faculty of feeling pleasure and displeasure does not rest exclusively on empirical grounds but may rather rest also on *a priori* principles, a third *Critique* dedicated to this faculty is still needed.

In sum: Kant first (A) doubts that feeling might rest on *a priori* principles; however, he then (B) considers the determination of the will in the moral case

---

[537] EEKU, AA 20: 207.09–19: "Da nun in der Zergliederung der Gemüthsvermögen überhaupt ein Gefühl der Lust, welches, von der Bestimmung des Begehrungsvermögens unabhängig, vielmehr einen Bestimmungsgrund desselben abgeben kan, unwidersprechlich gegeben ist, zu der Verknüpfung desselben aber mit den beyden andern Vermögen in einem System erfodert wird, daß dieses Gefühl der Lust so wie die beyde andere Vermögen, nicht auf blos empirischen Gründen, sondern auch auf Principien *a priori* beruhe, so wird zur Idee der Philosophie, als eines Systems, auch, (wenn gleich nicht eine Doctrin, dennoch) eine Kritik des Gefühls der Lust und Unlust, sofern sie nicht empirisch begründet ist, erfodert werden"; CPJ p. 12.

and the linked moral feeling; on the basis of the considerations on moral feeling Kant comes to consider (C) an *a priori* connection of the faculty of feeling pleasure and displeasure and the faculty of desire and, consequently, (D) the possibility of the existence of an *a priori* principle, on which the faculty of feeling rests. In this way, (E) since the moral case testifies that the "feeling of pleasure, like the other two faculties, not rest on merely empirical grounds but also on *a priori* principles", the necessity of a critique of the faculty of feeling also follows.

The central role that the analysis dedicated to the feeling of respect might have played in Kant's project of a *Critique of the Power of Judgement* seems to find confirmation also in the fact that Kant himself speaks of his decision to write a work on the faculty of feeling in a letter addressed to Karl Leonhard Reinhold dated the 28th-31st of December 1787, after he had completed the *Groundwork* (1785) and the second *Critique* (1787).[538]

In this letter Kant (1) overtly mentions the tripartite division of mental faculties ("there are three faculties of the mind: the faculty of cognition, the faculty of feeling pleasure and displeasure, and the faculty of desire");[539] he furthermore (2) acknowledges that the first and second *Critique* are respectively dedicated to the faculty of theoretical cognition and the faculty of desire ("In the Critique of Pure (theoretical) Reason, I found a priori principles for the first of these, and in the Critique of Practical Reason, *a priori* principles for the third");[540] conclusively, he (3) refers to his work on a critique of taste and the discovery of a third possible *a priori* principle, on which the remaining faculty rests and which consents to ground a third part of his philosophical system, i.e. the part dedicated to teleology ("I am now at work on the critique of taste, and I have discovered a new sort of *a priori* principle, different from those observed. [...] I tried to find [*a priori* principles] for the second [faculty, i.e. feeling] as well, and though I thought it impossible to find such principles, the analysis of the previously mentioned faculties of the human mind (*Gemüt*) allowed me to discover a systematicity, giving me ample material at which to marvel and if possible to explore, material sufficient to last me

---

538 Cf. Letter 313, Br, AA 10: 514.24–37, 515.01–05, *Correspondence*, pp. 271–273. Nonetheless, it should be remembered that the project of a "Critique of Taste" does not correspond to the project of the third *Critique*, as I will mention in the sections below.
539 Letter 313, Br, AA 10: 514.26–27: "Denn die Vermögen des Gemüths sind drey: Erkenntnisvermögen, Gefühl der Lust und Unlust und Begehrungsvermögen"; *Correspondence*, p. 272.
540 Letter 313, Br, AA 10: 514.27–29: "Für das erste [Vermögen des Gemüths = das Erkenntnisvermögen] habe ich in der Critik der reinen (theoretischen) für das dritte [Vermögen des Gemüths = das Begehrungsvermögen] in der Critik der practischen Vernunft Principien *a priori* gefunden"; *Correspondence*, p. 272.

for the rest of my life").[541] As I will briefly show, Kant will not succeed in founding this third part of the philosophical system, so that the real part of the system of philosophy will remain bipartite (on the one hand, philosophy of nature; on the other hand, philosophy of morals) and teleology will not have a part *per se* in this system. Nonetheless, the critical enterprise will be on any account enriched by a third part, that is the part dedicated to the analysis of the faculty of feeling and, in turn, of the analysis of the higher cognitive faculty of judgement.

If we now go back to the analysis of the 'First Introduction', we note that Kant ends its delineation of the structure of the mind (*Gemut*) after explaining the way in which he came to consider a critique of the faculty of feeling to be necessary. In order to do so, he refers to the connection between all general fundamental faculties of the human mind and the specific higher cognitive faculties that contain the a priori principles of the fundamental faculties.

With regard to the parallel that he aims to institute, Kant stresses that, as "the faculty of cognition in accordance with concepts has its *a priori* principles in the pure understanding (in its concept of nature)", in the same way "the faculty of desire" correspondingly has its *a priori* principles "in pure reason (in its concept of freedom)".[542] From these two correlation, it seems to Kant that another follows and "there remains among the properties of mind in general (*Gemüthseigenschaften überhaupt*) an intermediate faculty or receptivity (*ein mittleres Vermögen oder Emp-*

---

541 Letter 313, Br, AA 10: 514.24–26,30–35: "So beschäftige ich mich jetzt mit der Critik des Geschmaks bey welcher Gelegenheit eine neue Art von Principien *a priori* entdeckt wird als die bisherigen. [...] Ich suchte sie [=Principien *a priori*] auch für das zweyte [Vermögen des Gemüths = das Gefühl der Lust und Unlust] und ob ich es zwar sonst für unmöglich hielt, dergleichen zu finden, so brachte das Systematische was die Zergliederung der vorher betrachteten Vermögen mir im menschlichen Gemüthe hatten entdecken lassen und welches zu bewundern und wo möglich zu ergründen mir noch Stoff gnug für den Uberrest meines Lebens an die Hand geben wird mich doch auf diesen Weg"; *Correspondence*, p. 272. The letter goes on: "so daß ich jetzt drey Theile der Philosophie erkenne deren jede ihre Principien *a priori* hat die man abzählen und den Umfang der auf solche Art moglichen Erkentnis sicher bestimmen kan – theoretische Philosophie, Teleologie und practische Philosophie von denen freylich die mittlere als die ärmste an Bestimmungsgründen a priori befunden wird. Ich hoffe gegen Ostern mit dieser unter dem Titel der Critik des Geschmaks ein Mscpt. obgleich nicht im Drucke fertig zu seyn", Letter 313, Br, AA 10: 514.36–37, 515.01–05, *Correspondence*, p. 272. Of course, nonetheless, it has to be remembered that a *Critik des Geschmaks* is not the same as the *Kritik der Urteilskraft*. For an introduction on this theme, see HEINER F. KLEMME, "Einleitung", in IMMANUEL KANT, *Kritik der Urteilskraft – Beilage: Erste Einleitung in die Kritik der Urteilskraft*, edited by HEINER F. KLEMME, with explanatory notes by PIERO GIORDANETTI, Hamburg, Meiner 2006, pp. XVII-CI.
542 EEKU, AA 20: 207.20–23: "Nun hat das Erkenntnißvermögen nach Begriffen seine Principien *a priori* im reinen Verstande (seinem Begriffe von der Natur), das Begehrungsvermögen in der reinen Vernunft (ihrem Begriffe von der Freyheit)"; CPJ p. 12.

fänglichkeit), namely the feeling of pleasure and displeasure, just as there remains among the higher faculties of cognition an intermediate one, the power of judgement".[543] But now, Kant additionally wonders: "what is more natural than to suspect that the latter will also contain *a priori* principles for the former?".[544]

As I will show in the following section of my work, the answer to this question is given in the last section of the 'First Introduction', which Kant dedicates to an 'Encyclopaedic Introduction of the Critique of the Power of Judgement into the System of the Critique of Pure Reason',[545] while at this stage he does not extensively explain this parallel regarding the three *a priori* principles.[546]

4.9 Kant's "Encyclopaedic Introduction" of the Mental Faculties in the 'First Introduction' to the *Critique of the Power of Judgement*

In section XI of the 'First Introduction', Kant focuses more closely on the parallels between the three general faculties of cognition, feeling and desire, and the particular cognitive faculties providing *a priori* principles, i.e. understanding, power of judgement, and reason, by means of what he calls an "encyclopaedic" introduction: in contrast to "propaedeutic introductions", which are "the customary ones" and prepare the presentation of a doctrine "by adducing the precognition which is necessary for that from doctrines or sciences already to hand", an encyclopaedic introduction presupposes "the idea of a system which will first become complete through the latter".[547]

An encyclopaedic introduction is needed for the determination of the *a priori* principle pertaining to the power of judgement. By means of this introduction Kant identifies the *a priori* principle of the power of judgement in the purposiveness of nature.[548]

---

543 EEKU, AA 20: 207.23–26: "und da bleibt noch unter den Gemüthseigenschaften überhaupt ein mittleres Vermögen oder Empfänglichkeit, nämlich das Gefühl der Lust und Unlust, so wie unter den obern Erkenntnißvermögen ein mittleres, die Urtheilskraft, übrig"; CPJ p. 12.
544 EEKU, AA 20: 207.26, 208.01–02: "Was ist natürlicher, als zu vermuthen: daß die letztere zu dem erstern ebensowohl Principien *a priori* enthalten werde"; CPJ p. 12.
545 Cf. EEKU, AA 20: 241–251, CPJ pp. 41–51.
546 Cf. EEKU, AA 20: 208.03–18; CPJ pp. 12–13.
547 Cf. EEKU, AA 20: 241.31–34; 242.07–10; CPJ pp. 41–42. On the significance of this encyclopaedic introduction cf. the corresponding section of H. MERTENS, *Kommentar zur Ersten Einleitung in Kants Kritik der Urteilskraft*, cit.
548 Cf. EEKU, AA 20: 242.33–36, 243.01–06, CPJ p. 42.

Kant is now in possession of all the *a priori* principles on which each higher cognitive faculty rests and he considers this acquisition an important stage in the process of filling "a gap in the system of our cognitive faculties".[549] As Kant observes, the third *Critique* discloses "a striking and in my [=Kant's] view very promising prospect for a complete system of all the powers of the mind, insofar as they are related in their vocation not only to the sensible but also to the supersensible, yet without upsetting the border posts which a strict critique has imposed on the latter use of them".[550]

The last quotation has to be emphasized in many respects: (A) it focuses on the centrality of the third *Critique* for a comprehensive understanding of the critical enterprise; (B) it confirms the correspondence of the system of the *Critiques* to the classification of the mental faculties; (C) it mentions the possibility of reaching the field of the supersensible (*das Übersinnliche*) and, this way, introduces one of the fundamental themes of the *Critique of the Power of Judgement*.[551] Nevertheless, Kant's reference to the supersensible field in this passage is very brief, since he only rapidly alludes to it before passing to the now more pressing presentation of the outline of the systematic connection of the third *Critique* to the first two. This outline is introduced by means of a very neat picture of the systematic classification of the mental faculties with, on the one hand, the principles on which these faculties rest and, on the other hand, with the products deriving from the application of these faculties.

Kant again repeats that:

---

549 EEKU, AA 20: 244.31–32: "eine Lücke im System unserer Erkenntnißvermögen"; CPJ p. 44.
550 Here the whole passage of EEKU, AA 20: 244.29–35, 245.01–02: "Die Geschmackskritik aber, welche sonst nur zur Verbesserung oder Befestigung des Geschmacks selbst gebraucht wird, eröfnet, wenn man sie in transscendentaler Absicht behandelt, dadurch, daß sie eine Lücke im System unserer Erkenntnißvermögen ausfüllt, eine auffallende und, wie mich dünkt, viel verheißende Aussicht in ein vollständiges System aller Gemüthskräfte, so fern sie in ihrer Bestimmung nicht allein aufs Sinnliche, sondern auch aufs Übersinnliche bezogen sind, ohne doch die Grenzsteine zu verrücken, welche eine unnachsichtliche Kritik dem letzteren Gebrauche derselben gelegt hat"; CPJ p. 44.
551 On the concept of the supersensible [*das Übersinnliche*] cf. ANSELM MODEL, "Zur Bedeutung und Ursprung von 'übersinnlich' bei Immanuel Kant", in *Archiv für Begriffsgeschichte*, Volume 30 (1986), pp. 182–191; ANSELM MODEL, "Anmerkungen zum Terminus 'übersinnlich' bei Jacob Böhme und Immanuel Kant", in *Erkenntnis und Wissenschaft, Jacob Böhme (1575–1624). Internationales Jacob-Böhme-Symposium, Görlitz 2000. Neues Lausitzisches Magazin*, Volume 2, Görlitz (Zittau), Oettel 2001, pp. 158–163; CLEMENS SCHWAIGER, "Denken des 'Übersinnlichen' bei Kant. Zu Herkunft und Verwendung einer Schlüsselkategorie seiner praktischen Metaphysik", in NORBERT FISCHER (ed.), *Kants Metaphysik und Religionsphilosophie*, Hamburg, Meiner 2004, pp. 331–345.

(A) all the faculties of the mind can be reduced to the faculty of cognition, the feeling of pleasure and displeasure, and the faculty of desire;[552]

(B) a distinct cognitive faculty in accordance with *a priori* principles is the basis for the application of each of them, so that (B1) the higher cognitive faculty of understanding gives an *a priori* principle to the faculty of cognition, (B2) the higher cognitive faculty of the power of judgement gives an *a priori* principle to the feeling of pleasure and displeasure, and the higher cognitive faculty of reason gives an *a priori* principle to the faculty of desire;[553]

(C) every single higher cognitive faculty "contains its own special principles *a priori*" for the respective general faculty, so that the specific *a priori* principles of each higher cognitive faculty determine the corresponding general power of the mind.[554]

However, in the context of these observations, Kant also names all the *a priori* principles on which the faculties rest, i.e. the principle of lawfulness for understanding, the one of purposiveness for the power of judgement, and the one of obligation (a purposiveness that is at the same time law) for reason.

Once he reaches the comprehensive system of all the faculties, all the higher cognitive faculties and all the *a priori* principles on which the faculties rest, Kant further names their products, i.e. the fields pertaining to each faculty and each principle.[555] In this way, a comprehensive system is finally reached.

---

552 Cf. EEKU, AA 20: 245.07–11, CPJ p. 44: "Die Vermögen des Gemüths lassen sich nämlich insgesammt auf folgende drey zurückführen: Erkenntnißvermögen / Gefühl der Lust und Unlust / Begehrungsvermögen".

553 Cf. EEKU, AA 20: 245.12–20, CPJ pp. 44–45: "Der Ausübung aller liegt aber doch immer das Erkenntnißvermögen, ob zwar nicht immer Erkenntniß, (denn eine zum Erkenntnißvermögen gehörige Vorstellung kann auch Anschauung, reine oder empirische, ohne Begriffe sein) zum Grunde. Also kommen, so fern vom Erkenntniß ermögen nach Principien die Rede ist, folgende obere neben den Gemüthskräften überhaupt zu stehen: Erkenntnißvermögen – Verstand / Gefühl der Lust und Unlust – Urtheilskraft / Begehrungsvermögen – Vernunft".

554 Cf. EEKU, AA 20: 245.21–34, CPJ p. 45: "Es findet sich, daß Verstand eigenthümliche Principien *a priori* für das Erkenntnißvermögen, Urtheilskraft nur für das Gefühl der Lust und Unlust, Vernunft aber blos fürs Begehrungsvermögen enthalte. Diese formale Principien begründen eine Nothwendigkeit, die theils objectiv, theils subjectiv, teils aber auch dadurch, daß sie subjectiv ist, zugleich von objectiver Gültigkeit ist, nach dem sie durch die neben ihnen stehende obere Vermögen, die diesen correspondirende Gemüthskräfte bestimmen: Erkenntnißvermögen – Verstand – Gesetzmäßigkeit / Gefühl der Lust und Unlust – Urtheilskraft – Zweckmäßigkeit / Begehrungsvermögen – Vernunft – Zweckmäßigkeit, die zugleich Gesetz ist (Verbindlichkeit)".

555 Cf. EEKU, AA 20: 246.01–02, CPJ p. 45: "Endlich gesellen sich zu den angeführten Gründen *a priori* der Möglichkeit der Formen, auch diese, als Producte derselben".

Kant schematises the comprehensive division as follows:

Faculty of the mind	Higher cognitive faculties	*A priori* principles	Products
Faculty of cognition	Understanding	Lawfulness	Nature
Feeling of pleasure and displeasure	Power of judgement	Purposiveness	Art
Faculty of desire	Reason	Purposiveness that is at the same time law (Obligation)	Morals[556]

He explains the previous table with the following words:

> Thus nature grounds its lawfulness on *a priori* principles of the understanding as a faculty of cognition; art is guided *a priori* in its purposiveness in accordance with the power of judgement in relation to the feeling of pleasure and displeasure; finally morals (as product of freedom) stand under the idea of a form of purposiveness that is qualified for universal law, as a determining ground of reason with regard to the faculty of desire. The judgements that arise in this way from *a priori* principles peculiar to each of the fundamental faculties of the mind are theoretical, aesthetic and practical judgements.[557]

By means of the last table and the corresponding explanation, Kant is in a position to comprehensively explain the inseparable relation between the faculties

---

556 Cf. EEKU, AA 20: 246.03–15, CPJ p. 45:

Vermögen des Gemüths	Obere Erkenntnisvermögen	Principien *a priori*	Producte
Erkenntnißvermögen	Verstand	Gesetzmäßigkeit	Natur
Gefühl der Lust und Unlust	Urtheilskraft	Zweckmäßigkeit	Kunst
Begehrungsvermögen	Vernunft	Zweckmäßigkeit die zugleich Gesetz ist (Verbindlichkeit)	Sitten

557 Cf. EEKU, AA 20: 246.16–25: "Die Natur also gründet ihre Gesetzmäßigkeit auf Principien *a priori* des Verstandes als eines Erkenntnißvermögens; die Kunst richtet sich in ihrer Zweckmäßigkeit *a priori* nach der Urtheilskraft in Beziehung aufs Gefühl der Lust und Unlust; endlich die Sitten (als Product der Freyheit) stehen unter der Idee einer solchen Form der Zweckmäßigkeit, die sich zum allgemeinen Gesetze qualificirt, als einem Bestimmungsgrunde der Vernunft in Ansehung des Begehrungsvermögens. Die Urtheile, die auf diese Art aus Principien *a priori* entspringen, welche jedem Grundvermögen des Gemüths eigenthümlich sind, sind theoretische, ästhetische und practische Urtheile"; CPJ pp. 45–46.

and the critical enterprise. While in the first and the second *Critique* we have to derive the classifications of the faculties from many different references made by Kant unsystematically throughout the whole of these works, in the 'First Introduction' we find the system of the faculties explicitly represented in its comprehensive unity.

As Kant himself notes, the exhaustive classification of the 'First Introduction' reveals,

(A) on the one hand, the system of the powers of mind in its relation to the bipartite philosophical system of nature and of morals,[558]

(B) and, on the other hand, what is most noteworthy, a transition (*Übergang*), which a third faculty, i.e. the power of judgement, renders possible, and which "connects the two parts through its own special principle, namely from the sensible substratum of the first part of philosophy to the intelligible substratum of the second".[559]

We have now before us Kant's complete and extensive division of the faculties. As I will now illustrate, this classification occurs almost unchanged in the context of the published introduction to the *Critique of the Power of Judgement* (1790) and will be presented once again, this time with some more specific information about the field of morality, at the beginning of the general introduction to the *Metaphysics of Morals* (1797/1798).

4.10 Kant's Classification of the Faculties in the Preface and in the Published Introduction to the *Critique of the Power of Judgement*

Immediately in the first lines of the Preface to the *Critique of the Power of Judgement* published in 1790 Kant resumes the discussion of the faculties as a funda-

---

558 Cf. EEKU, AA 20: 246.26–30, CPJ p. 46: "So entdeckt sich ein System der Gemüthskräfte, in ihrem Verhältnisse zur Natur und der Freyheit, deren jede ihre eigenthümliche, bestimmende Principien *a priori* haben und um deswillen die zwey Theile der Philosophie (die theoretische und practische) als eines doctrinalen Systems ausmachen".
559 EEKU, AA 20: 246.30–33: "[So entdeckt sich] zugleich ein Übergang vermittelst der Urtheilskraft, die durch ein eigenthümliches Princip beide Theile verknüpft, nämlich von dem sinnlichen Substrat der ersteren, zum intelligibelen der zweyten Philosophie"; CPJ p. 46.

mental topic that has to be comprehended if we aim to gain a correct understanding of the whole of the critical enterprise.[560]

Kant first dedicates a long explanation to the fact that a critique of reason aims to investigate the boundaries and possibilities of the application of our cognitive faculty in general while the work entitled *Critique of Pure Reason* is dedicated to the faculty of pure reason in its theoretical application and the *Critique of Practical Reason* is dedicated only to the analysis of reason in its practical application.[561] Kant admits that the first *Critique* deals only with the fundamental faculty of cognition in the narrow sense and the corresponding peculiar cognitive faculty of understanding, while no room is given either to the other two general fundamental faculties, i. e., the feeling of pleasure and displeasure and the faculty of desire, or to their corresponding specific cognitive faculties, i. e. the power of judgement and reason in its narrow sense.[562] Kant explains that in

---

560 For a discussion concerning the history of the genesis of the third *Critique*, cf. H. F. KLEMME, "Einleitung", in IMMANUEL KANT, *Kritik der Urteilskraft – Beilage: Erste Einleitung in die Kritik der Urteilskraft*, edited by H. F. KLEMME, cit., pp. XVII-CI (and in particular the section I. Zur Entstehungsgeschichte, pp. XVII-XXV); for some interpretive suggestions concerning the philosophical origin of the third *Critique* and some observations on the relation of the origin of this work and the faculties topic, see also PIERO GIORDANETTI, "Kants Entdeckung der Apriorität des Geschmacksurteils. Zur Genese der *Kritik der Urteilskraft*", in HEINER F. KLEMME – BERND LUDWIG – MICHAEL PAUEN – WERNER STARK (eds.), *Aufklärung und Interpretation – Studien zu Kants Philosophie und ihrem Umkreis. Tagung aus Anlaß des 60. Geburtstags von Reinhard Brandt*, Würzburg, Königshausen und Neumann 1999, pp. 171–196; REINHARD BRANDT, "Schön, Erhaben, nicht Häßlich. Überlegungen zur Entstehung und Systematik der Kantischen Theorie des ästhetischen Urteils", in HEINER F. KLEMME – MICHAEL PAUEN – MARIE-LUISE RATERS (eds.), *Im Schatten des Schönen. Die Ästhetik des Hässlichen in historischen Ansätzen und aktuellen Debatten*, Bielefeld, Aisthesis 2006, pp. 65–92; HEINER F. KLEMME, "The Origin and Aim of Kant's *Critique of Practical Reason*", in ANDREWS REATH – JENS TIMMERMANN (eds.), *Kant's Critique of Practical Reason. A Critical Guide*, Cambridge/New York, Cambridge University Press 2010, pp. 11–30.

561 KU, AA 05: 167.03–09: "Man kann das Vermögen der Erkenntniß aus Principien a priori die reine Vernunft und die Untersuchung der Möglichkeit und Gränzen derselben überhaupt die Kritik der reinen Vernunft nennen: ob man gleich unter diesem Vermögen nur die Vernunft in ihrem theoretischen Gebrauche versteht, wie es auch in dem ersten Werke unter jener Benennung geschehen ist, ohne noch ihr Vermögen als praktische Vernunft nach ihren besonderen Principien in Untersuchung ziehen zu wollen"; CPJ p. 55.

562 The first *Critique* "pertains solely to our faculty for cognizing things a priori, and thus concerns itself only with the faculty of cognition, excluding the feeling of pleasure and displeasure and the faculty of desire; and among the faculties of cognition it concerns itself only with the understanding in accordance with its a priori principles, excluding the power of judgement and reason (as faculties likewise belonging to theoretical cognition), because in the course of that work it turns out that no faculty of cognition except for the understanding can yield constitutive principles of cognition a priori", KU, AA 05: 167.09–18; CPJ p. 55.

the *Critique of Pure Reason* he aimed to establish "the understanding, which has its proper domain indeed in the faculty of cognition, insofar as it contains constitutive principles of cognition *a priori*", in a "secure and unique possession against all other competitors",[563] while in the *Critique of Practical Reason* he intended to focus on the territory of "reason, which contains constitutive principles *a priori* nowhere except strictly with regard to the faculty of desire".[564]

By means of an overview of his critical enterprise, Kant explains the relation between the critique and the division of the faculties and is now ready to pass to the analysis of a third general fundamental faculty and its corresponding more particular cognitive faculty in the *Critique of the Power of Judgement*. This is shown by the fact that the third *Critique* is concerned with finding an answer to the three following questions:

(A) "whether the power of judgement, which in the order of our faculties of cognition constitutes an intermediary between understanding and reason, also has *a priori* principles for itself";[565]

(B) "whether these are constitutive or merely regulative (and thus do not prove the power of judgement to have its own domain)";[566]

(C) "whether the feeling of pleasure and displeasure, as the intermediary between the faculty of cognition and the faculty of desire, gives the rule *a priori* (just as the understanding prescribes *a priori* laws to the former, but reason to the latter)".[567]

From this, it follows that the *Critique of the Power of Judgement* focuses on the fundamental faculty of feeling, on the cognitive faculty of the power of judgement, and on the *a priori* principles given from the cognitive faculty of the power of judgement to the faculty of feeling. Already at the very beginning of the third *Critique*, not only the core argument of the whole work is elucidated,

---

563 Cf. KU, AA 05: 168.06 – 10; CPJ p. 56.

564 KU, AA 05: 168.10 – 13: "Eben so ist der Vernunft, welche nirgend als lediglich in Ansehung des Begehrungsvermögens constitutive Principien a priori enthält, in der Kritik der praktischen Vernunft ihr Besitz angewiesen worden"; CPJ p. 56.

565 KU, AA 05: 168.14 – 16: "Ob nun die Urtheilskraft, die in der Ordnung unserer Erkenntnißvermögen zwischen dem Verstande und der Vernunft ein Mittelglied ausmacht, auch für sich Principien a priori habe"; CPJ p. 56.

566 KU, AA 05: 168.16 – 17: "ob diese [Principien a priori] constitutiv oder bloß regulativ sind (und also kein eigenes Gebiet beweisen)"; CPJ p. 56.

567 KU, AA 05: 168.17 – 21: "ob sie [=die Principien a priori] dem Gefühle der Lust und Unlust, als dem Mittelgliede zwischen dem Erkenntnißvermögen und Begehrungsvermögen, (eben so wie der Verstand dem ersteren, die Vernunft aber dem letzteren a priori Gesetze vorschreibt) a priori die Regel gebe"; CPJ p. 56.

but also the position of the work in the context of the whole critical enterprise is pointed out – and this all happens through a reference to the system of the faculties.[568]

As the passages show, Kant's classification of the faculties influences fundamentally the constitution of Kant's critical work and its systematisation. That is why only at this stage and with this work Kant can be sure to have brought his "entire critical enterprise to an end" and "shall proceed without hindrance to the doctrinal part", i.e., the metaphysics of nature and the metaphysics of morals.[569]

Already in the 'First Introduction' Kant refers to the difference between a tripartite system for the domain of the critical analysis and a bipartite system for the domain of what he calls the real part of philosophy. Nonetheless, in that context the difference between a tripartite critical analysis and a bipartite system seems to be inexact, since in the 'First Introduction' Kant assesses that both divisions of the critique and of philosophy must be brought back to the division of the faculties, which is tripartite. In contrast to the 'First Introduction', in the published introduction to the third *Critique* Kant gives a clear explanation of the difference between a bipartite philosophical system and a tripartite division of the critical enterprise. This differentiation is due to the fact that the critique is said to be based on the analyses of the three fundamental faculties, while the bipartite constitution of the real part of the system of philosophy derives from the presence of only two kinds of concepts: the concepts of nature and the concepts of freedom.[570]

This consideration arises from the section of the published introduction to the *Critique of the Power of Judgement* that Kant entitles 'On the Division of Philosophy'.[571] In a similar way as in the first section of the 'First Introduction', which Kant entitles 'On Philosophy as a System', in this section from the published introduction Kant distinguishes between philosophy of nature and moral philosophy.

Nonetheless, while in the 'First Introduction' Kant states that the division of the higher cognitive faculties is also the basis for the division of philosophy, in the published introduction Kant notes that "if one divides philosophy [...] into theoretical and practical, as is customary, then one proceeds entirely correct-

---

568 On the "architectonical" importance of the third *Critique* in Kant's critical enterprise, cf. FRANK PIEROBON, "L'architectonique et la faculté de juger", pp. 1–17, and ALEXIS PHILONENKO, "L'architectonique de la *Critique de la faculté de juger*", pp. 41–52, both in HERMAN PARRET (ed.), *Kants Ästhetik / Kant's Aesthetics / L'esthétique de Kant*, cit.
569 Cf. KU, AA 05: 170.20–27, CPJ p. 58.
570 Cf. KU, AA 05: 171.13–15, CPJ p. 59.
571 *Von der Eintheilung der Philosophie*, KU, AA 05: 171–173, CPJ pp. 59–61.

ly":[572] this is due to the fact that "there are [...] only two sorts of concepts that allow an equal number of distinct principles of the possibility of their objects, namely the concepts of nature and the concepts of freedom".[573]

From this, it follows that "philosophy is justifiably divided into two parts, entirely distinct as far as their principles are concerned, namely, the theoretical, as philosophy of nature, and the practical, as moral philosophy".[574]

In contrast to the 'First Introduction', Kant does not ground the division of the system of the real part of philosophy on the system of the fundamental mental faculties. In the published introduction to the third *Critique* he rather brings back the philosophical division to the distinction between the two fundamental kinds of concepts with which philosophy is concerned, i.e. the concepts of nature and freedom. Nonetheless, in a way, also this bipartition is derived from the mental faculties (even if not exactly from the way they are classified), insofar as Kant assesses that "our cognitive faculty as a whole has two domains, that of the concepts of nature and that of the concept of freedom" and the cognitive faculty "is *a priori* legislative through both".[575] The tripartite division of the critical enterprise is still based on the tripartite classification of the faculties, as in the 'First Introduction'. This is due to the fact that the critique is not a doctrine but has rather "to investigate whether and how a doctrine is possible through it given the way it is situated with respect to our faculties".[576]

---

572 Here the whole passage of KU, AA 05: 171.04–12: "Wenn man die Philosophie, sofern sie Principien der Vernunfterkenntniß der Dinge (nicht bloß wie die Logik Principien der Form des Denkens überhaupt ohne Unterschied der Objecte) durch Begriffe enthält, wie gewöhnlich in die theoretische und praktische eintheilt: so verfährt man ganz recht. Aber alsdann müssen auch die Begriffe, welche den Principien dieser Vernunfterkenntniß ihr Object anweisen, specifisch verschieden sein, weil sie sonst zu keiner Eintheilung berechtigen würden, welche jederzeit eine Entgegensetzung der Principien der zu den verschiedenen Theilen einer Wissenschaft gehörigen Vernunfterkenntniß voraussetzt"; CPJ p. 59.

573 KU, AA 05: 171.13–15: "Es sind aber nur zweierlei Begriffe, welche eben so viel verschiedene Principien der Möglichkeit ihrer Gegenstände zulassen: nämlich die Naturbegriffe und der Freiheitsbegriff"; CPJ p. 59.

574 KU, AA 05: 171.20–24: "[...] so wird die Philosophie in zwei den Principien nach ganz verschiedene Theile, in die theoretische als Naturphilosophie und die praktische als Moralphilosophie (denn so wird die praktische Gesetzgebung der Vernunft nach dem Freiheitsbegriffe genannt), mit Recht eingetheilt"; CPJ p. 59.

575 KU, AA 05: 174.23–25: "Unser gesammtes Erkenntnißvermögen hat zwei Gebiete, das der Naturbegriffe und das des Freiheitsbegriffs; denn durch beide ist es a priori gesetzgebend"; CPJ p. 62.

576 Here the whole passage of KU, AA 05: 176.19–23: "Die Kritik der Erkenntnißvermögen in Ansehung dessen, was sie a priori leisten können, hat eigentlich kein Gebiet in Ansehung der

This investigation first presents, on the one hand, understanding as the faculty that legislates with regard to the concepts of nature and, on the other hand, reason as the faculty that legislates with regard to the concept of freedom.[577] Eventually, it shows how the power of judgement is "a means for combining the two parts of philosophy into one whole".[578] It is now in this context that Kant refers to this faculty as an "intermediary between the understanding and reason" and introduces it "in the family of the higher faculties of cognition".[579]

As a consequence, the tripartite division of the faculties still remains equivalent to the one of the 'First Introduction', denoting the same correspondences between general fundamental faculties, higher cognitive faculties, and *a priori* principles.[580]

In the published introduction to the third *Critique* this comprehensive, schematic presentation of the classification of all the mental faculties is not presented as part of what Kant in the 'First Introduction' calls an "encyclopaedic introduction". In contrast to the 'First Introduction' Kant now generally refers only to a 'Connection of the Legislations of Understanding and Reason through the Power of Judgement'.[581] Moreover, in the published introduction Kant does not present the comprehensive table of all the mental faculties after detailed clarifications, but he rather very briefly explains how each particular cognitive faculty relates to the respective fundamental mental faculty by means of constitutive principles *a priori*.[582] However, the table proposed is nearly identical to the final one proposed in the 'First Introduction':

Objecte: weil sie keine Doctrin ist, sondern nur, ob und wie nach der Bewandtniß, die es mit unseren Vermögen hat, eine Doctrin durch sie möglich sei, zu untersuchen hat"; CPJ p. 64.

577 Cf. KU, AA 05: 176.29–33, CPJ p. 64: "Die Naturbegriffe, welche den Grund zu allem theoretischen Erkenntniß a priori enthalten, beruhten auf der Gesetzgebung des Verstandes. – Der Freiheitsbegriff, der den Grund zu allen sinnlich=unbedingten praktischen Vorschriften a priori enthielt, beruhte auf der Gesetzgebung der Vernunft".

578 Cf. the title of section III: "Von der Kritik der Urtheilskraft, als einem Verbindungsmittel der zwei Theile der Philosophie zu einem Ganzen", KU, AA 05: 176, CPJ p. 64.

579 KU, AA 05: 177.04–06: "Allein in der Familie der oberen Erkenntnißvermögen giebt es doch noch ein Mittelglied zwischen dem Verstande und der Vernunft. Dieses ist die Urtheilskraft"; CPJ p. 64.

580 Cf. KU, AA 05: 177.17–20, 178.01–11; CPJ pp. 64–66.

581 *Abschnitt IX. Von der Verknüpfung der Gesetzgebungen des Verstandes und der Vernunft durch die Urtheilskraft*, KU, AA 05: 195–198, CPJ pp. 80–83.

582 Cf. KU, AA 05: 196.23–28, 197.01–05: "In Ansehung der Seelenvermögen überhaupt, sofern sie als obere, d. i. als solche, die eine Autonomie enthalten, betrachtet werden, ist für das Erkenntnißvermögen (das theoretische der Natur) der Verstand dasjenige, welches die constitutiven Principien a priori enthält; für das Gefühl der Lust und Unlust ist es die Urtheilskraft unabhängig von Begriffen und Empfindungen, die sich auf Bestimmung des Begehrungsver-

All the faculties of the mind	Cognitive faculty	*A priori* principles	Products
Faculty of cognition	Understanding	Lawfulness	Nature
Feeling of pleasure and displeasure	Power of judgement	Purposiveness	Art
Faculty of desire	Reason	Final end	Freedom[583]

This table differs from the one occurring in the 'First Introduction' on three points:

(A) first, in this table from the published introduction Kant does not refer to nature, art, and morals as the "products" of the activity of the mental faculties; he rather speaks of an "application" of the faculties to different philosophical domains, so that the different fields of nature, art, and freedom are regarded only as the fields of application of each faculty;

(B) second, the last domain of application of the faculties is here called "freedom", while, as we remember, in the table from the 'First Introduction' Kant refers to "morals" as the product of freedom that is derived from the application of the faculty of desire according to the *a priori* principle furnished by the cognitive faculty of reason;

(C) third, the *a priori* principle furnished by the cognitive faculty of reason, on which the faculty of desire rests, is called a "final end" (*Endzweck*) in the published introduction, while in the 'First Introduction' Kant refers to this principle calling it obligation and defining it as a "purposiveness that is at the same time law".[584]

---

mögens beziehen und dadurch unmittelbar praktisch sein könnten; für das Begehrungsvermögen die Vernunft, welche ohne Vermittelung irgend einer Lust, woher sie auch komme, praktisch ist und demselben als oberes Vermögen den Endzweck bestimmt, der zugleich das reine intellectuelle Wohlgefallen am Objecte mit sich führt"; CPJ p. 82.

583 Cf. KU, AA 05: 198, CPJ p. 83:

Gesammte Vermögen des Gemüths /	Erkenntnisvermögen /	Principien *a priori* /	Anwendung auf
Erkenntnißvermögen	Verstand	Gesetzmäßigkeit	Natur
Gefühl der Lust und Unlust	Urtheilskraft	Zweckmäßigkeit	Kunst
Begehrungsvermögen	Vernunft	Endzweck	Freiheit

584 Cf. EEKU, AA 20: 245–246, CPJ pp. 45–46.

With regard to this last point, it is particularly noteworthy that Kant changes his mind on the way in which the third *a priori* principle should be called. Here, Kant seems to consider a gained importance of the concept of "final end" and, with it, the necessity of more closely underlining a concept, which becomes central in the *Critique of the Power of Judgement*, but which in this table is rather introduced with regard to moral philosophy. As we see from the table, the concept of final end is now mentioned as the *a priori* principle furnished by the cognitive faculty of reason in the narrow sense, on which the faculty of desire rests and which is applied to the domain of freedom. In contrast to the table of the 'First Introduction', Kant here does not mention the *a priori* principle of obligation anymore and seems to emphasize, for what concerns the domain of morals, not the mandatory feature of the law, but rather the doctrine of the highest good (*das höchste Gut*) that, nonetheless, he has already described in the *Critique of Practical Reason*.[585]

Eventually, a last difference between the table of the 'First Introduction' and the one of the published introduction to the *Critique of the Power of Judgement* has to be analysed. As I have already mentioned, it regards the way in which the two tables are introduced. While in the 'First Introduction' Kant appeals to an "encyclopaedic introduction" in order to justify his composition of the table, he substitutes the reference to this method with an explanation, in the footnote, of what a "synthetic" division is. In this way, Kant notes that, even though "it has been thought suspicious that [... his] divisions in pure philosophy almost always turn out to be threefold", he nonetheless aims to assess that a tripartite way of introducing the critical enterprise and the faculties "is in the nature of the matter", since "if a division is to be made *a priori*, then it will either be analytic, in accordance with the principle of contradiction, and then it is always twofold (*quodlibet ens est aut A aut non A*). Or it is synthetic".[586] In consideration

---

585 In these years, Kant deals with the doctrine of the highest good in the context of his writings on philosophy of history in particular. On this point cf. LUCA FONNESU, "Kants praktische Philosophie und die Verwirklichung der Moral", in HERTA NAGL-DOCEKAL – RUDOLF LANGTHALER (eds.), *Recht – Geschichte – Religion. Die Bedeutung Kants für die Gegenwart*, Berlin, Akademie Verlag 2004, pp. 49–61; LUCA FONNESU, "Entwicklung und Erweiterung der praktischen Absicht", in STEFANO BACIN – ALFREDO FERRARIN – CLAUDIO LA ROCCA – MARGIT RUFFING (eds.), *Kant and Philosophy in a Cosmopolitan Sense / Kant und die Philosophie in weltbürgerlicher Hinsicht. Akten des XI. Internationalen Kant-Kongresses*, Boston-New York, de Gruyter 2013, volume 3, pp. 173–184.

586 KU, AA 05: 197.18–22: "Man hat es bedenklich gefunden, daß meine Eintheilungen in der reinen Philosophie fast immer dreitheilig ausfallen. Das liegt aber in der Natur der Sache. Soll eine Eintheilung a priori geschehen, so wird sie entweder analytisch sein nach dem Satze des Widerspruchs; und da ist sie jederzeit zweitheilig (*quodlibet ens est aut A aut non A*). Oder sie ist

of this assessment, and since the table in question concerns the faculties and their corresponding fields of application and it pertains to a synthetic division derived from concepts *a priori*, it follows that the table has to show a tripartite division, because "in accordance with what is requisite for synthetic unity in general, namely (1) a condition, (2) something conditioned, (3) the concept that arises from the unification of the conditioned with its condition, the division must necessarily be a trichotomy".[587]

These considerations conclude Kant's presentation of the classification of the faculties in the published introduction to the third *Critique*. Correspondingly, with the analyses of these passages we have considered Kant's most comprehensive theorizing on the classification of the faculties.

In the following section, I aim to present Kant's classification of the faculties in the general introduction to the *Metaphysics of Morals*, which is particularly noteworthy in that it introduces some closer insights into the way in which Kant contextualises the systematisation of the faculties in his studies dedicated to moral philosophy.

4.11 A Last Clear and Comprehensive Classification of the Faculties of the Human Mind: The General Introduction to the *Metaphysics of Morals*

In the *Metaphysics of Morals* Kant refers to the classification of the mental faculties in the section of the general introduction entitled 'On the Relation of the Faculties of the Human Mind to Moral Laws'.[588] This text was published in the first of the two parts of the *Metaphysics of Morals* (*Die Metaphysik der Sitten*

---

synthetisch"; CPJ pp. 82–83. Kant refers here to Johann Schultz – cf. R. BRANDT, *Die Bestimmung des Menschen bei Kant*, cit., p. 592. Brandt proposes, however, that not really a tripartite division, but rather a quadruple partition should be taken to be characteristic of Kant's philosophical investigation (that is why Brandt also suggests to take into consideration the possibility of speaking of a "fourth *Critique*"). These considerations are also to be found in the just mentioned book.

587 Here the whole passage of KU, AA 05: 197.22–27: "[wenn die Einteilung synthetisch ist und soll] aus Begriffen *a priori* (nicht wie in der Mathematik aus der a priori dem Begriffe correspondirenden Anschauung) [...] geführt werden, so muß nach demjenigen, was zu der synthetischen Einheit überhaupt erforderlich ist, nämlich 1) Bedingung, 2) ein Bedingtes, 3) der Begriff, der aus der Vereinigung des Bedingten mit seiner Bedingung entspringt, die Eintheilung nothwendig Trichotomie sein"; CPJ p. 83.

588 *Von dem Verhältniß der Vermögen des menschlichen Gemüths zu den Sittengesetzen*, Cf. MS, AA 06.211–214; MM pp. 373–376.

in zwei Theilen. Abgefaßt von Immanuel Kant. Königsberg, bey Friedrich Nicolovius): this part, i.e. the one dedicated to the *Doctrine of Right*, which also includes the general introduction to the work, appeared for the first time in 1797. This edition of the *Doctrine of Right* is followed by a second, revised edition in 1798 (*Die Metaphysik der Sitten. Abgefaßt von Immanuel Kant. Erster Theil. Metaphysische Anfangsgründe der Rechtslehre. Zweyte mit einem Anhange erläuternder Bemerkungen und Zusätze vermehrte Auflage. Königsberg, bey Friedrich Nicolovius*). The second part of the *Metaphysics of Morals*, i.e. the one dedicated to the *Doctrine of Virtue*, appears also in 1798 (*Zweyter Theil. Metaphysische Anfangsgründe der Tugendlehre. Königsberg, bey Friedrich Nicolovius*).[589] Without taking up the discussion concerning the controversial editorial history of the work, I limit myself to quoting the *Metaphysics of Morals* on the basis of the Academy text, while in the footnotes I also refer to the page numbers of the Cambridge edition.[590]

I will begin my presentation of the section of the general introduction to the *Metaphysics of Morals* where Kant gives a very broad overview of the mental faculties and of their relation to the moral laws, i.e. the section entitled 'On the Relation of the Faculties of the Human Mind to Moral Laws'.[591]

Right at the beginning of this section Kant gives a definition of the faculty of desire (*Begehrungsvermögen*) and focuses his attention on the relation between this faculty and the faculty of feeling (*Gefühl*). In addition, Kant mentions the faculty of life (*Leben*), by which he explains the actions performed by the

---

589 For a first introduction concerning the editing of the text, cf. Paul Natorp's introduction to the Academy edition of the text of the *Metaphysics of Morals*, AA 06: 517–520.

590 This means that, for what concerns the way of quoting the sections of the general introduction, I follow also the section numbering of the Academy edition, which is based on the first and second editions of the *Doctrine of Right* mentioned above. Nonetheless, it must be emphasized that in other contemporary editions of this work, such as the Cambridge translation of the *Metaphysics of Morals*, the order in which the sections of the introduction appear has been altered, so that the sections occur in the following order: section II of the Academy edition becomes the first section, to which section I, IV, III of the Academy edition follow. This order follows the one suggested by Bernd Ludwig on the occasion of his *Philosophische Bibliothek* edition of the *Rechtslehre* (Hamburg, Meiner 1981), where he proposes to operate many changes on the original text. On these controversies, cf. MARY GREGOR, "Translator's note on the text of The metaphysics of morals", in IMMANUEL KANT, *Practical Philosophy*, cit., pp. 355–359, and in particular p. 356. Ludwig's justification of his edition of the *Rechtslehre* is to be found in BERND LUDWIG, *Kants Rechtslehre*, Hamburg, Meiner [Kant-Forschungen, volume II] 1988. Ludwig's reconstruction is also discussed in BERND LUDWIG, "'The Right of a State' in Immanuel Kant's Doctrine of Right", in *Journal of the History of Philosophy*, 27/3 (1990), pp. 403–415.

591 *Von dem Verhältniß der Vermögen des menschlichen Gemüths zu den Sittengesetzen*, cf. MS, AA 06.211–214, MM pp. 373–376.

human being in general, the faculty of sensibility (*Sinnlichkeit*), also in its particular form of sense (*Sinn*), by which sensations (*Empfindungen*) or pure intuitions (*reine Anschauungen*] can be gained, and the fundamental faculties of reason (*Vernunft*) and understanding (*Verstand*).

Afterwards, Kant deepens the analysis of the faculty of desire by referring to its special forms of the power of choice (*Willkür*) and the will (*Wille*). According to Kant, the power of choice can be either an animal (*tierische Willkür* – *arbitrium brutum*) or a human power of choice (*menschliche Willkür*) and, in turn, only the latter can be properly defined as free (*freie Willkür* – *arbitrium liberum*), in contrast to both the animal power of choice, which can be determined only by inclination (*Neigung*), and in contrast to the will, which is neither free nor unfree, but rather an autonomous faculty, since it corresponds to pure reason in its practical application.

Eventually, Kant mentions also the faculty of taste (*Geschmack*) as a special form of the faculty of feeling (*Gefühl*).[592]

From a first look at these pages from the *Metaphysics of Morals* we may notice the differences between this classification of the mental faculties and the classifications previously proposed by Kant and the richness of the subdivisions within every single fundamental faculty, which Kant introduces here in a systematic outline.

Let me now present the most important concepts, which Kant mentions in the first section from the general introduction to the *Metaphysics of Morals*. The most general faculty mentioned there is the faculty of

(1) Life (*Leben*), which Kant defines as "the faculty of a being to act (*handeln*) in accordance with its representations".[593] Thus, the concept of "acting" (*handeln*) here refers to the "activity" of the human mind (*Thätigkeit des menschlichen Gemüths*).

According to Kant, as we have seen in particular in the first *Critique* and in the 1798 *Anthropology*, also in the general introduction to the *Metaphysics of Morals* the faculty which corresponds entirely to the receptive aspect of the mind, i.e. to its receptivity or susceptibility (*Empfänglichkeit*), is called

(2) Sensibility (*Sinnlichkeit*). Kant notes that "one can characterize sensibility as the subjective aspect of our representations in general".[594] Two more specific

---

592 Cf. MS, AA 06.211–214, MM pp. 373–376.
593 MS, AA 06: 211.07–09: "Das Vermögen eines Wesens, seinen Vorstellungen gemäß zu handeln, heißt das *Leben*"; MM p. 373.
594 MS, AA 06: 211.23–24 (footnote): "Man kann Sinnlichkeit durch das subjective unserer Vorstellungen überhaupt erklären"; MM p. 373.

aspects of the faculty of sensibility are considered by Kant. On the one hand, Kant refers to the faculty of

(2.1) Sense (*Sinn*), which he considers as receptive to a representation in a way that it makes intuitions (*Anschauungen*) or sensations (*Empfindungen*) possible. In fact, he notes that "what is subjective in our representation may be such that it can also be referred to an object for cognition of it (either in terms of its form, in which case it is called pure intuition / *reine Anschauung*, or in terms of its matter, in which case it is called sensation / *Empfindung*); in this case sensibility (*Sinnlichkeit*), as susceptibility to such a representation, is sense (*Sinn*)".[595] On the other hand, Kant considers also the peculiar form of the faculty of sensibility that is not oriented towards the representation of an object for its cognition, but which is only oriented to the subjective state of mind that the object evokes in the subject. In this case, he calls the faculty of sensibility the faculty of

(2.2) Feeling (*Gefühl*) and defines it as "susceptibility to the representation [...], which contains the effect of a representation (that may be either sensible or intellectual) upon a subject and belongs to sensibility".[596] The faculty of feeling makes possible "what is subjective in our representations [that] cannot become an *element in our cognition* because it involves *only* a relation of the representation of the *subject* and nothing that can be used for cognition of an object".[597]

These passages point toward a central idea in Kant's system of the faculties: they distinguish, in sensibility, between the faculty of sense and the faculty of feeling and, in turn, emphasize that the faculty of sense enables the states of

---

595 MS, AA 06: 211.25–29 (footnote): "Nun kann das Subjective unserer Vorstellung entweder von der Art sein, daß es auch auf ein Object zum Erkenntniß desselben (der Form oder Materie nach, da es im ersteren Falle reine Anschauung, im zweiten Empfindung heißt) bezogen werden kann; in diesem Fall ist die Sinnlichkeit, als Empfänglichkeit der gedachten Vorstellung, der *Sinn*", MM p. 373.

596 MS, AA 06: 212.34–37 (footnote): "diese Empfänglichkeit der Vorstellung [heißt] *Gefühl*, welches die Wirkung der Vorstellung (diese mag sinnlich oder intellectuell sein) aufs Subject enthält und zur Sinnlichkeit gehört, obgleich die Vorstellung selbst zum Verstande oder der Vernunft gehören mag"; MM p. 373. I translate here (in contrast to the Cambridge edition): feeling "contains the effect of a representation" rather than feeling "is the effect of a representation", since at this stage Kant refers to the faculty of feeling rather than to the mental state acquired and modified by the representation and, in accordance with this consideration, he uses the word "*enthält*" to refer to it.

597 MS, AA 06: 212.32–34 (footnote): "das Subjective der Vorstellung kann gar kein *Erkenntnißstück* werden: weil es *blos* die Beziehung derselben aufs *Subject* und nichts zur Erkenntniß des Objects Brauchbares enthält"; MM p. 373.

mind of sensations and intuitions (which are connected with the cognitive aspects of our experience), while the faculty of feeling is directed only towards the mere subjective aspect of mental experience. Moreover, it is noteworthy that Kant does not indicate another word for referring to the mental states made possible by the faculty of feeling, but he rather uses the same word, feeling (*Gefühl*), both for the faculty of feeling (*Gefühl*) and the relative states of mind (*Gefühle*) made possible by this faculty; in the case of the faculty of sense, however, he uses two distinct words, i. e. sense (*Sinn*) for the faculty and sensations/intuitions (*Empfindungen/Anschauungen*) for the mental states made possible by the faculty of sense.

To sum up, Kant (A) distinguishes, within the faculty of sensibility, between the two peculiar aspects of sense and feeling and he then (B) emphasizes that sense makes sensations and intuitions possible, while *feeling* makes *feelings* possible.

Eventually, in addition to the faculties of sense and feeling, Kant mentions a third faculty, which he includes under the domain of sensibility. This is the faculty of

(2.2.1) Taste (*Geschmack*), which Kant presents as a specification of the faculty of feeling but does not analyse very closely. He limits himself to mentioning it as the faculty that makes possible a "merely contemplative pleasure or *inactive delight*", i. e. a pleasure "which is not necessarily connected with desire for an object, and so is not at bottom a pleasure in the existence of the object of a representation but is attached only to the representation by itself".[598]

The quoted passages show that the role of the faculty of feeling and the mental state (*Gemütszustand*) of pleasure (*Lust*) and displeasure (*Unlust*) gain great importance in Kant's thoughts in the context of the *Metaphysics of Morals*.[599] This importance is further testified by the fact that Kant refers to different nuances of the various forms of pleasure and displeasure for explaining some connections between the fundamental faculties. Thus, the characterization of the concept of feeling deserves a closer analysis and Kant himself dedicates to it a very extensive part of the section on the faculties in the general introduction

---

[598] MS, AA 06: 212.13–18: "man [würde] die Lust, die mit dem Begehren des Gegenstandes nicht nothwendig verbunden ist, die also im Grunde nicht eine Lust an der Existenz des Objects der Vorstellung ist, sondern blos an der Vorstellung allein haftet, blos contemplative Lust oder unthätiges Wohlgefallen nennen können. Das Gefühl [... dieser] Art von Lust nennen wir Geschmack"; MM p. 374.

[599] However, it has to be remembered that Kant focuses his attention on these very topics also at the beginning of the *Critique of the Aesthetic Power of Judgment*. Cf. KU, AA 05: 203 ff., CPJ pp. 89 ff.

to the *Metaphysics of Morals*. For instance, Kant first repeats that "the capacity for having pleasure or displeasure in a representation is called *feeling* because both of these involve what is *merely subjective* in the relation of our representation and contain no relation at all to an object for possible cognition of it (or even cognition of our condition)".[600] In this way, he explains the role of the faculty of feeling in the context of the occurrences of our mental states. Afterwards, he focuses on the mental states of feeling and explains that these states of mind always occur only in the form of pleasure or displeasure, such that every time a feeling occurs, the subject undergoes either a pleasant or unpleasant mental experience. Kant further stresses that "pleasure or displeasure [...] expresses nothing at all in the subject but simply a relation to the subject" and that "for this very reason pleasure and displeasure cannot be explained more clearly in themselves".[601] But even though the mental state of feeling "cannot be explained more clearly", it is nonetheless possible to shed light on this concept by referring to the relations among the mental faculties that are enabled by feelings. In this way, it is possible to distinguish between the already mentioned

(A) contemplative pleasure (*contemplative Lust*) or inactive delight (*unthätiges Wohlgefallen*), and the

(B) practical pleasure (*praktische Lust*), i. e. "that pleasure which is necessarily connected with desire (*Begehren*) (for an object whose representation affects feeling in this way) [...], whether it is the cause or the effect of the desire".[602] In

---

600 MS, AA 06: 211.19 – 22, 212.01: "Man nennt aber die Fähigkeit, Lust oder Unlust bei einer Vorstellung zu haben, darum *Gefühl*, weil beides das *blos Subjective* im Verhältnisse unserer Vorstellung und gar keine Beziehung auf ein Object zum möglichen Erkenntnisse desselben (nicht einmal dem Erkenntnisse unseres Zustandes) enthält"; MM p. 373.

601 Here the whole passage of MS, AA 06: 212.01 – 09: "da sonst selbst Empfindungen außer der Qualität, die ihnen der Beschaffenheit des Subjects wegen anhängt (z. B. des Rothen, des Süßen u. s. w.), doch auch als Erkenntnißstücke auf ein Object bezogen werden, die Lust oder Unlust aber (am Rothen und Süßen) schlechterdings nichts am Objecte, sondern lediglich Beziehung aufs Subject ausdrückt. Näher können Lust und Unlust für sich und zwar eben um des angeführten Grundes Willen nicht erklärt werden, sondern man kann allenfalls nur, was sie in gewissen Verhältnissen für Folgen haben, anführen, um sie im Gebrauch kennbar zu machen"; MM p. 373.

602 MS, AA 06: 212.10 – 13: "Man kann die Lust, welche mit dem Begehren (des Gegenstandes, dessen Vorstellung das Gefühl so afficirt) notwendig verbunden ist, praktische Lust nennen: sie mag nun Ursache oder Wirkung vom Begehren sein"; MM p. 374. For the analysis of this topic, cf. THOMAS HÖWING, *Praktische Lust. Kant über das Verhältnis von Fühlen, Begehren und praktischer Vernunft*, Berlin/Boston, de Gruyter 2013 and HEINER F. KLEMME, "Fühlen, Begehren, Erkennen – Selbstbesitz. Reflexionen über die Verbindung der Vermögen in Kants Lehre vom Kategorischen Imperativ", in INGA RÖMER (ed.), *Affektivität und Ethik bei Kant und in der Phänomenologie*, Berlin/Boston, de Gruyter 2014 (forthcoming).

this case, an account of the concept of pleasure can be gained through the consideration of the relation that this state of mind makes possible between the faculty of feeling and the faculty of desire. Moreover, Kant considers the case in which "the faculty of desire [...] is caused and therefore necessarily *preceded*" by practical pleasure and calls this kind of practical pleasure "*appetite (Begierde)* in the narrow sense", while the habitual appetite is called inclination (*Neigung*).[603] It is clear that, in the case of practical feeling, the state of mind of feeling that is made possible by the mental faculty of feeling is intrinsically connected to the faculty of desire and, in this way, constitutes the link between the two faculties.[604] The mediating character of the state of mind of feeling sheds light on the actual link between the faculty of desire and the faculty of feeling, such that it already becomes clear that these two faculties are intrinsically connected in Kant's reflections and, in particular, in the ones pertaining moral philosophy, as I will show in the last chapter of my work, where also a third kind of pleasure will play a role, i.e.

(C) intellectual pleasure (*intellectuelle Lust*), defined as the pleasure that "can only follow upon an antecedent determination of the faculty of desire".[605]

But let me now leave aside Kant's characterisation of the different mental states of feeling and come back to the definitions of the single faculties as they are presented in the general introduction to the *Metaphysics of Morals*. In this way, after having dealt with the various aspects of the faculty of sensibility, one must now come to the analysis of the other central faculty that plays a big role in the context of moral action, i.e. the

(3) Faculty of desire (*Begehrungsvermögen*), as Kant defines it right at the beginning of the first section of the general introduction to the *Metaphysics of Morals* and also later. This faculty is characterised as "the faculty to be, by means of

---

603 MS, AA 06: 212.10 – 13: "Was aber die praktische Lust betrifft, so wird die Bestimmung des Begehrungsvermögens, vor welcher diese Lust als Ursache nothwendig vorhergehen muß, im engen Verstande Begierde, die habituelle Begierde aber Neigung heißen"; MM p. 374.

604 This is also true for the case of concupiscence, which Kant defines as "lusting after something" and which must "be distinguished from desire itself, as a stimulus to determining desire", in that concupiscence "is always a sensible modification of the mind but one that has not yet become an act of the faculty of desire" ["Noch ist die Concupiscenz (das Gelüsten) von dem Begehren selbst als Anreiz zur Bestimmung desselben zu unterscheiden. Sie ist jederzeit eine sinnliche, aber noch zu keinem Act des Begehrungsvermögens gediehene Gemüthsbestimmung"], MS, AA 06: 213.10 – 13, MM p. 374.

605 MS, AA 06: 212.27 – 29: "wenn die Lust nur auf eine vorhergehende Bestimmung des Begehrungsvermögens folgen kann, so wird sie eine intellectuelle Lust"; MM p. 374.

one's representations, the cause of the objects of these representations".[606] In addition, Kant notes that feeling, as a susceptibility to *pleasure* or *displeasure*, is "always connected with desire (*Begehren*) or aversion (*Verabscheuen*)", even though "the converse does not always hold".[607] It is questionable whether this assessment should not be put the other way around, i.e. whether Kant made a mistake here and should have more rightly said: "desire is always connected with feeling and the converse does not always hold". In fact, as we can note from what Kant assesses immediately afterwards, "there can be a pleasure that is not connected with any desire for an object but is already connected with a mere representation that one forms of an object (regardless of whether the object of the representation exists or not)".[608]

Also in consideration of the general theory of the faculties proposed by Kant, one should then observe that (a) desire is always connected with feeling, but feeling does not always necessarily precede desire; (b) feeling is not always connected to desire, since there are cases where feeling is directed just to a representation of an object without any reference to its realisation (like in the case of taste).

In sum, Kant states that the faculty of desire is always linked with either pleasure or displeasure and that pleasure or displeasure might be evoked by a desire or aversion for an object but also by the mere representation of the object and not necessarily by the object itself. He notes the mental states of pleasure or displeasure are not always needed for the activation of the faculty of desire: "pleasure or displeasure in an object of desire does not always precede the desire and need not always be regarded as the cause of the desire but can also be regarded as the effect of it".[609] Thus, Kant corroborates what he stated already in the *Groundwork*, as well as in the second and third *Critique*, i.e. he makes room for the consideration of a modified sentimental state of mind that follows an act of volition in the *Metaphysics of Morals* as well and, in this way, we are reminded of the case of the moral law, which is a volition and, at the same time, an obli-

---

606 MS, AA 06: 211.06 – 07: "*Begehrungsvermögen* ist das Vermögen durch seine Vorstellungen Ursache der Gegenstände dieser Vorstellungen zu sein"; MM p. 373.

607 MS, AA 06: 211.10 – 12: "Mit dem Begehren oder Verabscheuen ist *erstlich* jederzeit *Lust* oder *Unlust*, deren Empfänglichkeit man *Gefühl* nennt, verbunden; aber nicht immer umgekehrt"; MM p. 373.

608 MS, AA 06: 211.12 – 15: "es kann eine Lust geben, welche mit gar keinem Begehren des Gegenstandes, sondern mit der bloßen Vorstellung, die man sich von einem Gegenstande macht (gleichgültig, ob das Object derselben existire oder nicht), schon verknüpft ist"; MM p. 373.

609 MS, AA 06: 211.15 – 18: "Auch geht *zweitens* nicht immer die Lust oder Unlust an dem Gegenstande des Begehrens vor dem Begehren vorher und darf nicht allemal als Ursache, sondern kann auch als Wirkung desselben angesehen werden"; MM p. 373.

gation, that is not caused by a feeling, while it is rather a feeling (of respect) which is evoked in the faculty of feeling by this volition, i. e. the moral law.

On the basis of these more general considerations on the (in)dependence of feeling and desire, Kant now more closely analyses the faculty of desire. He states that

(2) the "faculty of desire (*Begehrungsvermögen*) in accordance with concepts, insofar as the ground determining it to action lies within itself and not in its object" can also be defined as a "faculty to *do or to refrain from doing as one pleases* (*ein Vermögen nach Belieben zu thun oder zu lassen*)".[610] In the context of this faculty, we can distinguish between three particular conative aspects, so that a tripartite division of the faculty of desire can be provided. In consequence to this tripartite division, Kant also rethinks his theory concerning the freedom of the will and the freedom of choice as he presented it in the critical works.[611] Accordingly, Kant calls

(3.1) Power of choice (*Willkür*) the faculty of desire that "is joined with one's consciousness of the ability to bring about its object by one's action"[612] – this is the faculty that is most fundamentally concerned with action and properly makes possible the acts of deciding –; and, eventually, he refers to

(3.2) Will (*Wille*) as "the faculty of desire whose inner determining ground, hence even what pleases it, lies within the subject's reason".[613]

Therefore, Kant adds, the will is "the faculty of desire considered not so much in relation to action (as choice is) but rather in relation to the ground determining choice to action. The will itself, strictly speaking, has no determining

---

610 MS, AA 06: 213.14–17: "Das Begehrungsvermögen nach Begriffen, sofern der Bestimmungsgrund desselben zur Handlung in ihm selbst, nicht in dem Objecte angetroffen wird, heißt ein Vermögen nach Belieben zu thun oder zu lassen"; MM p. 374.

611 For a first introduction to the discussion of these themes cf. note 606 below. For the debate on this topic also in the light of contemporary Kant scholarship see my article (and the relative bibliography) ANTONINO FALDUTO, "Free will e Freie Willkür: Kant e Searle sulla libertà dell'azione umana", in *Methodus. Revista Internacional de Filosofia Moderna/An International Journal for Modern Philosophy*, 5 (2010), pp. 85–96.

612 MS, AA 06: 213.17–18: "Sofern es [=das Begehrungsvermögen] mit dem Bewußtsein des Vermögens seiner Handlung zur Hervorbringung des Objects verbunden ist, heißt es Willkür"; MM pp. 374–375.

613 MS, AA 06: 213.20–22: "Das Begehrungsvermögen, dessen innerer Bestimmungsgrund, folglich selbst das Belieben in der Vernunft des Subjects angetroffen wird, heißt der Wille"; MM p. 375. Between power of choice and will Kant also introduces the concept of "Wish" [*Wunsch*], which he defines as the faculty of desire that "is not joined with [one's consciousness of the ability to bring about its object by one's action]", MS, AA 06: 213.18–19 ("...ist es [=das Begehrungsvermögen] aber damit nicht verbunden, so heißt der Actus desselben ein Wunsch"); MM p. 375.

ground; insofar as it can determine choice, it is instead practical reason itself".[614] If, as I showed in my analyses dedicated to the second and third *Critiques*, pure practical reason was already strictly connected to the faculty of desire in its specification as pure will, in the *Metaphysics of Morals* Kant equates the concept of pure practical reason and the concept of will (more overtly explaining what he already noted in the *Groundwork*): reason does not simply provide the *a priori* principle for the application of the fundamental faculty of desire, but it even corresponds to the specification of the faculty of desire that is will.

The prior motivating force of the faculty of desire, i.e., precisely, of the will as lawgiving pure practical reason, is emphasized by Kant's words: "insofar as reason can determine the faculty of desire as such, not only choice, but also mere wish can be included under will".[615] The supremacy of the will over the other forms of the conative faculties preserves the overriding nature of morality. Moreover, in this passage the freedom of the human being to decide in favour of non-moral action is preserved, notwithstanding the moral law and the motivating power of the will as lawgiving pure practical reason. In order to explain freedom, Kant in fact introduces in this section of the *Metaphysics of Morals* a very clear description of the faculty that he calls the power of choice (*Willkür*).

This is not the first time that Kant deals with this concept, since in the context of the critical works as well Kant mentions the power of choice (for instance, in the context of the antinomies-chapter of the first *Critique*).[616] Nonetheless, here in the *Metaphysics of Morals* Kant very clearly distinguishes between different aspects of the power of choice and shows the difference between the power of choice and the will in detail by defining human choice as free and the will as autonomous (neither free nor unfree). With regard to the distinction of different aspects of the power of choice, he notes that

---

614 MS, AA 06: 213.22–26: "Der Wille ist also das Begehrungsvermögen, nicht sowohl (wie die Willkür) in Beziehung auf die Handlung, als vielmehr auf den Bestimmungsgrund der Willkür zur Handlung betrachtet, und hat selber vor sich eigentlich keinen Bestimmungsgrund, sondern ist, sofern sie die Willkür bestimmen kann, die praktische Vernunft selbst"; MM p. 375.

615 MS, AA 06: 213.27–29: "Unter dem Willen kann die Willkür, aber auch der bloße Wunsch enthalten sein, sofern die Vernunft das Begehrungsvermögen überhaupt bestimmen kann"; MM p. 375.

616 Cf. in particular the third section [*III. Auflösung der kosmologischen Ideen von der Totalität der Ableitung der Weltbegebenheiten aus ihren Ursachen*] of the chapter dedicated to the Antinomy of Pure Reason, KrV, A 531ff./B 559ff., AA 03: 362ff.; CpR pp. 375ff.

(3.1.A) Free power of choice (*freie Willkür* – *arbitrium liberum*) is "choice which can be determined by pure reason",[617] while

(3.1.B) Animal power of choice (*tierische Willkür* – *arbitrium brutum*) is the power of choice that "can be determined only by *inclination* (*Neigung*) (sensible impulse / *sinnlicher Antrieb, stimulus*)".[618]

In contrast to the animal power of choice, according to Kant only the

(3.1.C) Human power of choice (*menschliche Willkür*) can be free, since it "is a choice that can indeed be *affected* but not *determined* by sensible impulses, and is therefore of itself (apart from an acquired proficiency of reason) not pure but can still be determined to actions by pure will".[619]

The human power of choice may come to a decision and, in this way, be free, only if it is moved by the will, such that freedom is realized only when the will moves the power of choice. The free application of the faculty of choice is typical of human beings, not of animals, since it implies independence from all inclinations, which cannot be attained by animals. The reference to the freedom of the human power of choice (*arbitrium liberum*) and, at the same time, to the autonomous activity of pure practical reason that gives the law implies a reference to two distinct concepts of freedom: Kant mentions, on the one hand, a "negative" concept of freedom, i.e. the freedom of the power of choice and, on the other hand, a "positive" concept of freedom, i.e. the autonomy of the will: "*Freedom* of choice is this independence from being *determined* by sensible impulses; this is the negative concept of freedom. The positive concept of freedom is that of the ability of pure reason to be of itself practical. But this is not possible except by the subjection of the maxim of every action to the condition of its qualifying as universal law".[620] Afterwards, in the fourth section of the general introduction to the *Metaphysics of Morals*, which Kant dedicates to the outline of the

---

617 MS, AA 06: 213.29–30: "Die Willkür, die durch reine Vernunft bestimmt werden kann, heißt die freie Willkür"; MM p. 375.

618 MS, AA 06: 213.30–32: "Die [Willkür], welche nur durch Neigung (sinnlichen Antrieb, *stimulus*) bestimmbar ist, würde thierische Willkür (*arbitrium brutum*) sein"; MM p. 375.

619 MS, AA 06: 213.32–35: "Die menschliche Willkür ist dagegen eine solche, welche durch Antriebe zwar afficirt, aber nicht bestimmt wird, und ist also für sich (ohne erworbene Fertigkeit der Vernunft) nicht rein, kann aber doch zu Handlungen aus reinem Willen bestimmt werden"; MM p. 375.

620 MS, AA 06: 226.35–37, 227.01–04: "Die Freiheit der Willkür ist jene Unabhängigkeit ihrer Bestimmung durch sinnliche Antriebe; dies ist der negative Begriff derselben. Der positive ist: das Vermögen der reinen Vernunft für sich selbst praktisch zu sein. Dieses ist aber nicht anders möglich, als durch die Unterwerfung der Maxime einer jeden Handlung unter die Bedingung der Tauglichkeit der erstern zum allgemeinen Gesetze"; MM p. 375.

'Preliminary Concepts of the Metaphysics of Morals',[621] Kant defines only the activity of the power of choice as free, while he refers to the activity of the will as autonomous. He says that only the negative concept of freedom should properly be called freedom, while the positive concept of freedom should instead be called only autonomy. As we read in the fourth section, Kant links this distinction with the difference between the concepts of law and maxim and then explains that the will, in contrast to the power of choice, cannot be said to be properly free, since only the power of choice is free in the proper sense: "Laws proceed from the will, *maxims* from choice. In man the latter is a free choice; the will, which is directed to nothing beyond the law itself, cannot be called either free or unfree, since it is not directed to actions but immediately to giving laws for the maxims of actions (and is, therefore, practical reason itself). Hence the will directs with absolute necessity and is itself *subject to* no necessitation. Only *choice* can therefore be called free".[622] In contrast to the power of choice, which chooses the maxims and directs human actions, the will (which, we remember, corresponds to pure reason in its practical use) cannot be said to be either free or unfree, in that it necessarily directs the actions by its lawgiving, so that it would be better to define it as the faculty of human beings' autonomy.[623]

---

621 *Vorbegriffe zur Metaphysik der Sitten*, cf. MS, AA 06: 221–228, MM pp. 376–382 (in the English edition the fourth section becomes the third, according to Ludwig's proposal).
622 MS, AA 06: 226.04–11: "Von dem Willen gehen die Gesetze aus; von der Willkür die Maximen. Die letztere ist im Menschen eine freie Willkür; der Wille, der auf nichts Anderes, als bloß auf Gesetz geht, kann weder frei noch unfrei genannt werden, weil er nicht auf Handlungen, sondern unmittelbar auf die Gesetzgebung für die Maxime der Handlungen (also die praktische Vernunft selbst) geht, daher auch schlechterdings nothwendig und selbst keiner Nöthigung fähig ist. Nur die Willkür also kann frei genannt werden"; MM p. 375. These observations on the power of choice introduce the problem of the *libertas indifferentiae*. For an analysis of this concept in Kant, cf. among others HEINER F. KLEMME, "Necessità pratica e indifferenza del volere. Considerazioni sulla *'libertas indifferentiae'*", in LUCA FONNESU (ed.), *Etica e mondo in Kant*, Bologna, Il Mulino 2008, pp. 57–73. On the concepts of freedom and imputability in Kant's philosophy, see, among others, JOCHEN BOJANOWSKI, *Kants Theorie der Freiheit*, Berlin 2006 and JOCHEN BOJANOWSKI, "Kant und das Problem der Zurechenbarkeit", in *Zeitschrift für philosophische Forschung*, Volume 61/2 (2007), pp. 207–228
623 On the difference between will and power of choice on freedom, cf. in particular MARCO IVALDO, "Volontà e arbitrio nella *Metafisica dei Costumi*", in *Kant e la morale. A duecento anni da "La metafisica dei costumi". Convegno della Società Italiana di Studi Kantiani presso la Scuola Normale Superiore di Pisa*, Pisa-Roma: Istituti Editoriali e Poligrafici Internazionali 1999, pp. 41–67; CLAUDIO LA ROCCA, "La distinzione kantiana tra *Wille* e *Willkür* e il problema della libertà", in *Eticidad y Estado en el Idealismo Alemán*, Valencia, Natán 1987, pp. 19–40; RALF MEERBOTE, "*Wille* and *Willkür* in Kant's Theory of Action", in MOLTKE S. GRAM (ed.) *Interpreting Kant*, Jowa City, University of Jowa Press 1982, pp. 69–84; HENRY SIDGWICK, "The Kantian Conception of

By means of the analysis of the differences between the power of choice and the will we reach the end of the analysis of the system of the faculties, as Kant presents it in the *Metaphysics of Morals*. As is easy to notice, in the context of the *Metaphysics of Morals* as already took place in the second *Critique*, Kant mentions only briefly the faculty of cognition in the proper sense, i.e. the fundamental faculty of

(4.1) Understanding (*Verstand*), which is defined only briefly as the faculty "that first refers representations to an object, i.e., only it *thinks* something by means of them".[624] In this context, as it already happened in the second *Critique*, Kant needs nothing but a quick reference to this fundamental faculty, since, here in the *Metaphysics of Morals* as well as in the *Critique of Practical Reason*, the faculty of feeling and the faculty of desire are at the centre of his moral philosophical discussion.

4.12 Kant's System of the Faculties of the Human Mind: Some Concluding Remarks

With the presentation of the system of the faculties introduced by Kant in the general introduction to the *Metaphysics of Morals* we are now in possession of one of the last comprehensive classifications of the faculties proposed by Kant in his published works.

This classification also helps me to introduce the last chapter of my work, where I will interpret Kant's concept of moral feeling on the basis of his theory of the faculties, since the division of the faculties in the *Metaphysics of Morals* also gives some closer insights into Kant's contextualisation of the faculties in his studies dedicated to moral philosophy. In the last chapter of my work, I only aim to clarify the role played by just one of the faculties analysed up until this point in my study, namely the faculty of feeling, in the context of Kant's study of moral action.

In the present chapter I aimed only to give a description of the treatment of the faculties, as Kant proposes it in some of his pure philosophical works. I

Free Will", in *Mind – A Quarterly Review of Psychology and Philosophy*, 12/51 (1888), pp. 405–412; PIRMIN STEKELER-WEITHOFER, "Willkür und Wille bei Kant", in *Kant-Studien*, 81 (1990), pp. 304–320. On the parallels with Reinhold's concepts of will and power of choice, cf. VIOLETTA STOLZ – MARION HEINZ – MARTIN BONDELI (eds.), *Wille, Willkür, Freiheit. Reinholds Freiheitskonzeption im Kontext der Philosophie des 18. Jahrhunderts*, Berlin/Boston, de Gruyter 2012.
624 MS, AA 06: 211.24–25 (footnote): "der Verstand bezieht allererst die Vorstellungen auf ein Object, d. i. er allein *denkt* sich etwas vermittelst derselben"; MM p. 373.

found this necessary since an independent study of the role of the faculties in Kant's philosophy has often been underestimated. Such a study has been treated as a topic of secondary interest and subordinated in a way such that an overall treatment of the faculties has been considered solely in the context of a psychological or anthropological reading of Kant's philosophy. In contrast to this view, I found it necessary to give a precise description of the faculties as Kant discusses them in his critical works.

On the background of the present description of Kant's classification of the faculties in his pure philosophy, in the final chapter of my work (chapter 5 below) I shall only take into consideration the faculty of feeling and the more particular concept of moral feeling in the context of the theory of the faculties, in order to shed light on only one particular aspect of Kant's doctrine of the faculties, namely the analysis of the sensitive faculty and its role in moral action.

Chapter 5
Interpreting Kant's Concept of Moral Feeling on the Basis of His Theory of the Faculties

Even though Kant's own contemporaries expounded the problematic relation between his moral theory and the motivational force of feelings,[625] in the Twentieth Century Kant scholars have not dedicated adequate consideration to Kant's treatment of the specific concept of "moral feeling", at least not up until the last few decades, when a renaissance of studies on Kant and a particular interest in sentiments and emotions in the philosophy of mind and cognitive neuroscience have set a new trend.

In the treatment of the topic of moral feeling, until now Kant scholars have concentrated on a conceptual-historical analysis, dedicated to the influence of the moral sense school on Kant's ethics.[626] Or, as it happens in contemporary English-speaking Kant scholarship, a theoretical approach on the concept of moral feeling has produced some works on "Kantian virtue ethics".[627] Nonetheless, we also find other studies in Kant scholarship that appeal to moral feeling

---

625 Cf. among others the famous criticisms by FRIEDRICH SCHILLER, *Ueber Anmuth und Würde*, in *Neue Thalia* (1792–93), third volume (1793), pp. 115–230, Leipzig, G. J. Göschen'sche Verlagsbuchhandlung. Now easily available in the Reclam edition: FRIEDRICH SCHILLER, *Kallias oder über die Schönheit. Über Anmut und Würde*, Reclam, Stuttgart 2006.

626 Among others, cf. DIETER HENRICH, "Hutcheson und Kant", in *Kant-Studien*, 49 (1957/1958), pp. 49–69; DIETER HENRICH, "Kants früheste Ethik. Versuch einer Rekonstruktion", in *Kant-Studien*, 54 (1963), pp. 404–431. But cf. also LUC LANGLOIS, "Du sentiment moral à la raison pratique. Kant disciple et critique de Hutcheson", in ROBERT THEIS – LUKAS K. SOSOE (eds.), *Le sources de la philosophie kantienne aux XVIIe et XVIIIe siècles*, Paris, Vrin 2005, pp. 203–211; GIANCARLO LUNATI, "Il significato del 'sentimento' nel pensiero morale del Kant precritico", in *Annali della Scuola Normale Superiore*, 32 (1954), pp. 237–256; JOSEF SCHMUCKER, *Die Ursprünge der Ethik Kants in seinen vorkritischen Schriften und Reflektionen*, Meisenheim am Glan, Hain KG 1961.

627 For the idea of a Kantian virtue ethics which is based on a revaluation of the emotive field cf. MICHAEL SLOTE, *From Morality to Virtue*, Oxford/New York, Oxford University Press 1992 and, more recently, MICHAEL SLOTE, *Moral Sentimentalism*, Oxford/New York, Oxford University Press 2010, but also ROBERT B. LOUDEN, *Kant's Impure Ethics. From Rational Beings to Human Beings*, Oxford/New York, Oxford University Press 2000; ROBERT B. LOUDEN, *Kant's Human Being. Essays on His Theory of Human Nature*, Oxford/New York, Oxford University Press 2011; and, eventually, LAWRENCE JOST – JULIAN WUERTH (ed.), *Perfecting Virtue: New Essays on Kantian Ethics and Virtue Ethics*, Cambridge/New York, Cambridge University Press, 2011.

to explain overdetermined actions in morality or those studies that consider moral feeling among many other sorts of "Kantian emotions".[628]

This theoretical approach has followed a more "philologically" characterized research on the concept of "moral feeling", which has mostly concentrated on the analysis of the *Triebfedern-Kapitel*.[629]

However, a considerable gap in the studies dedicated to the concept of moral feeling in Kant's philosophy is still to be noted, namely the lack of contextualisation of the concept of moral feeling in the agent's mental life as Kant describes it. As a consequence, I aim to more closely analyse how it happens that, according to Kant, a human being is able to feel respect for the moral law. This question brings one far away from the field of moral philosophy and requires that, more generally, Kant's description of the functioning of the human subject's mental life and actions needs to be clarified first.

That is the reason why in this final chapter of my work I aim to interpret a fundamental feature of Kant's theory of moral action on the basis of my explanation of Kant's concept of the faculties. This fundamental feature is the concept

---

628 For an account of overdetermined actions in Kant's moral theory, cf. for instance BARBARA HERMAN, *The Practice of Moral Judgment*, Cambridge (Mass.), Harvard University Press 1993. For a more general account of "Kantian emotions" cf. two philosophers, Nancy Sherman and Marcia W. Baron, who underline the "emotivist vocation" of Kant's concept of moral feeling. For the first author, cf. MARCIA W. BARON, *Kantian Ethics Almost without Apology*, Ithaca (N. Y.)/London, Cornell University Press 1995; MARCIA W. BARON, "Kantian Ethics and the Claims of Detachment", in ROBIN MAY SCHOTT (ed.), *Feminist Interpretations of Kant*, University Park, Pennsylvania State Ubiversity Press 1997, pp. 145–170; MARCIA W. BARON, "Kantian Ethics", in MARCIA W. BARON – PHILIP PETTIT – MICHAEL SLOTE, *Three Methods of Ethics: A Debate*, Oxford/New York, Oxford University Press 1997, pp. 3–9. For the second author, cf. NANCY SHERMAN, "The Place of Emotions in Kantian Morality", in OWEN FLANAGAN – AMÉLIE OK-SENBERG RORTY (eds.), *Identity, Character, and Morality: Essays in Moral Psychology*, Cambridge (Mass.)/London, MIT Press 1990, pp. 149–170; NANCY SHERMAN, *Making a Necessity of Virtue. Aristotle and Kant on Virtue*, Cambridge/New York, Cambridge University Press 1997.

629 Among the numerous recent contributions, cf. PHILIP BLOSSER, "A Problem in Kant's Theory of Moral Feeling", in *Lyceum*, 3 (1991), pp. 27–39; ALEXANDER BROADIE – ELIZABETH M. PYBUS, "Kant's Concept of 'Respect'", in *Kant-Studien*, 66 (1975), pp. 58–64; PIERO GIORDANETTI, *Rivoluzione copernicano-newtoniana e sentimento in Kant*, Frankfurt am Main, Lang 2012; INA GOY, "Immanuel Kant über das moralische Gefühl der Achtung", in *Zeitschrift für philosophische Forschung*, LXI/3 (2007), pp. 337–360; HENRI LAUENER, "Der systematische Stellenwert des Gefühls der Achtung in Kants Ethik", in *Dialectica*, 35 (1981), pp. 243–264; STEPHEN PALMQUIST, "Is Duty Kant's Motive for Moral Action?", in *Ratio*, 28 (1986), pp. 168–174; STEFFI SCHADOW, *Achtung für das Gesetz. Moral und Motivation bei Kant*, Berlin/Boston, de Gruyter 2013; GEORGE SCHRADER, "The Status of Feeling in Kant's Philosophy", in PIERRE LABERGE – FRANCOIS DU-CHESNEAU – BRYAN E. MORRISEY (eds.), *Actes du Congrès d'Ottawa sur Kant dans les Traditions Anglo-Américaine et Continentale*, Ottawa, University of Ottawa Press 1976, pp. 143–164.

of moral feeling, which I aim to present as a central component of Kant's description of the moral life of finite, sensuous subjects.

In contrast to the aforementioned studies from the secondary literature, in this last chapter of my work I aim to explain why the concept of moral feeling plays a fundamental role for the concrete realisation of Kant's ethical theory in human life by first referring to two possible concepts expressed by the term "moral feeling" in Kant's philosophy and, second, by showing that the notion of moral feeling does not entirely correspond to the concept of respect for the moral law. In order to do this, I will consider the faculty of feeling pleasure and displeasure and I will elucidate the role played by this faculty in the concrete realisation of Kant's moral theory. As I will now explain, since the study of the faculty of feeling still pertains to the domain of the "aesthetic" (as Kant intends it), the consideration of Kant's "moral aesthetic", which represents the analysis of moral feeling and of the role played by feelings in moral action in general, will require a revaluation of Kant's theory of moral agency. Furthermore, the revaluation of Kant's moral aesthetic will support the thesis that Kant was profoundly interested in the way in which moral theory can be concretely realized in the life of a sensuous human agent. I will propose further arguments in defence of Kant's moral theory against the accusation of mere formalism.

In order to properly evaluate the role played by feeling in the realisation of Kant's moral theory, I shall go back to the fundamental tripartite division of the faculties and consider the role played by the faculty of feeling pleasure and displeasure and its relation to the more fundamental faculty of sensibility.

I shall thus start from Kant's analyses of sensibility and his account of the study of the "aesthetic" (section 5.1). Afterwards, I will begin my analysis of Kant's moral theory and, after briefly emphasizing its rationalistic character (section 5.2), I will shed some light on the distinction between moral sense and moral feeling (section 5.3).

These topics will introduce the analysis of Kant's treatment of the concept of respect (sections 5.4–5.5) and the analysis of the way in which Kant deals with the concept of feeling as receptivity in the *Doctrine of Virtue* (section 5.6). At this stage I want to stress that, in the following pages, I will confine myself to the analysis of Kant's treatment of the topic of moral feeling in his published works and that I will refer, in particular, to the *Groundwork*, the second *Critique*, and the *Doctrine of Virtue* from the *Metaphysics of Morals*. However, for a better understanding of the development of Kant's ideas on feeling in general and moral feeling in particular, a study of the student's notes of Kant's lectures on anthropology (in particular, of the *Anthropologie-Mrongovius* from the winter se-

mester 1784/1785, that is from the years in which Kant is working on the *Groundwork*) plays a capital role.[630]

My considerations of Kant's published works and, in particular, the analysis of Kant's presentation of feeling as receptivity in the *Doctrine of Virtue* will eventually bring me to my last interpretive proposal concerning Kant's "moral aesthetic" (section 5.7).[631]

5.1 Kant's Account of the Aesthetic: Some Brief Remarks

According to the definition of the term *Ästhetik* that Kant gives in the first *Critique*, the study of the "aesthetic" does not necessarily have to do with the concept of the beautiful. The term aesthetic should, in fact, simply designate the discipline dedicated to the analysis of the faculty of sensibility (*Sinnlichkeit*) in its various forms.[632]

This is what Kant expresses in the Transcendental Aesthetic section of the *Critique of Pure Reason*.[633] In this section, he defines transcendental aesthetic as "a science of all principles of *a priori* sensibility".[634] Furthermore, in a note he adds that "the Germans are the only ones who now employ the word 'aesthet-

---

630 For the treatment of this theme cf. HEINER F. KLEMME, "Fühlen, Begehren, Erkennen – Selbstbesitz. Reflexionen über die Verbindung der Vermögen in Kants Lehre vom Kategorischen Imperativ", in INGA RÖMER (ed.), *Affektivität und Ethik bei Kant und in der Phänomenologie*, Berlin/Boston, de Gruyter 2014 (forthcoming).

631 In writing this chapter, I have combined new materials with elements from two other texts of mine, revising and rearranging materials from both of the following articles: ANTONINO FALDUTO, "Das Gefühl als Empfänglichkeit und die Bedeutung einer Ästhetik der Sitten. Anmerkungen zu Birgit Recki", in ANTONINO FALDUTO – CAROLINE KOLISANG – GABRIEL RIVERO (eds.), *Metaphysik – Ästhetik – Ethik. Beiträge zur Interpretation der Philosophie Kants*, Würzburg, Königshausen & Neumann 2012, pp. 137–153; ANTONINO FALDUTO, "The Two Meanings of moralisches Gefühl in Kant's Doctrine of Virtue", in S. BACIN ET. AL. (eds.), *Kant and Philosophy in a Cosmopolitan Sense*, cit., volume 3, pp. 161–172.

632 In the English translation there is a difference between "aesthetics" as the study of concepts such that of beautiful and "aesthetic" as the analysis of the faculty of sensibility – the German word is, in both cases, *Ästhetik*.

633 On the place of the Transcendental Aesthetic in the first *Critique* cf. REINHARD BRANDT, "Transzendentale Ästhetik, §§ 1–3", in IMMANUEL KANT, *Kritik der reinen Vernunft (Klassiker Auslegen)*, edited by G. MOHR – M. WILLASCHEK, cit., pp. 91–106; LORNE FALKENSTEIN, *Kant's Intuitionism. A Commentary on the Transcendental Aesthetics*, Toronto, University of Toronto Press 1995.

634 KrV, A 21/B35, AA 04: 30.23–24/AA 03: 50.28–29: "Eine Wissenschaft von allen Principien der Sinnlichkeit a priori nenne ich die transscendentale Ästhetik"; CPR p. 156/173.

ics' to designate that which others call the critique of taste" and that "the ground for this is a failed hope, held by the excellent analyst Baumgarten, of bringing the critical estimation of the beautiful under principles of reason, and elevating its rules to a science".[635]

Here in the first *Critique* Kant considers this attempt of "bringing the critical estimation of the beautiful under principles of reason" as "futile" and proposes "either again to desist from the use of this term and preserve it for that doctrine which is true science [...], or else to share the term with speculative philosophy and take aesthetics partly in a transcendental meaning, partly in a psychological meaning".[636] In order to avoid this ambiguity, in the Transcendental Aesthetic of the *Critique of Pure Reason* Kant defines aesthetic as the science that also partly sheds light on the process of forming objective judgements, which concur to theoretical cognition.

In contrast to the first *Critique*, in the *Critique of the Power of Judgement* Kant considers a way of using the adjective "aesthetic" (*ästhetisch*) with regard to the domain of the beautiful and admits that, in accordance with this domain, it is not erroneous to speak of a "critique of the aesthetic power of judgement", even though this term no longer refers to the objectivity brought by intuitions (attained by sensibility) in theoretical cognition and the "aesthetic" aspect of the judgement refers only, in this case, to an expressly subjective aspect of these judgements. The critique of the faculty called 'power of judgement' (which is, we remember, the cognitive faculty that gives the *a priori* principle to the faculty of feeling pleasure and displeasure) is called "not aesthetics (as if it were a doctrine of sense), but a critique of the aesthetic power of judgement, because the former expression has too broad a meaning, since it could also signify the sen-

---

635 KrV A 50/B 35–36 – AA 04: 30/AA03: 50–51 footnote: "Die Deutschen sind die einzige, welche sich jetzt des Worts Ästhetik bedienen, um dadurch das zu bezeichnen, was andre Kritik des Geschmacks heißen. Es liegt hier eine verfehlte Hoffnung zum Grunde, die der vortreffliche Analyst Baumgarten faßte, die kritische Beurtheilung des Schönen unter Vernunftprincipien zu bringen und die Regeln derselben zur Wissenschaft zu erheben"; CPR p. 156/173. On the influence of Baumgarten's *Aesthetica*, see MARY J. GREGOR, "Baumgarten's Aesthetica", in *The Review of Metaphysics*, 37/2 (1983), pp. 357–385 and more generally on the origin and development of Kant's aesthetic G. TONELLI, *Kant, dall'estetica metafisica all'estetica psicoempirica*, cit.

636 KrV A 50/B 35–36 – AA 04: 30/AA03: 50–51 footnote (Kant slightly modifies this passage from the A edition): "es [ist] rathsam, diese Benennung entweder wiederum eingehen zu lassen und sie derjenigen Lehre aufzubehalten, die wahre Wissenschaft ist [...], oder sich in die Benennung mit der speculativen Philosophie zu theilen und die Ästhetik theils im transscendentalen Sinne, theils in psychologischer Bedeutung zu nehmen"; CPR p. 156/173.

sibility of intuition, which belongs to theoretical cognition and furnishes the material for logical (objective) judgements".[637]

Notwithstanding the differences between objective and subjective judgements to which the use of "aesthetic" is linked, in both the first and the third *Critique* Kant holds that the term "aesthetic" (*Ästhetik*) and the correspondent adjective "aesthetic" (*ästhetisch*) in all cases refer to the sensible domain, by reference to either the more general faculty of sensibility or a more particular aspect of sensibility, i. e. the faculty of feeling pleasure and displeasure. This means that both in the first and in the third *Critique* the original meaning of "aesthetic" as linked to the "sensible" field, the field of "*aisthesis*", is preserved.

Another element that corresponds to the characterisation of Kant's study of aesthetic can be found if we go back to the passage quoted above from the *Critique of Pure Reason* and try to correctly evaluate Kant's mention of Baumgarten.

In the quoted passage, Baumgarten is thought to be guilty of supporting the false hope that "the critical estimation of the beautiful" might be brought "under principles of reason" and that "its rules" might be elevated "to a science".[638] Despite the reference to this "fault", the role of Baumgarten in Kant's reflections on the study of aesthetic must not be underestimated. In fact, Baumgarten can rather be considered as the one who inspired Kant's discipline of the aesthetic in the sense of an analysis dedicated to the faculty of sensibility.[639] Naturally, Baumgarten's contribution to the development of Kant's thought surrounding the study of the aesthetic has to be situated in the context of the more general way of valuing the relation between the rational part and the emotional part of the human soul in the Eighteenth century.[640] Nevertheless, the "merit of promoting the topic of sensibility to a dignity of its own" belongs to Baumgarten

---

637 EEKU, AA 20: 247.06 – 11: "Wir werden die Kritik dieses Vermögens in Ansehung der ersteren Art Urtheile nicht Ästhetik (gleichsam Sinnenlehre), sondern Kritik der ästhetischen Urtheilskraft nennen, weil der erstere Ausdruck von zu weitläufigter Bedeutung ist, indem er auch die Sinnlichkeit der Anschauung, die zum theoretischen Erkenntniß gehört und zu logischen (objectiven) Urtheilen den Stoff hergiebt, bedeuten könnte"; CPJ p. 46.

638 KrV A 50/B 35 – 36 – AA 04: 30/AA03: 50 – 51 footnote: "Es liegt hier eine verfehlte Hoffnung zum Grunde, die der vortreffliche Analyst Baumgarten faßte, die kritische Beurtheilung des Schönen unter Vernunftprincipien zu bringen und die Regeln derselben zur Wissenschaft zu erheben"; CPR p. 156/173.

639 *Meditationes*, § 115: "Aesthetica (theoria liberalium artium, gnoseologia inferior, ars pulchre cogitandi, ars analogi rationis) est scientia cognitionis sensitivae".

640 For a recognition of the studies dedicated to the relation between the sensible and the emotive part of the mind in the Eighteenth century cf. H.-M. GERLACH, "Gefühl – Sinnlichkeit – Verstand", cit.

and, in this way, his influence on Kant's revaluation of the faculty of sensibility is undisputed.[641]

But there is certainly a fundamental and distinctive point that radically differentiates Kant's aesthetic from the traditional picture, namely Kant's view that an *a priori* use of the faculty of sensibility, both in theoretical, objective judgements, and in the subjective judgements on the beautiful, is possible.

It is certainly true, especially for what regards the first *Critique*, that Kant does not always use the term sensibility (*Sinnlichkeit*) unequivocally.[642] Nonetheless, the possibility of an *a priori* application of the faculty of sensibility is indisputable.[643]

The Transcendental Aesthetic of the *Critique of Pure Reason* and the first part of the *Critique of the Power of Judgement*, i. e. the Critique of the Aesthetic Power of Judgement, are very different in their scopes; nevertheless, they both intend to analyse the sensible faculty and, in particular, they both refer to various aspects of sensibility: in the first *Critique*, the Transcendental Aesthetic is properly a science (*Wissenschaft*), which contributes to clarifying the process of acquiring theoretical cognition and the formation of objective judgements by means of the analysis of the *a priori* intuition of space and time, which the subject secures through the faculty of sensibility in its specific application as sense (*Sinn*); in the third *Critique*, the Critique of the Aesthetic Power of Judgement concentrates instead on the analysis of the faculty of feeling pleasure and displeasure and,

---

641 ANGELICA NUZZO, "Kant and Herder on Baumgaten's Aesthetica", in *Journal of the History of Philosophy*, 44/4 (2006), pp. 577–597 (here in particular p. 579) and, on Baumgarten's *Aesthetica*, the already quoted article by M. J. GREGOR, "Baumgarten's Aesthetica", cit.

642 For a recognition of the problem from a linguistic viewpoint see T. ROELCKE, *Die Terminologie der Erkenntnisvermögen*, cit., pp. 84–86, who distinguishes between five different meanings of the term sensibility [*Sinnlichkeit*]: (1) sensibility as faculty [*Vermögen*]; (2) sensibility as perception in general [*Wahrnehmung*]; (3) sensibility as a peculiar kind of perception [*Wahrnehmungstyp*]; (4) sensibility as the faculty of desire [*Begehrungsvermögen*]; (5) sensibility as disposition [*Neigung*]. For the problems concerning the source criticism and the exposure of Kant's sources for the development of the concept of sensibility see, instead, TAKESHI NAKAZAWA, *Kants Begriff der Sinnlichkeit. Seine Unterscheidung zwischen apriorischen und aposteriorischen Elementen der sinnlichen Erkenntnis und deren lateinische Vorlagen*, Stuttgart/Bad Cannstatt, frommann-holzboog 2009.

643 Cf. BEATRICE CENTI, *Coscienza, etica e architettonica in Kant. Uno studio attraverso le Critiche*, Pisa-Roma, Istituti editoriali e poligrafici internazionali (Biblioteca di *Studi kantiani*) 2002, pp. 43 ff.; PATRICIA KITCHER (*Kant's Transcendental Psychology*, cit., p. 59), who emphasizes that "the most valuable and distinctive aspect of [... Kant's] work is precisely that most repugnant of his twentieth-century commentators: the thesis of transcendental psychology that there is a specific *a priori* form of human sensibility"; but also, in particular, the observations by G. GIGLIOTTI ("Il rispetto del tulipano", cit.), and ANGELICA NUZZO ("*Ideal Embodiment*, cit.).

with no reference to the objectivity of knowledge but only to the reflective relation of the subject to himself, sheds light on the possibility and appropriateness of aesthetic judgements. The "aesthetic" sections of the first and the third *Critique* are very different in their scopes, but they both refer to the fact that sensibility (either in its specific form of the faculty of sense or in its specific form of the faculty of feeling) has an *a priori* application.[644]

Kant equates the adjectives "sensible" and "aesthetic" (*ästhetisch, d.i. sinnlich*) in the context of pure philosophy, as it often happens in the *Critique of the Power of Judgement*. Nonetheless, the different roles sensibility plays either in the formation of objective judgements (as he expresses it in the form of the faculty of sense [*Sinn*] in the first *Critique* and which pertains to Transcendental Aesthetic as a science) or in the formation of purely subjective judgements (as Kant analyses it in its particular aspect of the faculty of feeling [*Gefühl*] pleasure and displeasure in the third *Critique* and which does not pertain to a science: "all determinations of feeling are merely of subjective significance, there cannot be an aesthetic of feeling as a science as there is, say, an aesthetic of the faculty of cognition") is always central.[645]

In sum, in contrast to the third *Critique*, Kant refers in the first *Critique* to (1) "aesthetic" as a science where the faculty of sensibility is analysed with regard to its role in the formation of objective judgements in theoretical cognition; however, (2) both in the first and in the third *Critique* the aesthetic discussion refers to the *a priori* application of the faculty of sensibility in the context of pure philosophy, even though (2a) in the *Critique of Pure Reason* sensibility is analysed with regard to its particular form as the "faculty of sense" (*Sinn*), i.e. as the faculty that makes the *a priori* intuitions of space and time possible, while (2b) in the *Critique of the Power of Judgement* sensibility is analysed with regard to its particular form as the "faculty of feeling" (*Gefühl*) pleasure and displeasure, i.e. as the faculty that makes possible an *a priori* subjective, reflective relation of the subject to himself and, consequently, the occurrence of the mental states of feelings.

---

644 As Kant already noted in a reflection from 1770/1771, one might also be allowed to speak of a "pure sensibility" and of the aesthetic as the study dedicated to it. Cf. Refl. 4276, AA 17: 492.18–22: "Reine Sinnlichkeit. Reine Vernunft. Vermischt. / ubi, quando. transscendentalis philosophia. / Aesthetik ist die philosophie über die Sinnlichkeit, entweder des Erkenntnisses / oder des Gefühls". On this Reflection, cf. G. GIGLIOTTI, "Il rispetto del tulipano", cit., p. 30, who notes that the relation between the Transcendental Aesthetic of the *Critique of Pure Reason* and the aesthetics of the *Critique of the Power of Judgement* has to do with this "discovery of a pure *a priori* sensibility".

645 Cf. for instance EEKU, AA 20: 221.27–34, 222.01–15, CPJ p. 24.

In other words, the discipline of the aesthetic is the study dedicated by Kant to analysing the faculty of sensibility, but the study dedicated to analysing feeling as a special form of the faculty of sensibility is not a science.

These considerations do not exclude the possibility of referring to an "aesthetic" also in the case of the study dedicated to a special form of the faculty of sensibility, i.e. feeling, as we will see in the case of morals. In fact, Kant uses the term "aesthetic" (*Ästhetik*) in the specific meaning of a "science of sensibility", which contributes to theoretical cognition and an objective knowledge, only with regard to the first *Critique* and the Transcendental Aesthetic, while he uses the term "aesthetic" (*Ästhetik*) in the context of his consideration of the subjective incentives of moral action as well.

This is the case for the expression "Aesthetic of pure practical reason", which Kant uses in the *Critique of Practical Reason*, namely in the Critical Elucidation of the Analytic of Pure Practical Reason. In this section Kant determines that the "Analytic" must be concluded by a chapter where he intends to talk about "the relation of pure practical reason to sensibility and about its necessary influence upon sensibility", as it is "cognized *a priori*, that is, about moral feeling (*moralisches Gefühl*)".[646] In contrast to the first *Critique* where "the Analytic of theoretical pure reason was divided into transcendental Aesthetic and transcendental Logic", Kant divides the Analytic of the *Critique of Practical Reason* in reverse order, i.e. "into Logic and Aesthetic of pure practical reason".[647]

One should thus wonder what the term "aesthetic" (*Ästhetik*) refers to in this case. In the domain of the study that Kant calls here "Aesthetic of pure practical reason", sensibility is analysed not "as a capacity for intuition at all but only as feeling (which can be a subjective ground for desire), and with respect to it pure practical reason admits no further division".[648] In contrast to the first *Critique*, the Aesthetic-chapter of the second *Critique*, i.e. the *Triebfedern-Kapitel*, is focused only on the analysis of the concept of feeling and, in particular, of moral feeling, as a modified state of mind which is caused by a particular appli-

---

646 KpV, AA 05: 90.06–09: "von dem Verhältnisse der reinen praktischen Vernunft zur Sinnlichkeit und ihrem nothwendigen, *a priori* zu erkennenden Einflusse auf dieselbe, d. i. vom moralischen Gefühle, den Theil beschließen"; CprR p. 212.
647 Cf. KpV, AA 05: 90.09–18; CprR p. 212.
648 KpV, AA 05: 90.18–22: "Die Ästhetik hatte dort noch zwei Theile wegen der doppelten Art einer sinnlichen Anschauung; hier wird die Sinnlichkeit gar nicht als Anschauungsfähigkeit, sondern blos als Gefühl (das ein subjectiver Grund des Begehrens sein kann) betrachtet, und in Ansehung dessen verstattet die reine praktische Vernunft keine weitere Eintheilung"; CprR p. 212.

cation of the faculty of sensibility in its specific aspect of the faculty of feeling pleasure and displeasure.

The best way to make sense of Kant's use of the term "aesthetic" (*Ästhetik*) in this case is by referring to Kant's point of view in the third *Critique*, so that it would then follow that the "aesthetic of the pure practical reason" is not to be considered as the science of sensibility as it is presented in the first *Critique*, but this use of the term "aesthetic" (*Ästhetik*) is rather due only to Kant's reference to the particular aspect of sensibility, i.e. to Kant's analysis of the faculty of feeling. In this case, even before the treatment of the *Critique of the Power of Judgement*, Kant uses the term "aesthetic" (*Ästhetik*) to denote the field of analysis dedicated to feeling.

Among others, a reference to Lewis W. Beck's interpretation of this passage sheds light on this point. In considering the reasons why Kant calls "aesthetic" the section dedicated to the analyses of the incentives of pure practical reason, Beck starts considering the obvious analogical intent, which Kant obeys when he uses the term *Ästhetik* in order to stress one more time "the analogies [...] between the analytical parts of the first two *Critiques*".[649] In considering "the extent to which this term is or is not suitable", Beck emphasizes that the term "aesthetic" (*Ästhetik*) "is suitable insofar as the word 'aesthetic' has general reference to the sensibility, in this case to feeling as a mode of sense".[650]

The thematic field involved in Kant's proposal of an "aesthetic of pure practical reason" and the connected exposition of an "aesthetic of morals" in the *Doctrine of Virtue* (on whose basis Kant furnishes a "subjective presentation"[651] of the metaphysics of morals) are far more ample and complicated. This necessitates also, as Beck rightly notes, "a study of how the subject, as a sensuous being, is affected [...] by the principles" of pure practical reason, i.e. a study dedicated to "an immanent phenomenological problem", which must be in charge of answering the question:

---

649 Lewis White Beck, *A Commentary on Kant's Critique of Practical Reason*, The University of Chicago Press, Chicago 1960, p. 211.

650 L. W. Beck, *Commentary*, cit., p. 212. Beck further adds (confirming again the thesis I proposed above) that "it would be a mistake to expect very much similarity between the two Aesthetics. In the first *Critique*, there is a Transcendental Aesthetic having to do with the sensible conditions of a priori synthetic knowledge", while in the second *Critique* Kant is not "concerned with the manner in which the *objects* of practical reason are given to knowledge".

651 MS, TL, § XIV, AA 06: 406.19–25: "Eine Ästhetik der Sitten [ist] zwar nicht ein Teil, aber doch eine subjektive Darstellung der Metaphysik derselben: wo die Gefühle, welche die nötigende Kraft des moralischen Gesetzes begleiten, jener ihre Wirksamkeit empfindbar machen [...], um der *bloß*-sinnlichen Anreizung den Vorrang abzugewinnen"; DV p. 534.

> How can a being in the phenomenal world, through his knowledge of the law of the intelligible, control his conduct so that this law does in fact become effective?[652]

As Beck remarks,

> to answer this question we need to know as much about man as about the law.[653]

Kant's analysis of the mental faculties contributes exactly to a better knowledge of the human being. That is why now, at the end of my analysis of Kant's classification of the faculties, it is not improper to direct myself to the treatment of the problems connected with the realisation of Kant's moral theory.

What I aim to show is, in fact, why the analysis of the faculties and, in particular, the comprehension of the role played by the faculty of feeling pleasure and displeasure in the context of the mental faculties should be considered an indispensable means for a correct comprehension of the way in which the categorical imperative finds its application in the world.

As Beck further notes, one of Kant's reasons "for giving an extensive analysis of the moral disposition and intention, within which the consciousness of the law is effective", is that "the proper object of moral judgement is not the law, but man".[654] In fact,

> we can never understand the subjective phenomena of morality or have a firm basis for either moral imputation or moral decision if we do not understand the way in which the moral law enters into consciousness and makes a clear demand upon our allegiance.[655]

In order to understand and properly solve the immanent phenomenological problem linked to the application of the categorical imperative, a closer look at the concept of moral feeling is now needed. This analysis will be preceded by some brief general remarks on Kant's moral theory.

---

652 L. W. BECK, *Commentary*, cit., p. 212.
653 L. W. BECK, *Commentary*, cit., p. 212.
654 L. W. BECK, *Commentary*, cit., p. 211.
655 L. W. BECK, *Commentary*, cit., p. 211.

5.2 Kant's Ethics: A Rationalistic Account and the Role of Feeling

Kant's ethics is rationalistic; there is no better way to put it. Reason through the moral law "determines (bestimme) the will immediately".[656] And the law given by pure practical reason is, at the same time, the incentive (Triebfeder) that subjectively moves the human being to act morally. Even though "how a law can be of itself and immediately a determining ground of the will is for human reason an insoluble problem",[657] Kant assesses nonetheless that the moral law constitutes the incentive and, consequently, that to look for an incentive other than the law would produce only "hypocrisy without substance".[658]

The rationalistic character of Kant's ethics and the fact that pure reason by means of its law constitutes the only subjective incentive of moral action nowadays has to be stressed, given in recent years many studies on Kant's "moral motivation" have been published and the opinion that respect is the subjective motivation of a moral action has become quite widespread.[659] That is why it is

---

656 KpV AA 05: 71.28–29: "Das Wesentliche alles sittlichen Werths der Handlungen kommt darauf an, daß das moralische Gesetz unmittelbar den Willen bestimme"; CprR p. 198. Here a very neat clarification is due: the German word "*bestimmen*", which is translated with the English word "determine", does not imply a necessity of acting morality but only the sufficient motivational force of the law to guide the action. The English translation "determine" might cause the confusion that Kant's moral theory does not contemplate the possibility of choosing the evil – obviously, this is not the case. Cf. among others the already mentioned article by H. F. KLEMME, "Die Freiheit der Willkür und die Herrschaft des Bösen", cit.

657 KpV AA 05: 72.21–23: "wie ein Gesetz für sich und unmittelbar Bestimmungsgrund des Willens sein könne (welches doch das Wesentliche aller Moralität ist), das ist ein für die menschliche Vernunft unauflösliches Problem"; CprR p. 198.

658 KpV AA 05: 72.12–19: "Da man also zum Behuf des moralischen Gesetzes, und um ihm Einfluß auf den Willen zu verschaffen, keine anderweitige Triebfeder, dabei die des moralischen Gesetzes entbehrt werden könnte, suchen muß, weil das alles lauter Gleißnerei ohne Bestand bewirken würde, und sogar es bedenklich ist, auch nur neben dem moralischen Gesetze noch einige andere Triebfedern (als die des Vortheils) mitwirken zu lassen: so bleibt nichts übrig, als blos sorgfältig zu bestimmen, auf welche Art das moralische Gesetz Triebfeder werde"; CprR p. 198.

659 Among the many texts, cf. STEPHEN ENGSTROM, "The *Triebfeder* of Pure Practical Reason", in ANDREWS REATH – JENS TIMMERMANN (eds.), *Kant's* Critique of Practical Reason. A Critical Guide, Cambridge/New York, Cambridge University Press 2010; HEINER F. KLEMME – MANFRED KUEHN – DIETER SCHÖNECKER (eds.), *Moralische Motivation: Kant und die Alternativen*, Hamburg, Meiner 2006; RICHARD R. MCCARTY, "Kantian Moral Motivation and the Feeling of Respect", in *The Journal of the History of Philosophy*, 31 (1993), pp. 421–435; IAIN MORRISSON, "Respect in Kant: How the Moral Feeling of Respect Acts As an Incentive to Moral Action", in *Southwest Philosophy Review* (Stillwater), 20 (2004), pp. 1–26; MARK PACKER, "Kant on Desire

important to underline once again that according to Kant only reason by means of the moral law is the incentive, also the subjective incentive, of moral action.

Once we have clear in mind that the faculty of reason plays the central role in Kant's ethics both as principium dijudicationis and as principium executionis, an attempt to shed light on the role of the faculty of moral feeling in particular and of moral feelings in general in Kant's ethics can be undertaken. The attempt to show what the moral law "effects (or, to put it better, must effect) in the mind insofar as it is an incentive"[660] is, in fact, not only noteworthy but rather unavoidable, if we are to understand how the moral law modifies the human mind and how it effects human beings, i.e. those beings that are at the same time rational and sensuous.

In order to shed light on these points, in contrast to the preceding chapters of my work where I discussed Kant's treatment of the mental faculties, in what follows I will refer also to particular mental states realised by means of the faculty of feeling. I will thus analyse those changes that the human mind undergoes in the case of moral decisions and actions. I will describe how the faculty of feeling pleasure and displeasure, which is a "feeling in posse, in possibility", i.e. the mere possibility of feeling, will become an effective feeling, a "feeling in esse, in actuality", i.e. the mental state of respect (Achtung).

The analysis of the faculty of feeling and the respective mental states that this faculty makes possible will give way to my interpretation of Kant's "moral aesthetic" as the particular analysis dedicated to sensibility in its particular aspect of feeling applied in the moral case, i.e. an analysis dealing with the faculty of feeling pleasure and displeasure and the very mental states that this faculty of feeling makes possible during the process of moral deliberation and moral action.

However, before showing the role of the faculty of feeling in the moral case, a short clarification concerning the difference between the concept of moral sense and that of moral feeling in Kant's works is due, since a neat separation of these two concepts is important for a clear identification of the notion of moral feeling.

---

and Moral Pleasure", in *The Journal of the History of Ideas*, 50 (1989), pp. 429–442; ANDREWS REATH, "Kant's Theory of Moral Sensibility. Respect for the Moral Law and the Influence of Inclination", in *Kant-Studien*, 80 (1989), pp. 284–302; MELISSA ZINKIN, "Respect for the Law and the Use of Dynamical Terms in Kant's Theory of Moral Motivation", in *Archiv für Geschichte der Philosophie*, 88 (2006), pp. 31–53.

660 KpV AA 05: 72.12–19: "Also werden wir nicht den Grund, woher das moralische Gesetz in sich eine Triebfeder abgebe, sondern was, so fern es eine solche ist, sie im Gemüthe wirkt (besser zu sagen, wirken muß), a priori anzuzeigen haben"; CprR pp. 198–199.

5.3 Moral Sense and Moral Feeling

In the last chapter I analysed how, in the context of the fundamental faculties, Kant introduces the faculty of feeling pleasure and displeasure (Gefühl der Lust und Unlust) between the faculty of cognition (Erkenntnisvermögen), on the one hand, and the faculty of desire (Begehrungsvermögen), on the other hand. Furthermore, I analysed how Kant underlines the differences between the faculty of feeling and the faculty of sense (Sinn) in a way that feeling is nonetheless not involved in anything that the subject uses for reaching some cognition of the object (as is the case for sense), even though with each of these terms he designates a specific form of the more general faculty of sensibility (Sinnlichkeit). Feeling rather involves only a subjective relation, i.e. it only has to do with the effect of the representation of an object upon the subject's mind.[661]

These considerations and, in particular, the distinction between the general faculties of sense and feeling, are deeply relevant in order to comprehend the distinction between moral feeling (moralisches Gefühl) and moral sense (moralischer Sinn) in Kant's philosophy, since the distinctive aspects of the general faculties of sense and feeling hold also in the moral application of these faculties.

This difference is still not prominent in the first half of Kant's works in the 1760s, when the notion of moral sense, as had been proposed by the philosophers of the British "moral sense school", played a role also in Kant's thoughts on ethics.[662] Nonetheless, already in the '70s and afterwards very clearly also in the twelfth section of the Introduction to the Doctrine of Virtue Kant notes that:

---

661 Cf. my analysis in chapter 4 above and, among others, MS, AA 06: 211 f. (footnote).

662 For the influence of the moral sense School on Kant's work see in particular UDGTM, AA 02: 300.19–25 and NEV, AA 02: 311.24–29. There are many works on the influence of the moral sense school on the evolution of Kant's thought. I limit myself here to mention the following ones: among the articles, cf. D. HENRICH, "Hutcheson und Kant", cit.; D. HENRICH, "Kants früheste Ethik", cit.; JENS KULENKAMPFF, "Moralisches Gefühl oder moral sense – wie berechtigt ist Kants Kritik?", in *Jahrbuch für Recht und Ethik/Annual Review of Law and Ethics*, 12 (2004), pp. 234–251; LUC LANGLOIS, "Du sentiment moral à la raison pratique", cit.; G. LUNATI, "Il significato del "sentimento" nel pensiero morale del Kant precritico", cit.; A. MURRAY MAC-BEATH, "Kant on Moral Feeling", in *Kant-Studien*, 64 (1973), pp. 283–314. Among the books, cf. the classic work by J. SCHMUCKER, *Die Ursprünge der Ethik Kants in seinen vorkritischen Schriften und Reflektionen*, cit., and HELKE PANKNIN-SCHAPPERT, *Innerer Sinn und moralisches Gefühl – Zur Bedeutung eines Begriffspaares bei Shaftesbury und Hutcheson sowie in Kants vorkritischen Schriften*, Hildesheim-Zürich-New York, Olms 2007. Among the dissertations, cf. JANINE MARIE GRENBERG, *Moral Feeling and Human Autonomy: A Kantian Account of Action*, Dissertation, Emory University, 1996; MING-HUEI LEE, *Das Problem des moralischen Gefühls in der Entwicklung der Kantischen Ethik*, Dissertation, Bonn 1997; CHAN-GOO PARK, *Das moralische Gefühl in der britischen moral-sense-Schule und bei Kant*, Dissertation, Tübingen 1995.

> It is inappropriate to call this feeling [= moral feeling] a moral *sense*, for by the word 'sense' is usually understood a theoretical capacity for perception (*Wahrnehmungsvermögen*) directed toward an object, whereas moral feeling (like pleasure and displeasure in general) is something merely subjective, which yields no cognition [...]. We no more have a special *sense* (*Sinn*) for what is (morally) good and evil than for *truth*, although people often speak in this fashion. We have, rather, a *susceptibility* on the part of free choice to be moved by pure practical reason (and its law), and this is what we call moral feeling (*Gefühl*).[663]

In this passage from the *Doctrine of Virtue*, as is the case in other published works, for instance in the *Groundwork of the Metaphysics of Morals* and in the *Critique of Practical Reason*, Kant states that there is no possibility of grounding ethics on a sense (*Sinn*). In this way, he aims to underline that, if a moral sense (*moralischer Sinn*), i. e. a faculty for perceiving moral good and evil, existed, then this faculty would have to be directed towards an object and would then yield some sort of cognition, i.e. a moral cognition. The fact that Kant uses the word "sense" (*Sinn*) to refer to an alleged (but not existing) faculty of moral cognition testifies to this. More precisely, if a moral sense were given, then this moral sense would have to shed light on the objects of moral good and evil. However, according to Kant the existence of such a faculty cannot be verified: the possibility of proving the existence of the faculty of moral sense is chimerical and there is no way of showing that human beings are provided with such a faculty.

As I shortly showed before, Kant's opinion is in this case different from the one that he holds in the first half of the Sixties, as some examples will now show. For instance, in the *Inquiry Concerning the Distinctness of the Principles of Natural Theology and Morality / Untersuchung über die Deutlichkeit der Grundsätze der natürlichen Theologie und Moral* (1762) Kant states that the human being might be provided with a faculty for perceiving good and evil and he is also inclined to believe that ethics can be derived from this faculty.[664] At the end of the

---

663 MS, TL, AA 06: 400. 05–20: "Dieses [moralische] Gefühl einen moralischen Sinn zu nennen ist nicht schicklich; denn unter dem Wort Sinn wird gemeiniglich ein theoretisches, auf einen Gegenstand bezogenes Wahrnehmungsvermögen verstanden: dahingegen das moralische Gefühl (wie Lust und Unlust überhaupt) etwas blos Subjectives ist, was kein Erkenntniß abgiebt [...]. Wir haben aber für das (sittlich-) Gute und Böse eben so wenig einen besonderen Sinn, als wir einen solchen für die Wahrheit haben, ob man sich gleich oft so ausdrückt, sondern Empfänglichkeit der freien Willkür für die Bewegung derselben durch praktische reine Vernunft (und ihr Gesetz), und das ist es, was wir das moralische Gefühl nennen"; DV p. 529. But see also Kant's position against a 'moral sense' in GMS, AA 04: 443 f. and in Refl 806, AA 15: 353.

664 Cf. UDGTM, AA 02. 299.19–21: "Man hat es nämlich in unsern Tagen allererst einzusehen angefangen: daß das Vermögen, das Wahre vorzustellen, die Erkenntniß, dasjenige aber, das Gute zu empfinden, das Gefühl sei, und daß beide ja nicht mit einander müssen verwechselt

Inquiry Kant nonetheless still appears undecided about the reference to a moral sense and wonders whether it is the faculty of cognition or a feeling that provides moral principles.[665] Afterwards, in the *Announcement of the Programme of His Lectures for the Winter Semester 1765–1766 / Nachricht von der Einrichtung seiner Vorlesungen in dem Winterhalbenjahre von 1765–1766*, Kant stresses that, in his lectures, he will shed light on the attempts by Shaftesbury, Hutcheson and Hume and these attempts will be further complemented and meliorated by means of Baumgarten's moral philosophical theories.[666] The development of Kant's ethics and its relation to the moral sense philosophers in the first half of the Sixties is, thus, quite complex, as the few texts quoted testify.[667] However, on the one hand, some studies on the developmental history of Kant's ethics can already be found in the secondary literature and, in addition to this and most importantly, a study of the debts of Kant's moral theory and of the works composed by him in the Sixties would cause me to lose the thread of my analysis dedicated to moral feeling in the published critical works.[668] This is why I limit myself to underlining these few attempts by Kant to assimilate some of the suggestions of the British moral sense school into the traditional universalistic and rational ethical doctrines, with which he was acquainted mainly by means of Baumgarten's texts.

---

werden". Kant further notes that "Hutcheson und andere haben unter dem Namen des moralischen Gefühls [...] einen Anfang zu schönen Bemerkungen geliefert" (UDGTM, AA 02. 300.23–25).

665 Vgl. UDGTM, AA 02. 300.26–33.

666 Cf. *M. Immanuel Kants Nachricht von der Einrichtung seiner Vorlesungen in dem Winterhalbenjahre von 1765–1766*, AA 02, 311.24–29: "Die Versuche des Shaftesbury, Hutcheson und Hume, welche, obzwar unvollendet und mangelhaft, gleichwohl noch am weitesten in der Aufsuchung der ersten Gründe aller Sittlichkeit gelangt sind, werden diejenige Präcision und Ergänzung erhalten, die ihnen mangelt".

667 Bacin speaks of an "eclectic approach" for Kant's way of combining "perspectives of divergent systems" in order to "accomplish new solutions to fundamental theoretical problems"; cf. STEFANO BACIN, *Il senso dell'etica. Kant e la costruzione di una teoria morale*, Naples, Istituto Italiano per gli Studi Storici – Il Mulino 2006, in particular p. 14.

668 For the development of Kant's ethics cf. among others FRIEDRICH WILHELM FOERSTER, *Der Entwicklungsgang der Kantischen Ethik bis zur Kritik der reinen Vernunft*, Berlin, Mayer & Müller 1893; DIETER HENRICH, "Über Kants Entwicklungsgeschichte", in *Philosophische Rundschau*, 13 (1965), pp. 252–263; PAUL MENZER, "Der Entwicklungsgang der Kantischen Ethik in den Jahren 1760 bis 1785", in *Kant-Studien*, 2 (1898), pp. 290–322–3 (1899), pp. 41–104; PAUL ARTHUR SCHILPP, *Kant's Pre-Critical Ethics*, Evanston, North-Western University Press 1960 (chapter IV, pp. 22–40) [this is a controversial account of Kant's pre-critical ethics – cf. for instance: KEITH WARD, *The Development of Kant's View of Ethics*, Oxford, Blackwell 1972]; J. SCHMUCKER, *Die Ursprünge der Ethik Kants*, cit., pp. 52–98.

Both the *Remarks on the Observations on the Feeling of the Beautiful and the Sublime / Bemerkungen zu den Beobachtungen über das Gefühl des Schönen und Erhabenen* (January 1764-December 1765) and the *Dreams of a Spirit-Seer Elucidated by Dreams of Metaphysics / Träumen eines Geistersehers, erläutert durch die Träume der Metaphysik* (1766) prepares the way for an assimilation of rationalism and sentimentalism in Kant's moral theory.[669] Afterward, in 1770 Kant clearly assesses that the existence of a faculty for the cognition of the objects of moral good and evil is not given: in the *Inaugural Disseration* (§§ 7ff.) he states that "moral concepts [...] are cognized not by experiencing them but by the pure understanding itself" and that "moral philosophy [...] is only cognized by the pure understanding".[670] From this text on, i.e. also afterwards in both the *Groundwork of the Metaphysics of Morals* and the *Critique of Practical Reason*, Kant holds that the emotional sphere cannot grant the necessary universality required by moral theory, even though this very emotional sphere still has to be considered in the context of moral theory: after 1770 it is clear to Kant that the grounding role of the emotional sphere must be clearly ruled out and there is no possibility of grounding morals on heteronomous principles, such as a sense or feelings.[671]

Nonetheless, a question still remains unanswered, i.e. the one concerning the place of moral feeling in ethics, since this concept does not vanish from Kant's texts. Neither the fact that (A) a moral sense (as a faculty for perceiving moral good and evil) is excluded from Kant's reflections on morals, nor the fact that (B) ethics cannot be grounded on the emotional sphere, implies (C) the ban of the emotional sphere and of moral feeling, in particular, from Kant's ethics. Nonetheless, during the middle of the Sixties the emotional

---

669 Cf. Bemerkungen zu GSE, AA 20: 145.06 – 12; AA 20: 145.16 – 23; AA 20: 146.02 – 09; AA 20: 137.01 – 02; AA 20: 168.07 – 15; TG, AA 02: 335.03 – 15.

670 Cf. MSI (*De mundi sensibilis atque intelligibilis forma et principiis*), AA 02: 385 – 419; English translation: IMMANUEL KANT, *Inaugural Dissertation (On the Form and Principles of the Sensible and the Intelligible World)*, in *Theoretical Philosophy, 1755 – 1770*, edited and translated by DAVID WALFORD, in collaboration with RALF MEERBOTE, Cambridge/New York, Cambridge University Press 1992, pp. 373 – 416. Here in particular § 7, AA 02: 395.08 – 09: "conceptus morales non experiundo, sed per ipsum intellectum purum cogniti [sunt]"; § 9, AA 02: 396.04 – 06: "Philosophia [...] moralis [...] non cognoscitur nisi per intellectum purum"; English translation pp. 387 – 388.

671 From the *Inaugural Dissertation* (1770) Kant considers reason (*Vernunft*) to be the *principium dijudicationis* in ethics – see also the *Moralphilosophie Kaehler-Collins*, the first *Critique*, and the students' notes of Kant's lectures on anthropology from the 1770ies (e.g. *Anthropologie Friedländer*, AA 25: 649: "Das Vermögen nach Grundsätzen und Maximen zu handeln, beruht darauf, daß der Mensch nach Begriffen handeln kann").

sphere, by means of moral sense, might have played a role as *principium dijudi-cationis* in Kant's moral theory, after 1770 this is not the case anymore: even in the most important works on ethics (in the *Groundwork*, in the second *Critique* or in the *Doctrine of Virtue*) where moral feeling (instead of moral sense) is mentioned, Kant describes it as a concept that has to be analysed in the context of the *Triebfeder* of practical reason, i.e. in regard to the question concerning the *principium executionis*.

After 1770 Kant excludes the possibility of a faculty for perceiving moral good and evil, i.e. a *moral sense*; nevertheless, at the same time, he assigns to *moral feeling* a central role in ethics.

Even though the concept of moral feeling is analysed in the secondary literature as equivalent to the one of respect for the most part, I now aim to show that a general account of the more general concept of feeling (as it is applied in ethics) is due in order to properly understand the functioning of mental events in the process of moral motivation.

5.4 Moral Motivation, Moral Incentives, and Respect

Kant's treatment of the moral feeling of respect has to be considered within the more general problem of moral motivation. More precisely, it has to be situated in what can be designated as a phenomenological problem concerning the way in which the moral law modifies the mind of a human being who is at the same time rational and sensuous. The human being and his mental faculties are thus, in this case, again at the centre of my analysis.

The new stress on the feeling of respect and its connection to the subjective incentive of moral action testifies to the reorientation of Kant's thought concerning the subjective and objective motivating force of a moral action.

Still in the *Critique of Pure Reason*, in the Transcendental Doctrine of Method, namely in the second section (On the Ideal of the Highest Good) of the Canon of Pure Reason, Kant first describes a sort of "religious eudaemonism".[672] He notes, for instance, that "without a God and a world that is now not visible to

---

672 Cf. KrV A589–590/B617–618, A633–635/B661–663, A810–819/B838–847; AA 03: 395, 421f., 526f., 528f.; CpR pp. 562–563, 585–586, 680–684 and L. W. BECK, *Commentary*, cit., p. 214: Kant seems "to have been so torn between two incompatible doctrines of the moral motive [...] that we find him espousing each of them on a single page"; but also SERGIO LANDUCCI, *Sull'etica di Kant*, Milano, Guerini e Associati 1994, p. 127: "Kant adottò la soluzione più a portata di mano, per individuare un movente della moralità [...]: il timor di Dio (e, s'intende, la speranza in lui)".

us but is hoped for, the majestic ideas of morality are, to be sure, objects of approbation and admiration but not incentives (*Triebfedern*) for resolve and realisation".[673] And, afterwards, he further notes that "happiness alone is far from the complete good for our reason".[674]

A different analysis is to be found in the *Groundwork of the Metaphysics of Morals*. There, Kant deals with the problem of the bindingness of the moral law and, in the Transition from Metaphysics of Morals to the Critique of Pure Practical Reason (more precisely, in the sections where he speaks Of the Interest Attaching to the Ideas of Morality and On the Extreme Boundary of All Practical Philosophy),[675] Kant aims to answer the related questions "why the universal validity of our maxim as a law must be the limiting condition of our action, and on what we base the worth we assign to this way of acting" and "how it happens that a human being believes that only through this does he feel his personal worth".[676] In sum, Kant wonders how human beings can take an interest in morality, i.e. he deals with a problem which is linked to the question: how can the moral law be itself an incentive for a rational and sensuous being? Even though he sustains the "impossibility of discovering and making comprehensible an *interest* which the human being can take in moral laws", Kant nevertheless affirms that the human being "does really take an interest in them, the foundation of which in us we call moral feeling".[677] Against the theory of the British philosophers who believed that a moral sense might constitute "the standard for our

---

673 KrV, A812–813/B840–841, AA 03: 527.26–29: "Ohne also einen Gott und eine für uns jetzt nicht sichtbare, aber gehoffte Welt sind die herrlichen Ideen der Sittlichkeit zwar Gegenstände des Beifalls und der Bewunderung, aber nicht Triebfedern des Vorsatzes und der Ausübung"; CpR p. 681.

674 KrV, A813/B841, AA 03: 527.33–34: "Glückseligkeit allein ist für unsere Vernunft bei weitem nicht das vollständige Gut"; CpR p. 681.

675 Cf. GMS, AA 04: 448–453, 455–463; *Groundwork*, pp. 96–100, 101–108.

676 GMS, AA 04: 449.32–36, 450.01–02: "warum denn die Allgemeingültigkeit unserer Maxime, als eines Gesetzes, die einschränkende Bedingung unserer Handlungen sein müsse, und worauf wir den Werth gründen, den wir dieser Art zu handeln beilegen, der so groß sein soll, daß es überall kein höheres Interesse geben kann, und wie es zugehe, daß der Mensch dadurch allein seinen persönlichen Werth zu fühlen glaubt, gegen den der eines angenehmen oder unangenehmen Zustandes für nichts zu halten sei"; *Groundwork*, p. 97.

677 GMS, AA 04: 459.32–33, 460.01–03: "Die subjective Unmöglichkeit, die Freiheit des Willens zu erklären, ist mit der Unmöglichkeit, ein Interesse ausfindig und begreiflich zu machen, welches der Mensch an moralischen Gesetzen nehmen könne, einerlei; und gleichwohl nimmt er wirklich daran ein Interesse, wozu wir die Grundlage in uns das moralische Gefühl nennen"; *Groundwork*, pp. 105–106.

moral appraisal", Kant states that moral feeling "must rather be regarded as the subjective effect (*die subjective Wirkung*) that the law exercises".[678]

I will show how Kant more precisely focuses on moral feeling in the second *Critique*, where he describes moral feeling as an effect on the faculty of feeling, i.e. a modification of this very faculty. However, before showing this, by means of the analysis of the *Triebfeder*-chapter of the second *Critique*, let me first have a closer look at Kant's theory of moral motivation in the *Groundwork* and, in particular, at Kant's account of moral feeling and the connected concept of respect (*Achtung*) in this work.[679]

In the last passage quoted we read that human beings take an *interest* in moral laws and that the foundation of this interest is called moral feeling. In a note where Kant diffusely explains what respect is, he says that "all so-called *moral interest* consists simply in *respect* for the law (*Achtung fürs Gesetz*)" and further explains that "though respect is a feeling, it is not one *received* by means of influence; it is, instead, a feeling *self-wrought* by means of a rational concept and therefore specifically different from all feelings of the first kind, which can be reduced to inclination or fear".[680] At this stage of his explanation, Kant aims to clarify that "an action from duty is to put aside entirely the influence of inclination and with it every object of the will; hence there is left for the will nothing that could determine it except objectively (*objective*) the *law* and subjectively (*subjective*) pure respect (*reine Achtung*) for this practical law".[681]

---

678 Cf. GMS, AA 04: 460.03–07; *Groundwork*, p. 106.

679 Kant sometimes also uses reverence [*Ehrfurcht*] to refer to the concept of respect [Achtung], for instance in the famous passage of the starry heavens: "Zwei Dinge erfüllen das Gemüth mit immer neuer und zunehmender Bewunderung und Ehrfurcht, je öfter und anhaltender sich das Nachdenken damit beschäftigt: der bestirnte Himmel über mir und das moralische Gesetz in mir", KpV AA 05: 161.33–36, CprR p. 269. Also in consideration of such passages, Paton suggests to translate the German word "Achtung" with the English term "reverence": "It is obvious to any attentive reader that Kant himself feels most intensively this emotion of reverence for the law, and that both from his description and from the language he uses the feeling in question is something almost akin to religious emotion. For this reason I have translated the German word Achtung by "reverence" and not by the word "respect", which is commonly used by English translators. [...] Its similarity to religious emotion is shown, I think, by the fact that in it I feel at once humbled and also uplifted or exalted", HERBERT J. PATON, *The Categorical Imperative. A Study in Kant's Moral Philosophy*, first edition London 1947, reprint (among others): Philadelphia (Penn.), University of Pennsylvania Press 1971, pp. 63–64. However, in my analysis I prefer the more traditional translation (respect), which has a less religious connotation.

680 GMS, AA 04: 401 (*passim*); *Groundwork*, p. 56. The term *Achtung* also occurs in GMS, AA 04: 403, 407–408.

681 GMS, AA 04: 400.30–33: "Nun soll eine Handlung aus Pflicht den Einfluß der Neigung und mit ihr jeden Gegenstand des Willens ganz absondern, also bleibt nichts für den Willen übrig,

The meaning of this passage becomes even clearer if we remember Kant's distinction between the objective ground of an action, which he calls "motive"/"determining ground" (*Bewegungsgrund/Bestimmungsgrund*), and the subjective motivating force, which he calls "incentive" (*Triebfeder*).[682] According to this distinction, Kant refers to respect as the incentive of a moral action and to the moral law as the determining ground of this action.

With this quick look at the *Groundwork*, we have already found some noteworthy assertions concerning the concepts of moral feeling and respect. Some of them are:

(A) Moral feeling (*moralisches Gefühl*) is linked to an interest in the moral law (in this passage Kant does not use the word respect);[683]

(B) Moral feeling (*moralisches Gefühl*) must "be regarded as the subjective effect (*die subjective Wirkung*) that the law exercises on the will";[684]

(C) Respect for the law (*Achtung fürs Gesetz*) is a feeling;[685]

(D) Respect for the law (*Achtung fürs Gesetz*) is the "so-called *moral interest*";[686]

---

was ihn bestimmen könne, als objectiv das Gesetz und subjectiv reine Achtung für dieses praktische Gesetz"; *Groundwork*, pp. 55–56.

682 Cf. GMS, AA 04: 427.26–30: "Der subjective Grund des Begehrens ist die Triebfeder, der objective des Wollens der Bewegungsgrund; daher der Unterschied zwischen subjectiven Zwecken, die auf Triebfedern beruhen, und objectiven, die auf Bewegungsgründe ankommen, welche für jedes vernünftige Wesen gelten"; *Groundwork*, p. 79. Already in the *Groundwork* Kant uses the term *Bestimmungsgrund* instead of *Bewegungsgrund* in order to refer to the determining ground of the action. Cf. GMS, AA 04: 459, note: "Ein unmittelbares Interesse nimmt die Vernunft nur alsdann an der Handlung, wenn die Allgemeingültigkeit der Maxime derselben ein gnugsamer Bestimmungsgrund des Willens ist"; *Groundwork*, p. 105. In the second *Critique* Kant uses nearly exclusively (and more than a hundred times) the term *Bestimmungsgrund* instead of *Bewegungsgrund*. See e. g. KpV, AA 05: 109.17–18: "Das moralische Gesetz ist der alleinige Bestimmungsgrund des reinen Willens".

683 GMS, AA 04: 460.01–03: "[der Mensch] nimmt wirklich daran [= an moralischen Gesetzen] ein Interesse, wozu wir die Grundlage in uns das moralische Gefühl nennen"; *Groundwork*, p. 106.

684 GMS, AA 04: 460.05–06; *Groundwork*, p. 106 (passage already quoted).

685 GMS, AA 04: 401 (footnote): "Man könnte mir vorwerfen, als suchte ich hinter dem Worte Achtung nur Zuflucht in einem dunkelen Gefühle, anstatt durch einen Begriff der Vernunft in der Frage deutliche Auskunft zu geben. Allein wenn Achtung gleich ein Gefühl ist, so ist es doch kein durch Einfluß empfangenes, sondern durch einen Vernunftbegriff selbstgewirktes Gefühl und daher von allen Gefühlen der ersteren Art, die sich auf Neigung oder Furcht bringen lassen, specifisch unterschieden"; *Groundwork*, p. 56.

686 GMS, AA 04: 401, footnote: "Alles moralische so genannte Interesse besteht lediglich in der Achtung fürs Gesetz"; *Groundwork*, p. 56.

(E) Pure respect for the practical law (*reine Achtung fürs practische Gesetz*) can subjectively (*subjective*) determine the will.[687]

As I already mentioned, Kant analyses the concept of respect and, more generally, the concept of feeling in relation to the moral field, most precisely in the second *Critique*, namely in the third chapter of the Analytic of Pure Practical Reason, *On the Incentives of Pure Practical Reason*.[688] There Kant assesses that
(A1) "respect for the moral law [is] an effect on feeling"[689] and that
(B1) "respect for the law is not the incentive to morality; instead it is morality itself subjectively considered as an incentive".[690]

These two points are connected to each other and, in turn, have to do with the interpretation of (1) what respect exactly is, (2) why Kant says that it is a feeling and at the same time an effect on feeling, and (3) whether moral feeling actually is the incentive of human moral action.

5.5 Respect, Incentive, Feeling

In my analysis I will now consider the last of the points mentioned, i. e. whether respect or rather the moral law is the incentive of a moral action. Here, Kant's opinion regarding the way of solving the problem concerning the incentive (*Triebfeder*) of a moral action seems somehow ambiguous. Let me first consider some passages from the chapter dedicated to the incentives of pure reason from the second *Critique*. The first passage is the just mentioned one:
(1) "respect for the law is not the incentive to morality; instead it is morality itself subjectively considered as an incentive".[691] The second passage reads, instead:

---

687 GMS, AA 04: 400.32–33: "...also bleibt nichts für den Willen übrig, was ihn bestimmen könne, als objectiv das Gesetz und subjectiv reine Achtung für dieses praktische Gesetz"; *Groundwork*, p. 56.
688 *Drittes Hauptstück. Von den Triebfedern der reinen praktischen Vernunft*, KpV, AA 05: 71–89; CprR pp. 198–211.
689 KpV, AA 05: 76.09: "die Achtung [ist] eine Wirkung aufs Gefühl"; CprR, p. 201.
690 Cf. KpV, AA 05: 76.04–08; CprR, p. 201.
691 KpV, AA 05: 76.04–05: "Und so ist die Achtung fürs Gesetz nicht Triebfeder zur Sittlichkeit, sondern sie ist die Sittlichkeit selbst"; CprR, p. 201.

(2) "respect for the moral law is the sole and also the undoubted moral incentive".[692]

(3) A third passage, also from the second *Critique*, reads as follows:

Respect for the moral law must be regarded [...] as a subjective ground of activity – that is, as the incentive to compliance with the law – and as the ground for maxims of a course of life in conformity with it.[693]

(4) Eventually, the last passage I aim to consider reads as follows:

From the concept of an incentive arises that of an interest, which can never be attributed to any being unless it has reason and which signifies an incentive of the will insofar as it is presented by reason. Since in a morally good will the law itself must be the incentive, the moral interest is a pure sensefree interest of practical reason alone.[694]

One might wonder: is the moral law both the objective ground (*Bewegungsgrund/ Bestimmungsgrund*) and the subjective ground (the incentive – *Triebfeder*) of moral action?

As Beck notes, "it is regrettable that Kant was not more careful [on this question]; though, had he been so, the race of Kant-commentators would have been unemployed".[695] The commentators of this passage certainly had a lot to say, as the long list of publication on this topic shows.[696] However, the directions of the interpretive readings dedicated to the doctrine of respect as an incentive in the second *Critique* can be basically divided into two big groups, i.e. into the group of internalist readings [I] and the group of externalistic readings [II].[697]

[I] According to the first reading, "'respect' for the moral law is just a term for denoting the immediate action of the very moral law on the human will (or, better said, the power of choice)".[698] This term alludes to a "feeling" but it is actual-

---

692 KpV, AA 05: 78.20 – 21: "Achtung fürs moralische Gesetz ist also die einzige und zugleich unbezweifelte moralische Triebfeder"; CprR, p. 203.

693 KpV, AA 05: 79.14 – 19: "Also muß die Achtung fürs moralische Gesetz [...] als subjectiver Grund der Thätigkeit, d. i. als Triebfeder zu Befolgung desselben, und als Grund zu Maximen eines ihm gemäßen Lebenswandels angesehen werden"; CprR, p. 204.

694 KpV, AA 05: 79.19 – 24: "Aus dem Begriffe einer Triebfeder entspringt der eines Interesse, welches niemals einem Wesen, als was Vernunft hat, beigelegt wird und eine Triebfeder des Willens bedeutet, so fern sie durch Vernunft vorgestellt wird. Da das Gesetz selbst in einem moralisch guten Willen die Triebfeder sein muß, so ist das moralische Interesse ein reines sinnenfreies Interesse der bloßen praktischen Vernunft"; CprR, p. 204.

695 L. W. Beck, *Commentary*, cit., p. 221.

696 Cf. note 641 above.

697 Cf. S. Landucci, *Sull'etica di Kant*, cit., p. 135.

698 S. Landucci, *Sull'etica di Kant*, cit., p. 135, my translation.

ly rather only a synonym for denoting the consciousness of the moral law.[699] This first reading is proposed, among others, by L. W. Beck, according to whom the consciousness of the moral law can be considered the incentive of moral action.[700]

Since (A) consciousness of the moral law corresponds to the moral feeling of respect and since (B) consciousness of the moral law corresponds to the incentive of moral action, then (C) the moral feeling of respect corresponds to the incentive of moral action: "to know what the law requires and to feel respect for it [...] are, for Kant, identical".[701]

[II] According to the second reading, instead, it is necessary to consider respect as a "term which actually mediates between the moral law [...] and the determination of the will to obey the law".[702] In this case, respect is "a proper *feeling*, even though a unique sort of feeling", which can determine the will.[703]

The most clear evidence which might support this second reading is to be found in the two passages quoted above, where Kant says that (1) "respect for the moral law is the sole and also the undoubted moral incentive"[704] and that (3) "respect for the moral law must be regarded [...] as a subjective ground of activity – that is, as the incentive to compliance with the law".[705]

Nonetheless, in the very text (4) that follows this last quotation, Kant speaks in a way that clearly contradicts this second reading and rather seems to support the first reading, for he underlines that "in a morally good will the law itself must be the incentive".[706]

As many other passages show, the interpretation of the incentive-problematic is quite complicated.[707] In order to shed light on this interpretive difficulty, let

---

699 S. Landucci, *Sull'etica di Kant*, cit., p. 135, my translation.

700 Cf. L. W. Beck, *Commentary*, cit., p. 221.

701 L. W. Beck, *Commentary*, cit., p. 222: "Hence we must ask: What is the nature of the consciousness of the law, such that it can be the incentive? If the *Critique* [*of Practical Reason*] leaves any room for doubt on this, it is removed by the *Metaphysics of Morals*. There Kant says: 'The respect for the law, which is, subjectively, called the moral feeling, is identical with the consciousness of our duty' [MS, TL, AA 06: 464]".

702 S. Landucci, *Sull'etica di Kant*, cit., p. 135, my translation.

703 S. Landucci, *Sull'etica di Kant*, cit., p. 135, my translation.

704 KpV, AA 05: 78.20 – 21; CprR, p. 203 (passage already quoted).

705 KpV, AA 05: 79.13 – 19; CprR, p. 204 (passage already quoted).

706 KpV, AA 05: 79.22 – 23; CprR, p. 204 (passage already quoted).

707 In the present chapter I limit myself to analyses some passages from the *Groundwork* and the second *Critique*. However, the complexity of this problem can also be gained by the reading of many other writings of Kant. Among others, the text *Über den Gemeinspruch: Das mag in der Theorie richtig sein, taugt aber nicht für die Praxis* (1793) [AA 08: 273 – 313] should be mentioned, since there Kant develops his ideas on the concept of *Triebfeder* in reply to a critique of Christian

me briefly report Kant's treatment of the concepts of moral feeling and respect in the *Triebfeder*-chapter.

Kant first speaks of a feeling of displeasure as the negative effect of the law on human inclinations. This displeasure is caused by the moral law, in that this law restricts and humiliates all human inclinations and first causes a sort of decline of self-esteem (even though, this self-esteem is a "false" esteem in that it is directed only to the sensible self of the human being and its inclinations):

> First the moral law determines the will objectively and immediately in the judgement of reason; but freedom, the causality of which is determinable only through the law, consists just in this: that it restricts all inclinations, and consequently the esteem of the person himself, to the condition of compliance with its pure law. This restriction now has an effect on feeling and produces the feeling of displeasure which can be cognized a priori from the moral law. [...] The effect of this law on feeling is merely humiliation (*Demüthigung*), which we can thus discern *a priori* though we cannot cognize in it the force of the pure practical law as an incentive but only a resistance to incentives of sensibility.[708]

In turn, Kant describes the other side of the coin and refers to the positive transformation of a human being's faculty of feeling. He refers namely to a pleasure, a feeling that contains something elevating, which is connected to the fact that the law shows the human being the way to free himself from the constraints of sensible inclinations. In this case, Kant calls this feeling respect and states that this feeling evokes self-approbation in the human being caused by the fact that he recognizes himself as determined solely by the law and by no other interests:

> But the same law is yet objectively – that is, in the representation of pure reason – an immediate determining ground of the will, so that this humiliation takes place only relatively to the purity of the law; accordingly, the lowering of pretensions to moral self-esteem – that is, humiliation on the sensible side – is an elevation (*Erhebung*) of the moral – that is, prac-

---

Garve (Garve's reviews can be found in ALBERT LANDAU (ed.), *Rezensionen zur kantischen Philosophie*, Bebra, Landau 1991).

708 KpV, AA 05: 78.22–29; 34–37, 79.01: "Zuerst bestimmt das moralische Gesetz objectiv und unmittelbar den Willen im Urtheile der Vernunft; Freiheit, deren Causalität blos durchs Gesetz bestimmbar ist, besteht aber eben darin, daß sie alle Neigungen, mithin die Schätzung der Person selbst auf die Bedingung der Befolgung ihres reinen Gesetzes einschränkt. Diese Einschränkung [der Neigungen] thut nun eine Wirkung aufs Gefühl und bringt Empfindung der Unlust hervor, die aus dem moralischen Gesetze a priori erkannt werden kann. [...] Die Wirkung dieses Gesetzes aufs Gefühl [ist] blos Demüthigung welche wir also zwar a priori einsehen, aber an ihr nicht die Kraft des reinen praktischen Gesetzes als Triebfeder, sondern nur den Widerstand gegen Triebfedern der Sinnlichkeit erkennen können"; CprR, p. 203.

tical – esteem for the law itself on the intellectual side; in a word, it is respect for the law, and so also a feeling that is positive in its intellectual cause, which is known *a priori*.[709]

The feeling of respect is, thus, a feeling of pleasure, which occurs at the same time with the mental state of displeasure, i.e. the feeling of humiliation (*Demüthigung*).

In the last quotation Kant clearly states that the law can be, objectively, the determining ground of the will. Nonetheless, there he does not refer to any subjective determining ground. Respect is only described as a feeling. There is no reference to it working as incentive. In the same way, respect is described again only in terms of a special sort of feeling in a longer passage as well, where Kant states that "the law that demands this respect and also inspires it is [...] none other than the moral law" and adds that, moreover, "the feeling that arises from consciousness of this necessitation is not pathological [...] but practical only, that is, possible through a preceding (objective) determination of the will and causality of reason".[710]

Also in this passage, as earlier, Kant refers to the fact that this feeling is possible only by means of a "preceding (objective) determination of the will and causality of reason" and, in this way, he underlines once again the role of the moral law as the objective determining ground of action. Nonetheless, here Kant says nothing about the possibility of respect being the subjective ground of human moral action.

A domain of uncertainty is left by another passage, where Kant clearly refers to the moral law as the determining ground of the action but further mentions respect in the following way:

> The moral law is [...] for the will of a perfect being a law of holiness, but for the will of every finite rational being a law of duty, of moral necessitation and of the determination of his action through respect for this law and reverence for his duty.[711]

---

709 KpV, AA 05: 79.01–08: "Weil aber dasselbe Gesetz doch objectiv, d. i. in der Vorstellung der reinen Vernunft, ein unmittelbarer Bestimmungsgrund des Willens ist, folglich diese Demüthigung nur relativ auf die Reinigkeit des Gesetzes stattfindet, so ist die Herabsetzung der Ansprüche der moralischen Selbstschätzung, d. i. die Demüthigung auf der sinnlichen Seite, eine Erhebung der moralischen, d. i. der praktischen Schätzung des Gesetzes selbst, auf der intellectuellen, mit einem Worte Achtung fürs Gesetz, also auch ein seiner intellectuellen Ursache nach positives Gefühl, das a priori erkannt wird"; CprR, pp. 203–204.
710 Cf. KpV, AA 05: 80.22–37; 81.01–09; CprR, pp. 203–204.
711 KpV, AA 05: 82.08–12: "Das moralische Gesetz ist nämlich für den Willen eines allervollkommensten Wesens ein Gesetz der Heiligkeit, für den Willen jedes endlichen vernünftigen Wesens aber ein Gesetz der Pflicht, der moralischen Nöthigung, und der Bestimmung der

In this passage, Kant only says that the moral law can be the determining ground of action through respect. However, from this it follows neither that the law is also the subjective ground (incentive) of the action, nor that respect is this incentive.

All in all, we are left with four clear passages concerning the subjective ground (incentive) of moral action. These passages are the ones already considered at the beginning of this section. However, now they can be eventually grouped as follows, in a way that it can be shown that two of them clearly support reading [II]:

(2) "respect for the moral law is the sole and also the undoubted moral incentive".[712]

(3) "respect for the moral law must be regarded as a subjective ground of activity – that is, as the incentive to compliance with the law".[713]

While two other passages support reading [I]:

(1) "respect for the law is not the incentive to morality; instead it is morality itself subjectively considered as an incentive [...] which alone has influence".[714]

(4) "in a morally good will the law itself must be the incentive".[715]

A definitive proof in favour of the first or the second interpretive proposal does not seem to be given. Nonetheless, in what follows I argue that reading [I] can be considered more convincing with regard to my interpretive proposal concerning some passages from the second *Critique* and, in particular, concerning Kant's thoughts on feelings in general and moral feeling in particular in the *Doctrine of Virtue*.

What I suggest, in fact, is that respect for the moral law is not the actual incentive (*Triebfeder*) of human moral action, but rather the subjective presentation of the moral law in the human being's mind.

An initial attempt in this direction has been made by Beck, who concisely observes that one of the meanings of "subjective" in the case of the moral incentive "refers to the workings of the moral principle, which is itself objective, upon

---

Handlungen desselben durch Achtung für dies Gesetz und aus Ehrfurcht für seine Pflicht"; CprR, p. 206.

712 Cf. KpV, AA 05: 78.20 – 21; CprR, p. 203 (passage already quoted).

713 Cf. KpV, AA 05: 79.13 – 19 (*passim*); CprR, p. 204 (passage already quoted).

714 Cf. KpV, AA 05: 76.04 – 08; CprR, p. 201 (passage already quoted).

715 Cf. KpV, AA 05: 79.22 – 23; CprR, p. 204 (passage already quoted).

the constitution of the human subject".[716] This way, "subjective" would merely mean "located in and thus in part depending upon the constitution of the subject".[717]

To what extent this suggestion, which Beck unfortunately does not go further into, might be promising as a clearer explanation of the concept of moral feeling and its importance becomes evident if we consider the "subjective" changes that happen in the human being's mind and if we refer to respect as the "subjective presentation" (*subjektive Darstellung*) of the moral law, as part of a "moral aesthetic" (*Ästhetik der Sitten*).[718] In other words, this becomes clear if we consider respect as the element that brings the moral law closer to the human being's everyday intuition.[719]

According to my proposal, I argue that only the moral law is the subjective incentive (*Triebfeder*) of moral action (as well as its objective ground); respect is the subjective presentation or, we might say, the sensible presentation of this incentive. Respect has not to do with the determination of the will in a moral action but only with the way in which the moral law modifies the human mind on its sensible (feeling) side.

This reading also has the advantage of clarifying the point that still remained unclear at the end of the last section, i.e. it explains why Kant can say with no contradiction that respect is, at the same time, a feeling and an effect on feeling. I argue in fact that the will (*Wille*), which corresponds to pure practical reason, gives a law, on which basis the human being, through the power of choice (*Willkür*), can formulate a moral maxim, and that to this process, which pertains to the human faculty of desire (*Begehrungsvermögen*), corresponds a change in the sensitive part of his mind (*Gefühl der Lust und Unlust*), in that the human being at the same time feels a determinate feeling, namely the feeling of respect. The feeling of respect is thus a mental state, i.e. a change in the mind of a human subject who becomes conscious of the moral law (given by the faculty of desire as lawgiving pure practical reason). This mental state is made pos-

---

716 L. W. BECK, *Commentary*, cit., pp. 216–217.

717 L. W. BECK, *Commentary*, cit., pp. 216–217.

718 Cf. MS, TL, § XIV, AA 06: 406.19–23: "Eine Ästhetik der Sitten [ist] zwar nicht ein Teil, aber doch eine subjektive Darstellung der Metaphysik derselben: wo die Gefühle, welche die nötigende Kraft des moralischen Gesetzes begleiten, jener ihre Wirksamkeit empfindbar machen"; MM, p. 534.

719 By means of an analogy, one might say that something similar happened through the three "ways of presenting the principle of morality", i.e. the three formulae of the categorical imperative, which are intended "to bring an idea of reason closer to intuition (by a certain analogy) and thereby to feeling" – GMS, AA 04: 436.12–13: "eine Idee der Vernunft der Anschauung (nach einer gewissen Analogie) und dadurch dem Gefühle näher zu bringen"; *Groundwork*, p. 85.

sible by the way in which the human subject is mentally constituted, i. e. by the constitution of the human mind as Kant maps it in his classification of the mental faculties (that I analysed in chapter 4).

What through the faculty of desire is evoked as the moral law, i. e. the decision of the good will, is evoked as the moral feeling of respect through the faculty of feeling pleasure and displeasure.

The possibility of feeling respect can be explained only by means of a reference to Kant's description of the human mind, which I have so far tried to analyse in my work. In this way, by means of a reference to Kant's theory of the faculties, I can now account for the way in which the mental state that Kant calls the feeling of respect occurs in the human mind and how it happens that the faculty of feeling pleasure and displeasure makes this feeling possible in the context of moral cases.

Eventually, the relation between the moral feeling of respect and the faculty of feeling pleasure and displeasure as I analysed it in the context of Kant's classification of the faculties has to be further considered, in order for a better understanding of Kant's "moral aesthetic" (*Ästhetik der Sitten*) to be made possible.[720] This is why I now try to shed some more light on this relation by reference to Kant's *Doctrine of Virtue*.

5.6 Feeling as Susceptibility in the *Doctrine of Virtue*

In the *Critique of Practical Reason* Kant often and clearly states that moral feeling is the effect of the moral law on the human mind and, in particular, on feeling itself: "respect for the moral law [is] an effect on feeling".[721] At first sight, Kant's statement that respect corresponds *to a feeling* (*Gefühl*) and, at the same time, *to an effect of the law on a feeling* (*Wirkung desselben aufs Gefühl*), could seem problematic. Nonetheless, this is not a problem anymore if we distinguish between a "realised" form of feeling and a "not-yet-realised" form of feeling, i. e. between respect and the faculty for feeling pleasure and displeasure in moral cases.

These distinctions help us to show why most of the studies dedicated to the role of moral feeling of respect in Kant's ethics are incomplete, since they limit themselves to merely equating the concept of moral feeling (*moralisches Gefühl*)

---

720 Cf. MS, TL, § XIV, AA 06: 406.19–21.
721 Cf. for instance KpV, AA 05: 76.09: "die Achtung [ist] eine Wirkung aufs Gefühl"; CprR, p. 201; cf. also KpV, AA 05: 79.14–15: "Achtung fürs Gesetz [muß als] Wirkung desselben aufs Gefühl angesehen werden", CprR, p. 204.

and the concept of respect (*Achtung*) without appropriately stressing the relation between the faculty for feeling pleasure and displeasure in its application in the context of moral cases and the moral feeling of respect for the law as the effect of the moral law on the mentioned faculty.[722]

What I mean is that Kant is allowed to speak of respect as feeling and as an effect on feeling at the same time since the expression "moral feeling" (*moralische Gefühl*) denotes both the *faculty of feeling* (*Gefühl der Lust oder Unlust als Vermögen*) in its application to moral cases and the *feeling of respect for the moral law* (*der moralische Gefühlszustand der Achtung fürs Gesetz*) that is made possible by this very faculty.

This reading might also be used to interpret those passages, where Kant refers to moral feeling also as a "capacity to take an interest in the moral law". Kant expresses himself in these terms already in the second *Critique*.[723] However, this connotation of moral feeling as a "capacity" is depicted well afterwards in the *Doctrine of Virtue*.[724]

---

722 Only very few authors have already made a clear distinction between *Achtung* and *Gefühl*. Cf. L. W. BECK, *Commentary*, cit., pp. 224–225; MING-HUEI LEE, *Das Problem des moralischen Gefühls in der Entwicklung der Kantischen Ethik*, Dissertation, Bonn 1986; FRIEDRICH F. BREZINA, *Die Achtung. Ethik und Moral der Achtung und Unterwerfung bei Immanuel Kant, Ernst Tugendhat, Ursula Wolf und Peter Singer*, Frankfurt a. M., Lang 1998; THOMAS HÖWING, *Praktische Lust. Kant über das Verhältnis von Fühlen, Begehren und praktischer Vernunft*, Berlin/Boston, de Gruyter 2013; HEINER F. KLEMME, "Fühlen, Begehren, Erkennen – Selbstbesitz. Reflexionen über die Verbindung der Vermögen in Kants Lehre vom Kategorischen Imperativ", in INGA RÖMER (ed.), *Affektivität und Ethik bei Kant und in der Phänomenologie*, Berlin/Boston, de Gruyter 2014 (forthcoming); DIETER SCHÖNECKER (with ALEXANDER COTTER, MAGDALENA ECKES, SEBASTIAN MALY), "Kant über Menschenliebe als moralische Gemütsanlage", in *Archiv für Geschichte der Philosophie*, 92 (2010), pp. 133–175. In addition, cf. my articles on the topic: A. FALDUTO, "Das Gefühl als Empfänglichkeit und die Bedeutung einer Ästhetik der Sitten", cit.; A. FALDUTO, "The Two Meanings of moralisches Gefühl in Kant's Doctrine of Virtue", cit..

723 Cf. KpV, AA 05: 80.08–18; CprR, p. 204.

724 L. W. BECK, *Commentary*, cit., pp. 224–225: Beck notes that in the *Metaphysics of Morals* Kant discusses feeling as a potentiality [*Empfänglichkeit*]. Nonetheless, he explains it by saying that the moral feeling of the *Doctrine of Virtue* does not correspond to the "feeling as a phenomenological state of consciousness", i.e. as moral feeling as respect is analysed in the second *Critique*. Even if I do not agree with this neat distinction of Kant's account of moral feeling in second *Critique* and the *Doctrine of Virtue*, it is nonetheless noteworthy what Beck notes about the concept of "*Empfänglichkeit*": "Naturally, this must precede, logically or temporally, the actual feeling of respect. But this statement does not conflict, except verbally, with the statement that there is 'no antecedent feeling tending to morality'; it is as if one were to say in English, 'A man must have feeling before he can have feeling' – perhaps a not very lucid way of saying a single thing, but certainly no evidence of fundamental confusion in the speaker's mind".

In this sense, in particular in the twelfth section of the Introduction to the *Doctrine of Virtue*, dedicated to the "Concepts of What Is Presupposed on the Part of Feeling by the Mind's Receptivity to Concepts of Duty As Such" (*Ästhetische Vorbegriffe der Empfänglichkeit des Gemüths für Pflichtbegriffe überhaupt*), deserves very close consideration.[725]

This section has received very little attention in Kant scholarship, notwithstanding its central role for the comprehension of a fundamental passage of Kant's description of moral action.[726] This is also due to the general underestimation of the *Doctrine of Virtue*, which has been closely considered only in the years right after its publication,[727] and which, afterwards, has been nearly forgotten by the critics, apart from some important exceptions.[728] This is in part due to the

---

725 Cf. MS, TL, AA 06: 399–403; MM, pp. 528–531.

726 The contributions published on this topic are very limited, and all are very recent. Apart from the quoted work by DIETER SCHÖNECKER, "Kant über Menschenliebe als moralische Gemütsanlage", cit., and my articles on the topics, cf. PAUL GUYER, "Moral Feelings in the Metaphysics of Morals", in LARA DENIS (ed.), *Kant's Metaphysics of Morals. A Critical Guide*, Cambridge/New York, Cambridge University Press 2010, pp. 103–151 and IDO GEIGER, "Rational Feelings and Moral Agency", in *Kantian Review*, 16 (2011), pp. 283–308.

727 Cf. JOHANN HEINRICH TIEFTRUNK, *Philosophische Untersuchungen über die Tugendlehre zur Erläuterung und Beurtheilung der metaphysischen Anfangsgründe der Tugendlehre vom Herrn Prof. Imm. Kant. Zweiter Teil. Ausführung der Pflichten der Menschen gegen einander nach den besondern Zuständen und Verhältnissen derselben*, Halle, Mengersche Buchhandlung 1805; JOHANN ADAM BERGK, *Reflexionen über Kant's metaphysische Anfangsgründe der Tugendlehre*, first edition: Gera 1798; reprint in *Aetas Kantiana* (vol. 34), Bruxelles, Culture et Civilisation, 1968; CHRISTOPH FRIEDRICH NICOLAI (ed.), *Neun Gespräche zwischen Chrisitan Wolff und einem Kantianer über Kants metaphysische Anfangsgründe der Rechtslehre und der Tugendlehre*, first edition: Berlin 1798; reprint in *Aetas Kantiana* (vol. 199), Bruxelles, Culture et Civilisation 1968.

728 The only relevant exception is the book by MARY J. GREGOR, *Laws of Freedom: A Study of Kant's Method of Applying the Categorical Imperative in the "Metaphysik der Sitten"*, Oxford, Blackwell 1963 and the articles by Anderson: GEORG ANDERSON, "Die 'Materie' in Kants Tugendlehre und der Formalismus der kritischen Ethik", in *Kant-Studien*, volume 26 (1921), pp. 289–311; GEORG ANDERSON, "Kants Metaphysik der Sitten. Ihre Idee und ihr Verhältnis zur Ethik der Wolffschen Schule", in *Kant-Studien*, volume 28 (1923), pp. 41–61. The attempt by MARKUS FORKL, *Kants System der Tugendpflichten. Eine Begleitschrift zu den 'Metaphysischen Anfangsgründen der Tugendlehre'*, Frankfurt a. M., Lang 2001, is unfortunately very superficial, while the book by ANDREA MARLEN ESSER, *Eine Ethik für Endliche. Kants "Tugendlehre" in der Gegenwart*, Stuttgart/Bad Cannstatt, Frommann-Holzboog 2004, is more directed to a theoretical development of Kant's *Doctrine of Virtue*. Only in the last years appeared a few commentaries on the *Metaphysics of Morals*, i.e. LARA DENIS (ed.), *Kant's Metaphysics of Morals. A Critical Guide*, Cambridge/New York, Cambridge University Press; MARK TIMMONS (ed.), *Kant's Metaphysics of Morals: Interpretative Essays*, Oxford/New York, Oxford University Press 2002; and WERNER EULER – BURKHARD TUSCHLING (eds.), *Kants "Metaphysik der Sitten" in der Diskussion. Ein Arbeitsgespräch an der Herzog August Bibliothek Wolfenbüttel 2009*, Berlin 2013, besides a work

fact that Kant's method of expression is, in this work, more obscure than in others, a fact that might have influenced many critics along with the belief that the *Doctrine of Virtue* is just a secondary product in the constellation of Kant's production on morals, a "late" work of an old man.

However, what has generally to be remembered when analysing this work, is that the *Doctrine of Virtue* is very different from Kant's grounding writings on morals. The theoretical goal that Kant intends to achieve is in fact, in the *Doctrine of Virtue*, quite different from the one he undertakes in the *Groundwork* and in the second *Critique*. He is now more focused on the actual realisation of the moral theory in action and this stronger orientation to the problem of moral realisation contributes to creating the myth that the *Doctrine of Virtue* is partly incongruent with the theories proposed in the *Groundwork* and in the second *Critique* and, consequently, less "Kantian".

In the following analysis of some sections from the *Doctrine of Virtue* the peculiarity of this work thus must always be remembered, without forgetting the centrality of the *Doctrine of Virtue* in Kant's outline of the way in which moral theory finds a presentation in the actual life of a human being, which Kant explains by means of a description of the internal constitution of the human mind with particular regard to its sentimental aspects.

With it, we are eventually ready to analyse the mentioned twelfth section of the Introduction to the *Doctrine of Virtue*, where Kant defines four fundamental "natural predispositions (*praedispositio*) of the mind for being affected by the concepts of duty", i.e. four "subjective conditions of receptiveness to the concept of duty".[729]

Here the introducing text of the paragraph:

> There are certain moral endowments such that anyone lacking them could have no duty to acquire them. – They are *moral feeling, conscience, love* of one's neighbour, and *respect* for oneself (*self-esteem*). There is no obligation to have these because they lie at the basis of morality, as *subjective* conditions of receptiveness to the concept of duty, not as objective conditions of morality. All of them are natural predispositions of the mind (*praedispositio*) for being affected by concepts of duty, antecedent predispositions on the side of *feeling*. To have these predispositions cannot be considered a duty; rather, every human being has them, and it is by virtue of them that he can be put under obligation.[730]

---

dedicated specifically to the *Doctrine of Virtue*: TRAMPOTA, ANDREAS – SENSEN, OLIVER – TIMMERMANN, JENS (eds.), *Kant's "Tugendlehre". A Comprehensive Commentary*, Berlin/Boston, de Gruyter 2013.
729 Cf. MS, TL, AA 06: 399.04–16; MM p. 528 (note below).
730 MS, TL, AA 06: 399.04–16: "Es sind solche moralische Beschaffenheiten, die, wenn man sie nicht besitzt, es auch keine Pflicht geben kann sich in ihren Besitz zu setzen. Sie sind das

My aim is to focus on the first of these concepts, i. e. on the concept of moral feeling (*moralisches Gefühl*). I closely focus on what I retain the most noteworthy passage of this section, at least for what regards my present analysis. This passage reads as follows:

> We have [...] a susceptibility (*Empfänglichkeit*) on the part of free choice (*der freien Willkür*) to be moved by pure practical reason (and its law), and this is what we call moral feeling (*das moralische Gefühl*).[731]

Here, Kant states that we, as human beings, have no duty to have or to acquire a capacity for "feeling morally". Instead, he affirms that all consciousness of our obligation presupposes a moral feeling (*moralisches Gefühl*), without which we would have no consciousness of the concept of duty at all. This means that each human being possesses a moral feeling, "he has it in him originally":

> since any consciousness of obligation (*alles Bewußtsein der Verbindlichkeit*) depends upon moral feeling to make us aware of the constraint present in the thought of duty, there can be no duty to have moral feeling or to acquire it; instead every human being (as a moral being) has it in him originally.[732]

What we cannot acquire is the faculty for feeling pleasure and displeasure: every man possesses such a faculty since the human mind, as Kant repeatedly affirms, is tripartite in such a way that the faculty of feeling has to be regarded as the middle fundamental faculty between the faculty of cognition and the faculty of desire. As a human moral being, i. e. as a being that is at the same time sensuous and rational, the subject feels respect every time he is conscious of the moral law:

---

moralische Gefühl, das Gewissen, die Liebe des Nächsten und die Achtung für sich selbst (Selbstschätzung), welche zu haben es keine Verbindlichkeit giebt: weil sie als subjective Bedingungen der Empfänglichkeit für den Pflichtbegriff, nicht als objective Bedingungen der Moralität zum Grunde liegen. Sie sind insgesammt ästhetisch und vorhergehende, aber natürliche Gemüthsanlagen (*praedispositio*) durch Pflichtbegriffe afficirt zu werden; welche Anlagen zu haben nicht als Pflicht angesehen werden kann, sondern die jeder Mensch hat und kraft deren er verpflichtet werden kann"; MM p. 528.

731 MS, TL, AA 06: 400.18–20: "Empfänglichkeit der freien Willkür für die Bewegung derselben durch praktische reine Vernunft (und ihr Gesetz), [...] das ist es, was wir das moralische Gefühl nennen"; MM p. 529.

732 MS, TL, AA 06: 399.28–32: "Nun kann es keine Pflicht geben, ein moralisches Gefühl zu haben, oder sich ein solches zu erwerben; denn alles Bewußtsein der Verbindlichkeit legt dieses Gefühl zum Grunde, um sich der Nöthigung, die im Pflichtbegriffe liegt, bewusst zu werden: sondern ein jeder Mensch (als ein moralisches Wesen) hat es ursprünglich in sich"; MM p. 528.

> No human being is entirely without moral feeling, for were he completely lacking in recep-
> tivity (*Unempfänglichkeit*) to it he would be morally dead.[733]

This means that every human being is provided with a faculty of feeling that reacts every time one is conscious of the moral law: the sensible aspect of the
human mind allows the human being to be morally alive and to feel respect.
That is why, in another passage of the twelfth section of the introduction to
the *Doctrine of Virtue*, Kant speaks of both the feeling of pleasure or displeasure
and moral feeling as a "sensible state" (*ästhetischer Zustand*):

> Every determination of choice proceeds *from the representation of a possible action* to the
> deed through the feeling of pleasure or displeasure (*Gefühl der Lust oder Unlust*), taking
> an interest in the action or its effect. The sensible state (*ästhetischer Zustand*) here (the
> way in which inner sense is affected) is either *pathological* or *moral*. – The former is that
> feeling which precedes the representation of the law; the latter that which can only follow
> upon it.[734]

While taking into consideration the concept of conscience (*Gewissen*), Kant also
refers to moral feeling as something affected rather than an effect of the process
of affection:

> conscience is practical reason holding the human being's duty before hum for his acquittal
> or condemnation in every case that comes under a law. Thus it is not directed to an object
> but merely to the subject (to affect moral feeling by its act).[735]

Eventually, Kant expresses himself similarly in section 43 of the *Doctrine of Virtue*, where he notes that the intentional spreading of defamation diminishes the
respect felt for humanity as such, by way of dulling our moral feeling and making the human being accustoming to defamation itself:

---

733 MS, TL, AA 06: 400.09–11: "Ohne alles moralische Gefühl ist kein Mensch; denn bei
völliger Unempfänglichkeit für diese Empfindung wäre er sittlich todt"; MM p. 529.
734 MS, TL, AA 06: 399.24–27: "Alle Bestimmung der Willkür aber geht von der Vorstellung der
möglichen Handlung durch das Gefühl der Lust oder Unlust, an ihr oder ihrer Wirkung ein
Interesse zu nehmen, zur That; wo der ästhetische Zustand (der Afficirung des inneren Sinnes)
nun entweder ein pathologisches oder moralisches Gefühl ist. – Das erstere ist dasjenige Gefühl,
welches vor der Vorstellung des Gesetzes vorhergeht, das letztere das, was nur auf diese folgen
kann"; MM p. 528.
735 MS, TL, AA 06: 400.26–30: "Gewissen ist die dem Menschen in jedem Fall eines Gesetzes
seine Pflicht zum Lossprechen oder Verurtheilen vorhaltende praktische Vernunft. Seine Beziehung also ist nicht die auf ein Object, sondern bloß aufs Subject (das moralische Gefühl
durch ihren Act zu afficiren)"; MM p. 529.

the intentional *spreading* (*propalatio*) of something that detracts from another's honour [...] diminishes respect for humanity as such, so as finally [...] to dull one's moral feeling by repeatedly exposing one to the sight of such things and accustoming one to it.[736]

All the mentioned passages from the *Doctrine of Virtue* provide room for considering moral feeling not only as the realised feeling of respect, but rather as the faculty of feeling pleasure and displeasure that reacts to the consciousness of the moral law and feels respect. In this case, "moral feeling" thus denotes only the readiness for feeling respect, i.e. the faculty which makes the realized mental state of respect possible, i.e. the "not-yet-realised" respect. "Moral feeling" has thus to be intended also as the faculty of feeling pleasure and displeasure in the moral case, which is a *"feeling in posse, in possibility"*, i.e. the mere possibility of feeling, and that becomes an effective feeling, a *"feeling in esse, in actuality"*, i.e. the mental state of respect (*Achtung*), every time the subject becomes conscious of the moral law.

One of the most important consequences of this interpretive proposal concerning the analysis of the faculty of feeling and the respective mental state that this faculty makes possible, i.e. the feeling of respect for the moral law, is that this analysis allows for an interpretation of Kant's concept of "moral aesthetic" as the particular field dedicated to deal with the pure *a priori* modification of the faculty of sensibility, in its particular aspect of feeling, in moral cases.

As I will now show, Kant's moral aesthetic deals exactly with the way in which the faculty of feeling pleasure and displeasure is *a priori* modified and realized in the mental state of the feeling of respect during the process of moral deliberation and action.

5.7 Kant's Moral Aesthetic

Until now, in Kant scholarship an analysis dedicated to the concept of moral aesthetic has barely been proposed. Exceptions are the contributions by Birgit Recki, who tries to give an alternative perspective on the feeling-problematic

---

736 Here the whole passage from MS, TL, AA 06: 466.18 – 25: "Die geflissentliche Verbreitung (propalatio) desjenigen die Ehre eines Andern Schmälernden, was auch nicht zur öffentlichen Gerichtbarkeit gehört, es mag übrigens auch wahr sein, ist Verringerung der Achtung für die Menschheit überhaupt, um endlich auf unsere Gattung selbst den Schatten der Nichtswürdigkeit zu werfen und Misanthropie (Menschenscheu) oder Verachtung zur herrschenden Denkungsart zu machen, oder sein moralisches Gefühl durch den öfteren Anblick derselben abzustumpfen und sich daran zu gewöhnen"; MM p. 582.

in Kant.[737] According to Recki's proposal, Kant's reference to an *Ästhetik der Sitten* in the *Doctrine of Virtue* has to be interpreted as the attempt to bridge the gap between ethics, on the one side, and aesthetics as the study dedicated to the concept of beautiful, on the other side. In the case of Recki's proposal, the German word *Ästhetik* would be better translated by "aesthetics".

However, as I showed at the beginning of this chapter, in Kant's philosophy the term *Ästhetik* refers also very generally to the study dedicated to the faculty of sensibility, i. e. the analysis of the philosophical field concerning generally the concept of "*aisthesis*", which in English is rendered as "aesthetic".

In the light of this last observation, and in contrast to Recki's proposal, I suggest to read Kant's *Ästhetik der Sitten* as a "moral aesthetic" as opposed to an "aesthetics of morals". In other words, I suggest that the reference to the "aesthetic aspect" of ethics points at the subjective presentation of ethics as it is depicted by the faculty of feeling pleasure and displeasure. As aesthetic is the study dedicated to the faculty of sensibility in its *a priori* application, moral aesthetic is the study of the *a priori* change of a particular aspect of the faculty of sensibility, i. e. the study of the *a priori* modification of the faculty of feeling pleasure and displeasure, when the human being becomes conscious of the moral law in his mind. As Kant clearly states in the *Doctrine of Virtue*,

> a moral aesthetic, while not indeed a part of the metaphysics of morals, is still a subjective presentation of it.[738]

---

737 Cf. in particular BIRGIT RECKI, *Ästhetik der Sitten. Die Affinität von ästhetischem Gefühl und praktischer Vernunft bei Kant*, Frankfurt a. M., V. Klostermann 2001. Among the many other contributions of the author on this topic, cf. also BIRGIT RECKI, "Achtung vor der zweckmäßigen Natur: die Erweiterung der Kantischen Ethik durch die dritte Kritik", in VOLKER GERHARDT – ROLF-PETER HORSTMANN – RALPH SCHUMACHER (eds.), *Kant und die Berliner Aufklärung. Akten des IX. Internationalen Kant-Kongresses*, Berlin/New York, de Gruyter 2001, Vol. 3 (Sections VI-X), pp. 296–304; BIRGIT RECKI, "Wie fühlt man sich als vernünftiges Wesen? Immanuel Kant über ästhetische und moralische Gefühle", in her book *Die Vernunft, ihre Natur, ihr Gefühl und der Fortschritt*, Paderborn, Mentis 2006; BIRGIT RECKI, "Kant: Vernunftgewirkte Gefühle", in HILGE LANDWEHR – URSULA RENZ (eds.), *Klassische Emotionstheorien. Von Platon bis Wittgenstein*, Berlin/New York, de Gruyter 2008, pp. 457–477; BIRGIT RECKI, "Kants 'Ästhetik der Sitten'. Ein Beitrag zum Problem der moralischen Motivation", in ANTONINO FALDUTO ET AL. (eds.), *Metaphysik – Ästhetik – Ethik*, cit., pp. 121–135. RECKI, BIRGIT, "Kant über Achtung und Glauben. Leistung und Probleme seines motivationstheoretischen Beitrags", in ANNE TILKORN (ed.), *Motivationen für das Selbst. Kant und Spinoza im Vergleich*, Wiesbaden, Harrassowitz 2012, pp. 49–68.
738 MS, TL, § XIV, AA 06: 406.19–21: "Eine Ästhetik der Sitten [ist] zwar nicht ein Teil, aber doch eine subjektive Darstellung der Metaphysik derselben"; MM p. 534.

This reading concerning Kant's moral aesthetic can help to better explain Kant's designation of the *Triebfedern*-chapter as the chapter dedicated to aesthetic.[739] However, more importantly, it helps to introduce the concept of respect in the background of Kant's *a priori* treatment of the faculties of the human mind, such that the feeling-problematic cannot be regarded as an almost empirical pendant of Kant's pure *a priori* ethics, but it rather has to be considered as a necessary element in the context of Kant's pure philosophical analysis.

In light of all these considerations, the fundamental importance of Kant's moral aesthetic eventually comes to the fore.

5.8 Concluding Remarks and Outlook

In this last chapter of my work I dealt with an aspect of Kant's ethical theory, i.e. with the role of feeling in ethics, and I focused on the modification of the faculty of feeling pleasure and displeasure in the moral case as to produce the mental state of feeling of respect for the moral law. Nevertheless, it has to be noted that this analysis represents just a small part of the just considered moral aesthetic, since Kant's analysis of the various feelings (e.g. disgust, horror) in the context of his metaphysics of morals would deserve a chapter on its own.[740]

As Kant says, in a moral aesthetic

> the feelings that accompany the constraining power of the moral law (e.g., disgust, horror, etc., which make moral aversion possible) makes its efficacy felt, in order to get the better of *merely* sensible incitements.[741]

---

739 Cf. the *Kritischen Beleuchtung der Analytik der reinen praktischen Vernunft* of the *Triebfedern*-chapter (AA 05: 71–89), but also, in particular, KpV, AA 05: 90.12–23: "Die Analytik der theoretischen reinen Vernunft wurde in transscendentale Ästhetik und transscendentale Logik eingetheilt, die der praktischen umgekehrt in Logik und Ästhetik der reinen praktischen Vernunft (wenn es mir erlaubt ist, diese sonst gar nicht angemessene Benennungen blos der Analogie wegen hier zu gebrauchen), die Logik wiederum dort in die Analytik der Begriffe und die der Grundsätze, hier in die der Grundsätze und Begriffe. Die Ästhetik hatte dort noch zwei Theile wegen der doppelten Art einer sinnlichen Anschauung; hier wird die Sinnlichkeit gar nicht als Anschauungsfähigkeit, sondern blos als Gefühl (das ein subjectiver Grund des Begehrens sein kann) betrachtet, und in Ansehung dessen verstattet die reine praktische Vernunft keine weitere Eintheilung"; CpR, p. 213.

740 For an overview on feelings in the context of Kant's moral philosophy, see OLIVER SENSEN, "The Role of Feelings in Kant's Moral Philosophy", in *Studi Kantiani*, vol. 25 (2012), pp. 45–58.

741 MS, TL, § XIV, AA 06: 406.21–24: "[... eine Ästhetik der Sitten,] wo die Gefühle, welche die nötigende Kraft des moralischen Gesetzes begleiten, jener ihre Wirksamkeit empfindbar machen

In consideration of this passage, not only the moral feeling of respect, which is a fundamental part of Kant's theory of morals and whose treatment pertains to pure philosophy, but also a varied range of other feelings that are evoked in moral action but do not essentially pertain to a pure philosophical treatment (and which might be better analysed in the context of the empirical study of anthropology) should also be taken into consideration.

The present study might thus constitute the starting point of a larger project dedicated to the analysis of Kant's subjective presentation of the way in which ethics radically influences the subject's sentimental life.

(z. B. Ekel, Grauen etc., welche den moralischen Widerwillen versinnlichen), um der bloß-sinnlichen Anreizung den Vorrang abzugewinnen"; MM p. 534 (translation slightly modified).

Bibliography and Abbreviations

All passages from Kant's works are cited by the volume, page and line number in the standard edition of Kant's works, *Kant's gesammelte Schriften*, edited by the Royal Prussian, later German, then Berlin-Brandenburg Academy of Sciences, 29 volumes (Berlin, Georg Reimer, later Walter de Gruyter & Co., 1900–). Citations from the *Critique of Pure Reason* are located also by reference to the pagination of Kant's first ("A") and/or second ("B") editions. Unless otherwise indicated, all translations are from the *Cambridge Edition of the Works of Immanuel Kant* (see bibliography below). In the following, I list in alphabetical order the abbreviations of Kant's works that are used throughout my work:

AA	Akademie-Ausgabe
Anth	Anthropologie in pragmatischer Hinsicht (AA 07)
BDG	Der einzig mögliche Beweisgrund zu einer Demonstration des Daseins Gottes (AA 02)
Br	Briefe (AA 10–13)
EEKU	Erste Einleitung in die Kritik der Urteilskraft (AA 20)
FM	Welches sind die wirklichen Fortschritte, die die Metaphysik seit Leibnizens und Wolff's Zeiten in Deutschland gemacht hat? (AA 20)
GMS	Grundlegung zur Metaphysik der Sitten (AA 04)
GSE	Beobachtungen über das Gefühl des Schönen und Erhabenen (AA 02)
GSK	Gedanken von der wahren Schätzung der lebendigen Kräfte (AA 01)
HN	Handschriftlicher Nachlass (AA 14–23)
KpV	Kritik der praktischen Vernunft (AA 05)
KrV	Kritik der reinen Vernunft
KU	Kritik der Urteilskraft (AA 05)
Log	Logik (AA 09)
MAN	Metaphysische Anfangsgründe der Naturwissenschaft (AA 04)
MS	Die Metaphysik der Sitten (AA 06)
	MS, RL: Metaphysische Anfangsgründe der Rechtslehre (AA 06)
	MS, TL: Metaphysische Anfangsgründe der Tugendlehre (AA 06)
MSI	De mundi sensibilis atque intelligibilis forma et principiis (AA 02)
NEV	Nachricht von der Einrichtung seiner Vorlesungen in dem Winterhalbenjahre von 1765–1766 (AA 02)
NG	Versuch, den Begriff der negativen Größen in die Weltweisheit einzuführen (AA 02)
OP	Opus Postumum (AA 21 and 22)
Prol	Prolegomena zu einer jeden künftigen Metaphysik (AA 04)
Refl	Reflexion (AA 14–19)
RGV	Die Religion innerhalb der Grenzen der bloßen Vernunft (AA 06)
TG	Träume eines Geistersehers, erläutert durch die Träume der Metaphysik (AA 02)
TP	Über den Gemeinspruch: Das mag in der Theorie richtig sein, taugt aber nicht für die Praxis (AA 08)
UD	Untersuchung über die Deutlichkeit der Grundsätze der natürlichen Theologie und der Moral (AA 02)

ÜE   Über eine Entdeckung, nach der alle neue Kritik der reinen Vernunft durch eine ältere
        entbehrlich gemacht werden soll (AA 08)
VAMS   Vorarbeit zur Metaphysik der Sitten (AA 23)
VKK   Versuch über die Krankheiten des Kopfes (AA 02)
V-Anth Anthropologie-Vorlesungen
        Vorlesungen Wintersemester 1788/1789 Busolt (AA 25)
        Vorlesungen Wintersemester 1772/1773 Collins (AA 25)
        Vorlesungen Wintersemester 1775/1776 Friedländer (AA 25)
        Vorlesungen Wintersemester 1781/1782 Menschenkunde, Petersburg (AA 25)
        Vorlesungen Wintersemester 1784/1785 Mrongovius (AA 25)
        Vorlesungen Wintersemester 1772/1773 Parow (AA 25)
        Vorlesungen Wintersemester 1777/1778 Pillau (AA 25)
V-Met-L2 Pölitz Metaphysik L2 (Pölitz, Original) (AA 28)
VRML   Über ein vermeintes Recht, aus Menschenliebe zu lügen (AA 08)
VT   Von einem neuerdings erhobenen vornehmen Ton in der Philosophie (AA 08)
VvRM Von den verschiedenen Racen der Menschen (AA 02)
WA   Beantwortung der Frage: Was ist Aufklärung? (AA 08)
WDO   Was heißt sich im Denken orientieren? (AA 08)
ZeF   Zum ewigen Frieden (AA 08)

Kant's works – English translations

KANT, IMMANUEL, *Critique of Pure Reason*, translated and edited by PAUL GUYER – ALLEN W.
    WOOD, Cambridge/New York, Cambridge University Press 1998 [quoted as CpR]
KANT, IMMANUEL, *Practical Philosophy*, translated and edited by MARY J. GREGOR, with an
    introduction by ALLEN W. WOOD, Cambridge/New York, Cambridge University Press 1996
    [quoted from this work: *Groundwork* (*Groundwork of the Metaphysics of Morals*); CpR
    (*Critique of Practical Reason*), MM (*Metaphysics of Morals*)]
KANT, IMMANUEL, *Lectures on Metaphysics*, translated and edited by KARL AMERIKS – STEVE
    NARAGON, Cambridge/New York, Cambridge University Press 1997 [quoted from this
    work: *Metaphysics L2*]
KANT, IMMANUEL, *Correspondence*, edited and translated by ARNULF ZWEIG, Cambridge/New
    York, Cambridge University Press 1999 [quoted as *Correspondence*]
KANT, IMMANUEL, *Opus Postumum*, edited and translated by ECKART FÖRSTER – MICHAEL
    ROSEN, Cambridge/New York, Cambridge University Press 1993
KANT, IMMANUEL, *Theoretical Philosophy after 1781*, edited by HENRY E. ALLISON – PETER L.
    HEATH, translated by HENRY E. ALLISON – MICHAEL FRIEDMAN – GARY HATFIELD – PETER
    L. HEATH, Cambridge/New York, Cambridge University Press 2002 [quoted from this
    work: *Prolegomena* (*Prolegomena to Any Future Metaphysics That Will Be Able to Come
    forward as a Science*); *Progress-Metaphysics* (*What Real Progress Has Metaphysics
    Made in Germany Since the Time of Leibniz and Wolff*)]
KANT, IMMANUEL, *Lectures on Logic*, edited and translated by J. MICHAEL YOUNG,
    Cambridge/New York, Cambridge University Press 2004 [quoted from this work: *Jäsche
    Logic*]
KANT, IMMANUEL, *Anthropology, History and Education*, edited by GÜNTER ZÖLLER – ROBERT B.
    LOUDEN, translated by MARY GREGOR – PAUL GUYER – ROBERT B. LOUDEN – HOLLY

WILSON – ALLEN W. WOOD – GÜNTER ZÖLLER – ARNULF ZWEIG, Cambridge/New York,
Cambridge University Press 2007 [quoted from this work: *Anthropology* (*Anthropology
from a Pragmatic Point of View*); "*From Soemmerring's On the Organ of the Soul*"; "*On
the Different Races of Human Beings*; *Observations on the Feeling of the Beautiful and
Sublime*"]

KANT, IMMANUEL, *Critique of the Power of Judgment*, edited by PAUL GUYER, translated by
PAUL GUYER – ERIC MATTHEWS, Cambridge/New York, Cambridge University Press 2000
(quoted as CPJ)

KANT, IMMANUEL, *Theoretical Philosophy, 1755–1770*, edited and translated by DAVID
WALFORD, in collaboration with RALF MEERBOTE, Cambridge/New York, Cambridge
University Press 1992 (quoted from this work: *Inaugural dissertation* (*On the Form and
Principles of the Sensible and the Intelligible World*)]

Kant's texts (not in AA)

KANT, IMMANUEL, *Erste Einleitung in die Kritik der Urteilskraft. Faksimile und Transkription*,
edited by NORBERT HINSKE – WOLFGANG MÜLLER-LAUTER – MICHAEL THEUNISSEN,
Stuttgart/Bad Cannstatt, Frommann-Holzboog 1965

KANT, IMMANUEL, *Bemerkungen in den "Beobachtungen über das Gefühl des Schönen und
Erhabenen"*, neu herausgegeben und kommentiert von MARIE RISCHMÜLLER, Hamburg,
Meiner 1991

*Reflexionen Kants zur kritischen Philosophie. Aus Kants handschriftlichen Aufzeichnungen
herausgegeben von* BENNO ERDMANN, Neudruck der Ausgabe Leipzig 1882/1884, neu
herausgegeben und mit einer Einleitung versehen von NORBERT HINSKE, Stuttgart/Bad
Cannstatt, frommann-holzboog 1992

IMMANUEL KANT, *Vorlesung zur Moralphilosophie*, edited by WERNER STARK, with an
introduction by MANFRED KÜHN, Berlin/New York, de Gruyter 2004

STARKE, FRIEDRICH CHRISTAN, i.e.: JOHANN ADAM BERGK, (ed.), *Immanuel Kant's
Menschenkunde oder philosophische Anthropologie. Nach handschriftlichen Vorlesungen
herausgegeben*, Quedlinburg/Leipzig 1831; 2. edition 1838 / reprint: Olms 1976

Other Primary Sources

ADELUNG, JOHANN CHRISTOPH, *Grammatisch-kritisches Wörterbuch der Hochdeutschen
Mundart mit beständiger Vergleichung der übrigen Mundart, besonders aber der
Oberdeutschen*, Leipzig, Johann Gottlob Immanuel Breitkopf und Compagnie 1793. First
edition 1774–1786; author's last revision (last authorized version): 1793–1801

BAUMGARTEN, ALEXANDER GOTTLIEB, *Metaphysica*, Halle, 1739 (first edition – 1779, 7th edition;
but see now ALEXANDER GOTTLIEB BAUMGARTEN, *Metaphysica – Metaphysik.
Historisch-kritische Ausgabe*. Translated, introduced and edited by GÜNTER GAWLICK –
LOTHAR KREIMENDAHL, Stuttgart/Bad Cannstatt, frommann-holzboog 2011; the historical
German translation is by GEORG FRIEDRICH MEIER, Halle 1766 – revised edition by
JOHANN AUGUST EBERHARD, Halle 1783. Baumgarten's *Metaphysica* is also entirely

reprinted in AA 17: 05–226, except for the text of the *Empirical Psychology*, which is reprinted in AA 15: 05–54)

BLUMENBACH, JOHANN FRIEDRICH, *Ueber den Bildungstrieb und das Zeugungsgeschäft*, several editions, 1781–1792

CAMPE, JOACHIM HEINRICH, *Die Empfindungs- und Erkenntniβkraft der menschlichen Seele: die erstere nach ihren Gesetzen, beyde nach ihren ursprünglichen Bestimmungen, nach ihrem gegenseitigen Einflusse aufeinander und nach ihren Beziehungen auf Character und Genie betrachtet*, Leipzig, Weygandsche Handlung 1776

EBERHARD, JOHANN AUGUST, *Allgemeine Theorie des Denkens und Empfindens*, Berlin, Voβ 1776 (reprint: Hildesheim, Zürich/New York, Olms, 1984)

FOUCAULT, MICHEL, *Introduction à l'anthropologie de Kant. Thèse complémentaire pour le doctorat dès Lettres*, Paris 1961

FRIES, JAKOB FRIEDRICH, *Neue oder anthropologische Kritik der Vernunft*, 2nd ed., 3 vols., Heidelberg, 1828

HEIDEGGER, MARTIN, *Kant und das Problem der Metaphysik*, Frankfurt a. M. 1973[4]

HERDER, JOHANN GOTTFRIED, *Vom Erkennen und Empfinden, den zwo Hauptkräften der Menschlichen Seele*, in JOHANN GOTTFRIED HERDER, *Sämtliche Werke*, edited by BERNHARD SUPHAN, Volume 1–33, Berlin 1877–1913 (reprint: Hildesheim, Olms 1968), volume 8, Berlin 1892, pp. 263–333

HERBART, JOHAN FRIEDRICH, *Lehrbuch zur Einleitung in die Philosophie*, Königsberg, 1813

HUSSERL, EDMUND, *Logische Untersuchungen. Erster Teil: Prolegomena zur reinen Logik*, Halle, Max Niemeyer 1900

LAMBERT, JOHANN HEINRICH, *Neues Organon oder Gedanken über die Erforschung und Bezeichnung des Wahren und dessen Unterscheidung vom Irrthum und Schein*, Leipzig 1764

LANDAU, ALBERT (ed.), *Rezensionen zur kantischen Philosophie*, Bebra, Landau 1991

LOCKE, JOHN, *An Essay concerning Humane Understanding*, London 1690

MENDELSSOHN, MOSES, *Phädon oder über die Unsterblichkeit der Seele*, Berlin 1767

PISTORIUS, HERMANN ANDREAS, "Erläuterungen über des Herrn Professor Kant Critik der reinen Vernunft von Joh. Schultze, Königl. Preußischem Hofprediger. Königsberg 1784.", in *Allgemeine deutsche Bibliothek*, Volume 66/1 (1786), pp. 92–123

PISTORIUS, HERMANN ANDREAS, "Grundlegung zur Metaphysik der Sitten von Immanuel Kant. Riga 1785.", in *Allgemeine deutsche Bibliothek*, Volume 66/2 (1786), pp. 447/463

PISTORIUS, HERMANN ANDREAS, "Critik der reinen Vernunft von Immanuel Kant, Prof. in Königsberg, der Königl. Akademie der Wissenschaften in Berlin Mitglied. Zweyte hin und wieder verbesserte Auflage, Riga 1787.", in *Allgemeine deutsche Bibliothek*, Volume 81/2 (1788), pp. 343/354

PISTORIUS, HERMANN ANDREAS, "Prüfung der Mendelssohnschen Morgenstunden, oder aller spekulativen Beweise für das Daseyn Gottes in Vorlesungen von Ludwig Heinrich Jakob, Doktor der Philosophie in Halle. Nebst einer Abhandlung vom Herrn Professor Kant. Leipzig 1786.", in *Allgemeine deutsche Bibliothek*, Volume 82/2 (1788), pp. 427–470

PISTORIUS, HERMANN ANDREAS, "Critik der praktischen Vernunft, von Immanuel Kant. Riga 1788.", in *Allgemeine deutsche Bibliothek*, Volume 117/1 (1794), pp. 78–105

PLATNER, ERNST, *Anthropologie für Aerzte und Weltweise*, Leipzig 1772

REINHOLD, KARL LEONHARD, *Versuch einer neuen Theorie des menschlichen Vorstellungsvermögen*, Prag und Jena 1789

REINHOLD, KARL LEONHARD, *Briefe über die kantische Philosophie*, 2 vols., Leipzig,
  1790–1792
SCHILLER, FRIEDRICH, *Ueber Anmuth und Würde*, in *Neue Thalia* (1792–93), third volume,
  pp. 115–230, Leipzig 1793
SOEMMERRING (also: SÖMMERING), SAMUEL THOMAS VON, *Über das Organ der Seele*.
  Königsberg 1796
SULZER, JOHANN GEORG, *Allgemeine Theorie der schönen Künste*, Leipzig 1771–1774
TETENS, JOHANN NICOLAS, *Philosophische Versuche über die menschliche Natur und ihre
  Entwickelung*, Leipzig 1777
WALCH, JOHANN GEORG, *Philosophisches Lexicon, Darinnen die in allen Theilen der
  Philosophie, als Logic, Metaphysic, Physic, Pneumatic, Ethic, natürlichen Theologie und
  Rechts-Gelehrsamkeit, wie auch Politic fürkommende Materien und Kunst-Wörter erkläret
  und aus der Historie erläutert; die Streitigkeiten der ältern und neuern Philosophen
  erzehlet, die dahin gehörigen Bücher und Schrifften aufgeführet und alles nach
  Alphabetischer Ordnung vorgestellet werden, mit nöthigen Registern versehen und
  herausgegeben*, Leipzig, Verlegts Joh. Friedrich Gleditschens seel. Sohn 1726
WOLFF, CHRISTIAN, *Vernünfftige Gedancken von Gott, der Welt und der Seele des Menschen,
  auch allen Dingen überhaupt*, Halle 1720
WOLFF, CHRISTIAN, *Psychologia empirica, methodo scientifica pertractata, qua ea, quae de
  anima humana indubia experientiae fide constant, continentur et ad solidam universae
  philosophiae practicae ac theologiae naturalis tractationem via sternitur*,
  Frankfurt/Leipzig 1732
WOLFF, CHRISTIAN, *Psychologia rationalis, methodo scientifica pertractata, qua ea, quae de
  anima humana indubia experientiae fide innotescunt, per essentiam et naturam animae
  explicantur, et ad intimiorem naturae ejusque autoris cognitionem profutura
  proponuntur*, Frankfurt/Leipzig 1734
WOLFF, CHRISTIAN, *Discursus praeliminaris de philosophia in genere*, in *Philosophia
  rationalis sive logica methodo scientifica pertractata, et ad usum scientiarum atque
  vitae aptata. Praemittitur discursus praeliminaris de philosophia in genere*,
  Frankfurt/Leipzig 1740 (new edition of the Latin text of Wolff's *Discursus*, comprehensive
  of a German translation: CHRISTIAN WOLFF, *Einleitende Abhandlung über Philosophie im
  allgemeinen*, edited, translated and with an introduction by GÜNTER GAWLICK – LOTHAR
  KREIMENDAHL, Stuttgart/Bad Cannstatt, Frommann-Holzboog 2006)
ZEDLER, JOHANN HEINRICH, *Grosses Vollständige Universal-Lexicon Aller Wissenschaften und
  Künste*, Halle/Leipzig 1732–1754

Secondary Sources

ABICHT, JOHANN HEINRICH, *Neues System einer philosophischen Tugendlehre aus der Natur
  der Menschheit entwickelt*, first edition: Leipzig, Barth 1790; reprint in *Aetas Kantiana*
  (vol. 6), Bruxelles, Culture et Civilisation, 1968
ALLISON, HENRY E., *Kant's Theory of Freedom*, Cambridge/New York, Cambridge University
  Press 1990
AMERIKS, KARL, *Kant's Theory of Mind. An Analysis of the Paralogisms of Pure Reason*,
  Oxford/New York, Oxford University Press 1982 (new edition: 2000)

AMERIKS, KARL, "Recent Work on Kant's Theoretical Philosophy", in *American Philosophical Quarterly*, 19/1 (1982), pp. 1–24

AMERIKS, KARL, "The Critique of Metaphysics: Kant and Traditional Ontology", in PAUL GUYER, *The Cambridge Companion to Kant*, Cambridge/New York, Cambridge University Press 1992, pp. 249–279

AMOROSO, LEONARDO, *Senso e consenso. Uno studio kantiano*, Napoli, Guida 1984

ANDERSON, GEORG, "Die "Materie" in Kants Tugendlehre und der Formalismus der kritischen Ethik", in *Kant-Studien*, volume 26 (1921), pp. 289–311

ANDERSON, GEORG, "Kants Metaphysik der Sitten – Ihre Idee und ihr Verhältnis zur Ethik der Wolffschen Schule", in *Kant-Studien*, 28 (1923), p. 41–61

AQUILA, RICHARD E., *Matter and Mind: A Study of Kant's Transcendental Deduction*, Bloomington, Indiana University Press 1989

ARNOLDT, EMIL, "Verhältnis von Kants physisch-geographischem Kolleg zu seinem anthropologischen", in DERS., *Gesammelte Schriften*, edited by OTTO SCHÖNDÖRFFER, vol. 4 (*Kritische Exkurse im Gebiete der Kantforschung – Teil 1*), Berlin, B. Cassirer 1908, pp. 400–420

ARNOLDT, EMIL, "Möglichst vollständiges Verzeichnis aller von Kant gehaltenen oder auch nur angekündigten Vorlesungen nebst darauf bezüglichen Notizen und Bemerkungen", in IDEM, *Gesammelte Schriften*, edited by OTTO SCHÖNDÖRFFER, vol. 5 (*Kritische Exkurse im Gebiete der Kantforschung – Teil 2*), Berlin, B. Cassirer 1909, pp. 173–344

AUBENQUE, PIERRE, *La prudence chez Aristote*, 3. éd. rev. et augm. d'un appendice sur *La prudence chez Kant*, Paris, Presses Univ. de France 1986

BACIN, STEFANO, *Il senso dell'etica. Kant e la costruzione di una teoria morale*, Napoli, Istituto Italiano per gli Studi Storici – Il Mulino 2006

BAEUMLER, ALFRED, *Das Irrationalitätsproblem in der Ästhetik und Logik des 18. Jahrhunderts bis zur Kritik der Urteilskraft*, Reprograf. ND. d. 2., durchges. u. Um e. Nachw. Erw. Aufl. Tübingen (1967). Darmstadt 1981

BARON, MARCIA W., *Kantian Ethics Almost without Apology*, Ithaca (N. Y.)/London, Cornell University Press 1995

BARON, MARCIA W., "Kantian Ethics and the Claims of Detachment", in ROBIN MAY SCHOTT (ed.), *Feminist Interpretations of Kant*, University Park, Pennsylvania State Ubiversity Press 1997, pp. 145–170

BARON, MARCIA W., "Kantian Ethics", in MARCIA W. BARON – PHILIP PETTIT – MICHAEL SLOTE, *Three Methods of Ethics: A Debate*, Oxford/New York, Oxford University Press 1997, pp. 3–9

BATTAGLIA, FIORELLA, "Leben als Erleben. Sechs Funktionen des phänomenalen Erlebens bei Kant", in MATTHIAS JUNG – JAN-CHRISTOPH HEILINGER (eds.), *Funktionen des Erlebens*, Berlin-New York, de Gruyter 2009, pp. 253–284

BATTAGLIA, FIORELLA, *Il sistema antropologico. La posizione dell'uomo nella filosofia critica di Kant*, Pisa, Plus 2010

BAUM, MANFRED, "Gefühl, Begehren und Wollen in Kants praktischer Philosophie", in *Jahrbuch für Recht und Ethik/Annual Review of Law and Ethics*, 14 (2006), pp. 125–139

BECK, LEWIS W., *A Commentary on Kant's Critique of Practical Reason*, The University of Chicago Press, Chicago 1960

BECK, LEWIS W., *Early German Philosophy. Kant and His Precedessors*, Cambridge (Mass.), The Belknap Press of Harvard University Press 1969

BERGK, JOHANN ADAM, *Reflexionen über Kant's metaphysische Anfangsgründe der Tugendlehre*, first edition: Gera 1798; reprint in *Aetas Kantiana* (vol. 34), Bruxelles, Culture et Civilisation, 1968

BESOLI, STEFANO, "Antropologia", in STEFANO BESOLI – CLAUDIO LA ROCCA – RICCARDO MARTINELLI (eds.), *L'universo kantiano. Filosofia, scienze, sapere*, Macerata, Quodlibet 2010, pp. 13–52

BIRD, GRAHAM H., "The Paralogism and Kant's Account of Psychology", in *Kant-Studien* 91 (2000), pp. 129–145

BLACKWELL, RICHARD J., "Wolff's Doctrine of the Soul", in *Journal of the History of Ideas*, 22/3 (1961), pp. 339–354

BLOSSER, PHILIP, "A Problem in Kant's Theory of Moral Feeling", in *Lyceum*, 3 (1991), pp. 27–39

BOJANOWSKI, JOCHEN, *Kants Theorie der Freiheit*, Berlin/Boston, de Gruyter 2006

BOJANOWSKI, JOCHEN, "Kant und das Problem der Zurechenbarkeit", in *Zeitschrift für philosophische Forschung*, Volume 61/2 (2007), pp. 207–228

BRANDHORST, MARIO – HAHMANN, ANDREE – LUDWIG, BERND (eds.), *Sind wir Bürger zweier Welten? Freiheit und moralische Verantwortung im transzendentalen Idealismus*, Hamburg, Meiner 2012, pp. 195–222

BRANDT, REINHARD, *D'Artagnan und die Urteilstafel. Über ein Ordnungsprinzip der Europäischen Kulturgeschichte 1, 2, 3/4*, new, revised edition: München, dtv 1998, pp. 195–196 (first edition: Stuttgart, Steiner 1991)

BRANDT, REINHARD, "Beobachtungen zur Anthropologie bei Kant (und Hegel)", in FRANZ HESPE und BURKHARD TUSCHLING (eds.), *Psychologie und Anthropologie oder Philosophie des Geistes. Beiträge zu einer Hegel-Tagung in Marburg 1989*, Stuttgart/Bad Cannstatt, Frommann und Holzboog 1991, pp. 75–106

BRANDT, REINHARD, "Kants pragmatische Anthropologie: Die Vorlesung", in *Allgemeine Zeitschrift für Philosophie*, 19 (1994), pp. 41–49

BRANDT, REINHARD, "Kants 'Paradoxon der Methode'", in ROLF W. PUSTER (ed.), *Veritas filia temporis? Philosophiehistorie zwischen Wahrheit und Geschichte*, Berlin/New York, de Gruyter 1995, pp. 206–216

BRANDT, REINHARD, "Transzendentale Ästhetik, §§ 1–3", in IMMANUEL KANT, *Kritik der reinen Vernunft (Klassiker Auslegen)*, edited by GEORG MOHR – MARCUS WILLASCHEK, Berlin, Akademie Verlag 1998, pp. 81–106

BRANDT, REINHARD, *Kritischer Kommentar zu Kants Anthropologie in pragmatischer Hinsicht (1789)*, Hamburg, Meiner 1999

BRANDT, REINHARD, "Die Leitidee der Kantischen Anthropologie und die Bestimmung des Menschen", in RAINER ENSKAT (ed.), *Erfahrung und Urteilskraft*, Würzburg, Königshausen und Neumann 2000, pp. 27–40

BRANDT, REINHARD, "Schön, Erhaben, nicht Häßlich. Überlegungen zur Entstehung und Systematik der Kantischen Theorie des ästhetischen Urteils", in HEINER F. KLEMME – MICHAEL PAUEN – MARIE-LUISE RATERS (eds.), *Im Schatten des Schönen. Die Ästhetik des Hässlichen in historischen Ansätzen und aktuellen Debatten*, Bielefeld, Aisthetis 2006, pp. 65–92

BRANDT, REINHARD, *Die Bestimmung des Menschen bei Kant*, Hamburg, Meiner 2007

BRANDT, REINHARD – STARK, WERNER, "Einleitung", AA 25 (*Kant's Vorlesungen über Anthropologie*), pp. VII-CLI

BREZINA, FRIEDRICH F., *Die Achtung. Ethik und Moral der Achtung und Unterwerfung bei Immanuel Kant, Ernst Tugendhat, Ursula Wolf und Peter Singer*, Frankfurt a. M., Lang 1998

BROADIE, ALEXANDER – PYBUS, ELIZABETH M., "Kant's Concept of 'Respect'", in *Kant-Studien*, 66 (1975), pp. 58–64

BROOK, ANDREW, *Kant's View of the Mind*, Cambridge/New York, Cambridge University Press 1994

BROOK, ANDREW, "Kant, Cognitive Science and Contemporary Neo-Kantianism", in *Journal of Consciousness Studies (JCS) – Controversies in Science & the Humanities. An International Multi-Disciplinary Journal*. Special number 11/2004 (No. 10–11), pp. 1–25

BROOK, ANDREW, "Kant's View of the Mind and Consciousness of Self", in *The Stanford Encyclopedia of Philosophy* (Winter 2008 Edition), Edward N. Zalta (ed.), URL = <http://plato.stanford.edu/archives/win2008/entries/kant-mind/>, last accessed on November, 19th, 2011

BRUMMACK, JÜRGEN – BOLLACHER, MARTIN, "Kommentar", in Johann Gottfried Herder, *Schriften zu Philosophie, Literatur, Kunst und Altertum 1774–1787*. In JOHANN GOTTFRIED HERDER, *Werke in zehn Bände*. Band 4. Edited by JÜRGEN BRUMMACK – MARTIN BOLLACHER, Frankfurt a. M. 1994, pp. 795–1407

BUBER, MARTIN, *Das Problem des Menschen*, Heidelberg, Lambert Schneider 1948

BURCHARDT, KURT, *Kants Psychologie im Verhältnis zur transzendentalen Methode*, Dissertation, Bonn 1911

CAMPO, MARIANO, *Cristiano Wolff e il razionalismo precritico*, 2 volumes, Milano, Vita e pensiero 1939 – both the volumes are reprinted in a single one, as part of *Christian Wolff: Gesammelte Werke. Materialen und Dokumente*, edited by J. ÉCOLE – J. E. HOFMANN – M. THOMANN – H. W. ARNDT – CH. A. CORR (eds.), Volume 9, Olms, Hildesheim/New York 1980

CASULA, MARIO, *La metafisica di A. G. Baumgarten*, Milano, Mursia 1973

CAYGILL, HOWARD, *A Kant Dictionary*, Oxford/Cambridge (Mass.), Blackwell 1995

CENTI, BEATRICE, *Coscienza, etica e architettonica in Kant. Uno studio attraverso le Critiche*, Pisa-Roma, Istituti editoriali e poligrafici internazionali (Biblioteca di *Studi kantiani*) 2002

CESA, CLAUDIO, "Natura e mondo in Kant", in LUCA FONNESU (ed.), *Etica e mondo in Kant*, Bologna, Il Mulino 2008, pp. 17–34

CHENET, FRANÇOIS-XAVIER, *L'assise de l'ontologie critique: l'esthétique transcendantale*, Lille, Presses Univ. de Lille, 1994

CIAFARDONE, RAFFAELE, "Kraft und Vermögen bei Christian Wolff und Johann Nicolaus Tetens mit Beziehung auf Kant", in JÜRGEN STOLZENBERG – OLIVER-PIERRE RUDOLPH (Hrsg.), *Christian Wolff und die europäische Aufklärung. Akten des 1. Internationalen Christian-Wolff-Kongresses, Halle (Saale), 4.–8. April 2004*. Teil 2 (System der Metaphysik-Logik-Ontologie-Psychologie), wolffiana II.2 (Reihe: Christian Wolff, *Gesammelte Werke*, III Abt., Materialien und Dokumente, Band 102), Olms, Hildesheim 2007, pp. 405–414

CUMMINS, ROBERT, "Functional Analysis", in *The Journal of Philosophy*, 72 (1975), pp. 741–765

DELEUZE, GILLES, *La philosophie critique de Kant. Doctrine des facultés*, Paris, Presses Universitaires de France 1963 (English translation by Hugh Tomlinson and Barbara

Habberjam: *Kant's critical philosophy. The doctrine of the faculties*, London, Athlone Press 1984)

DENIS, LARA (ed.), *Kant's Metaphysics of Morals. A Critical Guide*, Cambridge/New York, Cambridge University Press 2010

DENNETT, DANIEL C., "Artificial Intelligence as Philosophy and as Psychology", in DANIEL C. DENNETT, *Brainstorms* Cambridge (Mass.), Bradford Books, 1978, pp. 109 – 126

DESSOIR, MAX, *Geschichte der neueren deutschen Psychologie*, Berlin, Dunker 1902

DESSOIR, MAX, "Kant und die Psychologie", in *Kant-Studien*, 29 (1924), pp. 98 – 120

DE VLEESCHAUWER, HERMAN J., "La Cinderella dans l'œuvre Kantienne", in GERHARD FUNKE (ed.), *Akten des 4. Internationalen Kant-Kongresses, Mainz 6 – 10 April 1974*, Teil I, Berlin/New York, de Gruyter 1975, pp. 304 – 306

DI GIANDOMENICO, MAURO, "Kant, Soemmerring e il dibattito sulla 'sede dell'anima'", in COSTANTINO ESPOSITO – PASQUALE PONZIO – PAOLO PORRO – VENERANDA CASTELLANO (eds.), *Verum et Certum. Studi di storiografica filosofica in onore di Ada Lamacchia*, Bari, Levante 1998, pp. 167 – 191

ÉCOLE, JEAN, "De la conaissance qu'avait Kant de la métaphysique wolffienne, ou Kant avait-il lu les ouverages métaphysiques de Wolff?", in *Archiv für Geschichte der Philosophie*, 73 (1991), pp. 261 – 273

EISLER, RUDOLF, *Wörterbuch der philosophischen Begriffe*, Berlin, Mittler 1899

EISLER, RUDOLF, *Kant-Lexikon – Nachschlagewerk zu Kants sämtlichen Schriften, Briefen und handschriftlichem Nachlass*, Berlin, Mittler 1930

ENGSTROM, STEPHEN, "Reason, desire, and the will", in LARA DENIS (ed.), *Kant's Metaphysics of Morals. A Critical Guide*, Cambridge/New York, Cambridge University Press 2010, p. 28 – 50

ENGSTROM, STEPHEN, "The *Triebfeder* of Pure Practical Reason", in ANDREWS REATH – JENS TIMMERMANN (eds.), *Kant's Critique of Practical Reason. A Critical Guide*, Cambridge/New York, Cambridge University Press 2010

ERDMANN, BENNO, *Beiträge zur Geschichte und Revision des Textes von Kants Kritik der reinen Vernunft*, Berlin, G. Reimer 1900

ESSER, ANDREA MARLEN, *Eine Ethik für Endliche. Kants "Tugendlehre" in der Gegenwart*, Stuttgart/Bad Cannstatt, Frommann-Holzboog 2004

EULER, WERNER, "Die Suche nach dem 'Seelenorgan'. Kants philosophische Analyse einer anatomischen Entdeckung Soemmerrings", in *Kant-Studien*, 93 (2002), pp. 453 – 480

EULER, WERNER – TUSCHLING, BURKHARD (eds.), *Kants "Metaphysik der Sitten" in der Diskussion. Ein Arbeitsgespräch an der Herzog August Bibliothek Wolfenbüttel 2009*, Berlin, Duncker & Humblot 2013

FABBRI BERTOLETTI, STEFANO, *Impulso, formazione e organismo. Per una storia del concetto di Bildungstrieb nella cultura tedesca*, Firenze, Olschki 1990

FALKENSTEIN, LORNE, *Kant's Intuitionism. A Commentary on the Transcendental Aesthetics*, Toronto, University of Toronto Press 1995

FALDUTO, ANTONINO, Review of ANGELICA NUZZO, *Ideal Embodiment*, in *Kant-Studien*, 102/3 (2011), pp. 401 – 403

FALDUTO, ANTONINO, "*Free will* e *Freie Willkür*: Kant e Searle sulla libertà dell'azione umana", in *Methodus. Revista Internacional de Filosofía Moderna/An International Journal for Modern Philosophy*, 5 (2010), pp. 85 – 96

FALDUTO, ANTONINO, "Das Gefühl als Empfänglichkeit und die Bedeutung einer Ästhetik der Sitten. Anmerkungen zu Birgit Recki", in ANTONINO FALDUTO – CAROLINE KOLISANG –

GABRIEL RIVERO (eds.), *Metaphysik – Ästhetik – Ethik. Beiträge zur Interpretation der Philosophie Kants*, Würzburg, Königshausen & Neumann 2012, pp. 137–153

FALDUTO, ANTONINO, "The Two Meanings of moralisches Gefühl in Kant's Doctrine of Virtue", in STEFANO BACIN – ALFREDO FERRARIN – CLAUDIO LA ROCCA – MARGIT RUFFING (eds.), *Kant and Philosophy in a Cosmopolitan Sense / Kant und die Philosophie in weltbürgerlicher Hinsicht. Akten des XI. Internationalen Kant-Kongresses*, Boston-New York, de Gruyter 2013, volume 3, pp. 161–172pp.

FERRARIN, ALFREDO, *Saggezza, immaginazione e giudizio pratico. Studio su Aristotele e Kant*, Pisa, ETS 2004

FIRLA, MONIKA, *Untersuchungen zum Verhältnis von Anthropologie und Moralphilosophie bei Kant*, Frankfurt a. M., Lang 1981

FLOYD, JULIET, "Heautonomy: Kant on Reflective Judgment and Systematicity", in HERMAN PARRET (ed.), *Kants Ästhetik / Kant's Aesthetics / L'esthétique de Kant*, Berlin / New York, de Gruyter 1998, pp. 192–218

FOERSTER, FRIEDRICH WILHELM, *Der Entwicklungsgang der Kantischen Ethik bis zur Kritik der reinen Vernunft*, Berlin, Mayer & Müller 1893

FONNESU, LUCA, "Kants praktische Philosophie und die Verwirklichung der Moral", in HERTA NAGL-DOCEKAL – RUDOLF LANGTHALER (eds.), *Recht – Geschichte – Religion. Die Bedeutung Kants für die Gegenwart*, Berlin, Akademie Verlag 2004, pp. 49–61

FONNESU, LUCA (ed.), *Etica e mondo in Kant*, Bologna, Il Mulino 2008

FONNESU, LUCA, "Entwicklung und Erweiterung der praktischen Absicht", in STEFANO BACIN – ALFREDO FERRARIN – CLAUDIO LA ROCCA – MARGIT RUFFING (eds.), *Kant and Philosophy in a Cosmopolitan Sense / Kant und die Philosophie in weltbürgerlicher Hinsicht. Akten des XI. Internationalen Kant-Kongresses*, Berlin/Boston, de Gruyter 2013, volume 3, pp. 173–184

FORGIONE, LUCA, "I due volti della *Critica della ragion pura*: argomento analitico e psicologia trascendentale", in *Annali della Facoltà di Scienze della formazione dell'Università di Cagliari*, XXVIII/1 (2005), pp. 137–152

FORKL, MARKUS, *Kants System der Tugendpflichten. Eine Begleitschrift zu den 'Metaphysischen Anfangsgründen der Tugendlehre'*, Frankfurt a. M., Lang 2001

FRIERSON, PATRICK R., *Freedom and Anthropology in Kant's Moral Philosophy*, Cambridge/New York, Cambridge University Press 2003

FRIERSON, PATRICK R., "Kant on the Causes of Human Actions: A Brief Sketch", in VALERIO ROHDEN – RICARDO R. TERRA – GUIDO A. DE ALMEIDA – MARGIT RUFFING (eds.), *Recht und Frieden in der Philosophie Kants. Akten des X. Internationalen Kant-Kongresses*, Band 5, Berlin/New York, de Gruyter 2008, pp. 33–44

FRIERSON, PATRICK R., *What is the Human Being?*, Abingdon/New York, Routledge 2013

FUNKE, GERHARD, "'Achtung für das moralische Gesetz' und Rigorismus / Impersonalismus-Problem", in *Kant-Studien*, 65 (1974) / Akten des 4. Internationalen Kant-Kongresses. Mainz 1974, pp. 45–67

GAWLINA, MANFRED, *Das Medusenhaupt der Kritik. Die Kontroverse zwischen Immanuel Kant und Johann August Eberhard*, Berlin/New York, de Gruyter 1996

GEIGER, IDO, "Rational Feelings and Moral Agency", in *Kantian Review*, 16 (2011), pp. 283–308

GERHARDT, VOLKER, "Handlung als Verhältnis von Ursache und Wirkung: Zur Entwicklung des Handlungsbegriffs bei Kant", in GEROLD PRAUSS (ed.), *Handlungstheorie und Transzendentalphilosophie*, Frankfurt a. M., V. Klostermann 1986, S. 98–131

GERHARDT, VOLKER, *Immanuel Kant. Vernunft und Leben*, Stuttgart, Reclam 2002
GERLACH, HANS-MARTIN, "Gefühl – Sinnlichkeit – Verstand. Bemerkungen zu einem erkenntnistheoretisch-psychologischen Problem in der Philosophie der Aufklärung", in *Deutsche Zeitschrift für Philosophie* (Berlin) 32/11 (1984), pp. 991–999
GESANG, BERNWARD (ed.), *Kants vergessener Rezensent. Die Kritik der theoretischen und praktischen Philosophie Kants in fünf frühen Rezensionen von Hermann Andreas Pistorius*, Hamburg, Meiner 2007
GIGLIOTTI, GIANNA, "'Vermögen' e 'Kraft'. Una rilettura del concetto di 'sintesi' nella *Critica della ragion pura* di Kant", *Rivista di storia della filosofia*, 2/1995, pp. 255–275
GIGLIOTTI, GIANNA, "Naturale e artificiale: il problema del carattere in Kant", *Rivista di filosofia*, 92 (2001), pp. 411–433
GIGLIOTTI, GIANNA, "Il rispetto del tulipano. Riflessioni sul sistema kantiano delle facoltà", *Rivista di storia della filosofia*, 1/2001, pp. 25–61
GIORDANETTI, PIERO, "Kants Entdeckung der Apriorität des Geschmacksurteils. Zur Genese der *Kritik der Urteilskraft*", in HEINER F. KLEMME – BERND LUDWIG – MICHAEL PAUEN – WERNER STARK (eds.), *Aufklärung und Interpretation – Studien zu Kants Philosophie und ihrem Umkreis. Tagung aus Anlaß des 60. Geburtstags von Reinhard Brandt*, Würzburg, Königshausen und Neumann 1999, pp. 171–196
GIORDANETTI, PIERO, *Rivoluzione copernicano-newtoniana e sentimento in Kant*, Frankfurt am Main, Lang 2012
GISI, LUCAS MARCO, *Einbildungskraft und Mythologie. Die Verschränkung von Anthropologie und Geschichte im 18. Jahrhundert*, Berlin/New York, de Gruyter 2007
GOY, INA, "Immanuel Kant über das moralische Gefühl der Achtung", in *Zeitschrift für philosophische Forschung*, 61 (2007), pp. 337–360
GREGOR, MARY J., *Laws of Freedom: A Study of Kant's Method of Applying the Categorical Imperative in the "Metaphysik der Sitten"*, Oxford, Blackwell 1963
GREGOR, MARY J., "Baumgarten's Aesthetica", in *The Review of Metaphysics*, 37/2 (1983), pp. 357–385
GRENBERG, JANINE MARIE, *Moral Feeling and Human Autonomy: A Kantian Account of Action*, Dissertation, Emory University, 1996
GRENBERG, JEANINE M., "Anthropology from a Metaphysical Point of View", in *Journal of the History of Philosophy*, 37/1 (1999), pp. 91–115
GROVE, PETER, "Johann August Eberhards Theorie des Gefühls", in HANS-JOACHIM KERTSCHER – ERNST STÖCKMANN (edited by), *Ein Antipode Kants? Johann August Eberhard im Spannungsfeld von spätaufklärerischer Philosophie und Theologie*, Berlin/Boston, de Gruyter 2012, pp. 119–131
GUERRA, AUGUSTO, "Metafisica e vita morale nel primo scritto kantiano (1746–1747)", *De homine* 31/32 (1969), pp. 91–118
GUYER, PAUL, *Kant and the Claims of Taste*, Cambridge/New York, Cambridge University Press, 1997 (second edition)
GUYER, PAUL, "Moral Feelings in the Metaphysics of Morals", in LARA DENIS (ed.), *Kant's Metaphysics of Morals. A Critical Guide*, Cambridge/New York, Cambridge University Press 2010, pp. 103–151
HAAG, JOHANNES, *Erfahrung und Gegenstand. Das Verhältnis von Sinnlichkeit und Verstand*, Frankfurt a. M., Klostermann 2007
HANNA, ROBERT, *Kant and the Foundations of Analytic Philosophy*, Oxford, Clarendon Press 2001

HARNACK, ADOLF, *Geschichte der Königlich Preußischen Akademie der Wissenschaften zu Berlin*, 2 volums, Berlin 1900

HARTKOPF, WERNER, *Die Berliner Akademie der Wissenschaften: Ihre Mitglieder und Preisträger*, Berlin 1992

HATFIELD, GARY, *The Natural and the Normative: Theories of Spatial Perception from Kant to Helmholtz*, Cambridge (Mass.)/London, MIT Press 1990

HATFIELD, GARY, "Empirical, Rational, and Transcendental Psychology. Psychology as Science and as Philosophy", in PAUL GUYER (ed.), *The Cambridge Companion to Kant*, Cambridge, Cambridge University Press 1992, pp. 200–227

HATFIELD, GARY, "Kant and Empirical Psychology in the 18th Century", in *Psychological Science*, 9/6 (1998), pp. 423–428

HATFIELD, GARY, "The Cognitive Faculties", in MICHAEL AYERS – DANIEL GARBER (eds.), *The Cambridge History of Seventeenth Century Philosophy*, Cambridge, Cambridge University Press 1998, pp. 953–1002

HEINZ, MARION, "Moralpsychologie statt Metaphysik der Sitten. Untersuchungen zu Reinholds Konzeption von praktischer Vernunft", in VIOLETTA STOLZ – MARION HEINZ – MARTIN BONDELI (eds.), *Wille, Willkür, Freiheit. Reinholds Freiheitskonzeption im Kontext der Philosophie des 18. Jahrhunderts*, Berlin/Boston, de Gruyter 2012, pp. 167–191

HENRICH, DIETER, "Hutcheson und Kant", in *Kant-Studien*, 49 (1957/1958), pp. 49–69

HENRICH, DIETER, "Kants früheste Ethik. Versuch einer Rekonstruktion", in *Kant-Studien*, 54 (1963), pp. 404–431

HENRICH, DIETER, "Über Kants Entwicklungsgeschichte", in *Philosophische Rundschau*, 13 (1965), pp. 252–263

HENRICH, DIETER, "The Proof-Structure of Kant's Transcendental Deduction", in *The Review of Metaphysics*, Vol. 22/4 (1969), pp. 640–659

HERMAN, BARBARA, *The Practice of Moral Judgment*, Cambridge (Mass.)/London, Harvard University Press 1993

HESSBRÜGGEN-WALTER, STEFAN, *Die Seele und ihre Vermögen. Kants Metaphysik des Mentalen in der 'Kritik der reinen Vernunft'*, Paderborn, Mentis 2004

HINSKE, NORBERT, "Kants Idee der Anthropologie", in HEINRICH ROMBACH (ed.), *Die Frage nach dem Menschen. Aufriß einer philosophischen Anthropologie. Festschrift für Max Müller zum 60. Geburtstag*, Freiburg i.Br./München, Alber 1966, pp. 410–427

HINSKE, NORBERT, *Kants Weg zur Transzendentalphilosophie. Der dreißigjährige Kant*, Stuttgart/Berlin/Bonn/Mainz, Kohlhammer 1970

HINSKE, NORBERT, *Kant als Herausforderung an die Gegenwart*, Freiburg/München, Alber 1980

HINSKE, NORBERT, "Wolffs empirische Psychologie und Kants pragmatische Anthropologie. Zur Diskussion über die Anfänge der Anthropologie im 18. Jahrhundert", in NORBERT HINSKE (ed.), *Die Bestimmung des Menschen*, thematic volume of *Aufklärung*, 11/1 (1996), pp. 97–107

HINSKE, NORBERT, "Transzendental, das Transzendentale, Transzendentalien, Transzendentalphilosophie, V. 18 Jh.", in JOACHIM RITTER – KARLFREID GRÜNDER (eds.), *Historisches Wörterbuch der Philosophie*, volume 10, Darmstadt 1998, columns 1376–1388

HINSKE, NORBERT, "La psicologia empirica di Wolff e l'antropologia pragmatica di Kant. La fondazione di una nuova scienza empirica e le sue complicazioni", in GIUSEPPE CACCIATORE – VANNA GESSA-KUROTSCHKA – HANS POSER – MANUELA SANNA (eds.), *La*

filosofia pratica tra metafisica e antropologia nell'età di Wolff e Vico/Praktische Philosophie im Spannungsfeld von Metaphysik und Anthropologie bei Wolff und Vico, Napoli, Alfredo Guida Editore 1999, pp. 207–224

HINSKE, NORBERT, "Die Jäsche-Logik und ihr besonderes Schicksal im Rahmen der Akademie-Ausgabe", in REINHARD BRANDT – WERNER STARK (eds.), *Zustand und Zukunft der Akademie-Ausgabe von Immanuel Kants Gesammelten Schriften*, Sonderheft: *Kant-Studien*, 91 (2000), pp. 85–93

HINSKE, NORBERT, "Ein unbeachtet gebliebener Kommentar zu Kants *Grundlegung zur Metaphysik der Sitten* aus dem Jahre 1784", in STEFFEN DIETZSCH – UDO TIETZ (eds.), *Transzendentalphilosophie und die Kultur der Gegenwart*, Leipzig 2012, pp. 107–112

HINTIKKA, JAAKKO, "Transcendental Arguments: Genuine and Spurious", in *Noûs*, 6/3 (1972), pp. 274–281

HÖWING, THOMAS, *Praktische Lust. Kant über das Verhältnis von Fühlen, Begehren und praktischer Vernunft*, Berlin/Boston, de Gruyter 2013

HOLZHEY, HELMUT – MUDROCH, VILEM, *Historical Dictionary of Kant and Kantianism (Historical Dictionaries of Religions, Philosophies, and Movements, No. 60)*, Lanham (Maryland)/Toronto/Oxford, The Scarecrow Press 2005

HOPPE, HANSGEORG, *Synthesis bei Kant*, Berlin/New York, De Gruyter 1983

HOENEGGER, HANSMICHAEL, "Geist, mens, nous. Teleologia della filosofia e sistema teleologico delle facoltà in Kant", in EUGENIO CANONE (ed.), *Per una storia del concetto di mente*, vol. II, Firenze, Olschki 2007, pp. 327–368

IVALDO, MARCO, "Volontà e arbitrio nella *Metafisica dei Costumi*", in *Kant e la morale. A duecento anni da "La metafisica dei costumi". Convegno della Società Italiana di Studi Kantiani presso la Scuola Normale Superiore di Pisa*, Pisa-Roma, Istituti Editoriali e Poligrafici Internazionali 1999, pp. 41–67

JANSOHN, HEINZ, *Kants Lehre von der Subjektivität. Eine systematische Analyse des Verhältnisses von transzendentaler und empirischer Subjektivität in seiner theoretischen Philosophie*, Bonn, Bouvier 1969

JOST, LAWRENCE – WUERTH, JULIAN (ed.), *Perfecting Virtue: New Essays on Kantian Ethics and Virtue Ethics*, Cambridge/New York, Cambridge University Press, 2011

KAULBACH, FRIEDRICH, "Weltorientierung, Weltkenntnis und pragmatische Vernunft bei Kant", in FRIEDRICH KAULBACH – JOACHIM RITTER (eds.), *Kritik und Metaphysik. Studien. Heinz Heimsoeth zum achtzigsten Geburtstag*, Berlin, de Gruyter 1966, pp. 60–75

KERTSCHER, HANS-JOACHIM – STÖCKMANN, ERNST (eds.), *Ein Antipode Kants? Johann August Eberhard im Spannungsfeld von spätaufklärerischer Philosophie und Theologie*, Berlin/Boston, de Gruyter 2012

KERTSCHER, HANS-JOACHIM – STÖCKMANN, ERNST, "Einleitung", in HANS-JOACHIM KERTSCHER – ERNST STÖCKMANN (eds.), *Ein Antipode Kants? Johann August Eberhard im Spannungsfeld von spätaufklärerischer Philosophie und Theologie*, Berlin/Boston, de Gruyter 2012, pp. 1–3

KIM, SOO BAE, *Die Entstehung der Kantischen Anthropologie und ihre Beziehung zum empirischen Psychologie der Wolffschen Schule*, Frankfurt a. M., Lang 1994

KITCHER, PATRICIA, "Discovering the Forms of Intuition", in *The Philosophical Review*, XCVI/2 (1987), pp. 205–248

KITCHER, PATRICIA, "Kant's Dedicated Cognitivist System", in JOHN-CHRISTIAN SMITH (ed.), *Historical Foundations of Cognitive Science*, Dordrecht, Kluwer 1990, pp. 189–209

KITCHER, PATRICIA, *Kant's Transcendental Psychology*, Oxford/New York, Oxford University Press 1990

KITCHER, PATRICIA, "Kant's Transcendental Psychology", in GERHARD FUNKE (Hrsg.), *Akten des Siebenten Internationalen Kant-Kongresses. Kurfürstliches Schloß zu Mainz 1990* (volume II.1: Sektionsbeiträge. Sektionen A – F), Bonn, Bouvier 1991, S. 215–225

KITCHER, PATRICIA, *Kant's Thinker*, Oxford/New York, Oxford University Press 2011

KITCHER, PHILIP, "A Priori Knowledge", in *The Philosophical Review*, 89 (1980), pp. 3–23

KLEINGELD, PAULINE, "Moral Consciousness and the 'Fact of Reason'", in ANDREWS REATH – JENS TIMMERMANN (eds.), *Kant's Critique of Practical Reason. A Critical Guide*, Cambridge/New York, Cambridge University Press 2010, pp. 55–72

KLEMME, HEINER F., *Kants Philosophie des Subjekts. Systematische und entwicklungsgeschichtliche Untersuchungen zum Verhältnis von Selbstbewußtsein und Selbsterkenntnis*, Hamburg, Meiner [Kant-Forschungen, volume VII] 1996

KLEMME, HEINER F., "Die Freiheit der Willkür und die Herrschaft des Bösen. Kants Lehre vom radikalen Bösen zwischen Moral, Religion und Recht", in HEINER F. KLEMME – BERND LUDWIG – MICHAEL PAUEN – WERNER STARK (eds.), *Aufklärung und Interpretation – Studien zu Kants Philosophie und ihrem Umkreis. Tagung aus Anlaß des 60. Geburtstags von Reinhard Brandt*, Würzburg, Königshausen und Neumann 1999, pp. 125–151

KLEMME, HEINER F., "Einleitung" to "Erste Einleitung in die Kritik der Urteilskraft", pp. 473–483, in IMMANUEL KANT, *Kritik der Urteilskraft – Beilage: Erste Einleitung in die Kritik der Urteilskraft*, edited by HEINER F. KLEMME, with explanatory notes by PIERO GIORDANETTI, Hamburg, Meiner 2006

KLEMME, HEINER F., KUEHN, MANFRED, SCHÖNECKER, DIETER (eds.), *Moralische Motivation: Kant und die Alternativen*, Hamburg, Meiner 2006

KLEMME, HEINER F., "Moralisches Sollen, Autonomie und Achtung. Kants Konzeption der 'libertas indifferentiae' zwischen Wolff und Crusius", in VALERIO ROHDEN – RICARDA R. TERRA – GUIDO A. DE ALMEIDA – MARGIT RUFFING (eds.), *Recht und Frieden in der Philosophie Kants. Akten des X. Internationalen Kant-Kongresses*, Band 3: Sektionen III–IV, Berlin/New York, W. de Gruyter 2008, pp. 215–228

KLEMME, HEINER F., "Necessità pratica e indifferenza del volere. Considerazioni sulla '*libertas indifferentiae*'", in LUCA FONNESU (ed.), *Etica e mondo in Kant*, Bologna, Il Mulino 2008, pp. 57–73

KLEMME, HEINER F., "Immanuel Kant", in EIKE BOHLKEN – CHRISTIAN THEIS (eds.), *Handbuch Anthropologie. Der Mensch zwischen Natur, Kultur und Technik*, Stuttgart/Weimar, J. B. Metzler 2009, pp. 11–16

KLEMME, HEINER F., "The Origin and Aim of Kant's *Critique of Practical Reason*", in ANDREWS REATH – JENS TIMMERMANN (eds.), *Kant's Critique of Practical Reason. A Critical Guide*, Cambridge/New York, Cambridge University Press 2010, pp. 11–30

KLEMME, HEINER F. – KUEHN, MANFRED (eds.), *Dictionary of Eighteenth-Century German Philosophers*, Bristol, Thoemmes Continuum 2010

KLEMME, HEINER F., "Die rationalistische Interpretation von Kants 'Paralogismen der reinen Vernunft'", in CHOTAS JIRI – JINDRICH KARASEK – JÜRGEN STOLZENBERG (eds.), *Metaphysik und Kritik. Interpretationen zur "Transzendentalen Dialektik" der Kritik der reinen Vernunft*, Würzburg, Königshausen & Neumann 2010, pp. 141–157

KLEMME, HEINER F., "Spontaneität und Selbsterkenntnis. Kant über die ursprüngliche Einheit von Natur und Freiheit im Aktus des Denkens (1785–1787/88)", in MARIO BRANDHORST – ANDREE HAHMANN – BERND LUDWIG (eds.), *Sind wir Bürger zweier Welten? Freiheit und*

moralische Verantwortung im transzendentalen Idealismus, Hamburg, Meiner 2012, pp. 195–222

Klemme, Heiner F., "Erkennen, Fühlen, Begehren, – Selbstbesitz. Reflexionen über die Verbindung der Vermögen in Kants Lehre vom Kategorischen Imperativ", in Inga Römer (ed.), *Affektivität und Ethik bei Kant und in der Phänomenologie*, Berlin/Boston, de Gruyter 2014 (forthcoming)

Kulenkampff, Jens, "Moralisches Gefühl oder moral sense – wie berechtigt ist Kants Kritik?", in *Jahrbuch für Recht und Ethik/Annual Review of Law and Ethics*, 12 (2004), pp. 234–251

Landau, Albert (ed.), *Rezensionen zur Kantischen Philosophie, 1781–1787*, Bebra (Landau) 1991

Landucci, Sergio, *Sull'etica di Kant*, Milano, Guerini e Associati 1994

Langlois, Luc, "Du sentiment moral à la raison pratique. Kant disciple et critique de Hutcheson", in Robert Theis – Lukas K. Sosoe (eds.), *Le sources de la philosophie kantienne aux XVIIe et XVIIIe siècles*, Paris, Vrin 2005, pp. 203–211

La Rocca, Claudio, "La distinzione kantiana tra *Wille* e *Willkür* e il problema della libertà", in *Eticidad y Estado en el Idealismo Alemán*, Valencia, Natán 1987, pp. 19–40

La Rocca, Claudio, *Soggetto e mondo. Studi su Kant*, Venezia, Marsilio 2003

La Rocca, Claudio, "Psicologia", in Stefano Besoli – Claudio La Rocca – Riccardo Martinelli (eds.), *L'universo kantiano. Filosofia, scienze, sapere*, Macerata, Quodlibet 2010, pp. 391–435

Lauener, Henri, "Der systematische Stellenwert des Gefühls der Achtung in Kants Ethik", in *Dialectica*, 35 (1981), pp. 243–264

Lee, Ming-Huei, *Das Problem des moralischen Gefühls in der Entwicklung der Kantischen Ethik*, Dissertation, Bonn 1997

Lenoir, Timothy, "Kant, Blumenbach and Vital Materialism in German Biology", in *Isis*, 71/1 (1980), pp. 71–108

Linden, Mareta, *Untersuchungen zum Anthropologiebegriff des 18. Jahrhunderts*, Frankfurt a. M., Lang 1976

Longuenesse, Béatrice, *Kant et le pouvoir de juger: Sensibilité et discursivité dans l'Analytique de la* Critique de la raison pure, Paris, Presses Universitaire de France 1993; English translation by Charles T. Wolfe, *Kant and the Capacity to Judge: Sensibility and Discursivity in the Transcendental Analytic of the* Critique of Pure Reason, Princeton, Princeton University Press 1998

Louden, Robert B., *Kant's Impure Ethics. From Rational Beings to Human Beings*, Oxford/New York, Oxford University Press 2000

Louden, Robert B., *Kant's Human Being. Essays on His Theory of Human Nature*, Oxford/New York, Oxford University Press 2011

Ludwig, Bernd, *Kants Rechtslehre*, Hamburg, Meiner [Kant-Forschungen, volume II] 1988

Ludwig, Bernd, "'The Right of a State' in Immanuel Kant's Doctrine of Right", in *Journal of the History of Philosophy*, 27/3 (1990), pp. 403–415

Ludwig, Bernd, "Die 'consequente Denkungsart der speculativen Kritik'. Kants radikale Umgestaltung seiner Freiheitslehre im Jahre 1786 – und die Folgen für die Kritische Philosophie als Ganze", in *Deutsche Zeitschrift für Philosophie*, 58/4 (2010), pp. 595–628

Ludwig, Bernd, "Was weiß ich vom Ich? Kants Lehre vom Faktum der reinen praktischen Vernunft, seine Neufassung der Paralogismen und die verborgenen Fortschritte der

Kritischen Metaphysik im Jahre 1786", in MARIO BRANDHORST – ANDREE HAHMANN – BERND LUDWIG (eds.), *Sind wir Bürger zweier Welten? Freiheit und moralische Verantwortung im transzendentalen Idealismus*, Hamburg, Meiner 2012, pp. 155–194

LUNATI, GIANCARLO, "Il significato del 'sentimento' nel pensiero morale del Kant precritico", in *Annali della Scuola Normale Superiore*, 32 (1954), pp. 237–256

MACBEATH, A. MURRAY, "Kant on Moral Feeling", in *Kant-Studien*, 64 (1973), pp. 283–314

MAKKREEL, RUDOLF, "Kant on the Scientific Status of Psychology, Anthropology, and History", in ERIC WATKINS (ed.), *Kant and the Sciences*, Oxford, Oxford University Press 2002, pp. 185–201

MARQUARD, ODO, "Zur Geschichte des philosophischen Begriffs 'Anthropologie' seit dem Ende des achtzehnten Jahrhunderts", in *Collegium philosophicum. Studien Joachim Ritter zum 60. Geburtstag*, Basel-Stuttgart, Schwabe 1965, pp. 209–239

MARTINELLI, RICCARDO, "Ein 'so lange aufgenommener Fremdling'. Kant und die Entwicklung der Psychologie", in CINZIA FERRINI (ed.), *Eredità kantiane (1804–2004). Questioni emergenti e problemi irrisolti*, Napoli, Bibliopolis 2004, pp. 333–355

MCCARTY, RICHARD R., "Kantian Moral Motivation and the Feeling of Respect", in *The Journal of the History of Philosophy*, 31 (1993), pp. 421–435

MCLAUGHLIN, PETER, "Soemmerring und Kant: Über das Organ der Seele und den Streit der Fakultäten", in *Soemmerring-Forschungen*, 1 (1985), pp. 191–201

MEERBOTE, RALF, "*Wille* and *Willkür* in Kant's Theory of Action", in MOLTKE S. GRAM (ed.) *Interpreting Kant*, Jowa City, University of Jowa Press 1982, pp. 69–84

MEERBOTE, RALF, "Kant's Functionalism", in JOHN-CHRISTIAN SMITH (ed.), *Historical Foundations of Cognitive Science*, Dordrecht, Kluwer 1990, pp. 161–188

MENZER, PAUL, "Der Entwicklungsgang der Kantischen Ethik in den Jahren 1760 bis 1785", in *Kant-Studien*, 2 (1898), pp. 290–322; 3 (1899), pp. 41–104

MENZER, PAUL, *Kants Lehre von der Entwicklung in Natur und Geschichte*, Berlin 1911

MERTENS, HELGA, *Kommentar zur Ersten Einleitung in Kants Kritik der Urteilskraft. Zur systematischen Funktion der Kritik der Urteilskraft für das System der Vernunftkritik*, Berchmans, München 1975

MEYER, JÜRGEN BONA, *Kant's Psychologie. Dargestellt und erörtert von*, Berlin, Wilhelm Hertz (Bessersche Buchhandlung) 1870

MODEL, ANSELM, "Zur Bedeutung und Ursprung von 'übersinnlich' bei Immanuel Kant", in *Archiv für Begriffsgeschichte*, Volume 30 (1986), pp. 182–191

MODEL, ANSELM, "Anmerkungen zum Terminus 'übersinnlich' bei Jacob Böhme und Immanuel Kant", in *Erkenntnis und Wissenschaft, Jacob Böhme (1575–1624). Internationales Jacob-Böhme-Symposium, Görlitz 2000. Neues Lausitzisches Magazin*, Volume 2, Görlitz (Zittau), Oettel 2001, pp. 158–163

MORRISON, IAIN, "Respect in Kant: How the Moral Feeling of Respect Acts As an Incentive to Moral Action", in *Southwest Philosophy Review* (Stillwater), 20 (2004), pp. 1–26

MÜLLER, HANS-HEINRICH, *Akademie und Wirtschaft im 18. Jahrhundert. Agrarökonomische Preisaufgaben und Preisschriften der Preußischen Akademie der Wissenschaften. Versuch, Tendenzen und Überblick*, Berlin, Akademie-Verlag 1975

NAKAZAWA, TAKESCHI, *Kants Begriff der Sinnlichkeit. Seine Unterscheidung zwischen apriorischen und aposteriorischen Elementen der sinnlichen Erkenntnis und deren lateinische Vorlagen*, Stuttgart/Bad Cannstatt, Frommann-Holzboog 2009

NEIS, CORDULA, *Anthropologie im Sprachdenken des 18. Jahrhunderts: Die Berliner Preisfrage nach dem Ursprung der Sprache (1771)*, Berlin/New York, de Gruyter 2003

NICOLAI, CHRISTOPH FRIEDRICH (ed.), *Neun Gespräche zwischen Christian Wolff und einem Kantianer über Kants metaphysische Anfangsgründe der Rechtslehre und der Tugendlehre*, first edition: Berlin 1798; reprint in *Aetas Kantiana* (vol. 199), Bruxelles, Culture et Civilisation 1968

NOBBE, FRANK, *Kants Frage nach dem Menschen. Die Kritik der ästhetischen Urteilskraft als transzendentale Anthropologie*, Frankfurt a. M., Lang 1995

Nouveaux Mémoires de l'Academie Royale des Sciences et Belles-Lettres. Anné MDCCLXXIII. Berlin 1775

NUZZO, ANGELICA, "Kant and Herder on Baumgaten's Aesthetica", in *Journal of the History of Philosophy*, 44/4 (2006), pp. 577–597

NUZZO, ANGELICA, *Kant and the Unity of Reason*, West Lafayette, Indiana, Purdue University Press 2008

NUZZO, ANGELICA, *Ideal Embodiment. Kant's Theory of Sensibility*, Bloomington / Indianapolis, Indiana University Press 2008

OBERDORFER, BERND, "Sinnlichkeit und Moral. Zur Bedeutung der Erfahrungstheorie für die 'intellektuelle und moralische Bildung des Menschen' in Eberhards *Allgemeiner Theorie des Denkens und Empfindens*", in HANS-JOACHIM KERTSCHER – ERNST STÖCKMANN (eds.), *Ein Antipode Kants? Johann August Eberhard im Spannungsfeld von spätaufklärerischer Philosophie und Theologie*, Berlin/Boston, de Gruyter 2012, pp. 109–118

PACKER, MARK, "Kant on Desire and Moral Pleasure", in *The Journal of the History of Ideas*, 50 (1989), pp. 429–442

PALMQUIST, STEPHEN, "Is Duty Kant's Motive for Moral Action?", in *Ratio*, 28 (1986), pp. 168–174

PANKNIN-SCHAPPERT, HELKE, *Innerer Sinn und moralisches Gefühl – Zur Bedeutung eines Begriffspaares bei Shaftesbury und Hutcheson sowie in Kants vorkritischen Schriften*, Hildesheim-Zürich-New York, Olms 2007

PARK, CHAN-GOO, *Das moralische Gefühl in der britischen moral-sense-Schule und bei Kant*, Dissertation, Tübingen 1995

PARRET, HERMAN (ed.), *Kants Ästhetik / Kant's Aesthetics / L'esthétique de Kant*, Berlin/New York, de Gruyter 1998

PATON, HERBERT J., *The Categorical Imperative. A Study in Kant's Moral Philosophy*, first edition London 1947, reprint (among others): Philadelphia (Penn.), University of Pennsylvania Press 1971

PHILONENKO, ALEXIS, "L'architectonique de la *Critique de la faculté de juger*", in HERMAN PARRET (ed.), *Kants Ästhetik / Kant's Aesthetics / L'esthétique de Kant*, Berlin/New York, de Gruyter 1998, pp. 41–52

PIEROBON, FRANK, "L'architectonique et la faculté de juger", in HERMAN PARRET (ed.), *Kants Ästhetik / Kant's Aesthetics / L'esthétique de Kant*, Berlin/New York, de Gruyter 1998, pp. 1–17

PIRILLO, NESTORE, *L'uomo di mondo fra morale e ceto. Kant e le trasformazioni del Moderno*, Bologna, Il Mulino 1987

REATH, ANDREWS, "Kant's Theory of Moral Sensibility. Respect for the Moral Law and the Influence of Inclination", in *Kant-Studien*, 80 (1989), pp. 284–302

REATH, ANDREWS – TIMMERMANN, JENS (eds.), *Kant's Critique of Practical Reason. A Critical Guide*, Cambridge/New York, Cambridge University Press 2010

RECKI, BIRGIT, *Ästhetik der Sitten. Die Affinität von ästhetischem Gefühl und praktischer Vernunft bei Kant*, Frankfurt a. M., V. Klostermann 2001

RECKI, BIRGIT, "Achtung vor der zweckmäßigen Natur: die Erweiterung der Kantischen Ethik durch die dritte Kritik", in VOLKER GERHARDT – ROLF-PETER HORSTMANN – RALPH SCHUMACHER (eds.), *Kant und die Berliner Aufklärung. Akten des IX. Internationalen Kant-Kongresses*, Berlin/New York, de Gruyter 2001, Vol. 3 (Sections VI-X), pp. 296–304

RECKI, BIRGIT, "Wie fühlt man sich als vernünftiges Wesen? Immanuel Kant über ästhetische und moralische Gefühle", in EADEM, *Die Vernunft, ihre Natur, ihr Gefühl und der Fortschritt*, Paderborn, Mentis 2006

RECKI, BIRGIT, "Kant: Vernunftgewirkte Gefühle", in HILGE LANDWEHR – URSULA RENZ (eds.), *Klassische Emotionstheorien. Von Platon bis Wittgenstein*, Berlin/New York, de Gruyter 2008, pp. 457–477

RECKI, BIRGIT, "Kants 'Ästhetik der Sitten'. Ein Beitrag zum Problem der moralischen Motivation", in ANTONINO FALDUTO – CAROLINE KOLISANG – GABRIEL RIVERO (eds.), *Metaphysik – Ästhetik – Ethik. Beiträge zur Interpretation der Philosophie Kants*, Würzburg, Königshausen & Neumann 2012, pp. 121–135

RECKI, BIRGIT, "Kant über Achtung und Glauben. Leistung und Probleme seines motivationstheoretischen Beitrags", in ANNE TILKORN (ed.), *Motivationen für das Selbst. Kant und Spinoza im Vergleich*, Wiesbaden, Harrassowitz 2012, pp. 49–68

RICHARDS, ROBERT J., "Kant and Blumenbach on the *Bildungstrieb*: A Historical Misunderstanding", in *Studies in History and Philosophy of Biological and Biomedical Sciences*, 31 (2000), pp. 11–32

RIVERO, GABRIEL, "Zur Entstehung der Anthropologie Kants. Die Anthropologie im Hinblick auf den kantischen Metaphysikbegriff der Phase κ", in *Methodus. Revista Internacional de Filosofía Moderna/An International Journal for Modern Philosophy*, volume 6/2 (2011), pp. 179–204

RIZO-PATRÓN DE LERNER, ROSEMARY –VÁZQUEZ LOBEIRAS, MARÍA JESÚS (eds.), *La razón y sus fines. Elementos para una antropología filosófica en Kant, Husserl y Horkheimer*, Hildesheim, Olms 2013

ROELCKE, THORSTEN, *Die Terminologie der Erkenntnisvermögen. Wörterbuch und lexikosemantische Untersuchung zu Kants 'Kritik der reinen Vernunft'*, Tübingen, Max Niemeyer 1989

RUMORE, PAOLA, "La concezione kantiana della psicologia razionale", in STEFANO BACIN – ALFREDO FERRARIN – CLAUDIO LA ROCCA – MARGIT RUFFING (eds.), *Kant and Philosophy in a Cosmopolitan Sense / Kant und die Philosophie in weltbürgerlicher Hinsicht. Akten des XI. Internationalen Kant-Kongresses*, Boston-New York, de Gruyter 2013, volume 4, pp. 459–472

RYLE, GILBERT, *The Concept of the Mind*, London, Hutchinson 1949

SATURA, VLADIMIR, *Kants Erkenntnispsychologie in den Nachschriften seiner Vorlesungen über empirische Psychologie*, Köln, Bouvier 1971

SCHADOW, STEFFI, *Achtung für das Gesetz. Moral und Motivation bei Kant*, Berlin/Boston, de Gruyter 2013

SCHILPP, PAUL ARTHUR, *Kant's Pre-Critical Ethics*, Evaston (Ill.), Northwestern University Press 1970

SCHMIDT, CLAUDIA M., "The Anthropological Dimension of Kant's Metaphysics of Morals", in *Kant-Studien*, 96 (2005), pp. 66–84

SCHMIDT, CLAUDIA M., "Kant's Transcendental, Empirical, Pragmatic, and Moral Anthropology", in *Kant-Studien*, 98 (2007), pp. 156–182

SCHMITZ, WALTER – ZELLE, CARSTEN (eds.), *Innovation und Transfer. Naturwissenschaften, Anthropologie und Literatur im 18. Jahrhundert*, Dresden, Thelem 2004

SCHMUCKER, JOSEPH, *Die Ursprünge der Ethik Kants in seinen vorkritischen Schriften und Reflektionen*, Meisenheim am Glan, A. Hain 1961

SCHNEIDER, ULRICH JOHANNES (ed.), *Seine Welt wissen. Enzyklopädien in der Frühen Neuzeit. Katalog zur Ausstellung der Universitätsbibliothek Leipzig und der Herzog August Bibliothek Wolfenbüttel*, Darmstadt, Primus 2006

SCHÖNECKER, DIETER (with ALEXANDER COTTER, MAGDALENA ECKES, SEBASTIAN MALY), "Kant über Menschenliebe als moralische Gemütsanlage", in *Archiv für Geschichte der Philosophie*, 92 (2010), pp. 133–175

SCHRADER, GEORGE, "The Status of Feeling in Kant's Philosophy", in PIERRE LABERGE – FRANCOIS DUCHESNEAU – BRYAN E. MORRISEY (eds.), *Actes du Congrès d'Ottawa sur Kant dans les Traditions Anglo-Américaine et Continentale*, Ottawa, University of Ottawa Press 1976, pp. 143–16

SCHWAIGER, CLEMENS, *Kategorische und andere Imperative. Zur Entwicklung von Kants praktischer Philosophie bis 1785*, Stuttgart/Bad Cannstatt, Frommann-Holzboog 1999

SCHWAIGER, CLEMENS, "Denken des 'Übersinnlichen' bei Kant. Zu Herkunft und Verwendung einer Schlüsselkategorie seiner praktischen Metaphysik", in NORBERT FISCHER (ed.), *Kants Metaphysik und Religionsphilosophie*, Hamburg, Meiner 2004, pp. 331–345

SENSEN, OLIVER (ed.), *Kant on Moral Autonomy*, Cambridge/New York, Cambridge University Press 2012

SENSEN, OLIVER, "The Role of Feelings in Kant's Moral Philosophy", in *Studi Kantiani*, vol. 25 (2012), pp. 45–58

SHELL, SUSAN MELD, *The Embodiment of Reason: Kant on Spirit, Generation and Community*, Chicago, University of Chicago Press 1996

SHERMAN, NANCY, "The Place of Emotions in Kantian Morality", in OWEN FLANAGAN – AMÉLIE OKSENBERG RORTY (eds.), *Identity, Character, and Morality: Essays in Moral Psychology*, Cambridge (Mass.)/London, MIT Press 1990, pp. 149–170

SHERMAN, NANCY, *Making a Necessity of Virtue. Aristotle and Kant on Virtue*, Cambridge/New York, Cambridge University Press 1997

SIDGWICK, HENRY, "The Kantian Conception of Free Will", in *Mind – A Quarterly Review of Psychology and Philosophy*, 12/51 (1888), pp. 405–412

SIMMERMACHER, VOLKER, *Kants Kritik der reinen Vernunft als Grundlegung einer Anthropologia transcendentalis*, Heidelberg, Dissertation 1951

SLOAN, PHILLIP R., "Preforming the Categories: Eighteenth-Century Generation Theory and Biological Roots of Kant's A Priori", in *Journal of the History of Philosophy*, 40/2 (2002), pp. 229–253

SLOTE, MICHAEL, *From Morality to Virtue*, Oxford/New York, Oxford University Press 1992

SLOTE, MICHAEL, *Moral Sentimentalism*, Oxford/New York, Oxford University Press 2010

SOMMER, ROBERT, *Grundzüge einer Geschichte der Deutschen Psychologie und Aesthetik von Wolff-Baumgarten bis Kant-Schiller. Nach einer von der königlich preußischen Akademie der Wissenschaften in Berlin preisgekrönten Schrift des Verfassers*, Würzburg, Staehl 1892

STARK, WERNER, *Nachforschungen zu Briefen und Handschriften Immanuel Kants*, Berlin, Akademie Verlag 1993

STEKELER-WEITHOFER, PIRMIN, "Willkür und Wille bei Kant", in *Kant-Studien*, 81 (1990), pp. 304–320

STOCKHAMMER, MORRIS, *Kant Dictionary*, New York, Philosophical Library 1972
STÖCKMANN, ERNST, "Phänomenologie der Empfindungen – Kultivierung des
  Gefühlsvermögens. Aspekte der anthropologischen Empfindungstheorie der deutschen
  Spätaufklärung am Beispiel von Platner und Irwing", in WALTER SCHMITZ – CARSTEN
  ZELLE (eds.), *Innovation und Transfer – Naturwissenschaften, Anthropologie und Literatur
  im 18. Jahrhundert*, Dresden, Thelem 2004, pp. 75–96
STÖCKMANN, ERNST, *Anthropologische Ästhetik. Philosophie, Psychologie und ästhetische
  Theorie der Emotionen im Diskurs der Aufklärung*, Tübingen, Niemeyer 2009
STÖCKMANN, ERNST, "Psychologische versus transzendentale Ästhetik. Eberhards
  Kant-Polemik in der Ästhetik", in HANS-JOACHIM KERTSCHER – ERNST STÖCKMANN (eds.),
  *Ein Antipode Kants? Johann August Eberhard im Spannungsfeld von spätaufklärerischer
  Philosophie und Theologie*, Berlin/Boston, de Gruyter 2012, pp. 251–275 (Falsche
  Paginierung: Seite 275 entspricht die eigentliche Seite 281)
STOLZENBERG, JÜRGEN, "'Was jedermann notwendig interessiert'. Kants Weltbegriff der
  Philosophie", in HANS FEGER (ed.), *The Fate of Reason. Contemporary Understanding of
  Enlightenment*, Würzburg, Königshausen & Neumann 2013, pp. 171–179
STRAWSON, PETER FREDERICK, *The Bounds of Sense. An Essay on Kant's* Critique of Pure
  Reason, London, Methuen 1966
STREUBEL, THORSTEN, "Was ist der Mensch? – Das Gehirn-Geist-Problem aus kantischer
  Sicht. Plädoyer für eine transzendentale Anthropologie", in *Kant-Studien*, vol. 103/3
  (2012), pp. 370–377
STURM, THOMAS, *Kant und die Wissenschaften vom Menschen*, Bielefeld, Mentis 2009
STURM, THOMAS, "Kant on Empirical Psychology: How Not to Investigate the Human Mind", in
  ERIC WATKINS (ed.), *Kant and the Sciences*, Oxford/New York, Oxford University Press
  2001, pp. 163–184
STURM, THOMAS, "Freedom and the Human Sciences: Hume's Science of Man versus Kant's
  Pragmatic Anthropology", in *Kant Yearbook 2011 – Anthropology*. Volume 3, pp. 23–42
STURMA, DIETER, "Was ist der Mensch? Kants vierte Frage und der Übergang von der
  philosophischen Anthropologie zur Philosophie der Person", in DIETMAR H. HEIDEMANN
  – KRISTINA ENGELHARD (eds.), *Warum Kant heute? Systematische Bedeutung und
  Rezeption seiner Philosophie in der Gegenwart*, Berlin/New York, de Gruyter 2004,
  pp. 264–285
SVARE, HELGE, *Body and Practice in Kant*, Dordrecht, Springer 2006
TERUEL, PEDRO JESÚS, "Das Organ der Seele. Immanuel Kant y Samuel Thomas Sömmerring
  sobre el problema mente-cerebro", in *Studi kantiani*, XXI (2008), pp. 59–76
TERUEL, PEDRO JESÚS, "Significato, senso e ubicazione strutturale del termine *Gemüt* nella
  filosofia kantiana", in STEFANO BACIN – ALFREDO FERRARIN – CLAUDIO LA ROCCA –
  MARGIT RUFFING (eds.), *Kant und die Philosophie in weltbürgerlicher Hinsicht. Akten des
  XI. Internationalen Kant-Kongresses*, Boston-New York, De Gruyter 2013, volume 4,
  pp. 507–518
THIEL, UDO, *The Early Modern Subject. Self-Consciousness and Personal Identity from
  Descartes to Hume*, Oxford/New York, Oxford University Press, 2011
THOUARD, DENIS, *Schleiermacher: Communauté, Individualité, Communication*, Paris, Vrin
  2007
THURNHERR, URS, *Die Ästhetik der Existenz. Über den Begriff der Maxime und die Bildung von
  Maximen bei Kant*, Tübingen, Francke 1994

TIEFTRUNK, JOHANN HEINRICH, *Philosophische Untersuchungen über die Tugendlehre zur Erläuterung und Beurtheilung der metaphysischen Anfangsgründe der Tugendlehre vom Herrn Prof. Imm. Kant. Zweiter Teil. Ausführung der Pflichten der Menschen gegen einander nach den besondern Zuständen und Verhältnissen derselben*, Halle, Mengersche Buchhandlung 1805

TIMMONS, MARK (ed.), *Kant's Metaphysics of Morals: Interpretative Essays*, Oxford/New York, Oxford University Press 2002

TONELLI, GIORGIO, "La formazione del testo della *Kritik der Urteilskraft*", in *Revue internationale de philosophie*, volume 8 (1954), pp. 423–448

TONELLI, GIORGIO, *Kant, dall'estetica metafisica all'estetica psicoempirica. Studi sulla genesi del criticismo (1754–1771) e sulle sue fonti*, Torino, V. Bona 1955

TRAMPOTA, ANDREAS – SENSEN, OLIVER – TIMMERMANN, JENS (eds.), *Kant's "Tugendlehre". A Comprehensive Commentary*, Berlin/Boston, de Gruyter 2013

VAN DER BERG, HEIN, "Kant on Vital Forces. Metaphysical Concerns versus Scientific Practice", in ERNST-OTTO ONNASCH (ed.), *Kants Philosophie der Natur. Ihre Entwicklung im Opus postumum und ihre Wirkung*, Berlin/New York, de Gruyter , pp. 115–135

VAN DE PITTE, FREDERICK, *Kant as Philosophical Anthropologist*, The Hague, Martinus Nijhoff 1971

VIDAL, FERNANDO, "La psychologie empirique et son historicisation pendant l'Aufklärung", in *Revue d'Histoire des Sciences Humaines*, 2000/2, pp. 29–55

VIDAL, FERNANDO, *The Sciences of the Soul. The Early Modern Origins of Psychology*, Chicago 2011

WARD, KEITH, *The Development of Kant's View of Ethics*, Oxford, Blackwell 1972

WATSON, JOHN B., "Psychology as the Behaviorist Views It", in *Psychological Review*, 20 (1913), pp. 158–177

WAXMAN, WAYNE, *Kant's Model of the Mind. A New Interpretation of Transcendental Idealism*, Oxford/New York, Oxford University Press 1991

WAXMAN, WAYNE, "Kant's Psychologism I.", in *Kantian-Review*, 3 (1999), pp. 41–63

WAXMAN, WAYNE, *Kant and the Empiricists: Understanding Understanding*, Oxford/New York, Oxford University Press 2005

WENZEL, UWE JUSTUS, *Anthroponomie: Kants Archäologie der Autonomie*, Berlin, Akademie Verlag 1992

WILSON, HOLLY L., *Kant's Pragmatic Anthropology: Its Origin, Meaning, and Critical Significance*, New York, State University of New York Press 2006

WOOD, ALLEN W., "Kant and the Problem of Human Nature", in BRIAN W. JACOBS – PATRICK P. KAIN (eds.), *Essays on Kant's Anthropology*, Cambridge/New York, Cambridge University Press 2003, pp. 38–59

WUNSCH, MATTHIAS, "The Activity of Sensibility in Kant's Anthropology. A Developmental History of the Concept of the Formative Faculty", in *Kant Yearbook 2011 – Anthropology*. Volume 3, pp. 67–90

ZAMMITO, JOHN H., *The Genesis of Kant's Critique of Judgment*, Chicago, The University of Chicago Press 1992

ZAMMITO, JOHN H., *Kant, Herder, and the Birth of Anthropology*, Chicago/London, The University of Chicago Press 2002

ZINKIN, MELISSA, "Respect for the Law and the Use of Dynamical Terms in Kant's Theory of Moral Motivation", in *Archiv für Geschichte der Philosophie*, 88 (2006), pp. 31–53

Author Index

Abicht, Johann Heinrich   23
Ameriks, Karl   26, 37, 47
Amoroso, Leonardo   81
Anderson, Georg   234
Aquila, Richard E.   51
Arnoldt, Emil   54, 74, 85, 89, 95
Aubenque, Pierre   65

Bacin, Stefano   219
Baron, Marcia W   205
Battaglia, Fiorella   129
Baum, Manfred   142, 162
Baumgarten, Alexander Gottlieb   1f., 21f.,
    41–43, 55–61, 76, 92f., 119, 208–210,
    219
Beck, Lewis W.   128, 162, 213f., 221–233
Bergk, Johann Adam   63, 89, 234
Bird, Graham H.   41
Blackwell, Richard J.   42
Blosser, Philip   205
Blumenbach, Johann Friedrich   27–31
Bojanowski, Jochen   75
Bona Meyer, Jürgen   40, 128
Brandt, Reinhard   45, 54–61, 64, 67, 71–
    76, 78f., 87, 92, 102f., 110f., 119, 207
Brezina, Friedrich F.   233
Broadie, Alexander   205
Brook, Andrew   35–38, 40, 51f.
Brummack, Jürgen   19, 22
Buber, Martin   87f.
Burchardt, Kurt   129

Campe, Joachim Heinrich   2, 20
Campo, Mariano   42f.
Casula, Mario   55
Caygill, Howard   3, 83
Centi, Beatrice   210
Cesa, Claudio   63
Chenet, François-Xavier   91
Ciafardone, Raffaele   10
Cummins, Robert   47

de Vleeschauwer, Herman J.   57
Deleuze, Gilles   2, 129

Dennett, Daniel C.   46
Dessoir, Max   10, 128

Eberhard, Johann August   1, 19–21, 23
École, Jean   42, 59
Engstrom, Stephen   122, 215
Erdmann, Benno   58f., 74, 76, 84
Esser, Andrea Marlen   234
Euler, Werner   26

Fabbri Bertoletti, Stefano   28f.
Falduto, Antonino   198, 207, 233
Falkenstein, Lorne   207
Ferrarin, Alfredo   160
Firla, Monika   95
Floyd, Juliet   170
Foerster, Friedrich Wilhelm   219
Fonnesu, Luca   189
Forkl, Markus   234
Foucault, Michel   82
Frierson, Patrick R.   81, 129
Fries, Jakob Friedrich   34, 40

Geiger, Ido   234
Gerhardt, Volker   24, 88
Gerlach, Hans-Martin   142, 162, 209
Gesang, Bernward   140
Gigliotti, Gianna   10f., 129, 210f.
Giordanetti, Piero   183, 205
Gisi, Lucas Marco   23
Goy, Ina   205
Gregor, Mary J.   95, 191, 208, 210, 234
Grenberg, Janine Marie   129, 217
Grove, Peter   19f.
Guerra, Augusto   11
Guyer, Paul   170, 234

Haag, Johannes   135
Hanna, Robert   31f.
Harnack, Adolf   13–16
Hatfield, Gary   10, 34–43, 50, 52, 62
Heidegger, Martin   82
Henrich, Dieter   37, 204, 217, 219
Herbart, Johan Friedrich   34, 40

Herder, Johann Gottfried 2, 14, 16 – 22, 40, 61
Herman, Barbara 160, 205
Hessbrüggen-Walter, Stefan 2, 10 f., 121
Hinske, Norbert 45, 56, 59 – 61, 63 – 67, 71, 83 – 86, 89, 92
Hintikka, Jaakko 37
Hoenegger, Hansmichael 25
Hoppe, Hansgeorg 51
Höwing, Thomas 130, 195, 233
Husserl, Edmund 50

Ivaldo, Marco 201

Jansohn, Heinz 129

Kaulbach, Friedrich 62
Kim, Soo Bae 41, 53, 57, 82, 92, 95
Kitcher, Patricia 35, 40 f., 45 – 52, 210
Kitcher, Philip 31
Kleingeld, Pauline 149
Klemme, Heiner F. 26, 42, 45, 86, 92, 130, 140 f., 152, 162 f., 177, 183, 195, 201, 207, 215, 233
Kulenkampff, Jens 217

La Rocca, Claudio 25, 41, 86, 201
Lambert, Johann Heinrich 10
Landau, Albert 140, 228
Landucci, Sergio 221, 226 f.
Langlois, Luc 204, 217
Lauener, Henri 205
Lee, Ming-Huei 217, 233
Lenoir, Timothy 28
Linden, Mareta 56
Longuenesse, Béatrice 11
Louden, Robert B. 66, 82, 99 – 103, 204
Ludwig, Bernd 140, 191, 201
Lunati, Giancarlo 204, 217

MacBeath, A. Murray 217
Makkreel, Rudolf 41
Marquard, Odo 56
Martinelli, Riccardo 44 f., 56
McCarty, Richard R. 215
McLaughlin, Peter 26
Meerbote, Ralf 38, 45, 49, 201, 220

Mendelssohn, Moses 10, 15, 19 f.
Menzer, Paul 61, 114, 219
Mertens, Helga 129, 178
Model, Anselm 179
Morrisson, Iain 215
Müller, Hans-Heinrich 12, 14

Nakazawa, Takeschi 210
Neis, Cordula 13 f.
Nicolai, Christoph Friedrich 234
Nobbe, Frank 81
Nuzzo, Angelica 51 f., 130, 210

Oberdorfer, Bernd 23

Packer, Mark 215
Palmquist, Stephen 205
Panknin-Schappert, Helke 217
Park, Chan-Goo 205, 217
Philonenko, Alexis 185
Pierobon, Frank 185
Pirillo, Nestore 63
Pistorius, Hermann Andreas 140
Platner, Ernst 23., 56

Reath, Andrews 215 f.
Recki, Birgit 238 f.
Reinhold, Karl Leonhard 10 f., 34, 40, 137, 162, 176, 202
Richards, Robert J. 28
Rivero, Gabriel 44
Roelcke, Thorsten 2, 210
Rumore, Paola 50
Ryle, Gilbert 34, 46

Schadow, Steffi 205
Schiller, Friedrich 114, 204
Schilpp, Paul Arthur 114, 219
Schmidt, Claudia M. 81, 95
Schmucker, Joseph 114, 204, 217, 219
Schneider, Ulrich Johannes 8
Schönecker, Dieter 233 f.
Schrader, George 205
Schwaiger, Clemens 65, 179
Sensen, Oliver 240
Shell, Susan Meld 51
Sherman, Nancy 205

Sidgwick, Henry   201
Simmermacher, Volker   81–83
Sloan, Phillip R.   29
Slote, Michael   204
Soemmerring (also: Sömmering), Samuel
    Thomas von Sommer, Robert   26–28
Stark, Werner   45, 55, 59–61, 63, 92, 102
Stekeler-Weithofer, Pirmin   202
Stöckmann, Ernst   22 f.
Stolzenberg, Jürgen   63
Strawson, Peter Frederick   34, 46
Streubel, Thorsten   82
Sturm, Thomas   40, 45, 56, 61, 64, 86, 88,
    162
Sulzer, Johann Georg   1, 10, 18–20

Teruel, Pedro Jesús   25–27
Tetens, Johann Nicolas   1 f., 10, 23, 128
Thiel, Udo   42
Thouard, Denis   21
Thurnherr, Urs   160
Tieftrunk, Johann Heinrich   234

Timmermann, Jens   149, 183, 215, 235
Timmons, Mark   234
Tonelli, Giorgio   128, 162, 208
Trampota, Andreas   235

Van de Pitte, Frederick   88
van der Berg, Hein   28
Vidal, Fernando   23

Ward, Keith   219
Watson, John B.   46
Waxman, Wayne   31, 35, 37, 40 f., 136
Wenzel, Uwe Justus   95
Wilson, Holly L.   77–79
Wolff, Christian   1, 5, 10, 21, 41–43, 45, 57–
    61, 67, 89, 119
Wood, Allen W.   62
Wunsch, Matthias   101

Zammito, John H.   113 f., 129
Zinkin, Melissa   216

Subject Index

Aesthetic 51, 83, 91, 113 – 115, 130 – 135, 156 – 158, 206 – 213
– Moral Aesthetic 206 f., 216, 231 f., 238 – 240
Anthropology
– Pragmatic Anthropology 41, 53 – 56, 62 – 69, 76 – 80, 85 – 98, 110, 115, 120, 124 f.
– Transcendental Anthropology 54, 76 – 84
Autonomy 147, 200 f.

Capacity of choice (*Willkür*) 122, 149 f., 192, 198 – 202, 231, 236

Duty (*Pflicht*) 96 f., 150, 223, 227, 229 – 237

Epigenesis 28 – 32, 40

Faculty (*Vermögen*)
– Faculty of desire (*Begehrungsvermögen*) 1, 9, 11, 22, 61, 90, 119 – 123, 137, 140 – 148, 172 – 178, 180 – 184, 188, 191, 196 – 199, 210, 217, 231
– Faculty of cognition (*Erkenntnisvermögen*) 1, 24 f., 61, 79, 85, 90, 104 f., 119 f., 131, 136 f., 167, 181, 188, 210, 217
Feeling (*Gefühl*) 1, 22, 61, 85, 90, 119, 120 f., 123, 137, 140 f., 145, 147, 149 – 155, 172 – 178, 180 – 182, 184, 187 f., 191 – 197, 211, 217
– Moral Feeling (*moralisches Gefühl*) 149 – 155, 157, 205, 212, 217 – 241
Freedom 68, 164, 168 – 170, 174 – 177, 181, 185 – 189, 198 – 201, 228

Incentive (*Triebfeder*) 97, 151 – 160, 205, 215 f., 221 – 232
Inclination (*Neigung*) 15, 65, 121, 146, 149 f., 153 f., 158, 192, 196, 200, 210, 223 f., 228

Mind (*Gemüt*) 1 – 4, 7 – 13, 15, 17, 24 – 33, 34 – 52, 90 – 93, 101, 105, 111, 118 – 120, 123
Moral law 97, 122, 139, 146 – 148, 150 – 160, 190 f., 197 – 199, 205 f., 214 – 216, 221 – 238

Power (*Kraft*) 2, 9 – 13, 24 f., 33
Psychology
– Empirical Psychology 33, 35, 40 – 45, 47 – 52, 53 – 62, 69, 88, 92 – 94, 142, 166
– Rational Psychology 40 – 45, 50, 57
– Transcendental Psychology 33 f., 40 – 52

Reason (*Vernunft*) 4, 7, 29, 69 – 79, 81, 84, 94, 97, 124, 136, 144 – 149, 151, 154 – 158, 168 – 171, 174, 180 – 188, 192, 198 – 201, 207 – 216, 218, 220 – 229, 231, 236 f., 240
Respect (*Achtung*) 111, 205, 216, 223 – 233, 236, 238

Sense (*Sinn*) 99 f., 103 – 106, 108 – 110, 112, 121, 135, 145, 192 – 194, 210 – 221
Sensibility (*Sinnlichkeit*) 1, 23, 25, 39, 41, 51 f., 54, 79, 90 – 92, 98 – 101, 105, 107 – 125, 131 – 137, 157 – 162, 192 f., 207 – 214, 217, 228, 240
Soul (*Seele*) 1, 10, 12, 16 – 23, 24 – 28, 41 f., 53, 57 f.

Understanding (*Verstand*) 8 f., 29, 63, 66, 77 f., 81, 84 f., 90 – 92, 98 – 101, 104 – 125, 131 – 136, 145 – 148, 161 f., 168 f., 177 – 181, 187 f., 192 f., 196, 202, 209

Will (*Wille*) 8 f., 22, 123, 144 – 156, 174, 192, 195, 198 – 202, 215, 222 – 232

www.ingramcontent.com/pod-product-compliance
Lightning Source LLC
Chambersburg PA
CBHW070025100426
42740CB00013B/2593